The Handbook of Banking Technology

TIM WALKER
LUCIAN MORRIS

WILEY

This edition first published 2021.
© 2021 Tim Walker and Lucian Morris

Registered office
John Wiley & Sons Ltd, The Atrium, Southern Gate, Chichester, West Sussex, PO19 8SQ, United Kingdom

For details of our global editorial offices, for customer services and for information about how to apply for permission to reuse the copyright material in this book please see our website at www.wiley.com.

Library of Congress Cataloging-in-Publication Data is Available

ISBN 978-1-119-32801-8 (hardback) ISBN 978-1-119-32810-0 (ePub)
ISBN 978-1-119-32806-3 (ePDF) ISBN 978-1-119-32809-4 (Obook)

Cover Design: Wiley
Cover Image: © Phaigraphic/Shutterstock

Set in 10/12pt TimesNewRomanMTStd by SPi Global, Chennai, India
Printed and bound by CPI Group (UK) Ltd, Croydon, CR0 4YY

10 9 8 7 6 5 4 3 2 1

To Debbie, Tom, Holly and Emily.
– TJW

To Jo, Cameron and Amelie.
– LAM

Contents

Preface

Our goal in writing this book is to bring about a better understanding of the complex world of technology in banking. Of course, there are many books covering just about every aspect of technology, from mainframe computers to cloud computing and from the first programming languages such as COBOL to the latest such as Go. However, books that cover how technology is used in the banking industry are rare to non-existent, which means that those working in the industry have had to rely on documentation supplied by vendors, training courses, the Internet and, of course, by talking with their colleagues in the technology function. Throughout our careers working for many different types of banking and payment businesses, from one of the smallest with a single branch to the largest international banks and various start-ups along the way, we found documentation supplied by vendors, with some notable exceptions, is often incomplete or superficial, only available after attending a training course or only aimed at developers. Attending training courses is often expensive in terms of both money and time and Internet resources can be patchy, of variable quality and sometimes just wrong. One of the reasons we decided to write this book was to fill this gap.

This book is therefore targeted at all readers with an interest in banking and technology, not just technologists. It provides an introduction to the history of banking and an analysis of the current technology landscape that supports the major functions of modern banks, and looks at the opportunities and risks posed by the digital era that we are in. To read this book you do not have to be deeply technical, nor focused only on technology. Instead the book aims to provide all readers with a common understanding of the opportunities and challenges related to technology that all banking businesses must address.

Of course, if you are an executive or manager in the banking industry who wishes to improve your understanding of the technology used in the industry, this book is particularly relevant. It should also provide a good introduction for those who are embarking on a career in technology in the banking industry or who have changed roles in a banking technology function and need to familiarise themselves with the technology used in their new area. It's also useful for those looking to launch a new bank or fintech start-up, even if only to illustrate how technology should not be implemented!

We cover retail and commercial banking, which includes bank accounts, secured and unsecured lending, payments, and payment cards, across all the channels from branches to mobile banking that are in common use, and all of the functions that you'd expect to find in a modern bank, from operations and finance to marketing. We have focused on the technology behind basic bank accounts, payments, and customer interaction and been less detailed about the platforms that support specialised banking products. We don't cover investment banking, investment management, asset management or insurance, which would probably require books in their own right. We have drawn on our experience in the banking sector in Europe, the Middle East, and North America, although readers will quickly understand that we tend to draw most deeply on our experience in the UK, where we have spent most of our careers.

Of course, banking businesses are often complex and the technology they use is also complex, wide-ranging and anything from five or more decades old to right up to date. Our aim is to provide an overview of the technology in use so that if you are a manager or executive outside the technology function you should be able to have more informed conversations with your colleagues in the technology function, and if you are in the technology function you should better understand the wider context of the work you are doing or managing. If you need to get more technical, you can consult the references and further reading lists that we provide.

As we are covering technology in the banking industry, we often tend to use the term *bank* when in reality what we have written applies to businesses that provide banking services and which may not, strictly speaking, be banks. If we were to follow the UK's banking regulators, an organisation can only be called a bank if it is licensed to take deposits. For example, credit card issuers and lenders that do not take deposits are not banks but they do provide banking services, and many aspects of what we have written in this book are also relevant to them. Given that payments are integral to banking, we have devoted a chapter each to card payments and to interbank payments.

Acknowledgements

We started thinking about and then writing this book several years ago. However, progress was patchy as work and family life (including Lucian's cycling accidents and the death of Tim's teenage son from leukaemia) took priority. By the start of 2020 we had written less than a third of the final manuscript. However, we decided to take advantage of the lockdown due to the Covid-19 pandemic to focus on completing the book. Our families sustained us while we beavered away, for which we say a huge thank you.

Although we worked together previously, this exercise has taught us that co-authoring a book can be challenging but is ultimately rewarding. Reviewing each other's writing made us realise we had different writing styles and points of view on various topics, and that sometimes what one or the other of us had written was just plain wrong. At times we have even been a little short with each other. However, we were always able to discuss and resolve these differences with equanimity while also still striving for quality and completeness. If there are mistakes in this book, we accept joint responsibility.

Finally, the last two chapters are relatively opinionated. The reader is perfectly entitled to disagree with what we have written.

CHAPTER 1

Introduction

1.1   Banking and the Rise of Technology

The banking industry, in many varied forms, has verifiably been in existence for at least four millennia. Beginning as a simple money and commodity management activity that supported early merchants and royalty, banking has gradually evolved into today's model: a complex, highly connected network of businesses that spans the globe. While it can appear that the development of the banking industry has generally taken place at a rather sedate pace, in reality banks have been established, grown and consolidated into ever larger organisations seemingly non-stop for centuries.

The advent of computers and, later, the Internet have had a dramatic impact on how banking has been conducted in recent times and ended the long-standing trend of opening more and more branches across the globe. Banks have changed their products and services, developed credit and debit cards, introduced computers to improve efficiency, built multi-channel digital banking platforms and, in many geographies, significantly reduced their high street footprint. They are moving from being brick-and-mortar businesses to what seems often to be purely digital utilities. However, the emergence of digital-only propositions may allow new businesses to develop with a much lower cost to serve, better products and services and more convenient customer access. A *digital-first* world of banking, it is argued, would not only replace the legacy brick-and-mortar world, but has the potential to deliver business models that will out-compete the incumbents, businesses that have grown huge, cumbersome and complacent. Visionaries and digital advocates in the financial services market argue that incumbent banks are, like the dinosaurs, plodding slowly but surely towards their inexorable extinction. On the other hand, large incumbents have the advantage of huge economies of scale and existing customer bases, meaning they pay less for deposits and make more money from each of their existing customers. Although there is evidence to show that the costs of complex, legacy technology are higher than modern technology, the massive scale of incumbent banks may mean that this cost can be borne for long enough for these banks to modernise their technology estates. Thus, the stage is set for a struggle between the old and the new.

The outcome of this struggle is far from a foregone conclusion and, in fact, the history of banks and banking institutions implies that the bigger ones eventually acquire the smaller ones – for more than a century the total number of banks in developed markets has been declining and this trend continues even up to the present.

Some observers have predicted that the shift to digital will sideline incumbent organisations in a different way, akin to what happened in the mobile telecommunications industry, where huge and highly profitable new businesses offering a new paradigm – the smartphone – were built. The mobile network providers no longer have access to the bulk of the revenue in this industry and are purely utilities with varying levels of profitability and return on capital in different markets around the world. Could incumbent banks just become utilities providing vanilla banking products with the customer relationships intermediated by new organisations with better technology? In practice, many digital new entrants are offering just the same banking products as incumbents, with a better mobile app, and this doesn't feel like a paradigm shift like the smartphone was. Also, it appears likely that only some incumbents will manufacture products for others and the rest will resist being intermediated unless forced by regulators, such as in the EU, where the Payment Services Directive 2 (PSD2) has resulted in banks having to offer an open banking interface for use by third-party service providers.

There is a third point of view: that to even present the current situation as incumbents versus new entrants and fintech start-ups, or old versus new, may not even be an appropriate or accurate representation of the true picture.

Where many analysts and commentators originally expected conflict (as early as 1994 Bill Gates famously made his big bank dinosaur speech),[1] it is now becoming clear that the relationship between new and old will be much more nuanced, with start-ups as likely to cooperate with incumbents as they are to compete.

So, we believe that the predictions of apocalypse for the incumbents within the banking industry are far from certain. While the digital agenda is creating opportunities for new entrants and does pose a risk to incumbent organisations, the rise of innovative fintech solutions and business models also provides many opportunities for established entities. There is no doubt that a significant amount of work, both forward-looking and in remediation, must be carried out in order for the incumbents to remain competitive and position them to seize these new opportunities, but their size and scale offers stability, established market access, lower unit costs and the income to fund the required changes – all key attributes that the new entrants and fintech start-ups typically lack. Over the last seven decades the established banks have proven themselves more than capable of adjusting to, and adopting, new technologies (computers, ATMs and Internet banking, to name a few) and any suggestion that a new wave of technologies means certain destruction for them may therefore be premature or even wrong. Not only do they have a proven history of adaptation, but many also have the balance sheets to buy themselves out of trouble should they need to, either through investing in joint ventures with up-and-coming start-ups or through outright acquisition of potential competitors.

Incumbent organisations may well struggle to adapt and there will inevitably be some organisations that will fall by the roadside (which usually means being acquired), but any significant change in market conditions typically results in casualties among the established order in that market. To survive and prosper, the leadership of a bank needs to recognise that it is a fundamentally digital business and that having a sufficient understanding of technology, its uses and sources of competitive advantage is essential.

1.2   The Challenges of Technology in Large Banks

There are several typical challenges that a bank's leadership faces relating to technology. For example, the leadership will have to decide whether its bank can persist in using legacy banking platforms. In order to meet the demands of the new digital economy our incumbent banking organisations require substantial changes within their organisations, and not just in the technology itself. Bank leadership teams need to acknowledge that the banking business is essentially becoming one of technology. Banks are now, at their core, digital businesses, and the leadership team must accept that and ensure that it has the skills at the top of the bank to manage a technology organisation. One of the reasons we wrote this book is to help to raise the level of understanding of technology among bank management.

Many of the platforms and systems that sit at the core of banking businesses are legacy environments, containing dated software and hardware, that have been built up over many years. Stories continue to circulate about the age of some of these systems. For example, the UK newspaper *The Telegraph*, as recently as December 2016, published an article claiming that some banking platforms in the UK still run on pounds, shillings and pence,[2] the UK's currency before decimalisation in 1971. We do not know whether this story is really true or not, but it was certainly an urban myth that occasionally surfaced in our conversations across the industry during our careers. While the latest developments may have been carried out in modern software development languages, the core of these platforms is still legacy and is often complex and poorly understood and therefore prone to going wrong when changes are made. Not only are these platforms getting on in age, but so are many of the developers who understand them. Such systems are often blamed for the seemingly high cost base of technology, the shortcomings of various products offered by the bank, and the lack of flexibility to introduce new products and services. On the other hand, re-platforming is expensive and full of risk – we are aware of several banks around the world that spent huge sums replacing their core banking platforms, and some, such as TSB in the UK,[3] that ran into highly public difficulties.

In parallel with maintaining legacy banking platforms, it would appear that many banks have struggled to maintain appropriate controls over the ongoing development of their technology estates. Of course, there are many reasons for the huge diversity in technology estates, which include business-led decision-making with technology standardisation low on the list of priorities, ongoing developments in technology with consequent dead ends and obsolescence, and accumulation of technology variety through mergers and acquisitions. Consequently, modern banking technology estates are complex and often poorly understood, even by the technology functions that run them. Some estates are so large that even tracking the hardware and software within them can be a significant task and many large modern banks struggle to do even this effectively, let alone calculate the input costs for each service that they supply and for which they charge the business units that consume them. Of course, there are usually no easy solutions to the problems posed by this complexity and we are often reminded of the supposedly Irish response to a request by a lost traveller about how to get somewhere which goes *I wouldn't start from here if I were you*.

Banks' technology functions can be as complex and politically charged as any other function in a large business. In large international banks the internal technology organisations are often huge, containing tens of thousands of workers distributed across dozens of sites, and are dependent upon a diverse supplier ecosystem. The structure of these organisations varies from bank to bank and over any given period, often oscillating between business-aligned and technology-driven structures (as discussed in Chapter 9). When business alignment is the primary driver, individual technology functions align with business units and while this may provide greater control to the business units, it can also result in technology functions that associate more with their business unit than with the CIO's office. This can lead to political in-fighting and huge inefficiencies, such as duplication of roles, technologies and third-party relationships within the broader organisation as similar capabilities are established and technologies built to support the same general need. The alternative model, with alignment to technical horizontals, can deliver much greater technological competence, reduced potential for business-driven in-fighting and lower costs, but does so at the risk of alienating the business units when they cannot get the service they believe they need to support the ongoing running and development of their business. When this happens, we have seen business units develop their own in-house technology functions, resulting in additional technology costs, duplication of roles and systems and a lack of consistency across the technology estate, in much the same way as the business-aligned model.

On top of the challenges associated with managing an international technology organisation, the current low public regard for banking,[4] namely that it is a staid industry, full of untrustworthy middle-aged men in suits with outdated views on technology,[5] makes it harder to recruit graduates and technology professionals that can bring the much needed skills and mindset the industry needs to fully grasp the opportunities presented by the digital world. Also, the ambitious perceive they can have more impact and make more money elsewhere. The talent that is clearly needed in technology departments within incumbent banks is being drawn to the more dynamic environments of technology-centric companies such as Apple, Facebook and Google and the fintech companies that the incumbent banks fear.

Finally, the scale of technology functions, and the complexity and scale of the technology itself, present challenges for the processes used to manage and govern them. These processes often represent legacy practices that are engrained in the culture and mindset of the technology function. Changing these established ways of working requires a supreme effort and a determined executive team. Despite recent high-profile technology failures, or perhaps even because of them, internal technology functions are often conservative by nature and married to legacy processes and ways of working that are proven, despite being inefficient. In order to adjust to the threats and opportunities posed by the digital agenda, the technology functions will first need to address their legacy operating models and adjust to new ways of working.

1.3   Navigating This Book

In Chapter 2 we provide a review of the history of banking and a snapshot of the current state of the banking industry. This chapter is not essential reading, but it provides context for the rest of the book.

Chapter 3 provides a technology primer, building up a picture of the technology required to support a simple bank that provides bank accounts, credit cards and an Internet banking channel. It includes an overview of core banking platforms, databases, mainframe technology (which is still prevalent in large banks), how platforms are made highly available and how different platforms are integrated, including both service-oriented architecture and microservices. It finishes with a review of data analysis, touching on data warehouses, data marts and data lakes. Less technical readers may not wish to read all the sections in this chapter.

The remaining chapters are sequenced broadly according to the model of a bank we show in Figure 1.1. At the top, it shows the customer segments the bank serves – in this case retail customers, commercial customers (i.e. small and medium-sized enterprises) and corporate customers (i.e. large enterprises). Of course, some banks may use finer segmentation such as underbanked, mass retail and premier retail in place of a single retail segment. The largest banks are likely to have a wholesale segment, which includes the very largest corporations and other banks as their clients. Normally, each segment will have a corresponding business unit inside the bank with a member of the executive team heading it up and marketing, product management, relationship management and sales staff in the unit.

The customers and potential customers of the bank engage with it through various channels, as shown in alphabetical order in the second layer of Figure 1.1. Note that these channels may technically overlap – for example, emails are usually sent over the Internet, but both are regarded as distinct channels by our bank. Similarly, telephone calls may be made using standard telephone lines, from mobile phones or over the Internet. However, every bank needs to consider if and how it will deal with such a channel. Some channels will have corresponding business units, such as the chat, email, telephone and video channels which would be handled by the bank's contact centre(s). We cover the Internet channel in Chapter 3 and then the other channels in Chapter 4.

The business units that correspond to the first two layers of this model are occasionally called the *front office* of the bank.

The categories of products that the bank offers are shown in the third layer down in Figure 1.1. These are ordered so that the products with more relevance to commercial and corporate customers are to the right-hand side. Retail transaction banking covers retail current accounts and deposit accounts and retail lending encompasses both unsecured lending and lending secured on assets other than property (e.g. vehicle loans). Commercial finance includes asset-based lending, asset finance, leasing and sales finance such as invoice factoring and discounting. Transaction banking is the provision of bank accounts and services such as cash management to commercial and corporate customers. Syndicated lending is the participation in and organisation of loans underwritten by multiple lenders to corporate customers. For each product type there will sometimes be a corresponding business unit within the bank, particularly for credit cards (which, along with other payment cards, we cover in Chapter 6) and in some cases the product type will be owned and managed by the corresponding business segment. Many banks offer insurance products to their customers, but we do not cover these in this book. Some banks also offer specialist products based on derivatives to corporate clients to manage interest rate and foreign exchange rate risks, which we would class as investment banking products and so we do not cover them.

FIGURE 1.1 Operating model of a bank.

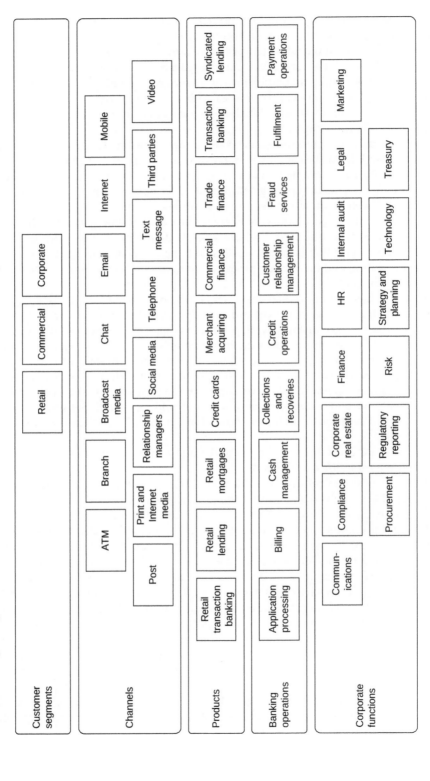

The products typically draw on some of the banking operations services shown alphabetically in the fourth layer of Figure 1.1, which are sometimes said to comprise the *middle office*. For example, application processing covers the processing of applications for products by new and existing customers, billing covers the billing of customers (typically more complex for larger corporate customers) and credit operations covers deciding whether to lend to a customer and at what interest rate. We cover these services in Chapter 5.

Finally, the lowest layer in Figure 1.1 shows the range of corporate functions a bank may have, i.e. the internal organisational units of the bank (apart from the customer-facing business units aligned with the customer segments in the first layer of the model). Many of these would be described as being in the *back office*, although this varies from bank to bank. In larger banks all the functions shown may exist, whereas in smaller banks some may be combined. For example, communications and marketing are often a single team and finance often includes regulatory reporting and treasury. We cover these functions in Chapter 8, apart from technology, which is the subject of Chapter 9.

Note that, although we have used the classification of front, middle and back office in this section, there are no standard definitions of what is included in each category and many banks do not use this terminology. Some banks use the classification of distribution (broadly equivalent to the sales functions in the front office plus marketing), manufacturing or production (covering the various products manufactured or produced by the bank and the servicing of them) and corporate services (equivalent to the back office). We will tend to avoid these classifications in the rest of the book.

1.4   References

1. Zack, J. (2015). Is Microsoft's Bill Gates right when he says banks are technology? *American Banker* 160 (5): 11A. https://www.americanbanker.com/news/is-microsofts-bill-gates-right-when-he-says-banks-are-technology (accessed 22 July 2020).
2. Evans, R. (2016). Some banks' systems still work in pounds, shillings and pence. That's a terrifying thought. *The Telegraph* (12 December). https://www.telegraph.co.uk/personal-banking/current-accounts/banks-systems-still-work-pounds-shillings-pence-terrifying-thought/ (accessed 2 June 2020).
3. Morrison, C. (2019). TSB IT meltdown cost bank £330m and 80,000 customers. *The Independent* (1 February). https://www.independent.co.uk/news/business/news/tsb-it-failure-cost-compensation-customers-switch-current-account-a8757821.html (accessed 22 July 2020).
4. White, L. (2018). British public don't trust banks 10 years after crisis, survey finds. *Reuters Business News* (16 August). https://uk.reuters.com/article/uk-britain-banks/british-public-dont-trust-banks-10-years-after-crisis-survey-finds-idUKKBN1L11EL (accessed 22 July 2020).
5. Hodge, N. (2016). U.K. boardrooms still 'pale, male, and stale'. *Compliance Week* (7 September). https://www.complianceweek.com/uk-boardrooms-still-pale-male-and-stale/2938.article (accessed 22 July 2020).

CHAPTER 2

The History and Current State of Banking

This chapter provides a brief introduction to the history of banking, the origins of cash and gold, and the importance of the branch in banking, before investigating the drive for scale that has been a defining element of the industry over the last century or so. We then look at the development of modern banking products and services and explore how technology has come to play such an important role in modern-day banking. The chapter ends with a review of the current state of banking.

When researching this chapter, it became apparent to us that what is accepted as historical fact is sometimes not correct, and sometimes there are conflicting or unsubstantiated claims for being the first to have done something. We have therefore provided extensive references in this chapter and in some cases we have qualified what we have written. There remains the risk that we have missed the actual first instance of a banking product or service because it isn't documented or because there were no references to it in the materials we consulted.

2.1 A Brief History of Banking

Much as it would be amusing to claim that banking is the earliest profession, this is, alas, untrue. One could argue, though, that without money, and therefore banking, it would be hard for any other walk of life to claim to be truly professional. The origins of banking can be traced back several millennia. From almost 2000 BCE there is evidence that the Babylonian temples provided a range of banking services, with their records kept on clay tablets.[1] Initially, as in other early cultures, this took the form of safeguarding of deposits of grain and then other agricultural products and ultimately precious metals.[2] Obviously, the receipt issued for a deposit had a value, which could be exchanged for other goods, and over time it also became possible to transfer the ownership of a deposit to another person. Another development was of temples making loans, initially of seed grain to be repaid after the harvest and then of money in the form of specific weights of metals such as silver, with interest payable by the debtor. Banking was important enough by this point in mankind's development that in the eighteenth century BCE, Hammurabi, the ruler of Babylon from around 1792 BCE, codified laws to govern banking practices such as the advancement of capital and the rate of interest to be paid on loans.[3] These laws were included in the Code of Hammurabi, the most famous copy of which was engraved on a stone slab (or stele) that was subsequently found in Iran in 1901 and is now in the Louvre Museum in Paris. So, in summary, the Babylonians developed three core aspects of banks: safekeeping of items of value, lending, and transfer of ownership of deposits (i.e. payments).

Mediterranean civilisations developed those early banking practices through the following 2,000 years, with the maritime nature of the Greek civilisation having a significant impact upon the development of moneylending. By the fourth century BCE, the civilisation of the ancient Greeks saw private individuals, temples and public bodies taking deposits, making loans, settling accounts (i.e. transferring the ownership of deposits) and changing money.[4] Changing money was required because by this period the Greek city states were separately issuing coins, and so travelling traders needed to be able to exchange coins from different city states. Maritime loans enabled traders to pay for cargoes, with the loan secured on the trader's ship, and the debt being cancelled if a trader's ship sank before returning home. The rate of interest charged was up to 30%, commensurate with the level of risk.[5]

In Egypt during the Ptolemaic era (305 BCE to 30 BCE), royal grain depositories were developed into royal banks that operated the first known giro system.[6] The basic concept of a giro system is that each customer of a bank has an account into which he or she makes deposits (often of grain, in this case) and that the bank records. Internally, the bank consolidates all the deposits and keeps them in one large store rather than keeping each customer's deposits separate.[7] A customer can then request that the bank transfer some of their deposits to another customer, and the bank updates its account records accordingly – without any physical transfer of the deposits. In particular, Egyptians could pay taxes to the government that were due on their produce through this procedure and the government made payment to its officials in the same way. This procedure is the equivalent of today's credit transfer. Records from the depositories and banks were sent to the equivalent of a central bank in the capital, Alexandria. In addition, a customer with deposits could issue a cheque to a third party, who could claim payment at any state bank.[8] Note how the cheque process differs from the giro or credit transfer process – the beneficiary presents a cheque to the bank and can receive payment in cash or equivalent, whereas the payer instructs the bank directly with a giro or credit transfer and payment is made into the beneficiary's account. It is the ability to use a network of banks with payments possible at different branches that marks out the Egyptian banking system of this era.

Over the following centuries, banking continued to grow in importance and eventually became such a key element of commerce that under the Romans it became regularised and various banking roles were recognised (and at times even appointed) by the state. Roman law even set out that bankers had unlimited liability for funds deposited with them (a principle that we will see later in eighteenth-century England) and how they should record transactions.[9] However, it is also recognised that the Romans did not develop a centralised network of banks and giro payments comparable with the Egyptian network.[10]

Of course, banking was not unique to the Mediterranean world. There is evidence from India during the early Vedic period (between 1500 BCE and 1200 BCE),[11,12] and from China in the third century BCE, of established banking practices.[13] In fact, it may well be that these cultures have a longer continuous history of banking practices than does the West.

There is little documentation of the history of banking in Europe after the fall of the Roman Empire until the eleventh century, and various authors record (see, for example, reference 2) that the main form of banking was money changing, given the issuing of different coins by many kingdoms. The influence of Christianity had a major impact on early banking – usury (originally defined as charging any interest on a loan) became frowned upon by Christian culture, banned for all clergy by the first council of Nicaea in 325 and was eventually prohibited altogether by Charlemagne in the ninth century.[14] Fortunately for the Western world, usury was not banned in all cultures. The Jewish faith, in common with Christianity and Islam, bans usury. However, Jewish law interprets the relevant verses in the Torah (Exodus 22:24, Leviticus 25:36–37 and Deuteronomy 23:20–21*) and other books in the Bible as specifically forbidding charging interest on loans to fellow Jews but allowing it to be charged on loans to non-Jews.[†] With moneylending being one of the few careers left open to them in Europe, many Jews entered the business, but at a cost of significant prejudice and jealousy from the majority non-Jewish population, who resented their wealth. This prejudice, and the ruthlessness of royalty and the Church, who coveted their wealth, resulted in pogroms that led to confiscation and theft of their wealth and the horrific treatment of Jews in general.[15]

During the twelfth century, the Crusades created demand for the development of a system of letters of credit, operated by the Knights Templar. A pilgrim or crusader could deposit money at a temple in their home city and receive a letter of credit in return, which they could exchange en route or at their destination.[16] The Templars also accepted valuable items for safe-keeping and used them as collateral for loans of money (which they had sourced from donations).

While it is true that in earlier periods (despite usury being frowned upon) many Christians, including the Church, had participated in or supported lending, in the thirteenth century Christians started to become more openly involved in banking. In Lombardy, the new breed of banker used double-entry bookkeeping,[‡] one of the backbones of modern accountancy.[17] This was the start of the growth of Italian banking. As the Italian merchant states grew in importance, so did the importance of banking to the merchant economy. In the fifteenth century, the Medici family established its famous banking dynasty, and in the sixteenth century, the first modern state-owned bank, Banco della Piazza di Rialto, was established in the Italian city-state of Venice to hold merchants' funds safely, more so than some private banks which had failed prior to its establishment.[18] Like the private banks before it, it enabled transactions to be made between merchants without the physical exchange of coins. The establishment

---

*The precise verse numbers may differ depending on the version and/or translation of the Torah.
†Given the Christian Bible contains the same verses, there was also a view that Christians could lend to non-Christians. Given there were many more Christians than Jews in the Middle Ages in Europe, Jewish lenders to Christians had a much bigger market than the other way round. Islam, on the other hand, prohibits all usury, even by those of other faiths.
‡We have seen claims that forms of double-entry bookkeeping may have been used by the Romans and the Muslim Empire before the Italian bankers, but these appear to be based on the fact that the Italian bankers drew on the teachings of the Muslim Empire via Jewish traders and that all of the basic technologies required for accounting (e.g. arithmetic, commerce, credit, capital, etc.) were in place in the Muslim Empire; see reference 17.

of state-owned banks was later followed by the creation of national banks, with the first example being the Bank of Sweden (or Riksbank) in 1668, followed by the Bank of England in 1694 and the Bank of Scotland in 1695. Governments created national banks for a variety of reasons. The Riksbank was instituted to provide commercial banking services (the safekeeping of deposits and lending) following the collapse of the first chartered Swedish bank, the privately owned Stockholms Banco, which was effectively controlled by the Swedish king. It had collapsed after issuing loan notes (including to the king) greater in value than the deposits it held, which were exhausted when recipients of the loan notes cashed them in.[19] With parallels in modern central banks being granted autonomy, the Swedish parliament, the Riksdag, had learnt from the collapse of Stockholms Banco and kept control of the Riksbank away from the king. The Bank of England was created to provide funds to the government to pay for its involvement in the Nine Years' War with France.[20] The Bank of Scotland was established as a commercial bank offering banking services to Scottish businesses and was originally prohibited from lending to the Scottish government. Within a year of being founded, the Bank of Scotland was issuing banknotes (which reduced the need to use heavy coins).[21] National banks have since often gone on to play fundamental roles in the banking industries of their respective nations, becoming central banks typically with remits to manage monetary policy (including controlling the issuing of banknotes), to provide settlement accounts for payment schemes and to regulate the banking industry.

2.2 Cash, Gold and Digital Money

While banking has existed since at least the eighteenth century BCE, the concept of money in the form of coins is a much later development. Prior to the development of coins, any manner of items was used as a means of stored value. Such commodity money[22] could range from pieces of precious metal including gold, lead, silver and tin, and stones (precious and otherwise) to animal teeth, cattle, feathers, fur, rice, salt, shells and other materials.[23] In ancient times, in the Middle East, specified weights of precious materials (mostly silver) were used as the basis of money. One such weight was referred to as a shekel, a term that became associated with the coinage that was developed. The shekel is probably the world's oldest term for a unit of value that is still in use today.[24]

The British Museum has in its collection some of the earliest known minted coins, dated around 550 BCE and which originate from the Kingdom of Lydia, in what is now western Turkey. A coin is typically defined as a metal object with a fixed weight and size (and therefore density and composition) for its value, and that is stamped to give it official standing. It is believed that the Lydians invented coinage about a hundred years earlier[25] and were possibly the first to do so because they had ample sources of gold in the form of electrum, a naturally occurring amalgam with silver.[26] It is also believed that coins were invented in China around the same time.[27] Following this, at various times, thought to be no earlier than 650 BCE and no later than 500 BCE, most of the Greek city-states started issuing their own coins.[28] As the first Lydian coins were made from electrum, in which the relative proportions of the constituents could vary, two coins of the same size and shape may not have weighed the same, casting doubt over their value. However, over time the Lydians found a method of making pure gold coins which meant that two coins of the same size and shape weighed the same, and so purity could be assured. The Lydians made coins in a range of sizes that adhered to strict weight criteria, which enabled a specific value to be allocated to each size of coin. This ability to maintain a specific value for any given coin is fundamental to the whole basis of coins.

The creation of a system of coinage is a significant step forward. It creates an easily portable and recognised source of value that can be traded for all manner of goods and services. While coins have always suffered from a risk of debasement, such as through forgery or coin clipping, from less reputable members of society, they have proven to be a remarkably resilient means of storing value since they were first created.

The key to the success of coinage (and, later, also banknotes) has been in its ability to maintain a value. The basic premise of stored value in coins throughout history typically came down to one of two approaches.

First, and originally, coins had intrinsic value, as they were made from precious metals. There is no dependence on the issuing authority to be able to refund the bearer of the coin and its value is arguably very stable (though, of course, if the value of the constituent metal or metals changes then the intrinsic value of the coin may change as well). While in practice it appears that there were many cases where the face value of the coin was actually slightly more than that of its constituent parts, this did not seem to matter as long as the participants in the market agreed that the face value was broadly representative of the coin's actual worth. A risk with this approach is that the metal used for coinage can become scarce as the economy develops and people are then forced to resort to other ways of exchanging value (such as promissory notes and receipts for deposits at banks).

Second, and as is seemingly universally the case today, coins had token-based value – where the value of a coin is different (typically greater) than the metal(s) it is made from and is based upon trust in the issuing authority. In this case, the issuing authority is held to account for that value and therefore is, in essence, issuing a promissory note. This is, of course, also the case with banknotes and is the origin of the promise to pay the bearer statements found on many modern notes. In theory, the holder or bearer of the currency can turn up at the issuing authority, hand in the coin or banknote, and be reimbursed the value in gold.

The second of these two approaches, which is termed representative money,[29] essentially requires the issuing authority to hold a reserve of gold to cover the value of the coins and banknotes it issues. Without this reserve, or at least the trust that the means to pay exists, the cash loses its value. From the eighteenth century onwards the use of a gold standard became widespread, with various nations implementing laws to enforce the direct relationship of their currency to their gold reserves. However, the ability to do this is obviously directly related to a country's ability to hold reserves and this was always an issue during periods of stress – civil wars, world wars and the depression of the late 1920s and 1930s all put pressure on the ability of many countries to maintain a gold standard as governments used up their reserves to pay for their armed forces or to fund social programmes. France and Germany suspended their gold standards in 1914 (although France returned to it in 1928, with the franc at a fifth of its value compared to when convertibility was suspended, and then left it in 1936), the UK abandoned it in 1931, followed by many countries in 1932, and then the US in effect suspended convertibility in 1933 by stopping banks issuing gold, preventing gold exports, making it illegal for people to hold gold bullion, getting the Federal Reserve to issue notes that were not backed by gold and implementing a policy of devaluing the dollar in terms of the gold equivalent.[30] In each case these governments worked on the basis of issuing fiat money – money that has value because the issuer says that it does.[31]

At the end of World War II, major western currencies agreed to adopt a gold exchange standard* with fixed exchange rates with the US dollar which was convertible to gold on demand by the participating countries. This arrangement lasted until 1971. The beginning of the end was arguably a decision by the French government in 1965 to convert its holding of US dollars to gold. By the start of the 1970s, the ability of the US to honour the agreement was under pressure due to the challenges the US had from funding the Vietnam War, high US unemployment and high US inflation, all of which were exacerbated by a balance of trade that moved from surplus to deficit.[32] This meant that the US had printed more dollars than it could convert to gold. West Germany withdrew from the standard in May 1971, after which other participants swiftly took steps to redeem their dollar reserves. The US effectively ended the agreement in August 1971 when President Nixon suspended convertibility of the dollar to gold. Over the course of the twentieth century there was a general move away from the use of gold standards and no countries were using them by the end of the century.

Today's position is therefore an interesting one in that we now live in a world of fiat currency – where currency is legal tender because the issuing nation declares it so. In practice, the issuing authority typically does not hold enough gold (and does not have to) to cover the value of the coins and banknotes that it has issued. In most cases this system runs well enough, but in periods of stress some struggling governments have been known to resort to money printing to address their immediate issues. While the printing of money may have appeal in addressing some short-term issues, it inevitably results in longer-term woes for the issuing authority. For example, in Germany in 1923,[33] in Uganda under Idi Amin in the 1970s,[34] in Zimbabwe under Robert Mugabe in 2007–2008[35] and in Venezuela under Nicolás Maduro in 2017–2019,[36] this policy led to massive hyperinflation. When this occurs, it damages the economy and renders savings worthless, often leading to a flight to more reliable currencies.

In the modern era the use of fiat currency has seen a significant move away from hard currency (coins and banknotes) towards digital money. In most modern economies this and modern banking methods mean that the amount of money in the economy is significantly higher than the actual value of minted currency and our dependence on coins and banknotes in support of our daily spending has been reduced significantly. Consider a customer taking out a loan with a bank. The act of the bank's setting up the loan is to set up a loan account on its banking platform (or in a paper ledger, before the days of computers) with a negative balance for the amount of the loan, and deposit the same amount into the account of the customer (i.e. add it to the account's balance recorded on the banking platform or in a paper ledger). In effect, by doing this the bank

---

*With a gold standard, a member of the public can exchange a banknote for the equivalent in gold, with the rate of exchange (the weight of gold received per unit of currency) normally fixed or at least stable. With a gold exchange standard, a group of countries agree to fix the exchange rates of their currencies relative to the currency of one of the group (the reserve currency). The reserve currency has a fixed rate of exchange to gold, so that if one country collects a large amount of the reserve currency, it can exchange it on demand for a known amount of gold. The Bretton Woods agreement of 1944 put in place a gold exchange standard based on the US dollar as the reserve currency with $1 worth 1/35 of a troy ounce of gold.

has created some money. If the customer uses the loan to pay another customer of the bank – a seller of goods, say – by transferring some money from their account to the account of the seller, no physical cash is required. In fact, if the bank's customers only pay each other by transferring money between their accounts at that bank, the bank never has to worry about having any assets to back up the money it created.* However, in reality, more often than not a customer of the bank will pay a seller who has an account at a different bank by transferring funds to the seller's account at the other bank (paying the seller using a debit or credit card ultimately has the same outcome). At this point, the first bank must transfer some assets to the second bank. In a modern payment system, these would be assets owned by the bank that the central bank or some other trusted party holds (typically called reserves), which could include gold but may just be money deposited by the bank at the central bank. Such reserves are of course finite, so a bank could run out of reserves if it issues too many loans. Banking regulators set limits on the amount of lending banks can do relative to their reserves to prevent this happening. Note that as a bank gets larger and increases its share of the banking market (e.g. through faster growth than its competitors, acquisition, or merger), on average a larger proportion of the money it creates stays with it. Also, there are typically millions of small interbank transfers a day, so to settle these payments only net amounts are transferred between the banks. Where electronic payments dominate, the value of digital money will outweigh the value of banknotes and coins in circulation, and this is indeed the case according to central bank data – in the UK only 3% of money is in the form of cash.[37] Also, banks do not have to cover all their deposits with reserves, but they do have to have enough reserves to cover their likely daily outflow of funds plus some extra for unusual levels of outflow. In the UK, 18% of money is held by the banks as reserves at the Bank of England and 79% as customer deposits at the banks.

While most countries around the world, with the obvious exception of those in the eurozone, still maintain their own currency we can now imagine a future where money becomes completely digital. We are now approaching a point where virtual currencies (Bitcoin, for example, which has no underlying guarantor of value) may offer potential alternatives to national currencies. While initial attempts to create virtual currencies have not so far been wholly successful, the ongoing development of technology, particularly concepts such as the blockchain and, even more importantly, cybersecurity (cryptocurrency exchanges, which facilitate the buying and selling of cryptocurrencies such as Bitcoin, have regularly been attacked by hackers[38]) are making them more viable. We return to virtual currency in Chapter 10.

2.3   Branch Centrism

The historical link between banking and physical currency meant that before the arrival of technology most banking products and services could only be provided through physical interactions. Where physical currency was in common usage, there was a natural requirement for bankers to have a physical presence in the market to provide funds. As noted at the start of this chapter, early forms of banking were often closely associated

---

*Note that this was equally true before banks used computers.

with temples, and even the Bible makes reference to money changers in the temples of Israel (Matthew 21:12–17, Mark 11:15–19, Luke 19:45–48 and John 2:13–16), but it was not long before bankers started to establish a separate presence within the marketplace itself. Due to the nature of trade, it was a natural logical extension to establish networks that could provide services at the ends of trade routes.

However, in Europe it was only in the later Middle Ages that banks established branch networks. The reliance on a physical presence as the only channel through which banks could engage with their customers dictated that in order to grow their businesses, until the twenty-first century, the banks' primary routes were therefore through the geographical expansion of their branch networks and the acquisition of other banks.

For a variety of reasons, including regulatory, cultural and geographic, banking has developed differently around the globe and this is reflected in the development of branch networks and the differing perceptions on the need for, and reach of, these networks. In some countries, banks limit themselves geographically. In Germany, for example, the regional banks or Landesbanken are publicly owned banks that originally funded local projects and provided wholesale banking services to the local savings banks called Sparkassen (legally and financially independent organisations that do not have owners or shareholders[39] focused on a specific geographical area) inside their respective regions.* There are also member-owned co-operative banks, Volksbanken and Raiffeisenbanken, also normally focused on a specific urban or rural geographical area.

Like Germany, Austria has a system of nearly 500 local Raiffeisenbanken that typically own regional Raiffeisenlandesbanken. It also has systems of local Sparkassen and Volksbanken, although these have not fared well. The Sparkassen saw various waves of consolidation from 124 in 1989 to 74 in 1994 and then 46 by 2016, with the majority becoming listed entities rather than member owned.[40] The Volksbanken came under pressure following the banking crisis in 2008, with 51 Volksbanken consolidated into 10 by 2015.[41]

In Spain too, the concept of local banking was embedded in the cajas (savings banks) and cajas rurales (rural savings banks), both of which were established in the nineteenth century. However, the geographical restrictions on the cajas were lifted in 1988[42] and many of them expanded rapidly outside their historical areas and diversified. After the banking crisis in 2008 a large number of the cajas failed, with local political interference in their management and operations having caused them to overextend and make risky loans suggested as a contributory factor.[43] The number of cajas dropped from 45 in 2007[44] to just two (Caixa Ontinyent and Colonya Caixa Pollença) by 2020, with the rest consolidated into various listed banking groups or bought by other banks.[45] In 2020, there were still 29 cajas rurales, down from 77 in the 1980s, all of whom were by that point members of a federated group that provides shared services to its members.[46]

---

*The Landesbanken were not formally geographically constrained and in the 1970s several developed their businesses internationally. After the EU banned the public guarantees the Landesbanken had, their internationalisation increased in the first decade of the twenty-first century, including involvement in the US mortgage market. This caused major issues for several of them after the banking crisis of 2008.

In the UK and the US, local and regional banks have been going through a period of significant consolidation since the 1970s and 1980s[*],[†] and arguably even longer in the UK, resulting in a small number of banks with extensive branch networks. That is not to say that local banks, credit unions and building societies do not exist or are on the cusp of extinction. In fact, the UK saw a growth in the popularity of credit unions in the second decade of the twenty-first century, with membership increasing from 1.66 million in 2013[50] to 2.14 million in 2019[51] with 437 credit unions.[52]

Consolidation in the number of different banks has driven a substantial reduction in the number of bank branches due to overlap of branch networks. For example, there are stories of Santander having three branches on some high streets after its acquisitive entry into the UK. Closures were inevitable. This, alongside the growth first in telephone banking and then later in online banking services, led many in the banking industry to believe that the concept of the local, branch-based retail bank was all but dead, although many also recognised that the size of a bank's customer base remained proportional to its branch footprint.

However, in 2008, Vernon Hill, following the sale of Commerce Bancorp in the United States, decided to enter the UK market. Having built Commerce Bancorp from a single branch in 1973 to 440 branches in 2007,[53] Vernon decided that his model should work equally well in the UK. He launched Metro Bank in 2010 and the concept of branch banking in the UK was, if not re-born, then certainly given a new lease of life. Metro Bank is not the only bank that recognises the branch as the core of its business. Handelsbanken, a Swedish bank with branches in the UK (and in Sweden, Denmark, Finland, Norway and the Netherlands),[54] has its entire model centred on the branch concept, making individual lending decisions at the branch level.

Despite these exceptions, branch banking does appear to be on the decline, with most banks seeking to retrench their branch networks and focus on high footfall locations. For many villages and small towns in the UK this is resulting in the closure of all branches.

2.4   Banking Consolidation

While there is a degree of smaller-scale local banking (such as credit unions and building societies and small-scale banks), in most geographies it is also true that much of the banking by value is concentrated in just a handful of banks in many countries. In the UK

---

[*]The UK had hundreds of local savings banks (termed trustee savings banks) in the nineteenth century. By 1975 there were 73, which were consolidated due to government action into 20 and then 16 regional savings banks. In 1983 these consolidated again into TSB England and Wales, TSB Northern Ireland, TSB Scotland and TSB Channel Islands. TSB England and Wales became a listed entity, TSB Group plc, in 1986, with TSB Northern Ireland and TSB Scotland fully owned subsidiaries. Allied Irish Banks bought TSB Northern Ireland in 1991 and TSB Channel Islands became a subsidiary of TSB Group in 1992. TSB Group merged with Lloyds Bank in 1995. Following UK government support during the 2008 credit crisis, the European Commission forced Lloyds to divest 632 branches which were formed into TSB Bank plc in 2013 (see reference 47). Spain's Banco de Sabadell purchased TSB Bank plc in 2015.
[†]There were 952 building societies in the UK in 1940, 481 in 1970, 273 in 1980, 101 in 1990, 67 in 2000, 49 in 2010 (see reference 48) and 43 in 2020 (see reference 49). Of those remaining, one building society had over 50% of the sector's total assets.

and US the consolidation of the banking industry, particularly in the last 40 years, has created banking entities of huge scale and scope. For example, we calculated from data publicly available from the Federal Deposit Insurance Corporation (FDIC) that 13 banks in the US held over 50% of all domestic deposits as of the end of June 2019. Similarly, in Great Britain in 2016 over 70% of personal current accounts were held with just four banks.[55]

2.4.1 Consolidation in UK Banking

Arguably the origins of the consolidation in British banking can be traced back to the Banking Co-Partnership Act of 1826. The act was made by the Parliament of the United Kingdom in response to the financial crisis of 1825, which had resulted in the failure of 93 banks in England and Wales (approximately 15% of the total).[56] Since 1709 until this act, banks that issued banknotes in England and Wales other than the Bank of England could not be incorporated and had to be run as unlimited liability partnerships with no more than six partners, and were called private banks. Following the act, such banks could still not be incorporated, but the number of partners allowed was unlimited for banks outside a 65-mile radius of London. The government's intent was for such *country banks* to increase the number of their partners by adding a few more partners, but in reality following the act new banks were established with hundreds of partners, which were in effect joint stock companies, i.e. companies that issued shares (to their partners) and for which the owners of the shares had unlimited liability[57] – although the individual risk was more diluted, given the much larger number of partners. By 1833, 34 joint stock banks had been successfully formed and were operating, and the Bank Charter Act of 1833 confirmed that it was legal to establish joint stock banks within the 65-mile radius of London, as long as they did not issue banknotes.*,[58]

The primary benefits of the act of 1826 were the establishment of the ability for banks to raise capital from a large group of shareholders (and use that to expand their businesses) and the ability for banks to merge with and acquire each other. Further legislation in 1858 and 1862 enabled joint stock banks to give limited liability to their shareholders. From 1826 until the early twentieth century this resulted in a shift in banking activity from private banks, which peaked at nearly 800 banks in 1813 and dropped to fewer than 100 in 1900, to joint stock banks. The number of joint stock banks peaked at 122 in 1875 and then reduced as they merged and acquired each other. At the same time, the number of bank branches grew from around 1,000 in 1813 to over 6,000 in 1900[59] and then 8,610 in 1913 with a total of 88 banks (both private and joint stock).[60] As Newton points out in her paper "Change and Continuity: The Development of Joint Stock Banking in the Early Nineteenth Century":

> *The absorption of small-scale joint stock and private banks into a national network of branches owned and controlled by large-scale, limited liability clearing banks was more or less complete by 1918.*[61]

---

*The Banking Co-Partnership Act of 1826 had actually left it open whether joint-stock banks that did not issue notes could be established within a 65-mile radius of London. After the 1826 act, the government obtained a ruling from the Court of King's Bench that they were legal, and the 1833 act regularised the situation.

The clearing banks were so called because they operated the cheque-clearing systems in England and Wales and in Scotland. Other banks and financial services businesses could only access cheque clearing via the clearing banks. The clearing banks also provided funding to smaller banks and other financial institutions. The situation described by Newton persisted for several decades, including through another world war, although consolidation continued. For example, 13 banks or banking groups owned the 16 clearing banks in England and Scotland in 1960.* At the start of 1970, although there were still nominally 14 English and Scottish clearing banks (according to the Bank of England),[62] these were owned by six banks or banking groups,† and during the course of 1970, the number of English and Scottish clearing banks dropped to 10 due to the consolidation of several by their owners.‡

Starting in the 1960s, though, the UK government came under growing pressure to increase competition in banking in response to complaints about the clearing banks' conservative lending policies (which in turn were heavily influenced by individual lending caps the Bank of England imposed on the clearing banks and other institutions) and their operation of a cartel.[63] Government action in the market and regulatory and legal changes seemingly abounded in the next two decades.

The UK government established the National Girobank in 1968 (initially called the Post Office Giro), which was seen as a means of providing a cheap and efficient money transfer system for retail and business customers through the existing network of post offices.[64] Although it took several years to establish itself, it became successful through providing cheap cash deposit facilities for businesses, distribution of government benefits and, from 1978, a free interest-bearing personal bank account[65] that spurred the large UK banks to respond in kind. At its peak it was the UK's sixth-biggest bank. It was

*The 16 London and Scottish clearing banks in 1960 comprised 12 banks or banking groups. Eight were independent London clearing banks (Barclays Bank, District Bank, Lloyds Bank, Martins Bank, Midland Bank, the National Bank, National Provincial Bank and Westminster Bank). There were three London clearing banks owned by other banks (Coutts & Co, owned by National Provincial Bank; Glyn, Mills & Co, owned by the Royal Bank of Scotland; and Williams Deacon's Bank, also owned by the Royal Bank of Scotland). There were four independent Scottish clearing banks (Bank of Scotland, Clydesdale Bank, National Commercial Bank of Scotland and the Royal Bank of Scotland Limited) plus The British Linen Bank which was owned by Barclays Bank but operated separately from it.
†At the start of 1970, there were 14 London and Scottish clearing banks which comprised six banks or banking groups. There were three independent London clearing banks (Barclays Bank, Lloyds Bank and Midland Bank). National Westminster Bank owned four London clearing banks (Coutts & Co, District Bank, National Provincial Bank and Westminster Bank) and the Royal Bank of Scotland owned three (Glyn, Mills & Co, the National Bank and Williams Deacon's Bank). There were two independent Scottish clearing banks (Bank of Scotland and The Royal Bank of Scotland) and two that were owned by other banks (Clydesdale Bank was owned by Midland Bank and The British Linen Bank had been sold in 1969 by Barclays Bank to Bank of Scotland for a 34.5% stake in the combined group, which Barclays Bank retained until 1985).
‡By the end of 1970 there were four independent London clearing banks (Barclays Bank, Lloyds Bank, Midland Bank and National Westminster Bank) and two that were owned by other banks (Coutts & Co was owned by National Westminster Bank and Williams & Glyn's Bank was owned by the Royal Bank of Scotland). There were still two independent Scottish clearing banks and two that were owned by other banks, although The British Linen Bank was absorbed into Bank of Scotland on 1 March 1971.

sold to Alliance & Leicester Building Society in 1990,[66] which was ultimately acquired by Santander.

In 1971 the UK government set up the Page Committee to review the financial and legal framework of the UK National Savings and associated money transmission facilities.[67] The review included examining the trustee savings bank (TSB) sector across the UK. TSBs had typically been set up as charities (overseen by trustees, hence the name) that provided a means for working people to save so that they had funds to draw on if they became ill or unemployed and as a source of funds during retirement. The first TSB was established in 1810 in Scotland.[68] Although there had been several hundred TSBs in the nineteenth century, by 1970 these had been consolidated to 73 and various laws restricted their activities. The committee's final report in 1973 reported that the ownership of the TSBs was unclear and that the liabilities of their trustees to the depositors was also unclear. Furthermore, it recommended that they should become mutual organisations owned by their members and that restrictions on the activities of the TSBs should be removed so that they could provide a competitive personal banking service. The Trustee Savings Bank Act 1976 only implemented the second of these recommendations and also established the Central Board of Trustee Savings Banks that oversaw the activities of the TSBs, could provide services to them and would also be the recipient of any surplus funds from closed TSBs.[69] In effect, the act enabled further consolidation of the TSBs (which duly took place) and further Trustee Savings Banks Acts in 1981 and 1985 resulted in the flotation and public listing of the TSB Group in 1986 – it became just another private bank and merged with Lloyds Bank in 1995.

The Bank of England abolished the clearing banks' interest rate cartel in 1971.[70] There were then some additions to the list of clearing banks with The Co-operative Bank in 1975, the Central Trustee Savings Bank* in 1975 and National Girobank in 1983. The number was further enlarged in 1985 with the establishment of an umbrella clearing organisation (APACS, with 17 members) and three clearing companies (the Cheque and Credit Clearing Company, the CHAPS and Town Clearing Company for high-value electronic payments and Bacs for bulk electronic payments) to operate the existing payment schemes.[71]

In 1979, the new UK government lifted controls that had limited foreign exchange to authorised UK banks, therefore allowing the free movement of capital in and out of the UK.[72] At the same time, the 1979 Banking Act came into effect. This established a statutory banking supervisory environment, creating a two-tier system of licensed deposit-taking institutions and recognised banks,[†] making it unlawful to take deposits without having a license or formal recognition. By implementing a framework with a basis in law for operating a banking business and opening the borders of the UK to

---

*The Central Trustee Savings Bank Ltd was set up by the TSBs in 1972 to provide processing services. It was different from the Central Board of the Trustee Savings Banks which was established by the Trustee Savings Bank Act 1976.

†A deposit-taking institution was permitted to accept deposits after it had demonstrated that it had sufficient quality of management, conducted its business prudently and was financially sound. A bank had to satisfy the same requirements and also demonstrate it had a *high reputation and standing in the financial community* and that it either supplied a wide range of banking services (as defined in the act) or was highly specialised (see reference 72). The two tiers were consolidated in the Banking Act of 1987 so that all deposit-taking entities were regulated as banks.

flows of capital, these changes provided a foundation for increasing competition in the banking markets, primarily from an influx of overseas banks.

The Big Bang of 1986 sought to remove anti-competitive practices in financial markets by opening up membership of the London Stock Exchange. This enabled several of the UK's clearing banks to diversify by acquiring stock exchange firms and building investment banking businesses and for foreign banks to start investment banking in London (often by acquisition).[73]

The building society sector in the UK was also busy consolidating. For example, there was a near 40% drop in the number of building societies between 1980 and 1985. The UK government passed legislation in 1986 that allowed building societies to diversify and demutualise, becoming banks in the process, with the second-largest society, Abbey National, demutualising in 1989. Consolidation in the sector continued nonetheless, with another near 40% drop in the number of building societies between 1985 and 1990, although the total number of building society branches peaked in 1987 and the total assets of the sector increased by 150% between 1985 and 1995.[74] In reality, the biggest impact of the change in law and the most significant blow to the sector took place between 1995 and 1997, when seven larger building societies demutualised (all of which were subsequently absorbed into other banking groups*), reducing the total assets of the building society sector and the total number of branches to less than half of what they had been at the start of 1995.[†]

The final round of consolidation of the clearing banks occurred between 1995 and 2010, starting with the merger of Lloyds Bank and TSB, then the acquisition of National Westminster Bank by the Royal Bank of Scotland in 2000, various acquisitions by Santander, the merger of Clydesdale Bank and Yorkshire Bank by their common owner in 2005, and ending with the acquisition of HBOS (which owned Bank of Scotland) by Lloyds in 2008. Further reorganisation of the UK payment clearing systems in the next decade made direct participation in the various forms of payment clearing significantly easier and many more institutions began to participate directly rather than through another clearing bank (the options for participation are covered in Section 7.6.14).

Following the banking crisis of 2008, George Osborne became the UK's Chancellor of the Exchequer in 2010. He immediately began to push the regulators to improve the bank licencing process by formalising the approach and timescales associated with it. Alongside this, in 2013 the Financial Standards Authority was split into two bodies, the Financial Conduct Authority and the Prudential Regulation Authority. The former is responsible for ensuring that banks protect customers and keep the industry stable and, significantly, for encouraging competition in the banking sector. It appeared that the

---

*Alliance & Leicester (demutualised in 1997 and acquired by Santander in 2008), Bristol & West (demutualised and acquired in 1997 by Bank of Ireland, which ultimately sold the branches to The Co-operative Bank), Cheltenham & Gloucester (demutualised and acquired by Lloyds TSB in 1995), Halifax (demutualised in 1997 and merged in 2001 with Bank of Scotland, which was acquired by Lloyds Banking Group in 2009), National & Provincial (demutualised and acquired in 1996 by Abbey National, which was subsequently acquired by Santander in 2004), Northern Rock (demutualised in 1997 and split up following its collapse in 2008), Woolwich (demutualised in 1997 and acquired by Barclays in 2000).

†The total amount of building society assets at the end of 1994 was £300,998 million and at the end of 1997 was £137,864 million. The number of building society branches at the end of 1994 was 5,566 and at the end of 1997 was 2,537 (see reference 74).

UK may have reached the end of consolidation of the banking sector, and that the UK government, the UK banking regulators and the European Commission would reverse the trend. In some ways, this appears to be the case. Metro Bank, the first new high street bank for 100 years, was launched. Also, the banking joint ventures involving two large UK supermarket retailer groups, Tesco with Royal Bank of Scotland and Sainsbury's with Lloyds Banking Group, were ended by the retailers buying out their banking partners and setting up their own banking operations and platforms. A new version of the TSB was split out of Lloyds Banking Group (and acquired by Spain's Banco de Sabadell). ClearBank, which claimed to be the first new bank to offer clearing services to other banks in 250 years, was launched. Several new banks were also launched, including Atom Bank, Monzo, Starling and Tandem (although strictly speaking Tandem gained its banking licence by virtue of acquiring Harrods Bank). The Bank of England, in its paper 'Evolution of the UK Banking System',[75] points out that the big four banking groups in the UK accounted for a smaller percentage of the deposit taking and lending market in 2014 than their constituent parts did in 1960. Additionally, according to the Bank of England in June 2020[76] there were 363 monetary financial institutions in the UK (which are licensed to accept deposits and include banks and building societies but not credit unions), of which 120 are native banking entities. Our analysis indicates that the total number of institutions increased by 11 from the start of 2015 to June 2020, with net 12 new banks.* It does look like the regulatory focus on increasing competition worked to some extent.

2.4.2   Consolidation in Global Banking

In the US, the story is very similar to that of the UK, but over a shorter timeframe. In 1995, The Brookings Institution published a paper titled 'The Transformation of the US Banking Industry: What a Long Strange Trip It's Been'[77] that detailed, at great length, the origins of US banking consolidation. They identified two core drivers at the heart of the process: first, the large numbers of regulatory changes from the early 1980s onwards, much of which sought to de-regulate banking, and, second, the advance of technology (including ATMs, increased computing power, improved telecommunications and automated credit scoring) that provided the technical means to improve profitability without being as dependent upon a branch network.

---

*The bulk of the list comprises branches and UK subsidiaries of international banks, which change frequently. In addition, during the period all the large UK banks were forced to ring-fence their UK retail banking operations into separate legal entities (as discussed in Section 2.9), and this caused many changes to the list. The total number of entities on the list increased by 11 between 1 January 2015 and 1 June 2020. Adding new entries to the list and subtracting removals from the list of entities offering retail, commercial, corporate and/or wholesale banking services (excluding branches and subsidiaries of international banks in London purely to gain access to wholesale markets), the net number of such entities increased by 12. This comprises 16 new entities (Allica Bank, Atom Bank, Castle Trust Capital, Charter Court Financial Services, ClearBank, Fineco Bank, GKBK, Masthaven, Monzo, N26, OakNorth, Oxbury FS, Redwood Bank, Revver, Starling Bank and Zopa) and four removed entities (Duncan Lawrie, GE Capital UK, Holmesdale Building Society and Redstone Mortgages). There were also entities that gained and then lost or handed back their licenses during this period, such as Civilised Investments (which then re-emerged as Allica Bank).

However, when the Brookings paper was written, the authors believed that the decline in bank numbers was coming to an end. This has clearly not been the case and, it could be argued, the drivers identified in the report are as much (or more) in evidence in the market in the twenty-first century as they were in the late twentieth century, although the regulatory changes switched to a focus on bringing in controls rather than de-regulating. FDIC data shows clearly the decline in the number of US commercial banks, from 14,482 in 1984[78] to 4,518 at the end of 2019.[79] It also records the number of bank failures from 2001 to the end of 2019 as 557,[80] during which time the number of banks reduced by 3,797. We conclude, therefore, that over 80% of the reduction in bank numbers between 2001 and 2019 was through mergers and acquisitions rather than failures* (assuming either zero or no more than a small number of banks voluntarily wound down). This was also observed by the FDIC in the period 1984 to 2003 which noted that the primary mechanism for the reduction in banking institutions was mergers and acquisitions.

The same process is equally as evident in savings institutions as it is for commercial banks. The FDIC data describes 3,368 savings institutions in 1984.[81] Comparable data indicates that at the end of 2019 that there were only 659 savings institutions recognised by the FDIC as operating in the US.[82]

The decline in the numbers of US and UK banking institutions has been blamed variously on several factors, and deregulation seems to be one of the most popular. However, the data is not convincing. For example, after 2008, the US authorities embarked on a period of unprecedented regulation and yet the decline in US banking institutions continued. Additionally, in the decade between the start of 2010 and the end of 2019, only 39 new commercial banks and four savings institutions were registered. Put another way, in the whole of that decade fewer new banks were registered than in any single year between 1944 and 2008 inclusive.

Of course, these trends have not been experienced only in the UK and the US. There are plenty of other geographies where there has been significant banking business consolidation and many developed markets demonstrate quite extreme examples of banking services concentration. For example, a study in 2003[83] showed that just three banks held a 75% share† or greater of the total banking assets in Austria, Cyprus, Denmark, Finland, Greece, Israel, the Netherlands, New Zealand, Norway, Sweden and Switzerland. For comparison, the same study showed the biggest three banks in the UK and US had 57% and 19% shares of total banking assets respectively. Given the impact of the 2008 banking crisis, we suspect many markets became more consolidated due to bank failures, and this was seen to be the case in at least one study.[84]

Four Nordic countries featured in the list of concentrated markets in the previous paragraph. The largest bank in the Nordics is Nordea, which achieved its current form between 1997 and 2000 through the combination of four Nordic banks – Unibank of Denmark, Merita Bank of Finland, Kreditkassen (Christiania Bank og Kreditkasse) of Norway and Nordbanken of Sweden. It can trace its roots to more than 300 banks across the Nordic region, dating back to a bank founded in 1820 (Sparekassen for Kjøbenhavn og Omegn).[85] Arguably Nordea is one of the most compelling examples of banking consolidation in the world.

---

*Most US commercial bank failures result in the deposits and assets of the failed bank being acquired by another bank, sometimes by what the FDIC terms an assisted merger. For the statistics presented here we do not count these as mergers, but as failures.
†Averaged over the period 1988–1997.

2.4.3   An Alternative Form of Consolidation

Consolidation of banking institutions in the twentieth and twenty-first centuries seems to have been inexorable in developed countries, and we are unaware of any such countries that provide a different history. However, the rate of consolidation appears to have varied significantly. Regulation may have restricted it in some countries. We saw in Section 2.4.1 how lifting the limitation of banks to unlimited liability partnerships with no more than six partners in England and Wales in 1826 enabled consolidation of the banking industry. In the US, consolidation across state boundaries was difficult, if not impossible, until 1995, when the Riegle-Neal Interstate Banking and Branching Efficiency Act of 1994 took effect. Yet there are countries where there are still relatively high numbers of local banks, including Austria (with nearly 500 local Raiffeisenbanken), Germany (with 839 Volksbanken and Raiffeisenbanken as at the end of 2019[86]), Norway (with 95 savings banks[87]), Spain (with 29 cajas rurales), Switzerland (with 229 Raiffeisenbanken[88]) as well as the US (with 659 savings institutions, the vast majority of which are local). Note that this remains the case in some markets even when the majority of banking assets are concentrated into a small number of large national banking groups, such as in Austria, Norway and Switzerland (see Section 2.4.2). Although such local savings banks are normally independent, they typical draw on the services of either a central organisation or from one of a small number of service providers. For example, in Germany, Fiducia & GAD IT operates a core banking platform (among other platforms) for the Volksbanken and Raiffeisenbanken that processes nearly 100 million accounts[89] and Finanz Informatik likewise processes 120 million accounts for the Sparkassen,[90] and in Switzerland all the Raiffeisen banks moved to a single core banking platform, Avaloq, in 2019.[91] In the US there are several third-party processors that provide centrally operated and shared banking platforms to the savings banks. This is, of course, one way in which small banks can get similar levels of automation and economies of scale as large corporate banks.

Contrast that with the UK, where in 2013 we were asked by the board of a small bank about the possibility of moving its customers' accounts (including current accounts) onto a shared, outsourced platform in order to reduce operating costs, to which we answered there was no such platform in the UK.* That bank no longer exists. We also explored with a small group of building societies the possibility of offering current accounts on a shared platform. The absence of any third-party processors offering such a shared platform meant that the start-up costs would have been prohibitive. Since then, several organisations have started offering outsourced core banking platforms in the UK covering the full range of retail bank accounts, although none have anything like the scale of such providers in other countries.

However, federated structures such as a group of independent banks sharing ownership of a central services organisation as described previously can still come under pressure to change. We covered the consolidation, flotation and eventual acquisition of the UK's trustee savings banks in Section 2.4.1. As another example, the Netherlands had a system of independent, member-owned co-operative local Rabobanks that owned a central organisation, Rabobank Nederland, that provided services to the

---

*At the time there was at least one third-party organisation that processed savings accounts for banking institutions, but none that could process current accounts.

local Rabobanks and, significantly, also supervised them. However, on 1 January 2016 the structure was radically changed so that Rabobank Nederland and the 106 local Rabobanks merged to form a single co-operative bank.[92] It appears that the new structure enabled the costs of operating over 100 separate local banks to be reduced (with significant job losses), by centralising activities that weren't customer-facing and removing those that were no longer needed.

We have a theory that strong, independent local banks can only survive where they combine resources, although this can result in a loss of autonomy. Also, having geographical limits on the scope of those individual local banks can foster co-operation, as it can mean that such banks do not compete with each other.

2.5   The Development of Modern Banking Products and Services

From a banking product perspective, many of the basic banking products were already in existence thousands of years ago. Basic loans and deposits, merchant lending facilities and foreign exchange all existed by the time of the Romans. However, more sophisticated products and services continued to be developed, with the odd pause when empires collapsed, and the basis of modern banking products (sophisticated commercial lending, payments networks, payment cards, etc.) can only really be said to have come into existence in relatively recent times.

Many of the products and services that we would recognise, in an updated form, today have been developed in the last few hundred years, with some products being much older. This section provides a selection of some of the more notable developments.

2.5.1   Banknotes

Banknotes were developed in China during the Tang and Song dynasties[93] from the ninth century to the thirteenth century. In the Tang dynasty, a trader could take goods to the capital and then bank the proceeds at a chancellery, the representative office of the government of the region the trader came from, in return for a receipt called *feiqian* or flying money. Once back in his region, the trader could exchange the note for cash.[94] Unfortunately, no examples of these notes remain. Following the development of printing on paper during the Song dynasty, at the start of the eleventh century several merchant houses in Sichuan were licensed to issue notes (called *jiaozi*) in exchange for coin deposits. These notes could be used to purchase goods from traders in place of coins. Eleven years later the government had to step in after one of the merchant houses failed (i.e. could not cover redemptions of jiaozi with coins) and from 1160 had a monopoly on the issue of jiaozi.

Of course, the basic concept of a banknote is that it represents a deposit held safely by a bank, and we can find plenty of examples where receipts for deposits were used in effect as banknotes. Mass issue of banknotes in the Western world had to wait until printing was established there. In Europe and the United States, many banks issued their own banknotes and the practice became widespread in the seventeenth century. However, over time central banks tended to take over the issue of banknotes (as happened in eleventh-century Sichuan), probably for two reasons – one was to raise funds for the government in the form of gold deposits and the other to increase the security of such banknotes, which lost all value if a bank failed and could cause significant economic damage. We cover the issuance of banknotes and coins in more detail in Chapter 7.

2.5.2   Cheques

Precursors of the modern cheque go back well over two millennia. Some form of letters of credit (*adesha*) in India are referenced in the *Arthashastra*,[95] which is thought to date from between the start of the Mauryan period (322 BCE) to around 200 CE. Promissory notes (in effect, a written promise to pay someone an amount on a future date) were used by the Romans in wooden tablet form over 2,000 years ago.[96] In the third century, banks in the Persian Sassanid Empire issued letters of credit called *chak*,[97] which is believed to be the origin of the Arabic word *sakk*, used for letters of credit in the Muslim Empire in the seventh century, and from which it is believed the English term *cheque* originates.[98] As we have already mentioned, in twelfth- and thirteenth-century Europe, pilgrims and crusaders travelling to Jerusalem could deposit money at a local temple of the Knights Templar in exchange for a letter of credit that they could cash in Jerusalem. In China, there is a record from the start of the thirteenth century that the army of the Song dynasty issued paper bearer notes (i.e. a cheque that is payable to anyone who presented it for payment) for purchases.[99] Italian bankers issued bills of exchange in the fourteenth century that could be cashed in their branches across Europe, North Africa and the Near East.

The modern cheque emerged in the sixteenth and seventeenth centuries in England, with the earliest remaining handwritten example dating from 16 February 1659.[100]

The boom in the usage of cheques in the second half of the twentieth century – for example, the volume of cheques used in the US grew from 8 billion in 1952 to 13 billion in 1960[101] – required various technological developments, including magnetic ink so that cheques could be machine read, and cheque-sorting machines, which we explore in Section 2.6.1.

The volume and value of cheques used has typically fallen both relatively and absolutely compared to other payment methods throughout the twenty-first century, but their use is still popular. We cover the use of cheques in more detail in Chapter 7.

2.5.3   Centralised Cheque Clearing

The 1770s saw the advent of centralised cheque clearing in London.[102] A group of banks in London had been operating a process of bilateral exchange of cheques, with clerks of each bank making daily rounds of the other banks. Around 1770 this changed to a daily meeting at the Five Bells tavern in Lombard Street. The group of banks involved eventually formed the Committee of London Clearing Bankers, which became the Bankers' Clearing House, with its members known as the London clearing banks, a classification the Bank of England continued to use until the 1980s when the UK's clearing systems were reorganised. See Section 2.4.1 for more on the history of the UK's clearing banks.

Similar manual cheque-clearing arrangements were established in many countries in the nineteenth century and the US established a national cheque-clearing service operated by the Federal Reserve Banks in 1914.[103] Generally, such systems involved the bank to which a cheque had been submitted presenting the cheque to the bank that had issued it and receiving payment in return.

Centralised systems typically netted off all the payments between the banks so that either one side of each pair of banks made a net payment to the other one of the pair (which is only practical with a relatively small number of banks, given the rapid increase in possible combinations as the number of banks involved increases), or an overall netting arrangement in which there was a net transfer of assets owned by each bank held in a central reserve (typically at the central bank). We cover the topic of settlement in more detail in Chapter 7.

Clearing of cheques by transmitting the information from a cheque electronically rather than physically transporting the cheques began in the US in the 1990s, between banks and the Federal Reserve, and was made legal in the UK in 1996. Recipients of cheques in various countries have increasingly been able to submit an electronic image of the cheque to their bank for collection, often enabled by changes in the law to remove the requirement for physical cheques to be submitted and the introduction of smart-phones with cameras.

2.5.4 Traveller's Cheques

Circular notes, the precursor of traveller's cheques, were issued by banks in England in the eighteenth century. These enabled noteholders to withdraw cash from an overseas branch of the same bank or a correspondent bank. The oldest known remaining example is from the 1770s and was issued by the Paris branch of Sir Robert Herries and Co., London.[104] The modern form of traveller's cheques was launched by American Express in 1891,[105] along with a campaign to promote acceptance by banks and retailers around the world. The widespread adoption and acceptance of payment cards severely reduced the demand for traveller's cheques.

2.5.5 Wire Transfers and Electronic Payments

Western Union, established in 1856 from the merger of other telegraph companies, was the operator of a telegraph network* in the United States and in 1871 introduced a money transfer service, so that a person in one location could send money to another per-son, potentially on the other side of the country. The concept of such person-to-person cash transfers survived, and they are still used extensively for cross-border personal remittances to less developed countries, although they now use modern communication methods.

The same technology – telegraphic communications – was used in 1918 by the recently established Federal Reserve to set up an interbank network between all the Federal Reserve Banks, the Federal Reserve Board and the US Treasury. Alongside the Gold Settlement Fund comprising deposits from the regional Federal Reserve Banks held by the US Treasury, this enabled the Federal Reserve Banks to rapidly settle payments between banks in different districts (and therefore with different Federal Reserve Banks) without any physical movement of cash or gold.[106] Each payment was settled individually, and so this was in effect a real-time gross settlement (RTGS) system. Of course, when it was introduced, payment instructions were sent and received manually

---

*Initially, Morse code was used to transmit messages over a telegraph connection, which predated the telephone system by several decades.

and then the payment was processed manually and the confirmation transmitted back. However, over time, communications were upgraded to telex (which is a faster and more user-friendly way of sending text messages over telegraphic connections, using teletype machines) and then to use proprietary networks with the submission and processing of payment instructions performed by computers. The service is called Fedwire and runs on the same basis today.[107]

Many other interbank electronic payment systems* work in a similar fashion, the main variation being how settlement takes place. In summary, a bank submits a payment instruction to a payment scheme to make a payment to an account at another bank. With a net settlement system, the payment scheme works out the net positions of all the banks that submitted and received payments in a period (typically a day) and then debits or credits the settlement account (typically at a central bank) of each participant. This is how automated clearing house (ACH) payment schemes work. With a real-time gross settlement system like Fedwire and the UK's equivalent, CHAPS, each payment is settled as it is processed, with funds being transferred from the settlement account of the paying bank to the settlement account of the beneficiary bank. Net settlement is typically used by low-value, high-volume payment schemes where time is not critical and RTGS by high-value, low-volume payment schemes where speed and certainty of payment are critical.

Of note is the UK's introduction of the first high-volume immediate-payment scheme, Faster Payments, in 2008. This is a low-value, high-volume immediate-payment scheme, in which payments are made usually in near-real time (typically within seconds) between accounts at different banks. The customers of the banks get the benefit of the near-immediate transfer, whereas the actual settlement takes place periodically at several times during each day, on a net settlement basis. Most low-value, high-volume payment schemes originally processed payments overnight at best, or even over several days (the UK's predominant low-value, high-volume scheme before this, Bacs, takes two nights or three days). Many developed countries have since moved to schemes similar to Faster Payments.

2.5.6 Charge and Credit Cards

Shortly after the US Civil War ended in 1865, retailers in the US started issuing charge coins made initially of celluloid and then various metals to customers who they deemed worthy of receiving credit.[108] A customer would show the coin to the retailer to identify themself and the retailer would check the standing of their account. Such coins were the precursor of store cards and could only be used at a specific retailer.

In 1880, vouchers were issued in the UK by Bradford-based Provident Clothing & Supply Co Ltd (which became Provident Financial Group). Customers were issued with vouchers that they could use in a range of pre-agreed shops. Payment was later made in instalments to a representative who would call at the customer's home.[109]

Then in 1928 embossed metal plates with a paper signature strip were first issued to customers of larger retail stores. A holder of such a plate could use it to purchase goods in the issuing store and pay for them later.[110] The embossing meant that the store

---

*Often also called electronic funds transfer (EFT) systems.

personnel could rapidly take an imprint of the card,[111] an idea that was carried over to plastic cards.

In 1950, the first charge card to gain widespread acceptance, the Diners Club Card, was launched in the US.* Initially launched with a membership of just 200, the scheme grew to 20,000 members within the first year.[112] Diners Club was quickly joined by other issuers of charge and credit cards, including BankAmericard and American Express. The first cards were made of cardboard[113] and by the late 1950s, cards made of plastic with embossed text on them were being issued.† Originally, taking an imprint of a card using a so-called zip-zap machine with a multilayer payment voucher, on which the retailer wrote the amount of the purchase and the cardholder signed, was the standard process at the point of sale for paying with a card. Given that most card payments are captured electronically, card payment schemes generally no longer insist that cards be embossed.

IBM engineer Forrest Parry developed the magnetic stripe on the back of plastic cards in the early 1960s, initially for an identification card to be issued by the CIA. The idea came from magnetic tape that was already being used to store data processed by computers. The magnetic stripe was included in a US card standard in 1969 and an international standard in 1971,[116] and quickly became a feature of virtually all plastic payment cards.

Around the first half of the 1970s, card schemes such as Mastercard and Visa built processing platforms that automated the handling of card payments, typically as a pair of systems – one that dealt with the authorisation requests that are made at the point of sale, and the other a clearing system that dealt with the vouchers that retailers submit to their acquiring bank which are used to record the card transactions. We explore how card payments work in Chapter 6.

2.5.7   Debit Cards

In his book *Looking Backward 2000–1887* published in 1888,[117] Edward Bellamy envisaged that by the year 2000 every person would be given a card linked to an account into which at the start of every year is deposited an equal share of the nation's annual product for the card holder to spend at public storehouses. Although Bellamy called such cards credit cards, they appear to function as debit cards.

In reality, it appears that the Bank of Delaware trialled the first debit card in 1966 with a chain of shoe stores, using a combination of technologies that is remarkable given the year.[118] A customer was issued with a plastic card that they could use to pay for goods by inserting the card into a reader attached to a telephone that dialled up the bank. The cashier followed the instructions from the computer's audio instructions and used the touchtone keypad on the telephone to enter the amount of the purchase.[119] Unlike a credit card, this debited the customer's current or checking account directly.

---

*There was at least one previous charge card that could be used at multiple stores, notably Charg-It, started by Flatbush National Bank in Brooklyn in 1946 (see reference 111), but this did not persist.
†We have seen various claims that American Express was the first issuer of plastic cards, often stating that it first issued them in 1959, but we could not validate this. What we found were an image of a plastic embossed BankAmericard that expired at the end of March 1959 (see reference 114) and an image of a plastic embossed American Express card that expired at the end of October 1959 (see reference 115).

Visa went on to launch its first debit card programme in 1975, in the US.[120] Debit cards were more widely issued from the 1980s onwards. The availability of automated, online authorisation at the point of sale was a precursor to the widespread acceptance by retailers of debit card transactions in place of cash and cheques, but had to wait for network connections and point-of-sale technology to become widely available.

The international card payment schemes took on the role of debit card payment switching, clearing and settlement in some countries, using essentially the same messaging protocols and infrastructure as they used for credit card payments. In other countries, local schemes were established, and in some countries both local schemes and the international card payment schemes were available. In many countries however, the international card payment schemes have acquired local payment card schemes (debit and ATM schemes), so to some extent they have been unified.

2.5.8   Direct Debits

We found evidence that standing orders, in which a customer instructs their bank to make periodic fixed value payments to a retailer or service provider, had been operated in the US at least as early as the 1960s.[121] Direct debits (sometimes called domiciliation), in which a bank customer authorises a retailer or service provider (such as a utility company) to debit their account with varying amounts, are common in developed countries. In our research we found references to direct debit payment being available to giro account holders in West Germany since the 1950s,[122] with 1964 being when the West German banking industry made an agreement for an industry-wide direct debit process[123] which went live in 1966. Direct debits were introduced in the UK in 1968.[124] Direct debit payment requests are usually exchanged electronically using the same networks as used for interbank payments.

In Austria and Germany, the direct debit system was extended so that it became possible to pay a retailer at the point of sale by direct debit, using ELV (Elektronisches Lastschriftverfahren). The account details were held on a payment card (which originally was also a cheque guarantee card and later a debit card), and a retailer swiped the card and got the customer to sign a payment slip. Unlike debit or credit card payments, the retailer took the risk that the payment was not honoured or that the card was stolen. For retailers, it had the advantage that the fees were lower than taking a credit or debit card payment.

2.5.9   Automated Teller Machines

The first automatic cash dispenser (the De La Rue Automatic Cash System or DACS) was installed by Barclays Bank in Enfield, UK, on 27 June 1967. Unlike modern ATMs, a customer had to obtain a paper voucher from the bank and could then use it to withdraw £10 from the machine in conjunction with a six-digit personal code number.[125] The vouchers were impregnated with carbon 14, which is radioactive, to provide a means for the dispenser to check they were valid[126] and had punched holes so the dispenser could read them. The vouchers were retrieved from the machine by bank staff and processed like cheques, so that the customer's account was debited after they made the withdrawal. Given that the dispenser was not online, customers could potentially go overdrawn using the dispenser, and so only preferred customers could get the vouchers. Nine days later, on 6 July 1967, an automatic dispenser manufactured by Metior was unveiled by Spar-främjandet, the central bank of the Swedish savings banks,[127] that took metal tokens with punched holes that it decoded. The MD2 automatic dispenser, manufactured by Chubb, was unveiled by Westminster Bank later the same month. This took plastic cards with punched holes and customers had a four-digit PIN, which the machine could check against the information represented by the punched holes using a complex algorithm.[128] Like the Barclays machine, it also retained the cards. Automatic cash dispensers from a range of manufacturers were quickly introduced all over the world.

The first modern ATM, manufactured by IBM, and branded a Cashpoint by Lloyds Bank was installed in December 1972.[129] This system contained several important developments. First, customers inserted a reusable plastic card with a magnetic stripe which was returned at the end of the transaction. Second, customers could choose the amount of cash to withdraw. Third, the ATM was online and got authorisation for the withdrawal while the customer waited. However, the customer's account was only debited overnight (probably due to the limitations of Lloyds Bank's core banking platform at the time).* However, the ATM didn't have a modern display, using illuminated text to give instructions.

A variety of manufacturers started to sell ATMs to banking institutions, with many subsequently merging to leave a small number of near-global suppliers. IBM eventually withdrew from the ATM business.

2.5.10   SWIFT

SWIFT, the Society for Worldwide Interbank Financial Telecommunication, was launched by 239 banks in 15 countries in 1973. In 1977, it launched a worldwide data network for the routing and exchange of financial messages between banks, and a standard format for those messages.[130] It replaced the use of telex machines and the telex network for international payments and other financial transactions, and enabled banks to automate and speed up international financial transactions. In 2020, SWIFT's website claimed that over 11,000 institutions were connected to its network.

SWIFT is not an electronic payment scheme (as in Section 2.5.5). Banks can send payment messages using it, but have to transfer the funds separately using correspondent banking relationships and payment schemes. This process is covered in more detail in Chapter 7.

Through its closed user groups, SWIFT can carry payment messages for payment schemes. For example, in the UK, the CHAPS high-value RTGS scheme uses SWIFT to send messages between banks including the payment instructions from the paying banks and settlement confirmations from the Bank of England.[131]

2.5.11   Online and Internet Banking

In 1980, the first online home banking service was launched by United American Bank in partnership with RadioShack. For a monthly fee, customers could access information on

---

*As a customer of Lloyds Bank in the 1980s, one of us worked out that immediately after withdrawing cash from a Lloyds Bank ATM, the balance available to the branch staff and at another ATM had not been reduced.

their bank accounts using their Tandy TRS80 home computer with a secure modem.[132] This was swiftly followed by a number of banks including Citibank, Chase Manhattan, Chemical Bank and Manufacturers Hannover in New York, and Nottingham Building Society in the UK.[133] The last, Homelink, was a joint development with Bank of Scotland launched in 1983, using the UK's Prestel dial-up videotex system. The most successful and well-known videotex system was France's Minitel that kept going until 2012[134] and could be used to access your bank. These solutions were a far cry from the Internet banking offerings we have today, providing limited capabilities in a text-only format.

It was the development of the Internet and the World Wide Web that transformed how customers could access information and services. Possibly the first true Internet banking solution was implemented by Stanford Federal Credit Union (SFCU) in 1993. This was text based, and used telnet to access the credit union via the Internet, but in 1994 SFCU launched a browser-based service that used the World Wide Web to access the credit union via the Internet.[135]

2.5.12   Telephone Banking

Using telephones to get account balance and transaction information was implemented by the Bank of Delaware in 1965, when it issued 87,000 plastic cards to its customers to provide them access to the service in its branches. When making a deposit or withdrawal, a customer would present their card to a bank teller, who inserted the card into a reader attached to a telephone.[136] This connected to a central computer, which then played back the balance of the account using a simulated voice, apparently constructing the audio from a selection of different pre-recorded words. The same system was used for the Bank of Delaware's debit card pilot described in Section 2.5.7, and apparently there were plans to pilot a bill payment system that customers could use from home. More sophisticated systems that used the touchtone keypad on a phone to select different services were implemented at around the same time by Wells Fargo Bank and Manufacturers National Bank and were used by bank employees rather than directly by customers.

Although we could not find documentation on when banks first rolled out telephone banking services to their customers, we know centralised telephone banking services were made available by many larger banks to their customers in the 1980s, and we assume some banks were providing such services in the 1970s. Of course, prior to this it was normally possible to call a branch of your bank if you were not able to visit in person, and credit card issuers and acquirers ran call centres to service cardholders and retailers requiring authorisations for purchases. There were (and are) essentially two flavours of telephone banking – a staffed call centre, so a customer of the bank could speak to a person, and an automated service powered by a voice response unit, using touchtones (and later spoken commands) to navigate through a menu of options and to issue requests to the bank. We cover these in more detail in Chapter 4. First Direct, a UK banking brand owned by HSBC, is claimed to have launched the first telephone-only bank in 1989,[137] although we were unable to validate whether this was genuinely the first instance of such an offering.

2.5.13   Smartcards and Contactless Cards

The first smartcard, a plastic card incorporating a microprocessor and memory, was launched in 1977, after being jointly developed by Bull and Motorola.[138] By 1993, all bank-issued payment cards in France had been converted to smartcards, to combat fraud enabled by copying cards with magnetic stripes. The French cards were a precursor of EMV payment cards,* for which specifications were developed, starting in 1994. Contactless cards followed in the 1990s, including for faster fuel payment for trucks in the United States,[139] automated transport tolls in France[140] and ski passes in Austria.[141] Credit cards that integrated a contactless smartcard were first issued in 1995 for Lufthansa, the German airline, to replace a previous version integrated with a regular smartcard. These cards removed the need for frequent travellers to have paper tickets and boarding cards,[142] although the smartcard functionality did not include any credit card payment mechanism. The first contactless transportation smartcard was launched in Seoul, Korea in 1996.[143] Over time charge cards, credit cards and debit cards became smartcards virtually universally, using the EMV standard.

2.5.14   Stored Value and Prepaid Cards

Various public pilots of stored value smartcards took place in the 1990s. The earliest ones that our research identified, both in 1992, were a stored value card, Danmønt, issued in Denmark initially as a public telephone payment card[144] and the addition of a stored value purse to the JerseyCard smartcard on the island of Jersey.[145] Banksys, a payment services company owned by Belgian banks at the time, started a pilot of its Proton stored value card in February 1995, followed by National Westminster Bank starting the pilot of its Mondex card in Swindon, UK, on 3 July and then Visa piloting the VISA Cash card in Australia in November[146] (after licensing the Danmønt system). These cards used an application on the chip inside the card to hold the value, and so did not need to be used online. Many modern prepaid cards and gift cards do not use this arrangement and typically are, in effect, debit cards that can only be used with an online authorisation.

2.5.15   Mobile Banking

With the advent of mobile data and simple web browsers on mobile phones in the late 1990s, some banks offered mobile banking services using WAP (Wireless Application Protocol), which provided primarily text-based user interfaces. Modern smartphones have fully fledged web browsers and modern mobile data networks offer much greater bandwidth, so WAP mobile banking has mainly, if not totally, disappeared. It may still be available from some banks, particularly where low-powered and cheap mobile phones are still widely used.

Perhaps the most well-known mobile money transfer system is M-Pesa, originally launched in 2007 in Kenya by Safaricom, a mobile network operator,[147] and subsequently implemented in various other countries. This allowed customers to deposit money into an account with Safaricom that was associated with their mobile phone, and then send money to and receive money from other mobile phone users. Money transfers were done by exchanging text messages, although this was transparent to users who would access the service through a menu on their phone. It used a network of agents across Kenya who could accept and dispense physical cash to add and withdraw funds from mobile phone accounts. In a country where ATMs and bank branches were not widespread, it gained

---

*Sometimes called Chip and PIN cards.

popularity quickly and became a way of paying for goods and services. In some ways (through the use of agents) it is similar to Western Union's money remittance service, apart from each user has an account that can hold money and can transact, and so physical cash need no longer be involved in a remittance. The M-Pesa service was not free, but it did undercut Western Union's remittance service and one operated by the Kenyan post office. M-Pesa saw significant success over the first decade of its operations, and by the end of 2018 its Kenyan customer base exceeded 25 million[148] and its customer base outside Kenya was over 13 million.[149] By this time, it offered other services in addition to money transfers.

Of course, M-Pesa was originally a limited service, with two key functions – deposit-taking and money transfer. The same year that M-Pesa was launched saw Apple launch its iPhone, the first widely used smartphone, followed by the first Android phone (from HTC) in 2008. Banks responded by developing mobile-friendly versions of their Internet banking sites and then banking apps. M-Pesa, too, provided apps for its customers to use its service.

2.6   Developments in Banking Technology

The use of information technology in banking has origins that stretch back into the mid-twentieth century. The first applications provided a mainly mechanical means of replacing laborious manual tasks and it indicated little to the casual observer, or indeed the seasoned banker, of what the longer-term implications of technology would be for the banking sector.

The most startling aspect of the use of technology in banking has been the pace and scale of change, particularly since the 1950s. In recent years we have seen an explosion in the proliferation of new applications right across the banking sector, with each new technology seemingly paving the way for further advances in a range of new directions. Figure 2.1 illustrates how the use of information technology in banking has expanded over the past century, and the rest of this section provides more details on these developments.

2.6.1   Cheque-sorting Machines

Arguably the earliest use of information technology in banking was that of cheque-sorting systems. As noted previously, the first modern cheques emerged in the late sixteenth and seventeenth centuries and required a clearing process – in which cheques are sorted and sent to the paying bank – to be developed. Historically, the first step of clearing took place in each bank branch, as that is where customers deposited cheques for payment into their accounts, as did the last step of clearing, in which the payers' accounts are debited after the paying bank branch has received the cheques to be paid out from its customers' accounts. In both steps, individual and various sub-totals of the cheque values must be recorded to make sure the right payments are received or sent and applied to individual customer accounts correctly. As banking became more popular and cheque volumes rose, so correspondingly did the effort to process cheques in each branch. To address this issue, bankers turned initially to sorting methods that in some ways replicated postal sorting and then to machines that could use mechanical methods

FIGURE 2.1   Information technology in banking over the past century.

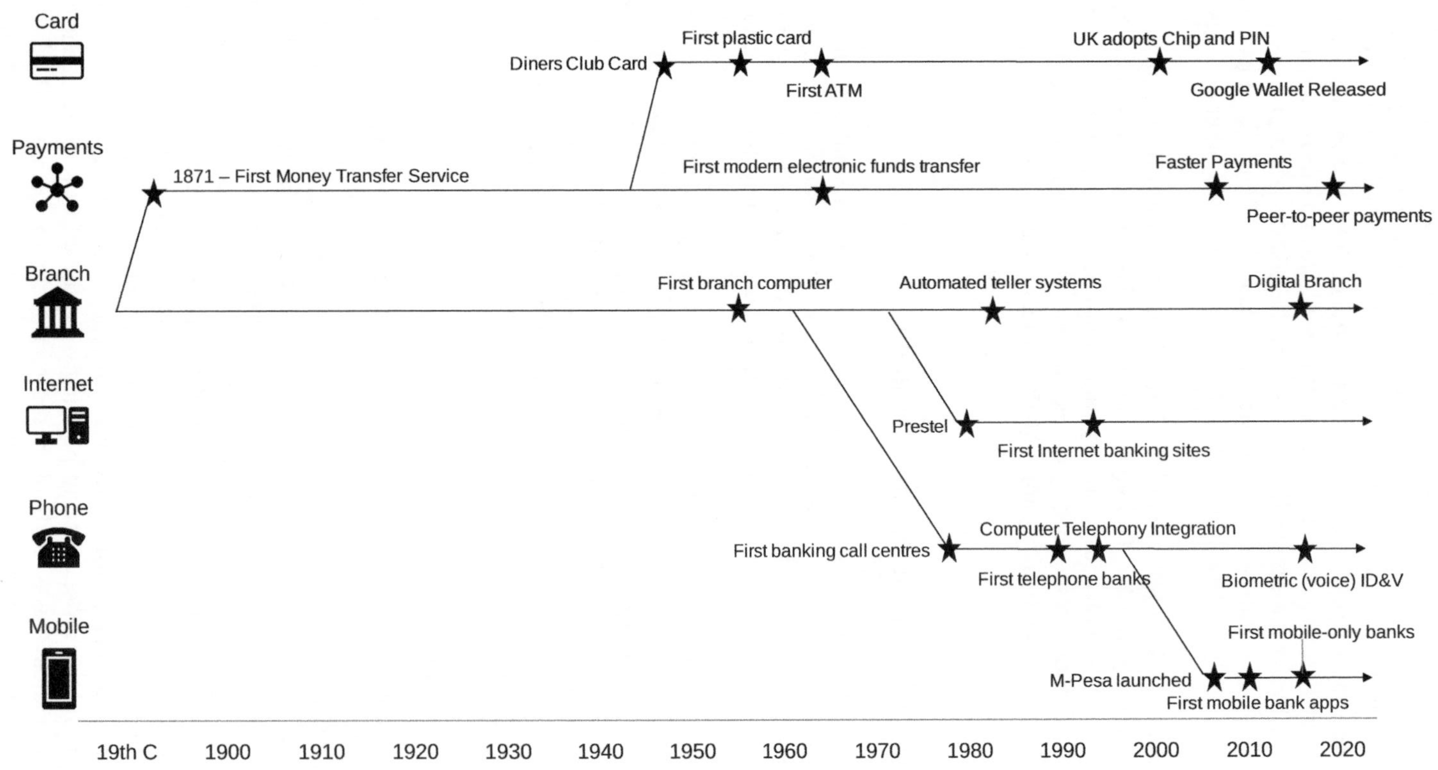

to sort cheques, endorse them and add up their values – such as IBM's 801 Bank Proof machine launched in 1934.[150] These machines relied on human data entry to read the cheque and enter its value and bank and account information. Further automation was possible when magnetic ink character recognition (MICR) was developed, with the E-13B font defined as a standard by the American Bankers' Association in 1958,[151] alongside standardisation of routing numbers (or sort codes, in the UK) and the format of account numbers across banks. Each character could be read using a magnetic head similar to what would have been found in a reel-to-reel tape player or cassette tape player. When used alone, the first machines to use MICR would sort cheques based on each character in turn (so each cheque would go through several rounds of sorting), but once machines were connected to a computer they could sort based on all the information read from a cheque. Optical character recognition (OCR) was also developed at the same time as MICR. In some markets, such as Spain, OCR was used for cheque sorting, and OCR could also be used to read the E-13B MICR characters.

2.6.2   Electronic Accounting Machines

Mechanical adding machines, cash registers, punched-card tabulators and typewriters have been available since before the end of the nineteenth century,[152] and banks were using these much like other businesses. For example, by the end of 1929, Lloyds Bank had implemented mechanical accounting machines in six branches.[153] There are many records of banks using punched cards to help automate accounting in branches and also what were called tronics or electronic bookkeeping machines that use cards with a magnetic stripe on the back to record the current balance of an account – such as the Burroughs Sensimatic.[154] The front of the card is printed with transactions, and the machine adds or subtracts the latest transaction (typed in by a human operator) from the balance held on the magnetic stripe and prints it on the front.

Even with the advent of computers, banks continued to use electromechanical machines in branches for many years. For example, transactions could be entered into a machine at a branch that would print them onto punched cards for submission to a central computer system, or into an accounting machine that punched them onto paper tape that could be transported or read and sent by telephone (at low speed) by a paper tape reader (the equivalent of a teletype machine) to the central computer centre. Many banks didn't automate less busy branches for many years – for example, in 1966 Barclays Bank had automated fewer than 100 of its 2,300 branches.[155]

2.6.3   Computers

The first recorded use of a computer by a bank was in 1955, when Bank of America implemented the IBM 702 computer in San Francisco for mortgage, instalment loan and central-office accounting.[156] Given the pace of development, this computer was in effect obsolete by the time Bank of America installed it,[157] and at its San Jose branch in 1956 it went on to implement a prototype called the Electronic Recording Machine-Accounting (ERMA) system that it developed with the Stanford Research Institute. Later that year it ordered 30 ERMA systems from General Electric, with the first deployed in 1958, comprising a GE100 computer, a cheque reader/sorter, a printer and magnetic tape units. The GE100 computers were based on transistor technology, which was a step up from the vacuum tubes used for the ERMA prototype. Many other larger banks followed suit, with evidence of computers being used by other banks from 1956 in the US and 1959 in the UK. In 1962, a Federal Reserve survey found 178 banks, representing 40% of all commercial bank deposits in the US, were either using computers or in the process of installing them.[158] Computers of that era were able to handle the processing require- ments of up to tens of branches, and so large banks would require many computers. However, by the mid-1960s, computers with much more processing power were avail- able. Such large computers – what we typically call mainframes – could be deployed centrally and get feeds from the electromechanical equipment in branches (see Sections 2.6.1 and 2.6.2). There is no standard definition of a mainframe, but they are typically highly reliable powerful programmable computers that can process large amounts of data and are targeted for use by large corporations. In terms of processing power they sit below supercomputers – which are often used in the defence sector, for meteorology and for scientific research – and above the minicomputers and midrange servers that are typically used in office settings (including single bank branches and small banks) as powerful workstations and more recently as the basis for scalable cloud infrastructure. The IBM System/360 series, launched in 1964, and its successors, culminating in the IBM zSeries range launched in 2000, came to epitomise the mainframe and dominate mainframe computing. There were other manufacturers prevalent in the 1950s, 1960s and 1970s such as Burroughs (which competed strongly with IBM in the UK banking sector in the 1960s), Control Data, EMI, Ferranti, Fujitsu, General Electric, Hitachi, Honeywell, ICL, NCR, NEC, Oki, Olivetti, RCA, Siemens, Sperry Rand, Tandem and Telefunken, but most of these have either disappeared (usually being acquired or merged with other infrastructure providers) or exited the mainframe business. The growth of mainframe processing power made it possible for even the largest banks to centralise their processing.

The price of computer power continued to fall for several decades as technology developed. Computers were initially constructed from electromechanical switches, then vacuum tubes, followed by transistors and then integrated circuits built on silicon chips invented in the late 1950s. Integrated circuits were capable of housing tens and eventually tens of billions of transistors, and eventually lowered the price of computing to the point where banking institutions of virtually any size could afford it.

2.6.4   Data Centres

The first computers were large and needed dedicated rooms (and sometimes entire build- ings) to house them. Initially, office buildings were adapted, but given the centralisation of processing, banks found or built premises as dedicated computer centres. Initially these were near the branches they were serving, so that telephone connections were short distance and physical transfer of paper or magnetic tapes was feasible. In the UK, the earliest reference we could find to the first data centre was to one being opened in the UK in 1961 on Drummond Street in central London by Barclays Bank,[159] which was only two years after it had ordered its first computer. It seems likely that banking data centres were also being set up in the US and other countries around the same time, if not earlier.

Although computers have become more powerful, and therefore for the same com- puting power have shrunk in size (several orders of magnitude), the overall usage of computer processing has increased inexorably and continues to do so, and so data centres housing thousands of servers are now common. The largest banks still operate their own data centres, but the advent of cloud processing means that many financial services organisations have no need to operate their own data centres or even to rent space in a third-party data centre.

2.6.5 Data Networks

Electrical data networks, in rudimentary form, existed from the time of the first telegraph wires and, as already mentioned in Section 2.5.5, were being used for wire transfers from 1871 in the US. Of course, initially there were humans transmitting and receiving the Morse code messages sent using the telegraph system. More sophisticated coding schemes were developed, such as Baudot codes, and by the 1920s, teletype machines, which had a keyboard similar to a typewriter and a mechanism for printing received messages, were gaining traction.[160] The history of several computer manufacturers (including Olivetti and Siemens) includes manufacturing teletype machines, and in fact teletype machines were later adapted to be used as computer terminals and the telegraph network (or by this time, the telex network) was adapted to connect equipment in branches to central computers. There were also dial-up systems that used regular telephone lines along with a modem (modulator/demodulator) that converted electrical signals to sounds and vice versa. Over time, these relatively slow methods were replaced with much-higher-speed digital signalling using a range of technologies.

When a bank has one large centralised computer, with peripheral equipment in branches that submit information over telephone lines, the data network is straightforward. However, as banks acquired more than one computer and often lots of terminals, it was necessary for them to communicate with each other, and so the concept of a local area network (LAN) was born. Initially, these were often aimed at enabling more terminals and other peripherals to be connected to mainframes and minicomputers – including IBM's SNA (Systems Network Architecture), Datapoint's ARCnet (Attached Resource Computer Network) and Digital Equipment Corporation's DECnet, which became available in 1974, 1977 and 1975 respectively. Apparently the first commercial installation of a LAN was at Chase Manhattan Bank in December 1977,[161] using ARCnet to connect Datapoint desktop computers and data entry terminals. SNA was used extensively in LANs involving IBM mainframes. The uptake of PCs and then the Internet increased demand for local area networks. Ultimately, the open and standards-based Ethernet, originally designed at Xerox's Palo Alto Research Center, won out and became the predominant wiring and signalling technology used for wired LANs (alongside Wi-Fi for wireless LANs), and it has been through several design evolutions that have increased its maximum bandwidth. A data network specification like Ethernet typically defines a set of physical attributes such as the design of wiring, physical connection methods and electrical signalling to be used, and how data is sent between two nodes (e.g. computers) connected to it. In order to make use of a data network, computers must use an agreed-upon network protocol, which defines how packets of data are addressed and routed to their destination, and the dominant network protocol in use is Internet Protocol (IP). SNA may still be in use with IBM mainframes in banks and other organisations, but it, too, can be used over data networks that use IP. Other network protocols have virtually disappeared.*

2.6.6   Batch and Real-time Processing

Computers in banking were originally used for batch processing. In other words, staff in a bank branch would type information from cheques, receipts for deposits, payment instructions and so on, into an electronic accounting machine that would output the data onto paper tape or magnetic tape, and that might also have done some basic record counting and subtotalling. The tapes so produced would be physically transported to the computer centre, or loaded into a tape reader that would transmit the data over a telephone or telegraph line to the computer centre (where the data would be output onto another paper or magnetic tape). Data (on tape or sent over a phone or telegraph line) would also be received from other banks or payment schemes. The mainframe computer would then work its way through all the data so received, updating the records of customers' accounts with all the transactions during the day and creating various reports that would be sent back to each branch (so a branch could know what the balance of each of its customers' accounts was) and to the bank's headquarters. It would also have to create reports to be sent to the payment scheme(s) and periodically calculate and apply interest and charges to customers' accounts. This end-of-day processing is still done today, because interest is calculated on a daily basis and applied periodically, and many payment schemes are essentially based on daily batch processing.

However, a purely batch approach was insufficient when online ATMs and then debit cards were introduced. In order to minimise fraud it was necessary to maintain an intra-day balance for all accounts that offered ATM withdrawals and/or debit cards and also a means to flag a payment card as having been lost or stolen. Similarly, customers who had deposited cash at a branch often wanted to be able to withdraw it later that day from an ATM. From our experience, many banks dealt with these challenges by retaining their batch-oriented systems of record and adding another system that maintained an intraday balance that could be queried online. In fact, ATMs typically connected to a central online system inside a bank that they used to get authorisation for a withdrawal, and such systems could be used to hold the intraday balances of all accounts. End-of-day processing on the batch-oriented mainframe computer would take all the ATM withdrawal and debit card transactions (which were submitted daily) and apply them, along with all the data received from the branches, and then reload the online system with the newly calculated available balance. Note in this scenario how the system of record is always the central, batch-oriented mainframe computer. The records managed by the computer maintaining the intraday balances are in effect wiped out when they are replaced by the balances calculated by the batch-oriented mainframe computer. Of course, the system of record is only correct as of last night, as banks would say to their customers.

So, this begs the question whether banks now have online, real-time systems of record (i.e. banking platforms) instead of batch-oriented systems of record. As well as solving

---

*There are other network protocols used in some forms of wireless communication such as Zigbee for home automation and medical devices and the protocols used by Bluetooth, contactless cards and RFIDs.

the challenge of maintaining intraday balances, online real-time banking platforms have other advantages – new accounts can be created immediately and customers can start using them straight away – something that Metro Bank in the UK does with instant account opening accompanied with instant issuance of plastic cards, PINs and cheque-books. Customer information can be changed and used in real time (e.g. for lending decisions). All modern commercially available banking platforms that we are aware of are online, and it is on the record that some banks have implemented online real-time banking platforms.* A well-documented example is that of the Trustee Savings Banks in the United Kingdom that had implemented an online banking platform in Northern Ireland as early as 1970,[162] and by 1986, after merging into a single bank and being floated on the stock market, the TSB was the only UK clearing bank with an online real-time banking platform (and may well have still been in that position in 1995).[163] What does not appear to be documented or so well known is that when the TSB was taken over by Lloyds Bank in 1995, the merged bank retained the TSB banking platform for its retail banking business, primarily because it made branch operations more efficient (and so required fewer branch staff). Lloyds Bank was still using the same platform after it separated TSB into a new bank in 2013. Of course, in order to support ATMs, debit cards, immediate payments, Internet banking and so on, all banks in effect have online real-time banking capability, but we expect many are still using batch-oriented systems of record based on applications first developed in the 1960s.

2.6.7   Cloud

For many years, large banks have been running their own data centres, increasingly full of commoditised mid-range servers typically running some variant of the UNIX operating system. In effect, they have been providing computing power on demand to their internal IT projects and then recharging the business units that use the applications the projects supply. However, increasingly banks have been exploring and using third-party cloud services to gain even greater economies of scale and, perhaps just as importantly, better service levels than their in-house IT organisations can provide at the same cost. In our experience, the larger banks often had major internal challenges with concerns over information security, but the cost savings available by moving to a cloud provider, alongside the experience the industry has nonetheless gained, have begun to outweigh such concerns. For start-up banks, cloud means they can reduce up-front capital expenditure in infrastructure and get the benefits of better availability from cloud suppliers and we expect that virtually all new banks are running on cloud infrastructure.

2.7   The Challenges of Technology in Banking

While technology has improved banking services, it has also hugely complicated matters. Banking technology departments now regularly account for 10% or more of a bank's operating expenses and technology staff make up an ever-growing percentage of a bank's

---

*In this paragraph, an online platform is one into which transactions can be entered during the course of the day (but are stored for later batch processing) and provides a facility for online queries (e.g. the latest available balance). However, most processing, including updating an account with the transactions, is done in batch. An online real-time platform has the same online query features, and accounts are updated as transactions are entered.

workforce. More importantly, with the continued growth in the use of technology in banks over the last half century we are now in a position where many banks have huge technology estates that feature systems running from legacy mainframe platforms to modern cloud-based channel platforms, with a dose of outsourced platforms, knitted together with thousands of interfaces.* The complexity that this creates has become a significant worry for banks, not just in terms of day-to-day operational management, but also in terms of the costs and risks associated with keeping the system maintained and continually updating it to provide new services or keep up with changes to regulation.

In recent years the growing complexity and age of banking systems have become more and more evident to banking customers with a series of high-profile systems failures. In the UK, Royal Bank of Scotland experienced a significant system outage in 2012 for which it received a fine of £42 million[164] and another outage in 2015,[165] and it is far from alone in its systems outages. Many of the UK banks have experienced system outages, as has Commonwealth Bank of Australia (including one on its new core banking platform on 17 October 2019[166]), Bank of America (30 October 2019[167]) and many other international and local banks. Such outages are typically only the failures that are visible, on platforms that are customer-facing such as Internet banking platforms or on platforms that we heavily rely upon for timely delivery of services such as payment platforms. There are many other banking system failures that are never directly observed by the banking public. Of course, one positive reason for this is that there are often other systems that take over when such failures happen, because banks have standby systems and processes or can divert processing to other systems.

Banks with legacy IT platforms can find themselves in a difficult position. Often, the grass looks greener on the other side – in other words, modern platforms appear to have many advantages, such as more functionality, easier (and cheaper) to support and extend (because they are written in programming languages that are current, for example), more secure (or at least not reliant on legacy operating systems that are no longer supported or hardware that can only be purchased second hand) and less complex (because one modern platform can take on the role of several legacy platforms, reducing the amount of integration). However, implementing a new banking platform is expensive and risky, as many banks have found out, sometimes with severe reputational damage and/or damage to careers. In addition, out of the box a new platform typically will not support all the products or product variants the bank has built over the years on its legacy platform. Nonetheless, there are some platform vendors and banks that have made a success of platform migrations. For example, starting in the 1990s, Banco Santander made several acquisitions of banks and banking operations around the world and typically migrated them to its Partenon core banking platform, on the basis that maintaining one core banking platform is cheaper than maintaining a diverse mixture of legacy platforms. TSYS has a business of processing credit card accounts for banks and has established a track record in successfully migrating millions of accounts onto its TS2 platform. It processes more credit card accounts than any single bank, and therefore potentially offers an economy of scale for credit card processing better than any bank.

---

*The IT architecture team at one of the largest UK banks created a diagram of all its platforms and interfaces around 2002, probably more as a shock tactic than for everyday use, and around the thousands of coloured boxes representing platforms (or applications) it was black with lines representing interfaces between them.

2.8   New Banking Models

Many of the modern products and services that banks now offer were only possible because of the use of technology to support their implementation. We have seen how new technology – such as printing and the telegraph – enabled new products and services (banknotes and long-distance cash transfers, respectively). Often, however, technology, such as adding machines and branch accounting platforms, was required only in a supporting role to the service or product and may well have been invisible or of little consequence to the customer – perhaps the most annoying aspect of automating cheque sorting for some customers was the fact they had to use cheques with strange characters at the bottom. However, the advent of ubiquitous networking – in other words, the Internet, whether carried over a physical connection or via a mobile or Wi-Fi connection – has enabled a plethora of new services and operating models, and along with cloud infrastructure has made it significantly easier to enter the banking sector and rapidly gain scale. Some bankers believe that banks that only offer Internet and telephone-based banking are becoming a viable proposition, and that the death of the branch is imminent.

2.8.1   The UK Market as an Example

Since around 1990, we have seen the launch of banks with a range of operating models. The UK provides a good set of examples of the two waves of new, direct banks that took place between 1995 and 2020, some of which we have also seen in other countries. At the same time, the UK also saw other types of banks being launched, which we will explore in this section.

In 1989, Midland Bank (subsequently acquired by HSBC) launched a telephone-only brand, First Direct,[168] which went on to offer Internet and mobile banking, but has never had physical branches. If a customer needed to deposit a cheque or withdraw a large amount of cash, they could use the bank's parent's branches. All the large banks in the UK launched their own telephone banking services around the same time, but these were typically added onto their branch-based banking operations as an additional service for existing customers, often with the aim of reducing transactions in branches and therefore the costs of branches.

The first wave of new, direct banks took place in the second half of the 1990s and for some time after the turn of the century. These banks had a focus on customer acquisition and servicing over the Internet, although in practice they also typically offered telephone servicing, and they were often attempts by existing banks to capture new customers and build a business that was independent from their branch networks. In 1999, The Co-operative Bank launched smile, which started as an Internet-only offering and then extended to a mobile app, with very limited telephone banking. Cahoot was a telephone and Internet banking brand launched by Abbey National in 2000, and after being acquired by Santander stopped accepting new customers. First-e was an Internet bank servicing the UK and Germany that only operated from 1999 to 2001, based in Ireland and drawing on a French banking licence from the privately owned Banque d'Escompte. ING launched ING Direct, which was a telephone and Internet bank, in the UK in 2003, but sold it in 2012, after which it was absorbed by Barclays Bank. Intelligent Finance was a telephone and Internet bank launched by Halifax in 1999, which ultimately ended up as part of Lloyds Banking Group, and stopped accepting new customers in 2014. Ivobank was a start-up privately owned Internet bank aimed at customers of gaming websites, which failed in 2009, after which its infrastructure was acquired by Virgin Money.

At broadly the same time as the first wave of direct banks, the UK saw several insurance companies launching banks, probably as an attempt to develop a bancassurance model and as a way of retaining customers when their insurance investments matured, although none of the banks survived. Scottish Widows opened a direct bank in 1995, but it was in effect absorbed into Lloyds TSB when it acquired Scottish Widows in 2000. Prudential launched Egg, a telephone and Internet bank, in 1998 and sold it in 2007 to Citigroup, which eventually sold its accounts to various other institutions. Egg had the unique feature of being able to present a consolidated view of a customer's accounts at their other banks by, in effect, logging onto their Internet banking sites and reading the information from them, well before open banking offered a way to do this. Of all the direct-only banks launched around the time of the dot-com boom in the UK, Egg had the highest profile. Standard Life Bank was launched in 1998 and then acquired by and absorbed into Barclays in 2009.

Broadly simultaneously with the development of direct Internet banks, retailers got into banking. In 1997, two large supermarket retailers, Tesco and Sainsbury's, set up joint venture banks with Royal Bank of Scotland and Bank of Scotland, respectively. These were aimed at cross-selling to supermarket shoppers by mining the data from their customer loyalty programmes and also hoped, by issuing their own payment cards, to capture some of the interchange payments that retailers in effect make to card issuers. After the banking crisis, both supermarkets ended the joint ventures and took full ownership of their banks and became direct Internet, mobile and telephone banks, providing some servicing in the associated supermarkets. It is worth pointing out that supermarkets are very wary of increasing the time customers spend at the checkout, as this represents more cost in terms of checkout staff and less revenue per second. Therefore, they aren't keen on offering any banking services at checkouts. However, retailer-owned banks can also experiment with new forms of payment such as higher value contactless payments using a mobile phone at their checkouts.

Other retailers also had banking offerings, typically centred around store cards that they converted to scheme-branded cards (i.e. Mastercard or Visa). Notably, two of the largest of these, Marks & Spencer's M&S Money and John Lewis Financial Services were sold by the retailers to HSBC. Virgin established Virgin Direct in 1995 offering a low-cost index tracker fund and then launched an offset mortgage product (i.e. a current account whose balance offsets the mortgage) in a joint venture with Royal Bank of Scotland in 1997, offered over the phone, Internet and through financial advisers. The initial aim was to cross-sell the mortgage product to Virgin Direct's customer base. However, Royal Bank of Scotland took over the joint venture in 2003. Virgin Direct, by then rebranded Virgin Money, acquired the failed Northern Rock bank during the banking crisis, and went on to merge with Clydesdale Bank and Yorkshire Bank. Finally, the UK's government-owned Post Office, which runs post office counters around the country, got back into banking, by distributing branded savings accounts, current accounts (which were subsequently withdrawn) and loans, all of which were issued and operated by the Bank of Ireland's UK entity. The Post Office also provided basic banking services on behalf of many banks, such as accepting cheque and cash deposits (which was probably an important part of many banks' strategy to close branches with low footfall).

The second wave of new, direct banks – the so-called neobanks – took place during the second decade of the twenty-first century. These often started as mobile-only offerings based around a prepaid card, so strictly speaking many were not banks initially, although some did gain full banking licenses. Some were focused on small to medium-sized businesses, offering easy integration with various accounting packages and included the likes of Anna, Cashplus and Tide. Direct banks launched between 2015 and 2020 included Atom Bank, Monzo, Revolut, Starling Bank and Tandem Bank. However, these new direct banks have so far struggled to demonstrate that they can be profitable, although in some cases they have demonstrated impressive growth in customer numbers and rapidly expanded into other countries (and some, such as N26, entered the UK from other countries). It appears that these attract new customers with a combination of price competition (e.g. offering free overseas ATM withdrawals, lower-cost foreign exchange, fee-free business banking), app-based servicing offerings (e.g. the ability to temporarily block a payment card, expenditure tracking and budgeting, integration with small business accounting packages) and marketing. However, the route to profitability appears to be hard, particularly when all surplus revenue must be ploughed back into activities to grow the business.

From a technology perspective, the neobanks were notably different from the first wave of Internet banks in at least three ways. First, they tended to be focused on acquisition and servicing via a mobile app, with support typically offered via online chat through their app and sometimes by telephone. Second, they tended to build their own platforms, sometimes with a stripped-down third-party core banking platform such as Mambu at the core providing little more than a ledger and acting as the system of record for customer accounts. Third, they typically ran their platforms on cloud infrastructure, therefore reducing up-front capital expenditure.

Finally, throughout all of this period, banking institutions focused on business banking (and in particular business lending) were also launched (or in some cases rebadged and refocused from older banks), such as Aldermore, Bank & Clients, OakNorth, Redwood Bank, Shawbrook and Tide. These tended to offer retail savings products as well – in other words, raising deposits from retail customers and using them to lend to business customers.

Nearly uniquely, Metro Bank, launched in 2010 as we have already covered, stood out as a branch-centric bank (with an Internet servicing capability), with its branches offering free-to-use coin counters, safe deposit boxes (which the big UK banks had all but phased out), instant issuance of payment cards and cheques to new customers (new to the UK), and extended seven-day-a-week full-service opening hours. It was replicating the model that its founder, Vernon Hill, had established at Commerce Bancorp in the US starting in the 1970s. Although Metro Bank went on to develop its Internet and mobile capability, it remained focused on extending its branch network, replicating the same format in every branch. Handelsbanken also entered the UK market, with a branch-centric approach of building relationships with local businesses and their owners.

Large banks continue to have the advantage of scale, so that their unit costs per transaction and per account are extremely low. If the history of the first Internet banks is anything to go by, the destination for smaller banks is still to be acquired by bigger banks.

2.8.2   North America

Across the rest of the globe direct-only banking models are arriving at varying rates of speed and in many locations are often new plays by established banks. Given the diversity and large number of banks in the US, there are examples of direct banks with many different heritages. Like in the UK, there was a boom in the founding of Internet banks in the second half of the 1990s, including Bank of Internet USA, CompuBank, EverBank, NetBank (initially Atlanta Internet Bank) and TAB (Transportation Alliance Bank, aimed at small to medium-sized businesses), of which only the first and last survived. Bank of Internet USA became Axos Financial, and along the way acquired several other institutions – or their accounts – in order to grow scale.

Several Internet direct banks were established by existing banks (reusing the existing banking licences) from around the turn of the millennium, such as Bank5 Connect (a division of Bank Five), Brio Direct (Sterling National Bank), Comenity Direct (Comenity Capital Bank), nbkc bank (founded in 1999 as Horizon National Bank with its first branch in Kansas City and renamed in 2004), Radius Bank (originally First Trade Union Bank, and after becoming Radius Bank in 2014 was acquired by Lending Club in 2020), Salem Five Direct and Vio Bank (MidFirst Bank).

In the second decade of the twenty-first century, the US, again like the UK, saw a large second wave of direct banks, the neobanks, such as Chime, Moven, Simple and Varo. In most cases these relied upon old-fashioned banks for account processing and their banking licenses. They were characterised by offering mobile apps as their primary channel. Chime was founded in 2013 and relied upon banking services and licenses from The Bancorp Bank and Stride Bank. Moven, founded in 2011 (and therefore possibly the first neobank anywhere) by the well-known banking author and industry observer Brett King, did not actually own a banking licence, but relied on CBW Bank for its operation and banking licence. However, Moven closed its banking business in 2020. Simple was launched to the public in 2012 and subsequently acquired by Spanish bank BBVA in 2014 – which went on to fund another neobank aimed at small businesses, Azlo, in 2017. Varo relied on The Bancorp Bank for its account processing and licence at launch in 2015. Quontic Bank was in effect a start-up, although it was founded through the acquisition of Golden First Bank in 2009. Large banks and financial institutions also established direct offerings, such as American Express National Bank, Capital One 360 (formerly ING Direct USA, although it was not purely a direct bank – it operated cafés with ATMs), Discover Bank, E-Trade Bank, HSBC Direct, Marcus by Goldman Sachs and TIAA Bank (formed from the acquisition of EverBank). Ally Financial rose out of the ashes of GMAC, which was rescued by the US Treasury after the banking crisis of 2008. At the same time as the launching of various neobanks, many local banks also started up, often with a direct offering, although at a lower rate than in previous periods.

In Canada, banking is dominated by five large banks with direct banking arms and hasn't seen the same level of new bank activity as the UK or the US. Examples of Canadian direct banks include Simplii Financial, which was launched as President's Choice Financial as a joint venture between a supermarket chain and Canadian Imperial Bank of Commerce (CIBC) and rebranded in 2017 when CIBC took over the business, and Tangerine, which was launched by ING (of the Netherlands) in 1997 as ING Direct Canada, acquired by Scotiabank in 2012 and rebranded in 2014.* Zag Bank, originally

---

*Strictly speaking, Tangerine is not a pure direct bank, as it runs cafés providing banking facilities.

launched as Bank West in 2003, was acquired by Desjardins Group in 2011, after which it was rebranded. It was subsequently closed. Koho was one of the few neobanks in Canada, founded in 2014 and offering banking services around a prepaid card issued by Peoples Group – as such, as of 2020, it wasn't a bank.

2.8.3 Australia

The banking sector in Australia is highly concentrated, with four large national banks that successive governments have prevented from merging but have allowed to acquire smaller banks. Nonetheless, one of them, NAB, launched a direct brand called UBank in 2008 that drew on NAB's banking license but implemented its own core banking* and Internet banking platforms. It was widely marketed across the banking industry around the world as an example of what could be rapidly built with new technology. ING Direct, launched in Australia in 1999 by ING (of the Netherlands), was a success. It rebranded as ING in 2017. Like the UK and the US, in the second decade of the twenty-first century Australia saw the launch of several neobanks that went to market through mobile apps, including Judo Bank, Up Bank (launched as a direct brand of Bendigo and Adelaide Bank), Volt Bank, Xinja and 86 400. Relative to the UK, a higher percentage of the neobanks were based on fully functional third-party core banking platforms such as SAP Cloud for Banking and Temenos T24, but, like the UK, ran on cloud infrastructure. It could be that the software in these cases was already available with Australia-specific banking functionality, as other institutions had already implemented them.[†]

2.8.4 Europe

Many countries in continental Europe have seen their own neobanks, such as AION in Belgium, Qonto in France and Bnext in Spain. In addition, across Europe several organisations have gone on to offer services throughout most of the EU (including the UK before and after it left the EU), given the ease of passporting once licensed in one EU country and the Single European Payments Area making payment processing consistent. Several of them had similar models, in that they offered prepaid card accounts with low or zero fees for currency conversion (of little consequence inside the eurozone) and free (but often limited) pan-European ATM withdrawals, and often the appearance of local bank accounts in different countries (e.g. one account with several IBANs, each IBAN for a different country). These included Bunq, Fidor, Holvi, Monese, Monzo, N26 and Revolut, with all of these except Holvi and Monese having banking licenses. Bitwala was in some ways similar, but provided a Bitcoin wallet as well as a regular current account, although the latter was provided by solarisBank, another neobank focused on providing account processing (and its banking license) to other neobanks and businesses looking to hold deposits for customers and/or provide other banking and payment services.

---

*Oracle Flexcube.
[†]Commonwealth Bank of Australia had implemented SAP's core banking platform and Temenos T24 had been implemented by Rubik, a banking services provider to credit unions and was subsequently acquired by Temenos.

2.9 The Impact of the 2008 Banking Crisis

In 2007, an increased delinquency of US home loans started impacting investment trusts, funds and banks. In April of that year, New Century Real Estate Investment Trust filed for bankruptcy, followed by Bear Stearns liquidating two of its hedge funds and then American Home Mortgages collapsing. Banking institutions that were operating a leveraged model of issuing mortgages and then securitising them (in effect selling them to third-party investors) found that no-one wanted to buy them and so ran into liquidity problems. In the UK in September 2007, there was a run on Northern Rock, a former building society turned bank that operated this model, and the UK government stepped in to take it over and protect depositors. Then in 2008 the banking world was turned on its head with the failures of a string of US mortgage issuers and three major investment banks – Bear Stearns (acquired by JPMorgan Chase), Merrill Lynch (acquired by Bank of America) and Lehman Brothers (whose assets in North America were acquired by Barclays Bank and those elsewhere by Nomura). A large US bank, Washington Mutual, previously feted for its high growth rate, failed on 26 September (its assets were acquired by JPMorgan Chase) and in October, Royal Bank of Scotland was in effect taken over by the UK government. Around the world, governments stepped in to bail out banks. After the dust had settled the ensuing analysis of the causes of the banking crisis had potentially ruinous implications for both the reputations and the bottom lines of banks around the world. Banks were vilified for the way they had put profits before all else, with their cultures presented as being rotten to the core. In the US, the most obvious example of this profit-over-ethics mindset was mortgage mis-selling and over-leveraging, but since that point other examples of mis-selling, fraud and market manipulation were identified right across the globe – payment protection insurance mis-selling in the UK, market manipulation in Australia, France, the UK and the US (among other countries), enabling money laundering in Mexico, and the list goes on. The associated fines were arguably the lighter impact of these revelations, the more significant implications being vast amounts of new regulation, often implemented subtly differently across various regulatory regimes, and the press coverage resulting in a significant impact on customers' perceptions of their banks. The development of mobile-only banks meant that moving bank accounts became easier and at least some customers voted with their thumbs!

In some countries, the UK being a case in point, customer lethargy has historically worked in favour of the largest banks. Even with the implementation of guaranteed seven-day current account switching only about one million people (or roughly 2% of the adult population) switch accounts annually. In the UK, we are still statistically more likely to change our spouse than our bank accounts. However, account switching has grown in popularity as it became easier. Customers started to change age-old banking habits by switching on a more regular basis. For the period 1 January to 31 March 2020 a UK neobank (Monzo) became the biggest net recipient of switched retail current accounts in the UK for the first time.[169]

The consequences of the 2008 banking crisis were considerable, as we explore next.

First, in response to the banking crisis, regulators across the globe implemented broad-ranging changes to the regulatory environment within which banks operate. Additionally, the banks themselves, possibly feeling the threat of regulatory or even legal action (and in some cases following agreements with prosecutors) undertook programmes of work to implement globally consistent high standards. These changes, taken individually, were of significant scale but when considered together they were truly breathtaking in terms of their costs. For international banks, two aspects made the costs substantial. First, the regulatory changes varied from jurisdiction to jurisdiction. Second, international banks had to implement global standards programmes aimed at reinforcing control over distant operations and making sure that all such operations maintained high operational standards and compliance with local law and local and transnational regulation. In our experience it was not uncommon for international banks to be spending up to 40% of their technology change budgets (not to mention the cost of implementing these changes across their operations) in addressing regulatory and standards-based changes. For the larger banks, this amounted to sums ranging between hundreds of millions and billions of US dollars of technology change alone each year.

Second, regulators imposed structural changes on banking corporations. One of the lessons of the banking crisis of 2008 was that some universal banks were not appropriately segregating, and therefore protecting, customer funds from the banks' own trading funds. This created a clear risk to a bank's ability to guarantee its customers' deposits and a risk to the ongoing financial viability of a given bank, and possibly the entire market, should its trading business fail. Due to depositor protection schemes in various countries, it also meant that governments were in effect insuring a bank's customer deposits against all of the existential risks in each bank, and not just those risks that arose from retail and SME banking. In the US, the Volcker Rule, which came into effect in 2014, prohibited certain trading and high-risk activities in universal banks[170] (although it was subsequently relaxed under the Trump administration) and the UK took arguably the most draconian approach by forcing the UK retail and SME deposit-taking businesses of the largest banks to be ring-fenced from trading entities in order to avoid contagion from trading failures.[171] The EU stepped back from ring-fencing or its own version of the Volcker Rule, taking the view that its requirement for banks to increase capital buffers was sufficient.[172] Addressing these requirements required different approaches in each jurisdiction and, again, drove huge amounts of spending in the technology functions in order to deliver the required outcomes. In the UK, ring-fencing forced the five largest banking groups to restructure, with the resulting corporate structure typically one of the two options shown in Figure 2.2, with a listed holding company which owns separate entities for the ring-fenced retail/SME bank and the corporate/investment bank. The service company, which services both banks, is either a separate entity from the two banking entities or part of the ring-fenced retail/SME bank (potentially as a fully owned subsidiary of the ring-fenced banking entity). The reason for these two structures is that the banking groups took the view that it was totally infeasible to split servicing (particularly shared technology platforms) and keep the relevant parts with each banking entity. In practice,

FIGURE 2.2   Options for the structure of a banking corporation with a UK ring-fenced bank.

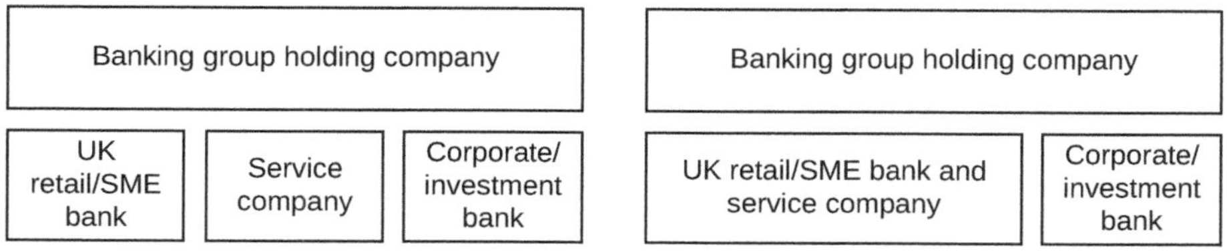

with a separate service company entity, nearly all employees, operations and technology ended up in the service company, with only employees in regulated roles (e.g. sales staff) in the two banking entities. Because of the interdependence of the banking entities and the service company, ring-fencing does not completely protect the retail/SME bank in either of the two structures from a failure of the corporate/investment bank. This is because the service company depended on income from the corporate/investment bank, so consideration had to be given to adequately capitalise it so that it could continue to operate after a failure of either or both of the banking entities for sufficient time for it either to downsize and reduce its cost base to match the reduced income or for the remnants of the banking business(es) to be sold. Of course, in reality, bank structures are more complex than we have shown here, with international subsidiaries (both banking and servicing entities), many special purpose vehicles and sometimes more than one UK ring-fenced licensed banking entity. Changing to these structures also caused issues with pension liabilities, required the ring-fenced bank to have its own governance and board and caused all the banking groups to re-examine recharging arrangements for technology and operations and put in place service agreements between the entities. Recharge models were often huge edifices built up over more than a decade, containing many special arrangements for particular businesses and not necessarily directly connected to actual usage or the input costs for each service. They were therefore politically challenging to change. These new structures and arrangements typically increase running costs, requiring more administration and reducing some economies of scale, and the cost of implementing the changes was considerable.

Third, many banks were subject to fines for supposed one-off illegal actions, the largest of which was $16.65 billion imposed on Bank of America in 2014 for financial fraud leading up to and during the banking crisis in the Merrill Lynch and Countrywide businesses it bought during the crisis[173] (and after it had already been fined $11.8 billion in 2012 for improper mortgage servicing and foreclosure practices up to 2010[174]). Other US banks received large fines for similar behaviour over the period of the banking crisis and its fallout. The US authorities fined many non-US international banks for breaches of US economic sanctions, the largest of which was a fine of $8.9 billion on BNP Paribas for breaches between 2004 and 2012.[175] In 2019, the UK's Financial Conduct Authority levied fines of over £392 million on organisations and individuals across the banking and insurance sectors, the largest of which was £102 million on Standard Chartered Bank for anti-money laundering (AML) breaches between 2010 and 2014.[176] We note that banks appear to incur fines on such a regular basis that the one-off status of fines appears to be a misnomer and could end up being regarded as the cost of doing business (albeit illegally). Remediation of sanctions and AML breaches (e.g. improving the enforcement of controls, typically through technology solutions and improvements to existing platforms) means more work for banks' technology organisations.

Fourth, a longer-term impact of the banking crisis which was then exacerbated by the Covid-19 pandemic was a prolonged period of exceptionally low inflation rates. During the pandemic central bank base rates stood at 0.1% in the UK, 0.25% in the US and 0% in the eurozone, and famously the Swiss Central Bank announced negative interest rates as early as December 2014.[177] A negative interest rate mortgage was offered by Jyske Bank in Denmark in 2019.[178] With low central bank rates, banks get squeezed on their net interest margins, that is, the difference between the interest they receive on lending and the interest they pay on deposits expressed as a percentage of the average amount on loan over the same period, and it is made worse because the interest they get on their reserves at the central bank (which are in effect loans to the central bank) is so low. There has been a long-term decline in the US banking industry's net interest margin since it peaked in 1994.[179] In the UK, average net interest margins[180] have bounced around with no apparent secular trend and it appears that periods of increased competition and economic downturns coincide with significant reductions in net interest margin followed by increases. What is clear from a survey and analysis conducted by the UK's Financial Conduct Authority in 2018[181] is that large banks pay lower interest on deposits (primarily due to customer inertia, with retail customers keeping their current account and savings accounts at the same bank), make more money from each current account (mainly because they have a higher mix of business current accounts which on average each earn 10 times as much as a personal current account across the UK banking sector), make more money from transactional fees (e.g. for payments) and have higher yields on lending products (primarily from credit cards and personal current account overdrafts). On the other hand, large banks' operating costs are higher per branch and IT costs, expressed as a percentage of lending assets, are higher, with these twice as high in banks incorporated more than 25 years ago compared to those incorporated within the past 25 years – in other words, it appears that maintaining and updating legacy technology platforms is expensive. Interestingly, the same study showed that the cost of operating a current account at a neobank was similar to the cost at the large banks, and so if neobanks could grow their account base significantly, they had the potential to compete against the large banks' net interest margin advantage.

So, the banking crisis typically increased a bank's cost base and reduced its revenue and so many banks' return on equity (ROE) was drastically reduced. ROE is a measure of profitability, in this case how well a bank uses its net assets to make a profit, and is defined as the net income of the bank (i.e. revenue less expenses such as operating costs, taxes, interest payments and payments to preferred shareholders) in a period (e.g. a year) divided by the shareholders' average equity over that period (e.g. the average of assets minus debts at the start and end of the period or the average of assets minus debts measured every month during the period). Of course, many banks responded by cutting costs, and this impacted their technology organisations due to the offshoring of roles to lower cost locations and rationalisation of the technology estate. For example, in June 2015, HSBC announced plans to reduce its headcount by 25,000 (around 10% of the workforce) and its annual run cost by $5 billion by 2018,[182] and then another cost-cutting drive in 2019, with a target of reducing headcount by 35,000 (14% of the workforce) and reducing its annual run cost by $4.5 billion by 2022,[183] alongside doubling the number of its mobile customers and continuing its pivot towards Asia. On 29 October 2015, Deutsche Bank provided details of its plan for 2020. This included targeting gross savings of almost $4 billion by 2018 and reducing its cost-to-income ratio from a planned 70% in 2018 to 65% by 2020.[184] In July 2016, Bank of America announced a drop in profits and the immediate implementation of a new expense target, with the objective of reducing its annual run cost by $3.3 billion by 2018.[185] In our experience with large UK banks, cost reduction is a never-ending programme and internally banks lose sight of their end customers, and we are not surprised that neobanks can offer more attractive roles to banking professionals given their focus on growth and customers. Having said all that, the FCA study in 2018[186] showed that large banks in the UK have a much higher ROE than smaller banks, with average underlying ROE before tax of 26% and 6% respectively, despite the higher costs – in other words, the net interest margin advantage of large banks still outweighs their higher cost bases.

While all this was going on, banks had to continue to invest in digital initiatives to stay competitive and increase automation to reduce operating costs. For international banks, the economies of scale they enjoy in their home markets often do not apply in many of the countries in which they operate, because their businesses can be small relative to large domestic banks, regulation and banking practices and products are different, they often haven't rationalised their platforms to use common technology in all their operating countries, and some countries (such as China, Indonesia, Russia and Saudi Arabia) insist that data, operations, infrastructure and capital are kept inside the country.

As a consequence of all these factors there was considerable pressure on banks' technology functions to meet the twin objectives of reducing costs and increasing the amount of automation and digitisation, including enhancing the banks' customer-facing digital presence. On the face of it these objectives appear to be contradictory in their nature – increasing automation and robotics requires additional investment in technology, which should therefore drive up the costs of the technology function within the bank. In reality, the belief within a number of banks is that technology has grown fat in recent years and there may well be an opportunity to take more than enough cost out to cover the additional investments. We could also make the point that banks have in effect become digital enterprises and so it is natural that the size of their technology cost base relative to the total cost base should rise as they digitise – the issue being that their ROE in many cases does not get close to the ROE that technology companies expect to make.

2.10   The Current State of Banking

We see four major strands in the history of banking and banks. First, there is a long history of banks forging relationships with other banks in order to support trade (and, more recently, tourism) that has become increasingly global, and, in the case of large international banks, entering new geographies for the same reason. Second, banks have sought economies of scale, often through mergers and acquisitions but also through the use of processors, joint ventures and membership associations. Third, banks have often diversified, increasing their range of products and services and customer segments. Fourth, banks have used automation and technology to reduce their unit costs and improve service levels, and, like other industries, have moved from developing technological solutions themselves to buying them from specialised suppliers – no modern bank would build its own computer hardware. Of course, we are not, and have never been, in a steady state where banks are concerned, and we can find examples of banks at different places in their evolution along these four strands. Finally, throughout the history of banking there have been crises and regulatory changes, some of which have resulted in structural changes to the banking sector.

2.10.1   Banking Organisations

Nearly every country has a central bank,* which is typically responsible for managing the reserves of banks in that country, regulating banks and banking-related entities such

---

*Countries that do not have their own central banks include Andorra and Monaco in Europe, both of which use the Euro as their currency, and various small countries in Oceania where either the Reserve Bank of Australia, the French Institut d'émission d'outre-mer, the Reserve Bank of New Zealand or the US Federal Reserve in effect perform the role.

as payment schemes, issuance of banknotes,* formulating monetary policy and lending to government.

The largest banks by assets in the world are state-owned Chinese banks such as Industrial and Commercial Bank of China, China Construction Bank, Agricultural Bank of China and Bank of China.[187] This is typically by virtue of having huge retail deposits in their home country, and they are not as diversified in terms of breadth of services, geographical presence or customer segments as the international universal banks. Universal banks offer the broadest range of services, including retail, SME and corporate banking and investment banking and often with asset management, private banking and wealth management. Although they may be present in many countries, most only have relatively large retail and SME banking operations in their home countries (where they are typically in the so-called big four or big five national banks). Such organisations include Bank of America, Barclays, BNP Paribas, Citigroup, Credit Suisse, Deutsche Bank, JPMorgan Chase, Mitsubishi UFJ Financial Group, Royal Bank of Canada and UBS. There are also large investment banks – notably Goldman Sachs, Morgan Stanley and Nomura – sometimes with (relatively small) retail banking businesses.

There are also large international banking organisations that offer retail, SME and corporate banking, often with significant scale in more than just their home markets and/or sizable trade finance businesses. These include Commerzbank, HSBC, ING, Nordea and Santander. Some of these are arguably international universal banks as they also have some investment banking operations. Below this scale, filling up the ranks of the big four or big five banks in each country, are the large domestic banks, of which there are many around the world, and include ABN AMRO, Bank of Nova Scotia, CaixaBank, Japan Post Bank, Lloyds Banking Group and National Australia Bank. Some banks have made a virtue of remaining focused (or often refocusing) on their home markets, although in reality many also have international businesses. Then there are relatively small domestic specialists – often focused around specific SME segments and sometimes with retail deposit taking.

Many countries have mutual banking organisations that range from large (i.e. in the big four or five in their domestic markets) such as Crédit Agricole in France and Rabobank in the Netherlands (both incidentally originating from agricultural banks) down through various sizes of building societies, co-operative banks, credit unions, savings banks and thrifts, with perhaps only a hundred or so members in the smallest cases. These mainly offer retail banking services, although larger ones typically diversify into SME lending and the largest have also built up international businesses.

Many countries, probably most famously Switzerland, have private banks offering banking and investment services to high-net-worth individuals and families. In some cases these are owned and operated by international banks (e.g. private banks in various countries operated by HSBC and UBS) and in others they remain privately owned.

Finally, neobanks typically focused on customer acquisition and servicing through mobile apps have captured retail and SME customers in many markets, as we explored in Section 2.8.

---

*Banks in Hong Kong and in the UK in Northern Ireland and Scotland still issue banknotes, although under supervision of the Hong Kong Monetary Authority and the Bank of England, respectively.

We covered historical bank consolidation in Section 2.4, and we expect bank consolidation to continue, but regulators and governments are likely to continue to place limitations on the largest domestic banks in the interests of promoting competition and stability of the banking system. This is likely to be the case in the EU if the European Commission carries over to the banking sector its view that there must be at least four large mobile operators in a country to promote competition.[*],[188] Whether this means that such banks will be allowed to acquire smaller domestic banks will probably vary from country to country (but regulators and governments may well have no choice if a smaller bank runs into trouble), and, similarly, cross-border acquisitions and mergers may still be permitted. However, the economies of scale available in a cross-border acquisition or merger involving a large domestic bank may be partially limited because regulators may insist on the domestic bank being run as a separate and adequately capitalised entity with withdrawals of capital to the overseas parent limited to dividend payments (e.g. Santander in the UK).

As well as bank consolidation, branch networks in developed countries appear to have peaked[†] and are being reduced because of less demand for physical servicing, alternatives to cheques (and the ability to submit cheque images digitally) and also as a result of bank consolidation. However, we believe lending, particularly business lending, will continue to involve face-to-face meetings and local knowledge and branches will remain important for marketing and customer origination purposes.

2.10.2   Bank Networks and Payment Schemes

Banks still require correspondent banking relationships to enable their customers to send international payments. In some ways these were the original interbank networks. As we mentioned in Section 2.5.10, many banks are now connected to the SWIFT messaging network, which enables them to exchange payment messages, and a whole variety of other financial messages. Even banks that aren't SWIFT members can usually access SWIFT through banks that are members. Given the threat of the US blocking access to the SWIFT network as part of its economic sanctions programmes, SWIFT itself has segregated its network into European and transatlantic zones,[191] and the Chinese and Russian governments have sponsored the development of their own interbank networks, the Cross-Border Interbank Payments System (CIPS) and the System for Transfer of Financial Messages (SPFS), respectively. However, SWIFT remains the de facto international interbank network. Also, many payments companies offer international payments and remittances, typically undercutting what a customer's bank would charge, and in many countries these use their own networks and international subsidiaries to make the transfer rather than using SWIFT and correspondent banking relationships.

Many countries have domestic electronic funds transfer schemes, often in two varieties. For low-value payments there are automated clearing house schemes (which

---

[*]Although in May 2020 the European Court of Justice reversed the European Commission's ruling that had forbidden the acquisition of O2 (owned by Telefónica) by Three (owned by Hutchison).
[†] *Which?*, a UK consumer affairs publication, reported that between January 2015 and August 2019, the number of branches of UK banks and building societies dropped from 9,803 to 6,549, including 49 new branches (see reference 189). In the United States, the total number of bank and thrift branches peaked in 2009 at just over 90,000 and then declined at just over 1% a year (see reference 190).

historically processed over one or more nights on business days, but trending in the twenty-first century towards new schemes with immediate payments operating 24 hours a day, seven days a week) operated by private companies owned by the participating banks or by the central banks. For high-value payments there are real-time gross settlement systems typically operated by the central banks and operating during business hours. We also note how schemes (which define the operating rules and contracts for scheme participation) are sometimes separate from the infrastructure (which is used to send payment messages and process payments). In the UK, the Faster Payments scheme runs on infrastructure provided by Vocalink,[192] a subsidiary of Mastercard, and the CHAPS RTGS scheme uses the SWIFT network for its payment messages.[193] In Australia, the New Payments Platform was designed with an Overlay Service to allow other payment applications to be built on top of it.[194] The Single European Payments Area (SEPA) payment scheme gives perhaps the most extreme example of scheme and infrastructure separation, probably because of the need to work with a highly federated system of different countries, each with its own central bank and existing payment networks and schemes. It allows payment service providers (PSPs, which are typically the banks whose customers initiate payments) to choose whatever clearing and settlement mechanism (CSM) they want to use as long as it adheres to the scheme rules[195] and requires CSMs to interact to ensure all PSPs can exchange payments. A CSM typically comprises a central bank such as Banca d'Italia or Deutsche Bundesbank, the European Central Bank's TARGET2 Instant Payment Settlement (TIPS) and a domestic payment scheme such as Belgium's Centre for Exchange and Clearing or Spain's iberpay. In reality this means that a bank can use its existing domestic payments scheme for both domestic and cross-border SEPA payments, with cross-border payments typically settled via its domestic central bank using TIPS. However, over time, different combinations, particularly using commercial infrastructure providers (that have typically emerged from the commercialisation and subsequent mergers of domestic payment infrastructure such as equensWorldline and Nets) that operate across SEPA are likely to be possible. Banks in Europe that still own domestic schemes may well decide to monetise their investments and sell the scheme infrastructure to commercial infrastructure providers (as has already happened in some countries), and therefore help enable pan-European payment infrastructure consolidation.

Card payment and ATM schemes appear to most end users to have all merged into a ubiquitous network where any card (or mobile payment method such as Apple Pay, Google Pay, Samsung Pay or WeChat Pay) is accepted at any point of sale, online retailer or ATM. Cardholders and retailers may of course end up paying different fees depending on the combination of card scheme, merchant acquirer, the issuer, ATM operator and so on, although from a cardholder's perspective such fees are often hidden because they are absorbed by the issuer or merchant. In reality there are multiple networks operated by many different schemes, some national (e.g. the UK's LINK ATM network) and some international (e.g. Mastercard and Visa) with merchant acquirers connecting to many different schemes and schemes also connecting to each other. Given all the interconnections among card payment schemes, merchant acquirers, payment service providers, banks and ATM operators that connect directly to schemes can often choose how they route payments, to minimise cost (for example). It also now appears possible for international retailers to use a single merchant acquirer covering nearly all markets around the world, due to international consolidation of merchant acquirers and partnerships between them, therefore reducing the effort required to administer multiple merchant acquirers. Merchant acquirers are increasingly able to acquire payments destined for non-card interbank payment schemes (e.g. iDEAL in the Netherlands), which often offer lower fees than the interchange on card payments and such schemes are likely to chip away at card-based schemes. Similar to their initiatives around financial networks, the Chinese and Russian governments sponsored the establishment of their own card networks, UnionPay and Mir, respectively. The former is now well established globally, and became the largest card payment network in the world in 2015 when measured by total annual value of payments,[196] although its size is because of its dominance in China.

2.10.3   Processors

Processors are well established in the US banking ecosystem, selling and operating core banking platforms and providing related services to banks, credit unions and thrifts. These include Fidelity National Information Services, Finastra, Fiserv and Jack Henry, which in combination were estimated to have had a 96% share of the US market in 2013[197] – although it is totally unclear what the split between software licences (in other words, on-premise core banking platforms installed at their bank clients), services and outsourced processing was and is. Our feeling is that these processors have not really established the greatest economy of scale – which would be a single multi-tenanted core banking platform. Where this does appear to be the case is in Germany, where, as we stated earlier, Finanz Informatik processes 120 million accounts for the Sparkassen[198] and Fiducia & GAD IT processes nearly 100 million accounts for the Volksbanken and Raiffeisenbanken.[199] As the latter arose from the merger of two processors, it actually had two core banking platforms but launched an initiative to merge these.[200] In the UK outsourced processing of current accounts was unavailable until the second decade of the twenty-first century, and there was some small-scale outsourced processing of deposit accounts.

Outsourced scale processing is firmly established in the credit card issuing area, where several suppliers such as equensWorldline, Fiserv (by virtue of its acquisition of FirstData), Nets and TSYS can process card accounts at scale. It's not always clear whether such organisations have achieved the target of a single multi-tenant process- ing platform – and in fact we believe this is unlikely given the heritage of most of these organisations through several mergers and acquisitions, although we are aware some were making steps to rationalise their card processing platforms. TSYS (which came out of the US bank Synovus) achieved impressive scale with its TS2 multi-tenant platform in the US and another in the UK, with tens of millions of card accounts processed on each plat- form. However, it too acquired another platform, now named TSYS Prime, which was positioned as a lower-cost, smaller-scale platform for smaller markets and could either be installed on-premise or operated by TSYS.

Of course, there are many other examples where banks have an option of outsourcing processing, some of which they have used for many years. Examples include fulfilment (e.g. statement printing, plastic card personalisation and chequebook printing), cheque processing, credit scoring, application processing, collections and recoveries, cash man- agement and identity verification.

2.10.4   Technology in Banks

This is, of course, the subject of this book. However, there are some general observations we will make. First, as we already pointed out in Section 2.9, according to the UK's FCA analysis older banks have technology that costs more to change and run than banks that were set up more recently, but this does not outweigh the advantages the large banks have in terms of net interest margins. However, it appears (at least in the UK) that neobanks' lower cost base may give them an opportunity to compete successfully against large banks if they can grow banking businesses centred around personal and business current accounts with a range of lending products. In general, the neobanks have used open source software as the basis of their own platforms and avoided using monolithic core banking platforms that try to do everything from digital and mobile banking through deposit, loan and current account processing. Some have even built their own ledger systems whereas some have used minimalist core banking platforms. This is based on the philosophy that large monolithic platforms remove flexibility and agility, and that building the platforms from microservices – components that each typically do only one thing and can be sequenced together to build more complex processes – promote agility, rapid test and learn, and enable a continuous pipeline of new functionality into production (as we describe in Chapter 3). Neobanks also typically use cloud infrastructure, therefore gaining the benefit of scalable, secure and highly available processing with minimal up-front expenditure.

In large and established banks, the use of cloud infrastructure as another means of getting economies of scale has started. Some investment banks have been forced down this route, as the economics of their business have been severely dented due to the reduction in trading volumes and therefore revenues since the banking crisis, and we think that even the large international and universal banks will embrace the use of third-party cloud infrastructure. They have already started using software as a service (SaaS) offerings in their back offices, with Oracle and SAP enterprise resource planning platforms now available in the cloud and some human resource platforms, training platforms and recruitment platforms only available as SaaS offerings, and of course started using processors for specific outsourcing decades ago.

2.11   Further Reading

There are some notable books on the history of banking and associated topics such as money which are included in the references in this chapter. Many of these are freely accessible at archive.org.

We enjoyed reading various papers by Bernardo Bátiz-Lazo (Professor of FinTech History and Global Trade at Northumbria University in the UK) and a range of co-authors, covering the history of developments in banking technology. These papers sometimes felt like the only reliable sources on some topics.

For a longer description of different types of money and monetary systems we recommend *Money and Banking* by William Gerdes.[201]

We relied upon O'Brien's *The Impact of Computers on Banking*[202] for its early history of computers in the US banking industry. In turn, it drew upon other publications such as *American Banker*. Although it is of little relevance to today's banks, we think it is an important record and it foresaw some of the challenges that banking and technology still have today.

We also enjoyed the website www.martinsbank.co.uk, which covers the UK's Martins Bank up to when it merged with Barclays Bank in 1969. The site feels like a labour of love. It has a useful collection of internal and external publications covering the introduction of various technologies in the 1960s. Some of the UK's large banks and the Bank of England maintain archives covering their histories and these were also useful.

2.12   References

1. Jastrow, M. (1911). *Aspects of Religious Belief and Practice in Babylonia and Assyria*. New York, NY: G.P. Putnam's Sons.

2. Orsingher, R. (1967*). Banks of the World* (trans. Ault, D.S.). New York, NY: Walker and Company.

3. Nagarajan, K.V. (2011). The Code of Hammurabi: An Economic Interpretation. *International Journal of Business and Social Science* 2 (8): 108–117. http://www.ijbssnet.com/journals/Vol._2_No._8;_May_2011/14.pdf (accessed 10 June 2020).

4. Hasebroek, J. (1933). *Trade and Politics in Ancient Greece* (trans. Fraser, L.M. and MacGregor, D.C.). London, UK: G. Bell and Sons.

5. Davies, G. (1996). *A History of Money from Ancient Times to the Present Day*. Cardiff, UK: Cardiff University Press.

6. Einzig, P. (1949). *Primitive Money in its Ethnological, Historical and Economic Aspects*. London, UK: Eyre & Spottiswoode.

7. Davies, G. (1973). *National Giro Modern Money Transfer*. London, UK: George Allen & Unwin.

8. Einzig. *Primitive Money*.

9. De Soto, J.H. (2006). *Money, Bank Credit and Economic Cycles* (trans. Stroup, M.A.). Auburn, AL: Ludwig von Mises Institute.

10. Davies. *National Giro*.

11. Macdonell, A.A. and Keith A.B. (1912). *Vedic Index of Names and Subjects*. London, UK: John Murray.

12. Jain, L.C. (1929). *Indigenous Banking in India*. London, UK: Macmillan.

13. Goetzmann, W.N. (2016). *Money Changes Everything: How Finance Made Civilization Possible*. Princeton, NJ: Princeton University Press.

14. Moehlmann, C.H. (1934). The Christianization of interest. *Church History* 3 (1): 3–15. doi:10.2307/3161033.

15. Holmes, G. ed. (2001). *The Oxford History of Medieval Europe*. Oxford, UK: Oxford University Press.

16. Goetzmann. *Money Changes Everything*.

17. Parker, L.M. (1989). Medieval traders as international change agents: A comparison with twentieth century international accounting firms. *The Accounting Historians Journal* 16 (2): 107–118.

18. Tucci, U. (1981). Il Banco della Piazza di Rialto, première banque publique vénitienne (The Banco della Piazza di Rialto, the first Venetian public bank). *Cahiers de la Méditerranée, hors série* 5: 155–169. doi:10.3406/camed.1981.1552.

19. Wetterberg, G. (2009). *Money and Power: from Stockholms Banco 1656 to Sveriges Riksbank Today*. Stockholm, Sweden: Sveriges riksbank.

20. Bank of England (2020). Our history. https://www.bankofengland.co.uk/about/history (accessed 11 June 2020).

21. Bank of Scotland Our heritage. https://www.bankofscotland.co.uk/helpcentre/our-heritage .html (accessed 11 June 2020).

22. European Central Bank (2015). What is money? https://www.ecb.europa.eu/explainers/tell-me-more/html/what_is_money.en.html (accessed 26 July 2020).

23. Einzig. *Primitive Money*.

24. Hockenhull, T. (2014). The shekel: A modern-day coin with 5,000 years of history. *Coin World* (14 November). https://www.coinworld.com/news/precious-metals/coin-world-shekel-history-numismatics-israel-world-coins-ancient-collecting-hobby.html (accessed 2 June 2020).

25. MacGregor, N. (2010). *A History of the World in 100 Objects*. London, UK: Allen Lane.

26. Einzig. *Primitive Money*.

27. Bowman, J.S. ed. (2000). *Columbia Chronologies of Asian History and Culture*. New York, NY: Columbia University Press.

28. Mundell, R.A. (2002). The birth of coinage. Columbia University Department of Economics Discussion Papers 0102-08. https://doi.org/10.7916/D8Q531TK (accessed 10 June 2020).

29. European Central Bank. What is money?

30. Ahamed, L. (2009). *Lords of Finance: The Bankers Who Broke the World*. London, UK: Penguin Books.

31. European Central Bank. What is money?

32. International Monetary Fund (2000). Money matters: The importance of global cooperation. https://www.imf.org/external/np/exr/center/mm/eng/mm_cc_01.htm (accessed 10 June 2020).

33. Ahamed. *Lords of Finance*.

34. Honey, M. and Ottaway, D.B. (1979). Idi Amin squandered the wealth of Uganda. *Washington Post* (29 May). https://www.washingtonpost.com/archive/politics/1979/05/29/idi-amin-squandered-the-wealth-of-uganda (accessed 3 June 2020).

35. Hanke, S.H. and Kwok, A.K.F. (2009). On the measurement of Zimbabwe's hyperinflation. *Cato Journal* 29 (2): 353–364. https://www.cato.org/sites/cato.org/files/serials/files/cato-journal/2009/5/cj29n2-8.pdf (accessed 3 June 2020).

36. Pons, C. and Armas, M. (2020). Venezuela's timid gains in taming inflation fade as food prices soar. *Reuters Business News* (11 May). https://www.reuters.com/article/us-venezuela-economy/venezuelas-timid-gains-in-taming-inflation-fade-as-food-prices-soar-idUSKBN22N26A (accessed 11 June 2020).

37. Bank of England. How is money created? https://www.bankofengland.co.uk/knowledgebank /how-is-money-created (accessed 18 June 2020).

38. Hickey, S. (2019). $32m stolen from Tokyo cryptocurrency exchange in latest hack. *The Guardian* (12 July). https://www.theguardian.com/technology/2019/jul/12/tokyo-cryptocurrency-exchange-hack-bitpoint-bitcoin (accessed 1 August 2020).

39. Simpson, C.V.J. (2013). *The German Sparkassen (savings banks)*. London, UK: Civitas. http://www.civitas.org.uk/content/files/SimpsonSparkassen.pdf (accessed 20 July 2020).

40. Die Erste Bank und Sparkassen (2019). Wir über uns (About us). https://www.sparkasse.at/ sgruppe/wir-ueber-uns (accessed 23 June 2020).

41. Atkins, T. (2015). Austria's Volksbanken shuts its doors, becomes 'bad bank'. *Reuters Banking and Financial News* (3 July). https://uk.reuters.com/article/austria-volksbanken-idUKL8N0ZJ19B20150703 (accessed 23 June 2020).

42. Hallerberg, M. and Markgraf, J. (2018). The corporate governance of public banks before and after the global financial crisis. *Global Policy* 9 (Suppl. 1): 43–53. doi:10.1111/1758-5899.12562.

43. Ibid.

44. Martin-Aceña, P. (2013). *The savings banks crisis in Spain: When and how?* Brussels, Belgium: World Savings and Retail Banking Institute. https://www.wsbi-esbg.org/SiteCollectionDocuments/Martin-AcenaWeb.pdf (accessed 5 June 2020).

45. CECA (2020). CECA Sector: regulatory and financial outlook. https://www.ceca.es/eng/wp-content/uploads/2020/04/Evolucion-regulatoria-y-financiera-16-4-2020.pdf (accessed 5 June 2020).

46. Asociación Española de Cajas Rurales (Spanish Association of Rural Savings Banks). Historical Review. https://www.ruralvia.com/cms/estatico/rvia/generico/ruralvia/en/particulares/informacion_institucional/grupo_caja_rural/asoc_espanola_cajas_rurales/index.html (accessed 10 June 2020).

47. Lloyds Banking Group. TSB Group. https://www.lloydsbankinggroup.com/Our-Group/our-heritage/our-history2/tsb/tsb-group (accessed 10 June 2020).

48. Building Societies Association (2019). *BSA Yearbook 2019/20*. Manchester, UK: Lansdowne Publishing Partnership.

49. Bank of England (2020). List of building societies as compiled by the Bank of England as at 1st June 2020. https://www.bankofengland.co.uk/-/media/boe/files/prudential-regulation/authorisations/which-firms-does-the-pra-regulate/2020/list-of-building-societies/building-societies-list-2006.pdf (accessed 10 June 2020).

50. Bank of England (2017). *Credit union annual statistics* – 2013. https://www.bankofengland.co.uk/statistics/credit-union/2013/2013 (accessed 5 June 2020).

51. Bank of England (2020). *Credit union quarterly statistics* – 2019 Q4. https://www.bankofengland.co.uk/statistics/credit-union/2019/2019-q4 (accessed 5 June 2020).

52. Bank of England (2020). List of authorised credit unions as at 1 January 2020. https://www.bankofengland.co.uk/-/media/boe/files/prudential-regulation/authorisations/which-firms-does-the-pra-regulate/2020/list-of-authorised-credit-unions/list-of-authorised-credit-unions-as-at-1-january-2020.pdf (accessed 12 June 2020).

53. Sparks, E. (2017). Nine young bankers who changed America: Vernon Hill. *ABA Banking Journal* (26 June). https://bankingjournal.aba.com/2017/06/nine-young-bankers-who-changed-america-vernon-hill/ (accessed 16 June 2020).

54. Handelsbanken (2020). About the Group: Locations. https://www.handelsbanken.com/en/about-the-group/locations (accessed 14 June 2020).

55. Competition & Markets Authority (2016). Retail banking market investigation – Final report (9 August). https://assets.publishing.service.gov.uk/media/57ac9667e5274a0f6c00007a/retail-banking-market-investigation-full-final-report.pdf (accessed 8 June 2020).

56. Newton, L. (2007). *Change and continuity: the development of joint stock banking in the early nineteenth century*. Centre for International Business History, University of Reading. http://www.reading.ac.uk/web/files/business/empd040-07.pdf (accessed 8 June 2020).

57. Barnes, V. and Newton, L. (2016). *The introduction of the joint-stock company in English banking and monetary policy*. Henley Business School, University of Reading. https://assets.henley.ac.uk/legacyUploads/pdf/research/papers-publications/IBH-2016-01_Barnes_and_Newton.pdf (accessed 8 June 2020).

58. Andreades, A. (1909). *History of the Bank of England* (trans. Meredith, C.). London, UK: P.S. King & Son.

59. Davies, R., Richardson, P., Katinaite, V. and Manning, M. (2010). Evolution of the UK banking system. *Quarterly Bulletin* 2010 *Q4: 321–332*. London: Bank of England. https://www.bankofengland.co.uk/-/media/boe/files/quarterly-bulletin/2010/evolution-of-the-uk-banking-system.pdf (accessed 8 June 2020).

60. Jeremy, D.J. (1998). *A Business History of Britain 1900–1990s*. Oxford, UK: Oxford University Press.

61. Newton. *Change and Continuity*.

62. Bank of England (1970). Statistical abstract. Number 1. https://www.bankofengland.co.uk/-/media/boe/files/archive/statistical-abstract/number-1-1970.pdf (accessed 9 June 2020).

63. Reveley, J. and Singleton, J. (2013). Business associations as legitimacy-seekers: The case of the Committee of London Clearing Bankers. Economic History Society Conference, University of York, UK (5–7 April 2013). https://www.ehs.org.uk/dotAsset/e38f1af6-e550-4820-8935-1acda7e8d993.pdf (accessed 20 July 2020).

64. National Archives. The National Giro. https://discovery.nationalarchives.gov.uk/details/r/ea8cf00b-5d7e-4c7c-b8fe-264110303bd1 (accessed 20 July 2020).

65. Collinson, P. (2003). Girobank brand laid to rest after 25 years. *The Guardian* (7 July). https://www.theguardian.com/money/2003/jul/07/business.postalservice (accessed 20 July 2020).

66. Rhodes, C., Hough, D. and Butcher, L. (2014). Privatisation. House of Commons Library Research Paper 14/61 (20 November). https://researchbriefings.files.parliament.uk/documents/RP14-61/RP14-61.pdf (accessed 20 July 2020).

67. National Archives. Committee to Review National Savings (Page Committee): Records. https://discovery.nationalarchives.gov.uk/details/r/C14043 (accessed 20 July 2020).

68. The World Savings and Retail Banking Institute/The European Savings and Retail Banking Group. Trustee Savings Banks in the UK 1810–1995. https://www.wsbi-esbg.org/About-us/History/Pages/HistoryUK.aspx (accessed 20 July 2020).

69. National Audit Office (1987). Trustee savings banks: Rights of ownership (27 February). https://www.nao.org.uk/pubsarchive/wp-content/uploads/sites/14/2018/11/Trustee-Savings-Banks-Rights-of-Ownership.pdf (accessed 20 July 2020).

70. Bank of England (1971). Competition and credit control. *Quarterly Bulletin* 1971 *Q2: 189–193*. London: Bank of England. https://www.bankofengland.co.uk/-/media/boe/files/quarterly-bulletin/1971/competition-and-credit-control-text-of-a-consultatice-document-issued-on-14-may-1971.pdf (accessed 20 July 2020).

71. Bank of England (1987). Recent developments in UK payment clearing systems. *Quarterly Bulletin* 1987 *Q3: 392–394*. London: Bank of England. https:// www.bankofengland.co .uk/-/media/boe/files/quarterly-bulletin/1987/recent-developments-in-uk-payment-clearing-systems (accessed 12 June 2020).

72. Bank of England (1980). *Report and accounts 1980*. London, UK: Bank of England. https://www.bankofengland.co.uk/annual-report/1980 (accessed 14 June 2020).

73. Jeremy. *A Business History of Britain*.

74. Building Societies Association. *BSA Yearbook 2019/20*.

75. Davies et al. Evolution of the UK banking system.

76. Bank of England (2020). Monetary Financial Institutions (MFI) list (updated 14 May 2020). https://www.bankofengland.co.uk/-/media/boe/files/statistics/data-collection/institutions/mfi-list.xlsx (accessed 11 June 2020).

77. Berger, A.N., Kashyap, A.K. and Scalise, J.M. (1995). The transformation of the U.S. banking industry: What a long strange trip it's been. *Brookings Papers on Economic Activity* 2: 55–218. https://www.brookings.edu/bpea-articles/the-transformation-of-the-u-s-banking-industry-what-a-long-strange-trip-its-been/ (accessed 10 June 2020).

78. Blair, C.E. and Kushmeider, R.M. (2006). Challenges to the dual banking system: The funding of bank supervision. *FDIC Banking Review* 18 (1): 1–23. Washington, DC: Federal Deposit Insurance Corporation. https://www.fdic.gov/bank/analytical/banking/br18n1full .pdf (accessed 12 June 2020).

79. Federal Deposit Insurance Corporation (2020). Statistics at a glance: FDIC historical trends – PDF. https://www.fdic.gov/bank/statistical/stats/2019dec/fdic.pdf (accessed 12 June 2020).

80. Federal Deposit Insurance Corporation (2020). Bank failures in brief – Summary 2001 through 2020. https://www.fdic.gov/bank/historical/bank/ (accessed 12 June 2020).

81. Blair and Kushmeider. Challenges to the dual banking system.

82. Federal Deposit Insurance Corporation. Statistics at a glance.

83. Beck, T., Demirgüç-Kunt, A. and Levine, R. (2003). Bank concentration and crises. NBER Working Paper Series 9921. doi:10.3386/w9921. https://www.nber.org/papers/w9921 (accessed 18 June 2020).

84. Álvarez, J.M., Deblas, C., Izquierdo, J.F. et al. (2017). The impact of European banking consolidation on credit prices. BBVA Research Working Paper 17/08. https://www.bbvaresearch .com/wp-content/uploads/2017/09/WP_Impact-Consolidation-on-Credit-Prices-vf_mod .pdf (acessed 18 June 2020).

85. Nordea (2020). Our history: Realising dreams for 200 years. https://www.nordea.com/en/ about-nordea/who-we-are/our-history/ (accessed 12 June 2020).

86. Bundesverband der Deutschen Volksbanken und Raiffeisenbanken (2020). All local cooperative banks as at December 31, 2019. https://www.bvr.de/p.nsf/0/D3E488DF22571CECC 1257D0A005439B7/$file/all%20local%20cooperative%20banks%20at%20December%2031, %202019.pdf (accessed 12 June 2020).

87. Finanstilsynet (2020). Reports: Banks, credit-, payment-, finance-, and E-money institutions in Norway. https://www.finanstilsynet.no/en/finanstilsynets-registry/reports/ (accessed 12 June 2020).

88. Raiffeisen Schweiz (2020). Medienmitteilung: Raiffeisen investiert in den Ausbau ihrer Marktstellung und entwickelt ihr Geschäftsmodell weiter (Press release: Raiffeisen invests in expanding its market position and is further developing its business model). https://www.raiffeisen.ch/content/dam/www/rch/ueber-uns/medien/medienmitteilungen/2020/ de/2020-06-20-medienmitteilung.pdf (accessed 23 June 2020).

89. IBM (2016). Fiducia & GAD IT AG: Bringing high-speed, low-cost, low-risk development to core banking systems. https://www.ibm.com/case-studies/t111146x01262w28 (accessed 14 June 2020).

90. financial.com. Finanz Informatik. https://www.financial.com/portfolio-item/finanz-informatik/ (accessed 20 July 2020).

91. Peyton, A. (2019). All Raiffeisen banks in Switzerland finally live on Avaloq. Fintech Futures (1 February). https://www.fintechfutures.com/2019/02/all-raiffeisen-banks-in-switzerland-finally-live-on-avaloq/ (accessed 23 June 2020).

92. Rabobank Group (2016). *Annual Report* 2015. https://www.rabobank.com/en/images/ rabobank-annual-report-2015.pdf (accessed 14 June 2020).

93. Bowman. *Columbia Chronologies of Asian History and Culture.*

94. Goetzmann. *Money Changes Everything.*

95. Banerjee, N.C. (1945). *Economic Life and Progress in Ancient India*. Calcutta, India: University of Calcutta.

96. Cheque & Credit Clearing Company. The advent of the cheque. https://www.chequeandcredit .co.uk/information-hub/history-cheque/advent-cheque (accessed 13 June 2020).

97. Safari, M. (2013). Contractual structures and payoff patterns of Sukūk securities. *International Journal of Banking and Finance* 10 (2): 81–110. https://papers.ssrn.com/sol3/papers.cfm?abstract_id=2386365 (accessed 14 June 2020).

98. Durant, W. (1950). *The Story of Civilization: The Age of Faith.* New York, NY: Simon & Schuster.

99. Goetzmann. *Money Changes Everything.*

100. Green, E. (1989). *Banking: An Illustrated History.* Oxford, UK: Phaidon Press.

101. O'Brien, J.A. (1968). *The Impact of Computers on Banking.* Boston, MA: Bankers Publishing Company.

102. Cheque and Credit Clearing Company. The clearings: Early days. https://www.chequeandcredit.co.uk/information-hub/history-cheque/clearings-early-days (accessed 15 June 2020).

103. Board of Governors of the Federal Reserve System (2016). *The Federal Reserve System Purposes & Functions* (tenth edition). Washington, DC: Federal Reserve System. https://www.federalreserve.gov/aboutthefed/files/pf_complete.pdf (accessed 18 June 2020).

104. Green. *Banking: An Illustrated History.*

105. American Express. Our history. https://about.americanexpress.com/our-history (accessed 13 June 2020).

106. Silver, F. (1920). *Modern Banking: Commercial and Credit Paper.* New York, NY: The Commercial and Financial Institute of America.

107. Board of Governors of the Federal Reserve System. *The Federal Reserve System Purposes & Functions.*

108. Koeppel, D. (2019). The first American credit card was a coin. *Wirecutter* (30 July). https://www.nytimes.com/wirecutter/blog/the-first-american-credit-card-was-a-coin/ (accessed 20 July 2020).

109. Provident Financial Group. Our heritage. https://www.providentfinancial.com/meet-pfg/our-heritage/ (accessed 13 June 2020).

110. Smithsonian Institute, *National Museum of American History.* Charga-plate in red leather case, United States, 1950s. https://americanhistory.si.edu/collections/search/object/nmah_1251614 (accessed 14 June 2020).

111. Fabry, M. (2016). Now you know: What was the first credit card? *Time* (19 October). https://time.com/4512375/first-credit-card/ (accessed 14 June 2020).

112. The UK Cards Association. *History of cards.* http://www.theukcardsassociation.org.uk/history_of_cards/index.asp (accessed 13 June 2020).

113. Diners Club International. The Diners Club legacy. https://www.dinersclub.com/about-us/history (accessed 13 June 2020).

114. Cashco. 1900–1950's: The beginnings. https://cashcofinancial.com/2016/01/the-history-of-plastic-money/ (accessed 19 July 2020).

115. Deville, J. The matter of the credit card. In: *Transactions: A payments archive.* https://transactions.socialcomputing.uci.edu/post/58430974481/american-express-one-of-the-first-plastic-credit (accessed 19 July 2020).

116. IBM (2011). Icons of progress: Magnetic stripe technology. https://www.ibm.com/ibm/history/ibm100/us/en/icons/magnetic/ (accessed 14 June 2020).

117. Bellamy, E. (1888). *Looking Backward 2000–1887.* Boston, MA: Ticknor and Company.

118. Hayashi, F., Sullivan, R. and Weiner, S.E. (2003). *A guide to the ATM and debit card industry.* Kansas City, MO: Federal Reserve Bank of Kansas City. https://www.kansascityfed.org/publicat/psr/bksjournarticles/atmpaper.pdf (accessed 16 June 2020).

119. O'Brien. *The Impact of Computers on Banking.*

120. Sparks, E. (2017). Nine young bankers who changed America: Dee Hock. *ABA Banking Journal* (26 June). https://bankingjournal.aba.com/2017/06/nine-young-bankers-who-changed-america-dee-hock/ (accessed 16 June 2020).

121. O'Brien. *The Impact of Computers on Banking*.

122. Chargebee (2016). Honey, who moved my money? A Brief History of Direct Debit (23 November). https://www.chargebee.com/elementary/what-is-direct-debit/ (accessed 24 June 2020).

123. Strube, H. (2009). Lastschriftverkehr. In: *Handbuch zum deutschen und europäischen Bankrecht* (ed. Derleder, P., Knops, K.O. and Bamberger, H.), pp. 1285–1306. Berlin, Germany: Springer.

124. Collinson, P. (2015). Number of direct debit payments sets new record. *The Guardian* (4 August). https://www.theguardian.com/money/2015/aug/04/number-of-direct-debit-payments-sets-new-record (accessed 24 June 2020).

125. Barclays Group Archives. Cash machines. https://www.archive.barclays.com/items/show/5415 (accessed 16 June 2020).

126. Bátiz-Lazo, B. and Reid, R.J.K. (2008): Evidence from the patent record on the development of cash dispensing technology. MPRA Paper No. 9461. https://mpra.ub.uni-muenchen.de/9461/ (accessed 22 June 2020).

127. Bátiz-Lazo, B., Karlsson, T. and Thodenius, B. (2009). Building Bankomat: The development of on-line, real-time systems in British and Swedish savings banks, c1965–1985. MPRA Paper No. 27084. https://mpra.ub.uni-muenchen.de/27084/ (accessed 15 June 2020).

128. Bátiz-Lazo and Reid. Evidence from the patent record.

129. Bátiz-Lazo, B. (2007). Emergence and evolution of proprietary ATM networks in the UK, 1967–2000. MPRA Paper No. 3689. https://mpra.ub.uni-muenchen.de/3689/ (accessed 15 June 2020).

130. SWIFT. Serving our community for over 40 years. https://www.swift.com/about-us/history (accessed 15 June 2020).

131. Bank of England. CHAPS technical requirements. https://www.bankofengland.co.uk/-/media/boe/files/payments/chaps/chaps-technical-requirements.pdf (accessed 20 July 2020).

132. Sparks, E. (2017). Nine young bankers who changed America: Thomas Sudman. *ABA Banking Journal* (26 June). https://bankingjournal.aba.com/2017/06/nine-young-bankers-who-changed-america-thomas-sudman/ (accessed 16 June 2020).

133. Cronin, M.J. (1998). *Banking and Finance on the Internet*. New York, NY: Wiley.

134. Lean, T. (2016). Prestel: The British Internet that never was. *History Today* (23 August). https://www.historytoday.com/history-matters/prestel-british-internet-never-was (accessed 18 June 2020).

135. Rapport, M. (2004). Stanford FCU set to mark 10-year anniversary as first financial to offer online banking. *Credit Union Times* (3 February). https://www.cutimes.com/2004/02/03/stanford-fcu-set-to-mark-10-year-anniversary-as-first-financial-to-offer-online-banking (accessed 20 June 2020).

136. O'Brien. *The Impact of Computers on Banking*.

137. HSBC UK. *History timeline*. https://www.about.hsbc.co.uk/hsbc-uk/history-timeline (accessed 18 June 2020).

138. Fancher, C.H. (1999). In your pocket: Smartcards. *IEEE Spectrum* (4 January). https://spectrum.ieee.org/consumer-electronics/standards/in-your-pocket-smartcards (accessed 16 June 2020).

139. Smith, J. ed. (1993). SmartFuel system for trucks. *Smart Card News* (March), p. 45. https://www.smartcard.co.uk/members/newsletters/1993/mar93.pdf (accessed 16 June 2020).

140. Smith, J. ed. (1993). Toll system for France. *Smart Card News* (March), p. 44. https://www .smartcard.co.uk/members/newsletters/1993/mar93.pdf (accessed 16 June 2020).

141. Smith, J. ed. (1993). Smart ski cards in Austria. *Smart Card News* (March), pp. 52–53. https:// www.smartcard.co.uk/members/newsletters/1993/mar93.pdf (accessed 16 June 2020).

142. Finkenzeller, K. (2003). *RFID Handbook: Fundamentals and Applications in Contactless Smart Cards and Identification* (trans. Waddington, R.). Chichester, UK: Wiley.

143. NXP Semiconductors (2014). NXP celebrates 20th anniversary of MIFARE products (28 January). https://www.mifare.net/nxp-celebrates-20th-anniversary-mifare-products/ (accessed 16 June 2020).

144. Smith, J. ed. (1992). Denmark to launch first country-wide scheme. *Smart Card News* (October), pp. 22–26. https://www.smartcard.co.uk/members/newsletters/1992/oct92.pdf (accessed 16 June 2020).

145. Smith, J. ed. (1992). JerseyCard launches purse. *Smart Card News* (October), pp. 33–34. https://www.smartcard.co.uk/members/newsletters/1992/oct92.pdf (accessed 16 June 2020).

146. McKenna, J. and Ayer, K. (1997). Worldwide development and player motivations. In: *Smart Cards: Seizing Strategic Business Opportunities* (ed. Allen, C.A. and Barr, W.J.), 44–56. Chicago, IL: Irwin Professional Publishing.

147. Jack, W., Suri, T. and Townsend, R. (2010). Monetary theory and electronic money: Reflections on the Kenyan experience. *Economic Quarterly* 96 (1): 83–122.

148. Reuters. (2019). M-Pesa has completely changed Kenyans' access to financial services, this is how … (3 April). https://www.cnbcafrica.com/east-africa/2019/04/03/m-pesa-has-completely-changed-kenyans-access-to-financial-services-this-is-how/ (accessed 28 June 2020).

149. Alushula, P. (2019). M-Pesa users outside Kenya hit 13.4 million. *Business Daily* (29 January). https://www.businessdailyafrica.com/corporate/companies/M-Pesa-users-outside-Kenya-hit-13-4-million/4003102-4956208-16s8a9/index.html (accessed 28 June 2020).

150. IBM (2011). IBM 100: Icons of Progress – The Automation of Personal Banking. https://www.ibm.com/ibm/history/ibm100/us/en/icons/bankauto/ (accessed 22 June 2020).

151. Bashe, C.J., Johnson, L.R., Palmer, J.H. et al. (1986). *IBM's Early Computers*. Cambridge, MA: The MIT Press.

152. O'Brien. *The Impact of Computers on Banking*.

153. Lloyds Banking Group. Mechanised Accounting Begins. https://www.lloydsbankinggroup .com/Our-Group/our-heritage/timeline/1901-1950/ (accessed 22 June 2020).

154. Bátiz-Lazo, B. and Wardley, P. (2005). Banking on change: Information systems and technologies in UK High Street banking, 1919–1979. In: *L'entreprise, le chiffre et le droit* (ed. Degos, J.G. and Trébucq, S.), pp. 29–51. Bordeaux, France: Université Montesquieu.

155. Martin, I. (2012). Too far ahead of its time: Barclays, Burroughs and real-time banking. *IEEE Annals of the History of Computing* 34 (2): 5–19.

156. O'Brien. *The Impact of Computers on Banking*.

157. Bashe et al. *IBM's Early Computers*.

158. O'Brien. *The Impact of Computers on Banking*.

159. Martin, I. (2009). *Britain's first computer centre for banking: What did this building do? XVth World Economic History Congress (3 to 7 August)*, Utrecht, Netherlands. https://core.ac.uk/reader/2743 (accessed 24 June 2020).

160. Nelson, R.A. and Lovitt, K.M. ed. (1963). History of teletypewriter development. http://rtty .com/history/nelson.htm (accessed 24 June 2020).

161. Wood, L. (2008). The LAN turns 30, but will it reach 40? *Computerworld* (31 January).

https://www.computerworld.com/article/2538907/the-lan-turns-30--but-will-it-reach-40-.html (accessed 24 June 2020).

162. Bátiz-Lazo et al. Building Bankomat.

163. CBR Staff Writer (1995). Lloyds may move current accounts off IBM, onto Unisys (13 October). *Computer Business Review* (13 October). https://www.cbronline.com/news/lloyds_may_move_current_accounts_off_ibm_onto_unisys (accessed 24 June 2020).

164. Financial Conduct Authority (2014). FCA fines RBS, NatWest and Ulster Bank Ltd £42 million for IT failures (20 November). https://www.fca.org.uk/news/press-releases/fca-fines-rbs-natwest-and-ulster-bank-ltd-%C2%A342-million-it-failures (accessed 21 July 2020).

165. BBC (2015). RBS payments failure 'unacceptable' (18 June). https://www.bbc.com/news/business-33182798 (accessed 21 July 2020).

166. Bajkowski, J. (2019). Massive CBA outage traced to failed infrastructure upgrade. *iTnews* (18 October). https://www.itnews.com.au/news/massive-cba-outage-traced-to-failed-infrastructure-upgrade-532586 (accessed 30 June 2020).

167. Klebnikov, S. (2019). Bank of America's outage panics customers. Here's what we know so far. *Forbes* (30 October). https://www.forbes.com/sites/sergeiklebnikov/2019/10/30/bank-of-americas-outage-panics-consumers-heres-what-we-know-so-far/ (accessed 30 June 2020).

168. HSBC UK. *History timeline.*

169. Pay.UK (2020). Current account switch service dashboard Issue 26: Covering the period 1 January 2020 to 31 March 2020. https://www.wearepay.uk/wp-content/uploads/Q1-2020-CASS-Dashboard-issue-26.pdf (accessed 28 June 2020).

170. Securities and Exchange Commission (2011). Notice regarding Volcker Rule. https://www.sec.gov/spotlight/dodd-frank/volckerrule.htm (accessed 29 June 2020).

171. Financial Conduct Authority (2016). Ring-fencing. https://www.fca.org.uk/consumers/ring-fencing (accessed 29 June 2020).

172. Jones, H. (2017). EU scraps its answer to U.S. Volcker Rule for banks. *Reuters Business News* (24 October). https://www.reuters.com/article/us-eu-banks-regulations/eu-scraps-its-answer-to-u-s-volcker-rule-for-banks-idUSKBN1CT285 (accessed 29 June 2020).

173. Department of Justice (2014). Bank of America to pay $16.65 billion in historic Justice Department settlement for financial fraud leading up to and during the financial crisis (21 August). https://www.justice.gov/opa/pr/bank-america-pay-1665-billion-historic-justice-department-settlement-financial-fraud-leading (accessed 29 June 2020).

174. Schwartz, N.D. and Creswell, J. (2012). Mortgage plan gives billions to homeowners, but with exceptions. *New York Times* (9 February). https://www.nytimes.com/2012/02/10/business/states-negotiate-26-billion-agreement-for-homeowners.html (accessed 29 June 2020).

175. Department of Justice (2014). BNP Paribas agrees to plead guilty and to pay $8.9 billion for illegally processing financial transactions for countries subject to U.S. economic sanctions (30 June). https://www.justice.gov/opa/pr/bnp-paribas-agrees-plead-guilty-and-pay-89-billion-illegally-processing-financial (accessed 29 June 2020).

176. Financial Conduct Authority (2020). 2019 fines (20 January). https://www.fca.org.uk/news/news-stories/2019-fines (accessed 29 June 2020).

177. Maclucas, N., Blackstone, B. and Morse, A. (2014). Swiss Central Bank to introduce negative interest rates. *Wall Street Journal* (18 December). https://www.wsj.com/articles/swiss-central-bank-introduces-negative-interest-rates-1418888001 (accessed 29 June 2020).

178. Collinson, P. (2019). Danish bank launches world's first negative interest rate mortgage. *The Guardian* (13 August). https://www.theguardian.com/money/2019/aug/13/danish-bank-launches-worlds-first-negative-interest-rate-mortgage (accessed 21 July 2020).

179. Federal Financial Institutions Examination Council (2020). Net interest margin for all U.S. banks [USNIM]. https://fred.stlouisfed.org/series/USNIM/ (accessed 30 June 2020).

180. World Bank (2019). Bank's net interest margin for United Kingdom [DDEI01G BA156NWDB]. https://fred.stlouisfed.org/series/DDEI01GBA156NWDB (accessed 30 June 2020).

181. Financial Conduct Authority (2018). Strategic review of retail banking business models: Final report (December). https://www.fca.org.uk/publication/multi-firm-reviews/strategic-review-retail-banking-business-models-final-report.pdf (accessed 1 July 2020).

182. Alliance News (2015). HSBC aims to cut USD5.0 billion from cost bill in 2.5 years. Morningstar (9 June). https://www.morningstar.co.uk/uk/news/AN_1433856584037153900/4th-update-hsbc-aims-to-cut-usd50-billion-from-cost-bill-in-25-years.aspx (accessed 29 June 2020).

183. Lovett, S. (2020). HSBC to cut 35,000 jobs as profits fall by a third. *The Independent* (18 February). https://www.independent.co.uk/news/business/news/hsbc-jobs-cut-profits-news-uk-banking-latest-a9341376.html (accessed 29 June 2020).

184. Deutsche Bank (2015). Deutsche Bank announces details of Strategy 2020 (29 October). https://www.db.com/newsroom_news/2015/medien/deutsche-bank-announces-details-of-strategy-2020-en-11247.htm (accessed 29 June 2020).

185. Freed, D. and Shankar, S. (2016). Bank of America sets new cost target under pressure from low rates. *Reuters Business News* (18 July). http://www.reuters.com/article/us-bank-of-america-results-idUSKCN0ZY17E (accessed 29 June 2020).

186. Financial Conduct Authority. Strategic review of retail banking business models.

187. Ali, Z. (2020). The world's 100 largest banks, 2020. *S&P Global Market Intelligence* (7 April). https://www.spglobal.com/marketintelligence/en/news-insights/latest-news-headlines/the-world-s-100-largest-banks-2020-57854079 (accessed 30 June 2020).

188. European Commission (2016). Mergers: Commission prohibits Hutchison's proposed acquisition of Telefónica UK (11 May). https://ec.europa.eu/commission/presscorner/detail/en/IP_16_1704 (accessed 1 July 2020).

189. Brignall, M. (2019). More than a third of UK bank branches have closed since 2015. *The Guardian* (24 September). https://www.theguardian.com/money/2019/sep/24/more-than-a-third-of-uk-bank-branches-have-closed-since-2015 (accessed 1 July 2020).

190. Stackhouse, J. (2018). Why are banks shuttering branches? Federal Reserve Bank of St. Louis (26 February). https://www.stlouisfed.org/on-the-economy/2018/february/why-banks-shuttering-branches (accessed 1 July 2020).

191. SWIFT. Distributed architecture. https://developer.swift.com/glossary/distributed-architecture (accessed 1 July 2020).

192. Vocalink. About us. https://www.vocalink.com/about-us/ (accessed 1 July 2020).

193. Bank of England. CHAPS Technical Requirements.

194. New Payments Platform. The Platform. https://nppa.com.au/the-platform/ (accessed 30 June 2020).

195. European Payments Council. Clearing and settlement mechanisms. https://www.europeanpaymentscouncil.eu/what-we-do/sepa-payment-scheme-management/clearing-and-settlement-mechanisms (accessed 30 June 2020).

196. Rolfe, A. (2018). China UnionPay Eyes Major European Expansion with UK Launch. Payments Cards & Mobile (19 September). https://www.paymentscardsandmobile.com/china-unionpay-eyes-major-european-expansion-with-uk-launch/ (accessed 1 July 2020).

197. Crosman, P. (2013). Can big four core banking vendors' oligopoly be broken? *American Banker* (7 October). https://www.americanbanker.com/news/can-big-four-core-banking-vendors-oligopoly-be-broken (accessed 1 July 2020).

198. finance.com. Finanz Informatik.

199. IBM. Fiducia & GAD IT AG.

200. Bruns, K.-P. (2016). Gemeinsam etwas Großes auf die Beine stellen (Putting something big together). *Börsen-Zeitung* 107 (B): 2. https://www.boersen-zeitung.de/index.php?li=1&artid=2016107701&titel=Gemeinsam-etwas-Grosses-auf-die-Beine-stellen (accessed 1 July 2020).

201. Gerdes, W.D. (2017). *Money and Banking* (second edition). New York, NY: Business Expert Press.

202. O'Brien, J.A. (1968). *The Impact of Computers on Banking*. Boston, MA: Bankers Publishing Company.

CHAPTER 3

An Introduction to Banking Technology

3.1 Introduction

In Chapter 2 we covered the history of banking and the use of technology in banking. In this chapter we start looking in more detail at the technology used in banking. We're going to cover various historical technologies that you may still come across as well as those technologies that you would be implementing in a new banking institution or using to replace legacy technology in an existing institution. In order to do this we are going to consider a simple banking institution initially and then expand on this to cover larger and more complex institutions over the course of this chapter.

3.2 A Model of a Simple Bank

We start with a small, simple bank that offers deposit accounts (including current accounts), unsecured loans and secured loans (including mortgages) to retail and business customers through a single branch. For whatever reason, this bank hasn't embraced ATMs, the Internet, smartphone apps or contact centres. Customers can either go into or phone the branch to do their banking. We actually came across a bank similar to this in the UK in 2010. The diagram in Figure 3.1 represents the channels through which a customer can interact with the bank and the single technology platform it uses to conduct its business. A diagram like this is intended to logically group the functions that are carried out inside a bank (e.g. a branch has certain functions such as a teller servicing a customer), with a business process comprising a route through one or more groups (for example, a customer mailing in a cheque results in a business process that starts in the post channel and carries on into the core banking platform).

The core banking platform that this bank uses is what is often called a bank in a box. Not only does it manage bank accounts and customer records, but it has rudimentary finance functions (including the bank's general ledger), treasury functions and reporting functions (e.g. to provide operational, management, statutory and regulatory reports). Anything else, including customer authentication, know your customer checks, payment screening and submission of regulatory reports, is done manually or using office applications such as Microsoft Excel or by using a third party (e.g. chequebook printing). This model was relatively common, often in overseas branches of banks (e.g. this could be what the branch of a Greek bank based in Paris would have).

FIGURE 3.1   A model of a simple bank.

A note on terminology: we define a platform as an application comprising one or more programs and an associated datastore (which may be one or more databases, files or some other storage mechanism) – the meaning of all these terms will become clear in this chapter. We use the term platform because generally it can be used for a range of products and services, which can be changed over time, and so is a platform on which an organisation can build its offerings. A platform may be composed of one or more systems. We usually think of a system as either a piece of hardware such as a computer (e.g. a mainframe, a minicomputer, a mid-range server or a PC) and the operating system running on it (such as Linux, various flavours of UNIX, Windows, z/OS and so on) or as a generic term for a technology component. However, other authors may use the term 'system' where we use 'platform'.

3.3   The Core Banking Platform

Our simple bank has only one platform – the core banking platform. This maintains a range of information on each account such as:

- The type of account, the account holder and the account number. How accounts are numbered is typically standardised in each country, as an account must be uniquely identifiable to be used to receive payments from and make payments via shared payment networks. Many current (or checking) accounts are now uniquely identifiable by their IBAN – an international standard for uniquely numbering bank accounts, which we cover in Section 7.6.8.
- Various balances, such as the available credit balance, the balance that is available to withdraw via an ATM (as banks typically limit daily ATM withdrawals), and a total balance (which incorporates items that have not yet cleared such as a cheque paid into the account before it has gone through the cheque clearing process).
- Historical transactions such as deposits, withdrawals, charges and interest debits and credits that have taken place on the account, along with historical balance information. This enables the core banking platform to generate statements for each account and calculate interest payments.
- Details of recurring payments set up on the account, e.g. direct debits and periodic payments out.
- Details of cheques issued on an account (e.g. cheque numbers and chequebooks issued).
- Details of cards such as debit cards or cash withdrawal cards linked to the account.

As well as this, the core banking platform must also enable different account types to be defined and therefore hold information on the characteristics of each account type, e.g. interest rates (different for credit and debit balances) and features available (such as whether cheques and cards can be issued on the account).

At a minimum, the core banking platform has the following functions:

- It calculates the interest on each account and applies this as a credit (for an account with a positive balance) or a debit (for a mortgage or loan account or a current account that is overdrawn).
- It maintains flags and status information on accounts (e.g. death of account holder, power of attorney in place), including holds on the account (e.g. account frozen because of a court order).
- It calculates charges such as a monthly fee or a per-transaction charge and applies these to each account where appropriate.
- It allows payments to be made from its accounts to accounts at other banks and to receive payments to its accounts from other banks. It would also be common for it to hold details of recurring payments to be maintained, for example, if a customer wishes to change the amount of a periodic outgoing payment, the core banking platform would offer a facility for doing this.
- It generates statements for accounts – typically these take the form of a file that is sent to a third-party statement printer for fulfilment (i.e. printing, putting in an envelope and posting to the account holder).
- It generates various reports used by the bank to manage its business and those required by banking regulators. However, this latter function may be done by a specialised platform that extracts the relevant information from the banking, treasury and finance platforms and combines it into the regulatory reports required by the banking regulator.
- It generates financial information (e.g. revenue from charges) that is used by the bank to manage its finances.

It may also perform other functions such as:

- Maintaining detailed records on each customer and linking these to all the accounts held by that customer. Modern banking platforms claim to be customer-centric, by which it is generally meant that each customer of the bank has a single record on the banking platform, which is linked to all their accounts, potentially even those held on other platforms in the bank (e.g. credit cards) – what is typically called a single customer view. The information on each customer would include an address, identification information such as the number from an official identification document such as a passport, their date of birth, contact details such as an email address and telephone numbers, a scan of the customer's signature, and so on.
- Providing the functionality to track applications by customers for accounts. For example, a mortgage application requires several steps, such as checking the identity of the customer, checking the customer's creditworthiness, checking and valuing the property to be mortgaged, releasing the funds to a third party and storing the mortgaged property's deeds.

- Handling the lifecycle of plastic cards, such as dealing with lost or stolen cards and issuing new cards to replace cards that are soon to expire.
- Issuing and keeping records of customer correspondence and customer contacts such as phone calls.
- Managing customer complaints. In some jurisdictions regulators require reporting on the management of customer complaints and impose mandatory standards for the maximum time taken to deal with a complaint.
- Managing the financial accounts of the bank itself – in other words, the bank's general ledger and associated reports. In the simple model shown in Figure 3.2 we have assumed this is indeed the case, although all but the simplest banks are likely to have a separate finance platform, in which case the core banking platform will have to generate information to feed into it.
- Providing simple treasury management – including tracking the inflows and outflows of cash and monitoring the bank's liquidity and capital position – typically incorporated within the financial management module. As with the finance functionality, all but the simplest banks will have a separate treasury platform which receives information from the core banking platform on outflows and inflows.

So, we can build up a logical picture for the various groups of functions that a core banking platform performs – in other words, a functional decomposition of it – as shown in Figure 3.2. We believe you would find these functions, to some extent, in just about every modern integrated core banking platform. Having said that, in large banks some of these functions may well be performed by different platforms that work together. For example, we're aware of one UK bank that has a different platform for managing details of future payments such as standing orders (where the account holder has set up

FIGURE 3.2   A logical view of the functions of a core banking platform.

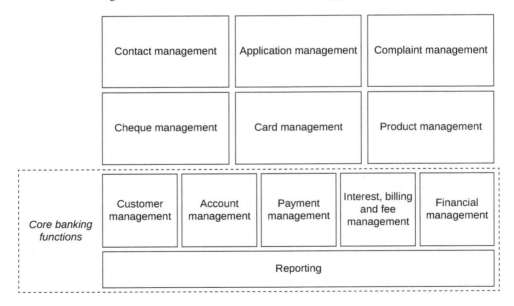

a payment to be made periodically) and direct debits (where a payment is initiated by the beneficiary), and this platform interfaces to the banking platform when these payments take place.

Historically, core banking platforms operated by processing transactions in a daily batch. This means that details of withdrawals and credits during the course of a day are stored up (originally on paper records) and then applied to the accounts in a process at the end of the day, followed by another process which calculates interest and charges on each account. During the period that batch processing is taking place, the core banking platform may not be available to human users. Outside the batch processing period, users could access the core banking platform to see the balance of the accounts on it for that day. This was a perfectly viable model of operating when payment networks processed payments overnight – each night the bank would submit a file of outgoing payments to the payment processor, and receive a file of incoming payments from the payment processor, then apply these to the customer accounts on the core banking platform. If a customer needed to withdraw cash during the day, he or she would go into a branch where a teller would access the account record and check the account balance at the end of the processing the night before and then if any other withdrawals had been made during that day. However, with the growth of ATM networks in the 1970s and 1980s followed by the introduction of debit cards, this mode of operation stopped being viable, as it was necessary to check a withdrawal against the account balance at any time of the day or night to avoid customers being able to go overdrawn without authorisation and to limit withdrawals in case a customer's card was misused. Modern core banking platforms work differently and are always available to their users, which means that as a customer of a bank you can withdraw cash or use your debit card at any time of day or night. Having said that, there will still be an end-of-day process on a modern banking platform, during which, for example, interest is calculated and batch payments take place, and during this process some functionality may not be available to users.

The core banking platform architecture can be represented as shown in Figure 3.3. This diagram is intended to show that there is a program (or set of programs) called the core banking application, which manages the banking data in another system called the banking database that is in some way separate (for example, it could reside on a different server). It's a different type of diagram from what we have shown earlier in this chapter, and is intended to show the technical components that are involved in a platform and indicate relationships between them – we could call it a technical architecture diagram. We are going to investigate this architecture, starting with how the banking database is designed.

FIGURE 3.3   Basic core banking platform architecture.

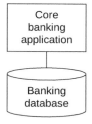

3.4   Database Architectures

In this section we cover how databases are architected. Our most basic model of an application (such as a banking application) accessing a database where it holds its data is shown in Figure 3.4. The application needs to store various types of records – for example a core banking application would need to maintain a list of accounts, a list of all transactions on those accounts, a list of payments to be made from the accounts and so on.

The database could be constructed in various ways. The simplest way would be to use a set of files. For the core banking platform at our simple bank, there could be a file containing all the details of accounts, another file containing all the transactions on the accounts and so on.

Let's look at how we might organise such files internally. An excerpt of the file containing account records might look like the following:

```
1000000982ARFTD0026100000034720180829_____
1000000983XRIAS0008100009354420180829020200105
1000000984CBFTD0006100000049020180829020190828
```

We have shown three records in this excerpt. Each record represents one account and contains information on that account. Each record is also a fixed length – in this example, 45 characters – and comprises several fixed-length fields, which are:

Characters 1 to 10 are the internal account number (e.g. 1000000982 in the first record shown). In this example, we have decided that account numbers do not start with 0, so that they are always 10 digits long and humans will be less tempted to leave off leading 0s. Assuming that the account numbers start at 1000000001 and there are no gaps in account numbers, the location of any record in the file can be calculated from its account number, using a very simple algorithm:

1. Reduce the left-hand digit of the account number by 1. This is necessary because we have decided that our account numbers will not start with 0.
2. Subtract 1 from the modified account number.
3. Multiply this number by the length of each record (45 in our example).

So, the very first account in the file would be numbered 1000000001 and start at location 0 in the file (using the convention in computer systems that the first location is numbered 0). The first record in our excerpt of the file would be located at position 981

FIGURE 3.4   Basic model of an application and database.

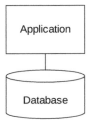

times 45, that is, position 44,145. In reality it is not ideal to have to ensure that there are no gaps in account numbers. For example, historically storage was expensive and limited and so it would have been preferable to delete records of accounts that had long been closed, which would have also had the benefit of reducing the time required to search through the accounts. This is the first problem we come across when using a file-based database, and in our example it could be solved by having a second file that is used to index the account records file – that is, it contains records to say where in the account records file each account record is located.

An important point to emphasise is that the account numbers we are using in this example are internal to the bank. If these accounts are going to accept payments from other institutions, they would also have to have external account identifiers consistent with the payment schemes in the country of operation, so we would have to add these to our records. For example, standard account identifiers in the UK comprise a six-digit sort code (historically representing a bank branch) and an eight-digit account number. We could potentially use the standard external account identifier as the internal account number, but this may not be sensible if there is account number portability in the country of operation and it may affect our application's ability to rapidly locate accounts in the file.

Character 11 indicates the status of the account, with A meaning active, X cancelled (one possible usage of this is because the fixed-term account represented by the record was never funded and so lapsed) and C closed.

Characters 12 to 15 are the account type. Here, RFTD means a retail fixed-term deposit account, RIAS means a retail instant access savings account and BFTD means a business fixed-term deposit account.

Characters 16 to 19 indicate the product version. For example, this is 0026 in the first record shown previously. This indicates version 26 of the retail fixed-term deposit account type. This version number may be used to distinguish between different variants of the same basic product type, for example, which differ in the interest rate or have different term lengths.

Characters 20 to 29 are the customer number. In the first record shown, this is 1000000347. If we were to look in the file containing the customer records, we should find a corresponding record beginning with this number. Pointing to a record in the customer file rather than putting the customer information into the account record allows the bank to have a single customer record for a customer who holds more than one account with it.

Characters 30 to 37 hold the date the account was opened, in the format yyyymmdd. In reality, the core banking platform could well use an internal representation for dates, such as the number of days since a specific date. For example, UNIX systems originally represented dates (and times) as the number of seconds since 00:00:00 UTC on 1 January 1970. Many older computer systems used only two digits to represent the year, which was the source of the infamous Y2K issue (or non-issue, as it turned out) which in summary meant that such systems would potentially act like the year was 1900 instead of 2000.

Characters 38 to 45 hold the date the account was closed, also in the format yyyymmdd. For the first record shown, the account is still open and so the record holds blanks, indicated by the open box symbols (␣).

A real core banking platform is likely to need to store much more information on each account and so a record would be much longer than we have shown here.

FIGURE 3.5   Contents of the index file.

ID	Location
1000000001	0000000000
1000000002	0000000035
1000000005	0000000070
...	...
1000000982	0000020685
1000000983	0000020720
1000000984	0000020755
...	...

Index file contains

10000000010000000000100000000200000000351000000005000000070...
1000000982000002068510000009830000020720100000098400000020755...

Data file contains

ARIAS0001100000000120130410ⱵⱵⱵⱵⱵⱵ
CRFTD0001100000000220130410 20140409
CRFTD0001100000000420130410 20140409
...
ARFTD0026100000034720180829ⱵⱵⱵⱵⱵⱵ
XRIAS00008100009354420180829 20200105
CBFTD00006100000004902018082920190828
...

One other note: we have shown each record on a new line. In reality, all the records could be concatenated without anything to indicate where one record ends and another one begins, although there may be a reason for having something to indicate the end of a record such as a special character or sequence of characters. This could make it quicker to navigate through the records and could also make it easier to detect and fix corruptions to the files.

You are unlikely to come across a core banking platform or any other complex modern platform directly using files as its database. We've already met one challenge to the use of files – the need to deal with gaps in the account numbers in our example – and various further challenges stand out. In addition, the application has to know the precise details of how the data is stored and so changing the database, e.g. because you want to add an additional field to a record, also requires the application (and any other applications that use the same data files) to be changed to cope with the new record length and all the existing records would have to be rewritten to include the new field. There are, of course, ways around this – for example, you could pad each record with blank characters from the start, so that if you want to add a new field you start using some of the blank space, which is fine until you use up all the blank space with new fields.

These challenges can be eased by introducing the notion of an index on the file. This is another file that contains records with two entries – a value and a position where the corresponding record for the value can be found in the data file. So, in the example, we would have an index file for the account number, as shown in Figure 3.5. Note how we have removed the account number from the data file and used it as the ID in the index file. Note also how it is possible to skip account numbers – in our example, account numbers 1000000003 and 1000000004 are missing. The use of an index file also allows variable-length data records in the corresponding data file.

In the 1950s and 1960s, storage was expensive and necessarily limited. The first hard disk drive, the IBM 350 Disk File launched by IBM in 1956, could hold five million seven-bit characters, approximately equivalent to 4.2 megabytes, and was roughly the size of a washing machine.[1] By the early 1960s there were hard drive storage units that could hold around 200 megabytes. Any practical storage method had to consider how hard drives themselves worked, and the Indexed Sequential Access Method (ISAM) was developed to do this. A hard disk drive stores data in concentric tracks on a spinning disk coated with a magnetic material, and has a head that is moved radially across the spinning disk that reads and writes the tracks – it can only read or write one track at a time. A hard disk drive unit could have several disks that rotate together on the same spindle, each with their own head (which moves in line with all the other heads), so you can envisage each track being part of a cylinder, and so we think of groups of data records being stored on different cylinders. ISAM builds on the index file approach set out earlier, with the account records stored sequentially in order of account number in each cylinder and the index file contains the highest value record ID in each cylinder. So, for example, the first cylinder (numbered zero) might contain account records with account numbers between 1000000001 and 1000000130, as shown in Figure 3.6. So, our three sample records (the first of which has the account number beginning 1000000982) are stored on cylinder 7. Note, once again, that we have to store the ID (i.e. the account number in our example) with each data record, as the index file doesn't contain every ID, just the highest ID of the records in each cylinder. The index file is now much smaller because it isn't holding every account ID.

Typically, some space is left in each cylinder for records to be inserted, which can be done without having to update the index file. When a cylinder becomes full, a record to be inserted is written to an overflow cylinder (typically another cylinder in the same hard drive storage unit). When looking for a specific record, ISAM will first check the cylinder indicated by the contents of the index file, and if a record isn't found will then check the overflow cylinder for it. Over time, more and more records would end up in the overflow cylinder and the time taken to find a record would increase. Therefore it was necessary to periodically reorganise the location of records in the storage system to move records from the overflow cylinder into the main storage cylinders, shift records between cylinders to free up space and update the index file accordingly. While this was being done, the database was unavailable (and probably so was the core banking application).

There have been many implementations of ISAM, typically in the form of software libraries that are embedded in business applications, some of which are still available today. Perhaps the most well-known implementation – and, from what we can determine, the first use of the term ISAM – was by IBM in the 1960s, which provided routines for its mainframe computers to manage ISAM data sets stored on IBM storage devices.[2] ISAM is still available in various database management systems today, as it can provide very fast read access with an ability to insert new records very quickly, although its connection with how disk storage systems are constructed is normally less relevant.

FIGURE 3.6   Contents of an ISAM index file.

ID	Cylinder	Index file contains
1000000130	000	1000000130000100000022400110000000398002... 100000009060061000001016007...
1000000224	001	
1000000398	002	
...	...	
1000000906	006	
1000001016	007	
...	...	

In our example it is very quick to find a specific account record if you know the account number. However, if you want to find a record based on something else, such as customer number (imagine the scenario where you want to see what accounts a customer has), the application has to search the whole account file to find the records. This can be solved by having another index file which contains records that indicate for each customer number where to locate the corresponding accounts (i.e. the accounts held by each customer) in the accounts file.

Most real-world applications have multiple processes running simultaneously, all of which probably need to access the same database. The application would have to be written to handle contention between processes for accessing and updating the same files and records. It was a natural progression to separate the management of the data files away from the applications that read and wrote the data and into separate database management systems that could be accessed by multiple processes and applications at the same time, and that handled the contention for reading from and writing to the database. Such database management systems could also manage the relationships between different types of records (e.g. which customers owned which accounts) to make sure these stayed in sync. In the first half of the 1960s, Charles Bachmann created the Integrated Data Store (IDS) at General Electric, as part of a project to develop a standard system to be rolled out to GE's various businesses to manage stock inventories.[3] IDS ran as an application in its own right and other applications would call it to access and update the data it was managing. To some extent it hid the physical storage of data from the calling applications. It also provided a mechanism for relating different types of records, so that in the example of our banking system it would be possible to find all the account records from a customer record. Notably, it allowed many-to-many relationships between records. So, for example, it would support more than one customer having the same bank account. As such it supports what are called network data models.

Also, during the 1960s, IBM developed its Information Management System (IMS), originally to manage the bill of materials for the *Saturn V* rocket used by the Apollo moon landing programme. Launched in 1969,[4] IMS, like IDS, ran as an application in its own right. It allowed different types of records to be linked in a hierarchy so that a parent record could have multiple child records related to it. In our banking database example, a customer record could have multiple account records related to it, but an account record couldn't have more than one customer record related to it. Such a hierarchical model is not as flexible as the network data model approach offered by IDS but can have the advantage of greater speed. IMS was – and still is – used extensively to manage very large databases, such as those used by telephone companies, to maintain details of customers, lines and call data records, and IBM claims it is used by banks around the world (which doesn't surprise us given the 1960s heritage of mainframe-based banking platforms in many large banks) – for example, Fiducia & GAD IT AG uses it to process nearly 100 million accounts for the German Volksbanken and Raiffeisenbanken.[5]

There were many other examples of database management systems developed in the 1960s, quite often specific to a server platform, and these live on today in various products. IDS was ported to various platforms and although the original IDS product is no longer available, CA-IDMS, which originated as a port of IDS, is available for various platforms.

Relational databases were the next type of database model to be developed. The concept of a relational database was defined by E. F. Codd in his seminal paper of 1970,[6] and the first commercially available relational database management systems became available in the second half of the 1970s. These systems store records of the same type in a table (so all account records would be stored in the Account table), and are able to link records of different types together using the concept of a foreign key, in which a field in a record in one table (say the Account table) holds a unique identifier of a record in another table (say the Customer table). A relational database should be used to store data in a normalised form, which in essence means minimising duplication of data by using tables and relationships between tables that respect the real relationships between pieces of data. There are various levels of normalisation, which textbooks and other sources explain. Such a system can link any records, including those in many-to-many relationships by using intermediate tables. How tables are stored is totally hidden from the calling applications, although in practice many relational databases originally used variants and extensions of the ISAM approach and may still have that as an option. Extending the data model (e.g. adding a field to each record in a table) typically does not mean the calling applications have to be changed. Applications use Structured Query Language (SQL) to read and update the information inside the database.

Figure 3.7 shows an example of an extremely simple relational data model to store information on customers and the accounts that they hold. This diagram uses so-called crow's foot notation and tells us that a customer can have zero to many accounts (indicated by the symbol on the right-hand end of the line connecting the two boxes). Alternatively, an account must have one or more customers (reading the symbol on the left-hand end of the line).

In an RDBMS, this would be implemented as three tables, shown in Figure 3.8, with some example data (copying some of the data from our data file example above). In this figure the top table is the Customer table. In our example, a customer record has six fields (or columns) – ID, Prefix, First_Name, Family_Name, Birth_Date and Gender. The ID field must always contain a unique value (i.e. no two customers can have the same ID), cannot be empty, and is what is called the primary key for the Customer table – which means we can uniquely identify any row in the table by its value. The bottom table is the Account table. In our example, an account record also has six fields – ID, Status, Type, Product_Version, Opened_Date and Closed_Date. The ID field is the primary key.

The middle table is where the information about which customers hold which accounts is stored. We could call this the Customer_Account table. Each entry in this table has two fields, namely Customer_ID and Account_ID, and these are what are called foreign keys into the Customer and Account tables respectively. This means that they must contain a value from the primary key of each table respectively and therefore point us to specific records in these two tables (they could also contain no value). Looking at the first row of data in this table, the customer with ID 1000020822

FIGURE 3.7   A simple relational data model.

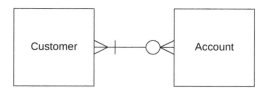

FIGURE 3.8   Tables in an RDBMS required for our simple data model.

ID	Prefix	First_Name	Family_Name	Birth_Date	Gender
1000020822	Miss	Elise	Wong	31/03/1968	Female
1000030444	Mr	Kevin	Smith	20/10/1991	Male
1000057934	Mrs	Hannah	Smith	03/07/1990	Female

Customer_ID	Account_ID
1000020822	1000000982
1000030444	1000000983
1000057934	1000000983

ID	Status	Type	Product_Version	Opened_Date	Closed_Date
1000000982	A	RFTD	26	29/08/2018	
1000000983	X	RIAS	8	29/08/2018	05/01/2020

has account with ID 1000000982, so Miss Elise Wong has the retail fixed-term deposit account (the one with type RFTD). Then the next two rows tell us that Mr Kevin Smith and Mrs Hannah Smith jointly hold the retail instant savings account (the account with type RIAS).

So, suppose our core banking platform had a means to look up the open accounts held by any customer by entering the customer's ID – let's use Miss Elise Wong's ID which is 1000020822. The core banking application would send the following SQL statement to its RDBMS:

```
SELECT Account.ID, Account.Type, Account.Product_Version, Account.Opened_Date
FROM Account, Customer_Account
WHERE Customer_Account.Customer_ID=1000020822
     AND Account.ID=Customer_Account.Account_ID
     AND Account.Status="A"
```

This tells the RDBMS to look in the Customer_Account table to find all values of Account_ID which have Miss Elise Wong's customer ID of 1000020822, and then load four fields from the records in the Account table which have those ID values and for which the account status is A (i.e. active). The RDBMS would return the following data to the core banking application:

```
1000000982, RFTD, 26, 29/08/2018
```

The core banking application would (we hope) display this in a user-friendly format.

There are also SQL statements that allow the core banking application to create new records (INSERT statements), update existing records (UPDATE) and delete records (DELETE). SQL statements can also be used to create, modify and delete databases, the tables within them and the columns the tables hold, which tend to be used by database administrators rather than the applications accessing the RDBMS. Note that although there are various standards for the SQL language, in reality every RDBMS has its own variations and additions to the standards and so business applications typically only support a small number of RDBMS platforms.

In practice, you could expect the RDBMS for a core banking platform to manage anywhere from around a hundred tables (which would be a very simple core banking platform) to several thousand tables. These represent both the fundamental business entities such as retail and corporate customers, accounts, products and transactions, and the relationships between them.

RDBMSs often also offer what are called stored procedures. These are programs that run on the RDBMS itself and are sometimes written in proprietary languages (i.e. specific to each RDBMS platform), including extended versions of SQL. Some RDBMS products also support more general programming languages such as JavaScript for stored procedures. You would typically consider implementing a stored procedure when there are many SQL statements to be executed to perform part of a business process. For example, determining the bank's view of the creditworthiness of a customer as part of a loan application may involve looking at lots of different information held on that customer and it would be quicker to execute this directly on the RDBMS rather than getting the application that uses the RDBMS to issue lots of different SQL statements and manipulate the records that are returned. There are pros and cons of using stored procedures, with application designers having strong views on when it is and isn't desirable to embed business logic in the database. We have seen plenty of commercial applications that use them extensively, often with the result that such applications require a specific vendor's RDBMS platform given stored procedure languages are often specific to each RDBMS platform.

Examples of RDBMSs include commercial systems such IBM Db2, Microsoft SQL Server and Oracle RDBMS and open-source systems such as MariaDB, MySQL and PostgreSQL.

Most complex platforms you may come across in a bank (and probably any other industry) that were developed from the mid-1980s onwards use an RDBMS to manage their data. The main reasons for this are the flexibility offered by an RDBMS, the ease with which an RDBMS-based database can be maintained and updated and the fast pace at which applications using an RDBMS to manage their data can be developed, plus the fact that they offer atomicity, consistency, isolation and durability (ACID) transaction properties.

Atomicity means that when an application modifies information in the database – what is called a transaction and typically represents a step in a business process – the changes are all made or they all fail. For example, if a customer makes a transfer between two accounts, the core banking platform has to debit the funds from one account (which means writing a row in the database table that holds all banking transactions) and credit the other account with the funds (which means writing another row in the banking transaction table). These records both have to be written, or all fail to be written – we can't debit one account and not credit the other, for example.

Consistency means that when an application performs a transaction on the database (i.e. updates, inserts or deletes data in the database), the database will only allow it to do so in line with the data model. This means that only valid values are written to each field (e.g. the database will only allow valid dates in fields that are intended to hold dates) and the relationships between entities are maintained (so in our simple relational model in Figure 3.7, every account must have at least one customer). If our core banking application tries to make changes to data in the database that aren't in line with the data model, the RDBMS will reject the transaction.

Isolation refers to the property that ensures that transactions do not interfere with one another. Our core banking platform may have hundreds of users accessing it, making updates, adding records and so on. Every transaction must be carried out sequentially, so that it is impossible for one transaction to see any intermediate changes being performed by a different transaction. For example, when we issue a loan to a customer we think of it as debiting the loan account and then crediting the customer's current account, and the database will do this as a single transaction. It must not be possible for another user of the database to see only the loan account as having been debited before the current account has been credited.

Durability is the property that guarantees that once a transaction has completed, it will not be lost. In effect this means the database is held on non-volatile or permanent storage such as hard drives and not just in volatile memory that could be lost if the database server crashed.

RDBMSs offer all these properties. For banks this is nearly always ideal – we normally need all these properties so that we know our data is secure, there is a totally reliable single source of truth and our customers and the bank do not lose money even if systems fail. A generation of developers, IT architects and business analysts have been brought up with RDBMSs and there is often a sense of great comfort in knowing that an organisation's data is safely held in an RDBMS. However, the limitations of RDBMSs have been exposed by the need for very highly available and very highly scalable Internet-based services that are accessed by people using web browsers and smartphone apps, and we explore alternatives to them in Section 3.21.

3.5   Making Platforms Highly Available

The availability of a platform is defined as the minimum percentage of the time it is designed to be available. Over what period it applies should be specified. For example, a platform that is 99% available over a year has been designed to be available to users for at least 361.35 days of the year, that is, when measured across a year it should be unavailable for no more than 87 hours and 36 minutes. So, theoretically, such a platform could be unavailable for a single period of more than three days in one year and still meet its availability target, although many commercial service-level agreements work on a monthly basis so the actual maximum outage would be roughly one twelfth of this (just over 7 hours per month). Core banking platforms couldn't be offline for this sort of period – even 99% available over a day translates to 14 minutes offline if there is a failure. For example, you expect to be able to withdraw cash from an ATM at any time of day or night. Let's look at this more closely. An individual ATM may not be functioning or may have run out of cash, but find one that is functioning and you expect to be able to withdraw cash without any problem. Your bank's core banking platform must be able to authorise the cash withdrawal, so it (or at least the functionality that authorises ATM withdrawals) must be highly available. In reality, banks often design their core banking platforms to be up to 99.999% available over a year, which translates to no more than 5 minutes 15.36 seconds downtime per year (although we note that in practice some banks appear to have planned outages as frequently as once a month, typically early on Sunday mornings and often affecting a subset of functionality, such as the ability to make payments, rather than complete outages).

Note that when we talk about designing a platform for a certain availability in a certain period of time, we are really designing for the worst-case duration the platform should be unavailable in that period. On the other hand, if there are no outages, the platform could end up as having been 100% available. As a user, we don't care what causes a platform to be offline, whether through a failure of some piece of technology equipment or for routine servicing such as updating a server's operating system or the application software. However, it is common to see availability specifications excluding such planned downtime, which may be specified separately.

Typically, just specifying the percentage availability is not sufficient; we also need to specify how quickly a platform can be recovered and to what point in time. The recovery time objective (RTO) is the maximum duration that it is planned it would take to recover the platform so it is available again. So, we may want our core banking platform to have 99.999% availability over a year with an RTO of one minute – which means that up to five outages per year that each take up to a minute to recover from would be within the availability target. The recovery point objective (RPO) is the point in time before the outage to which the platform has to be recovered – for example, in some cases we may be okay with a platform having an RPO of 1 hour, i.e. we will tolerate data loss of up to an hour before the platform failed, probably because we have some other means of recovering the lost data or recreating it. This may well be appropriate for a finance platform in a bank (and we have seen an RPO for a bank's finance platform that was 1 hour), as we can normally replay feeds into it from other platforms and ask the staff who use it to redo their last hour's work. For a core banking platform, we may well want an RPO of zero, which means no data loss, as we couldn't afford for records of transfers between accounts to be lost, for example. If you are relying on a third party to implement or operate a platform for you (or the infrastructure on which it runs), you may well end up with these specifications in the contract.

Finally, when designing a platform or contracting with a third party to supply or operate a platform with a specific availability, RTO and RPO, we typically also have to think about which type of failure and disaster scenarios we are going to allow for and which ones we will exclude. So, we may well specify what we require in the case of a server failure, hard disk failure, network outage affecting a data centre, power cut to a data centre, flood affecting a data centre, aeroplane crashing into a data centre, localised terrorist action and so on. However, we will probably exclude events that would end civilisation as we know it such as nuclear war, large meteorite impact or a super volcano eruption. Also, business recovery from an outage or disaster is not just a matter of getting the platforms restarted or failing over – ensuring that the bank's staff can still work and customers can still access the bank's services are equally important.

In the rest of this section we're going to look at how a core banking platform can be made highly available. Let's consider our core banking platform, which we showed simplistically in Figure 3.3 as the core banking application accessing the banking database. Well, in reality we need to think of it as shown in Figure 3.9, in which the core banking application accesses the RDBMS, which stores the core banking application's data in a storage system – this could be one or more hard drives inside the same server as the RDBMS or it could be hard drives inside a specialised storage system that the RDBMS

FIGURE 3.9   Core banking platform expanded.

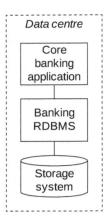

accesses over a very fast connection (such storage systems are often called Storage Area Networks, or SANs). In addition, the storage system would have been configured so that if a hard drive inside it failed, no data would be lost. In our experience and that of others (see, for example, reference 7), hard drives (whether the original spinning disks of magnetic material or solid-state devices) do fail, so this approach is necessary. Such a storage system would also normally support replacing a failing or failed hard drive while the storage system keeps running (so-called hot swapping), which means we don't have to stop the RDBMS or core banking application. The simplest approach is to keep a duplicate copy of the data on separate hard drives from the original, and in reality storage systems often implement a range of approaches using arrays of hard drives (hence the term Redundant Array of Inexpensive Disks, or RAID). The RDBMS does not need to be aware of the data duplication or how the hard drives are managed – storage systems do this automatically. When the core banking application performs a transaction (e.g. transfers funds from one account to another) the RDBMS sends a command to the storage system to write the data changes to disk, and the storage system replies when it has done so. At this point, the RDBMS replies to the core banking application that it has committed the transaction that required the data changes to be written.

We would also expect the data centre where our core banking platform is housed to be resilient by virtue of having two separately routed electricity supplies, plus backup batteries and generators to keep it going if the electricity supply fails completely, fire protection systems, physical security to prevent unauthorised access and two separately routed network or Internet connections.

However, how would we architect this to deal with a data centre outage (e.g. due to a fire, local natural disaster, aeroplane crash and so on)? We need another data centre, with two separately routed network connections to the first data centre. Let's consider the arrangement shown in Figure 3.10.

In this arrangement the storage system in data centre 1 is automatically sending a copy of all data and changes to it to the storage system in data centre 2. There is a standby RDBMS and core banking application in data centre 2. If data centre 1 becomes unavailable, the standby systems will be made live and users of the core banking platform can be

FIGURE 3.10   Core banking platform in two data centres.

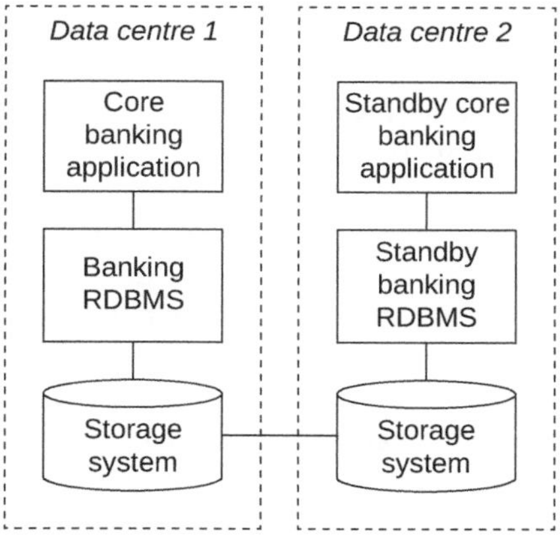

automatically routed to data centre 2 using network routing or by setting up their devices to automatically re-route to data centre 2. It may be possible to do all of this automatically, and there are specialised computer management systems that do this (normally called cluster management software). To ensure no data loss the storage system must save a copy of any data in both data centres before communicating back to the RDBMS that it has saved the data – this is called synchronous replication. In normal operation, the time taken (or latency) to send the data from data centre 1 to data centre 2 and then send back a confirmation the data has been saved becomes the limiting factor. The fastest that data can be sent is theoretically at the speed of light, and in practice at about 70% of the speed of light using fibre optic cable. This means that a round trip between two data centres 100 km apart will take a minimum of just less than 1 ms, with a dedicated fibre optic connection between them. In reality, few organisations would be able to afford such a dedicated link, and so the data would have to go across a telecommunication company's network and would likely take a little longer – for example, over the Internet you can get speeds up to the equivalent of approximately 45% of the speed of light, which would mean a round-trip time of 1.5 ms between our data centres. Nonetheless, such technology is used and the practical limitation on the distance between data centres using synchronous replication varies from tens to hundreds of kilometres depending on the acceptable latency – by which we mean that the performance of the RDBMS (and the applications using it) would suffer as it queues up transactions waiting for them to be saved to both data centres.

So, in order to meet our RPO of zero data loss, we need to install our platform in two data centres that are located close enough – typically in the same state or country. We have a live (or hot) core banking application and RDBMS in data centre 1, by which we mean they are running and being used, and a cold core banking application and RDBMS in data centre 2, by which we mean they are not actually running but have been installed on servers in data centre 2. However, this arrangement would almost certainly not provide an RTO of 1 minute, because the time taken to detect the outage, reconfigure the network and start up the RDBMS and core banking application in data centre 2 would be at best several minutes. To recover more quickly, the RDBMS and core banking application in data centre 2 need to be already running – what is called warm standby if we have to manually bring them into full operation in a failover scenario or hot standby if they automatically do this. This then means that the core banking application and RDBMS in data centre 2 need to be aware that they are operating as warm or hot standby systems, which in turn means they must have been designed to do this – most, if not all, enterprise scale RDBMSs do indeed support this.

There is yet another approach that is even more compelling, and that is to design the RDBMS so that both the primary and secondary RDBMS are live and can be used at the same time. The same approach could be used in the design of the core banking application. This is called a live-live configuration. In our experience the two RDBMS instances have to communicate directly with each other in this configuration, as this is quicker for sharing certain information than each of them just relying on the shared storage. This is because the direct sharing of information between each RDBMS instance is faster than one instance writing it to the shared storage system and the other instance reading it from the shared storage system. However, information shared directly could be lost in a data centre outage as it has not been securely written to the storage system – this places limitations on the usage of such information. The core banking application instances may also have to communicate with each other or at least be aware of each other (for example, to decide where the end-of-day processing is run). With the use of network technology (network load-balancing) that hides the two data centres behind one network address, users don't know (or care) which data centre they are accessing at any time and if there is a data centre outage, failover is either totally transparent or, at worst, a user has to reconnect to the banking application in the remaining data centre. This approach also enables us to manually divert all users to one data centre so that we can carry out planned work in the other data centre (e.g. replacing a failing server and upgrading server operating systems).

We have seen how we could potentially get very high availability, but with some constraints. First, the data centres must be close enough so that the storage system can save data synchronously in both locations in a small enough time – a small number of milliseconds at most – which would mean within hundreds of kilometres of each other. For some organisations, this still presents too great a risk that a major natural disaster could disrupt both data centres or prevent essential staff from working at both data centres, at their normal work locations or remotely – in which case, data centres would have to be located much further apart (e.g. on the other side of a continent or even on different continents) and data could not be written synchronously to both data centres. Therefore, the RPO could not be zero, but could be a few seconds – in other words, we could lose the last few seconds of data. In this case it would be unlikely that the core banking application could run in a live-live configuration either, because the two installations would see different versions of the data. Second, the core banking application and RDBMS must have been designed and implemented to run in a live-live configuration. We've used plenty of platforms, including core banking platforms, that have not been designed to do this (or even designed to be set up in a live-warm standby configuration). In this case, we have to accept the RTO will be longer – basically the time to start up the standby core banking application (and associated RDBMS), let it go through its start-up and recovery processes and become available.

There are also other considerations in designing for high availability – of which cost is probably the most important. Having two live RDBMSs and two live core banking applications could mean double the software license costs. Storage systems that work transparently across data centres tend to be expensive. There is also the cost of the additional hardware – in normal operation, less than 50% of the processing capacity of the servers would be in use, as in a failover scenario there has to be enough remaining capacity to take all the load. Furthermore, you need to be able to test the failover and falling back to normal operation as well as have a means to safely upgrade the live systems. So, in practice you may decide that you need yet another set of infrastructure (a third production environment) that you can use for these purposes. We remember advising one financial services organisation about this very point, but because of the additional cost it decided to not have a third environment. This seemed okay until it installed an upgrade to its platform (which was set up in a live-live configuration in two data centres and was designed to be 99.999% available over a year). The upgrade seemed to be working fine in data centre 1, so it went ahead and installed the upgrade in data centre 2 as well. Then the problems started, and both components of the platform crashed. After approximately four hours (well outside its 99.999% availability target), the organisation had removed the upgrade and restarted the systems in both data centres. Within a few days the organisation decided to implement a third environment in one of its existing data centres which was a replica of the other two environments. So now when it performs an upgrade, it can install the upgrade into the third environment for full-scale functional and non-functional testing. Once it is satisfied, it puts the third environment live and disconnects the first environment, upgrades it and puts it live, disconnecting the second environment. It keeps the second environment as a warm standby and doesn't upgrade it for some time until it is satisfied the two other environments are functioning correctly. Another important consideration is that choosing, designing, implementing and operating a high availability solution requires deep technical skills and a good knowledge of the high availability features available in storage systems, RDBMSs, cluster management software, network infrastructure and the business application being implemented.

Smaller organisations are likely to find that they do not have the means to implement such highly available platforms. However, much lower cost approaches – but with fewer guarantees around the time to recover from significant outages – are available. For example, enterprise RDBMSs often provide facilities for replicating data asynchronously between two RDBMS instances that do away with the need for shared storage. This would mean that the minimum RPO would be a few seconds but not zero because if the primary data centre is lost the RDBMS in the secondary data centre may not receive data that was in-flight at the time of the outage.

We'd like to make one final point about high availability. In our experience, the greatest likelihood of a failure occurring is when something is changed – such as an upgrade to the application software or some change to the configuration of the servers or network. Testing such changes before they are introduced and having a means to quickly fall back to the state prior to a change are the key ways to mitigate this risk.

3.6   Platform Architectures

We've covered how database systems have been architected, and in this section we cover how users access the applications that in turn use databases.

Historically, users logged onto a mainframe computer (and subsequently also less powerful systems that were termed minicomputers), with the sort of architecture shown

FIGURE 3.11   Terminals accessing a core banking platform running on a mainframe.

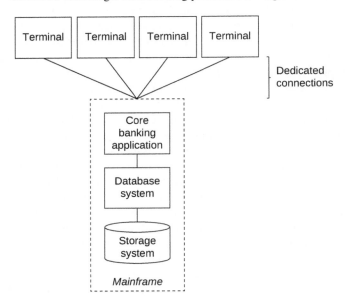

in Figure 3.11. A user sat in front of a terminal (sometimes colloquially called a green screen terminal because they used to display green text on a black background), which was connected directly to a mainframe computer, and logged onto the mainframe. The terminal had very little intelligence – it merely sent key presses to the mainframe and displayed what the mainframe sent back. When the user logged on, the mainframe automatically ran the core banking application which displayed, for example, a menu screen that the user could use to access various areas of the core banking application. Note that in reality the core banking application would be comprised of several different programs (e.g. one that handled user interaction and probably several that were called in sequence to execute the end-of-day processing and that each did specific things such as calculate interest, execute incoming payments, execute outgoing payments and so on), all of which accessed the banking database managed by the database system and held on the storage system.

You may still see this architecture in place today, although often the dedicated terminals have been replaced with terminal emulation software that runs on a PC. The terminal emulator connects to the mainframe across the corporate network, as shown in Figure 3.12.

With a simple terminal emulator, the PC will show pretty much what the green screen terminal would show, albeit in a window. Terminal emulator software can actually completely hide the mainframe screen view and present a more modern user interface – it does this by what is called screen scraping, which in effect means taking aspects of what the terminal screen would show and interpreting them so they can be displayed with a modern user interface, and translating what the user selects with the mouse and types with the keyboard into key presses the mainframe understands.

With the rise of RDBMSs, what is called client/server computing arose, illustrated in Figure 3.13. In this arrangement, the core banking client program is installed on each

FIGURE 3.12   Terminal emulators used to access a mainframe-based core banking platform.

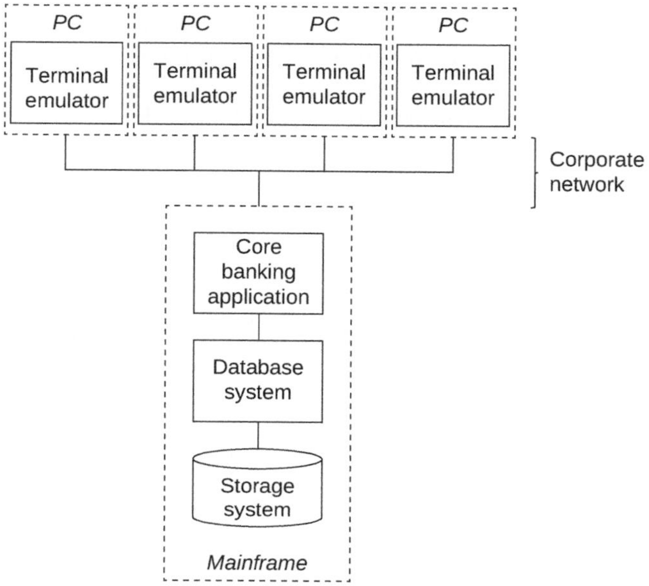

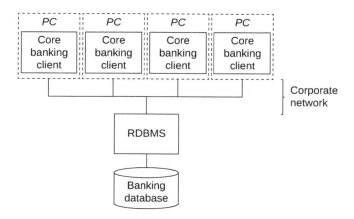

FIGURE 3.13   Basic client/server architecture.

user's PC. This program provides the user interface for the banking application, connects to the RDBMS across the corporate network and interacts with it by sending SQL queries to it and receiving the results back. It would contain a lot of business logic, so it would be a significant piece of software and so you may hear this sort of architecture called a thick client.

In reality, this arrangement would not be sufficient for operating a core banking platform because there has to be an end-of-day process and a way to provide ATM and debit card authorisations and support intraday payment schemes. So, you would also expect to have a core banking server running to perform these functions, as shown in Figure 3.14. The core banking server also sends SQL queries to the RDBMS across the network to read from and update the banking database, and receives the results back. It runs continuously and handles ATM and debit card authorisations and also executes the end-of-day process.

This architecture is fairly typical for the second half of the 1980s into the early 2000s and there were a range of programming languages for writing such thick clients, often termed fourth-generation languages (or 4GLs), perhaps the most notable of which is PowerBuilder (originally developed by PowerSoft and currently owned by SAP). However, this architecture requires relatively powerful PCs (which must be made secure and maintained) and a high-capacity network. Updates to the core banking platform must be rolled out to every PC. You may come across a variant of this, which improves the security and makes rolling out updates simple, which is a virtual desktop infrastructure (VDI), as shown in Figure 3.15.

FIGURE 3.14   Client/server architecture with a core banking server.

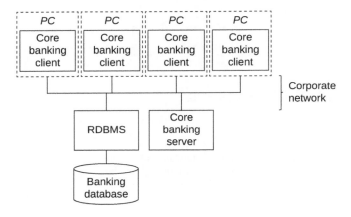

FIGURE 3.15   Virtual desktop infrastructure.

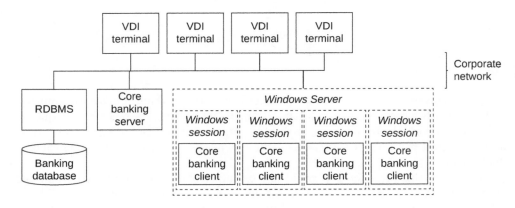

In this arrangement, rather than having a PC at each user's desk there is a VDI terminal – a low-powered computer to which a monitor, keyboard and mouse are connected and which displays the Microsoft Windows session that is actually running on a Windows server (or, more likely, a group of Windows servers) in a data centre. There is a Windows session on the Windows server for each user actively using a VDI terminal. Some organisations implemented this arrangement wholesale, as it removed the need to roll out PCs to all users and manage them remotely. The same technology can also enable remote working, as a laptop, tablet or even smartphone can be used as a VDI terminal – this is quite common, with vendors such as Citrix providing various solutions in this space.

The use of thick clients has declined and a more modern core banking platform has been architected so that users access it using web browsers, as illustrated in Figure 3.16. In this we have shown two core banking servers to provide better availability – the connections with the users could be shared across them. The core banking servers retrieve data from the banking database, generate webpages containing this data and serve them to each user's browser. They also receive input back from those users. As in previous diagrams, they perform other functions that don't have user interaction such as end-of-day processing and ATM and debit card authorisation.

This is an example of what is sometimes called a Web 1.0 architecture, which we can also illustrate as shown in Figure 3.17. The connections in this figure show which clients are using which core banking servers and the logical connections from the application servers to the RDBMS – in reality, all connections are made across the corporate network. The core banking server has two major components. First, it has a web server, normally a standard platform such as the Apache HTTP Server or Microsoft's Internet Information Server, to serve webpages to the user's browsers and receive input back from them. The pages themselves will typically display information specific to the work each user is doing. For example, a user may be talking to a customer in a branch and viewing information held on that customer. It is the job of the application server, the other major component of the core banking server, to provide that information to the web server, typically by looking it up in the banking database using SQL queries. The term application

FIGURE 3.16 Accessing the core banking platform using a web browser.

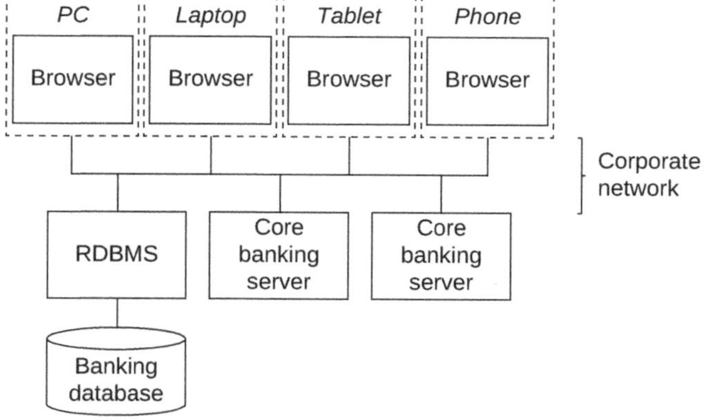

FIGURE 3.17   Web 1.0 core banking platform architecture.

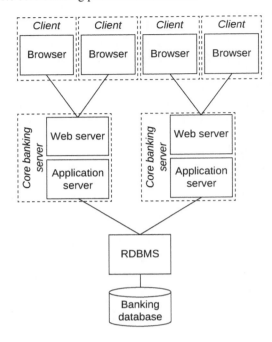

server can refer to many things. At its loosest, it is just a collection of programs to provide business functionality. A stricter definition is an environment that provides a set of
common services to programs that are run in it, such as database access, the interface to
the web server and methods to integrate with other platforms, along with tools to manage these programs, for example, to enable multiple copies of each program to be run
concurrently, to load balance across multiple servers, to handle failures of programs and
failover to other servers. One notable standard for such servers is Java Enterprise Edition
(Java EE, specified at www.jcp.org), which defines a large set of services and standards
with the intention that a JEE application server hosts programs written in the Java programming language. Notable application servers that conform to various versions and
aspects of Java EE include commercial products such as IBM WebSphere Application
Server, Oracle WebLogic Application Server and SAP Netweaver Application Server and
free and open-source products including Apache Tomcat, GlassFish, JBoss Enterprise
Application Platform and Payara.

Note that the distinction between web servers and application servers has blurred
over time, and some application servers include web serving capability, while some web
servers have been extended to include application server functionality. The term application server has also been applied to older products such as IBM's CICS and Oracle's
BEA Tuxedo, which were originally called transaction processing systems or transaction
processing monitors – these provide a means for applications to perform single transactions across multiple databases and other data sources, and the transaction-processing
capability can be spread across multiple servers. CICS is a common technology in banks
using IBM mainframes and you may find large core banking platforms that are based

FIGURE 3.18 Hybrid architecture.

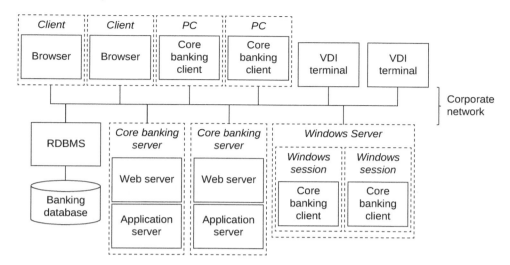

on it. These products have been extended to provide some of the same functions as the application servers described previously. IBM CICS, for example, can present webpages created dynamically from much older applications such as green screen mainframe applications. We examine CICS later in Section 3.9.

It wouldn't be odd to see a hybrid architecture, as shown in Figure 3.18, in which we have shown two users connecting to the core banking server using a web browser, two users who are using a core banking client (some form of thick client that may interact directly with the RDBMS and/or may interface to the core banking server) and two users using VDI terminals that display the core banking client running on a Windows server. This arrangement may be because:

- The PC users need a special core banking client because they are tellers and advisors in a branch, and their PCs are connected to local equipment such as card readers (that customers use to authenticate themselves with), specialised passbook readers, terminals used to capture customer signatures and cameras to take a photograph of a new customer.
- The VDI terminal users are contact centre agents who have a tightly controlled, lower-cost and highly reliable means of accessing the core banking platform.
- The users accessing the core banking platform using a browser (probably from a PC) are middle and back office workers who do not need any specialised equipment and have to perform a variety of tasks on the banking platform.

3.7 Revisiting Our Simple Model of a Bank

So, let's assume our simple bank now has several branches with ATMs and issues debit cards and credit cards. It has separate finance and treasury platforms, no longer relying

FIGURE 3.19   Expanded simple model of a bank.

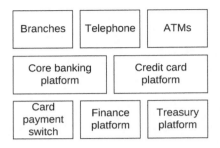

on the core banking platform for these functions. So, the functional model of our bank has expanded, as shown in Figure 3.19.

We could also expect to see an ATM management platform, but we have assumed that this is part of the card payment switch. The card payment switch is connected to the ATMs, to the core banking platform, to the credit card platform and to the card and ATM schemes in which the bank participates.

Note also that the core banking platform and credit card platform are entirely separate, and information on customers is often duplicated on both platforms. We'll cover integrating these later in this chapter. The core banking and credit card platforms create daily financial reports which are transferred to the finance and treasury platforms.

We're also assuming our bank has some form of contact centre. We explore the technology for this in Section 4.9.

3.8   Single Customer View

Now our bank has a core banking platform that manages customers' current accounts, deposit accounts and loan accounts, and a separate credit card platform. Two obvious questions are how does the bank get a complete view of a customer across all their accounts (banking and credit cards) – often termed a single customer view (commonly abbreviated to SCV) – and how can the bank provide servicing across all of their accounts? Some banks have ignored this challenge by operating their banking and credit card businesses virtually separately, with an inability to provide credit card servicing in the branches and separate contact centres for banking products and for credit cards. However, we are going to explore an integrated approach.

Here are some of the challenges. First, both the core banking platform and the credit card platform maintain details of the customers (i.e. their names, addresses and other information) with banking and credit card accounts, respectively. Some customers will have both types of account (e.g. a current account, maintained on the core banking platform, and a credit card account, maintained on the credit card platform). If a customer comes into a branch or calls the bank's contact centre, the customer service representative would have to look on both platforms to get a view of what products the customer has. If a customer with both types of product changes their address, both platforms must be updated. From a marketing perspective, the bank would almost certainly not want to market products to customers that already have those products, so ideally it needs to know what products each customer has. These challenges are compounded when a bank has even more platforms with products and accounts on them. In bigger banks it is not unusual for mortgage accounts to be on a separate platform from current, deposit and unsecured loan accounts. For business customers there can be even more platforms, reflecting a wider range of products that banks offer to businesses.

Let's start with how we may give banking users a single customer view in an environment where the bank has more than one platform for maintaining products and accounts, as illustrated in Figure 3.20.

In this arrangement, the core banking platform (comprising the core banking application and the banking database) and the credit card platform (comprising the credit card application and credit card database) both hold details of the customers who have accounts on those platforms. This would be normal in a big bank where banking and credit card operations and platforms are being run separately and where each division markets directly to potential customers. In order to have a readily accessible view of what customers have what products, the core banking platform and credit card platform both send a file at the end of every day with a list of new customers, or new products and accounts taken up by customers. These files go into a match process whose aim is to ensure that duplicate records for customers do not end up being created in the customer platform. For example, suppose there is a long-standing banking customer with a current account. They will have a record in the customer platform that shows they have a current account. If they then open a credit card account, the credit card platform sends their details to the match process. Now, if the customer supplied a unique ID (e.g. from a national identity card or passport), and the same ID had already been stored with the record for that customer in the customer platform, matching is straightforward and more or less certain. However, if matching is done on names and address, then the match may not be certain (e.g. parent and child with the same first and last names, living at the same address). So, normally, the match process must have a manual review step for matches that are uncertain. Once a customer is definitely matched or set up for the first

FIGURE 3.20   Simplified approach to get a single view of customer.

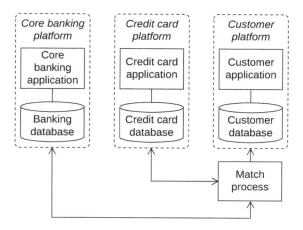

time in the customer platform, it would be sensible to send a unique ID back to the product platform that the new customer record came from, in case the customer changes what products they have that are maintained on that platform – hence the reason for the arrows on both ends of the lines between the core banking and credit card platforms and the match process.

This process isn't ideal because it isn't fully automated, but we have seen it done this way in a real, large bank. It suited that organisation because the product divisions were relatively autonomous with their own contact centres and Internet offerings. The branch network provided servicing for banking products only (i.e. those on the core banking platform or closely associated with it, such as payments) and marketing of other products (for example, you could pick up a brochure and application form for a credit card). There were some exceptions – if you walked into a branch to tell them your credit card had been stolen, the branch staff could do something about it, which was to tell the credit card division (we think they could send the equivalent of an email to the credit card division). At another large bank we saw a different process: if you went into a branch to apply for a product the first thing that happened is that a record was set up for you on the bank's customer platform (or if you were already a customer, your record on the customer platform was retrieved and checked). Then the product application was made. Even so, customer information was manually copied from one platform to another. Behind the scenes, there still had to be a mechanism for capturing from each product platform what new products and accounts were taken up by what customers, but the matching process was far more certain given the branch had already set up a customer record and unique ID for even potential customers. We've seen this problem addressed properly in two ways: either the bank has a single platform on which all its products are maintained, along with customer records, or the bank has been built from scratch with this problem addressed so that customer records are maintained and mastered in one location, and shared with platforms that need them. We'll go into this later.

What about providing joined up servicing for customers with products across multiple platforms? For example, I may want a single smartphone app that the customer in our example uses to access their accounts, including the current account and the credit card account. The app must access three platforms to do this – the customer platform, the core banking platform and the credit card platform. Similarly, I may want my branch staff to have a single platform they access to service customers who come into a branch and my contact centre staff to also have a single platform.

There are many ways to do this, and many books have been written over several decades that extensively cover the latest techniques of the time. We're going to cover several approaches in roughly chronological order, all of which still have relevance today.

One other note: platforms that provide a single customer view have often been extended into (or replaced with) customer relationship management (CRM) platforms. As well as providing a single customer view, such platforms can also keep a record of all interactions with customers, provide marketing and campaign management functionality (see Section 4.15), provide a means to update customer data, manage teams that interact with customers (such as relationship managers) and often have extended into application processing (see Section 3.19) or even being the user interface for all interaction with customers in the contact centre and branches.

3.9   IBM CICS

CICS, short for Customer Information Control System and pronounced *kicks*, is a proprietary commercial IBM product with a long pedigree. Initially launched in 1968,[8] it has been developed ever since. In our experience, many larger banks have used CICS extensively, with mainframe-based platforms built using it, including in-house core banking platforms and several core banking platforms that were (and in some cases still are) available commercially. Many of the ideas in CICS have been adopted or reinvented in more modern integration approaches, and CICS has also embraced more modern developments in technology such as Java and support for websites.

Mainframes were originally used primarily for batch-oriented applications. CICS is an environment that made it relatively straightforward to provide interactive business applications running on IBM mainframe computers to users using IBM green screen terminals (the original IBM model number for such a terminal was 3270, and you will often see this used as another name for such terminals). The business applications could process transactions on databases (e.g. IMS, VSAM and Db2, all available on IBM mainframes) where the business data was stored – in other words, they could create new records in those databases, update existing records and delete existing records, as well as read existing records. CICS manages many of the specific details of the hardware, operating system facilities and database platforms, so programs are typically focused on either how to present information and gather input from users or the business logic to process information entered by users and the commands entered by them. CICS also uses the underlying security mechanisms provided by the mainframe operating system, and it will ensure only authenticated users can access an application (typically each user has a unique login ID and password) and they can only perform the transactions that they are authorised to perform (typically each user is assigned one or more roles that permits them to access certain programs). A business application would normally comprise anything from a handful to tens or hundreds or even thousands of individual programs that would be chained together, depending on what each user decides to do in the application. For example, the user selecting an item in a menu could result in a program specific to that menu item being executed. Multiple copies of each program could be run simultaneously and independently, and so many users (in some cases, thousands) could use the same application simultaneously. By designing CICS programs properly, very high utilisation of the mainframe processing capacity is possible, and the same applications can be installed on multiple mainframes for even higher transaction throughput and very high availability.

As an example, imagine we have a simple application to view, edit, delete and add customer records. A user sits in front of a terminal, signs on to (i.e. logs into) the mainframe and runs the application (or, potentially, the application will run automatically immediately after login). A screen appears which allows the user to type in the number of an existing customer record and then view, edit or delete it, or alternatively the user can decide to add a new customer record without entering a customer record number. The user can also exit the application. If the user decides to view, edit, delete or add a customer record, the second screen is shown, with either details of the customer whose number they entered on the first screen or with blank fields for a new customer record. Once the user has either viewed the record, edited it, confirmed they wish to delete it or added the data for a new record, the application writes the changes to the database and returns to the first screen again.

FIGURE 3.21   Simple customer platform using IBM CICS.

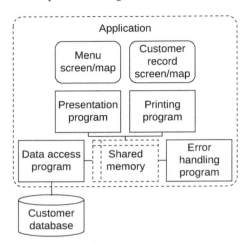

To implement this, we need to define a number of screens and programs, as shown in Figure 3.21. The two screens must be designed to fit the 80×24 character display on an IBM green screen (3270) terminal. The definition of each screen is called a map and all the maps for an application are usually put into one file, called a mapset. A map defines the layout of the screen, what each field can contain (e.g. the customer surname would be displayed in a field, and we might set this to hold up to 20 characters) and whether the user can edit each field or not.

In addition, we need a variety of programs, typically written in COBOL (Common Business Oriented Language, an early programming language used extensively on mainframes and minicomputers). One program displays the screens with appropriate titles and adjusts which fields are display-only or can be edited by the user (for example, if the user has decided to delete a customer record, the program would display the customer record to be deleted but with all the fields set to be display only, as there is no point in allowing the user to edit the record) and interprets the input from the user – this is the presentation program in Figure 3.21. Another program reads customer records from the database, writes new and updated customer records back to the database and deletes customer records from the database – but doesn't display them (as this is the function of the presentation program) – this is the data access program in Figure 3.21. Another program is required to gracefully handle any of the programs unexpectedly failing (an *abend*, in the terminology used by mainframe programmers and system administrators, short for abnormal end) or generating an error, so the user is informed and the failure or error is logged for later review by a system administrator. We could also provide a program to print a customer record (if we provided this as an option on the screen showing a customer record, for example). All the programs being run by one user share a common area of memory (in IBM's terminology, a communications area or COMMAREA and more recently a larger area that is called a channel), so, for example, if the user decides to edit an existing customer record, the presentation program places the customer number in this memory and then exits with a link to the data access program. The CICS environment starts the data access program which looks in the shared memory to get the customer record number and then uses this to read the customer record from the database. The data access program places all the values from the customer record (name, address and other information) in the shared memory and exits to CICS which restarts the presentation program that then displays the customer record details.

So, to edit an existing customer record, the sequence shown in Figure 3.22 takes place. In this diagram, each arrow represents control being returned to CICS, which then starts the next program shown. This bouncing between programs can seem odd to programmers used to writing monolithic applications (by which we mean applications that are comprised of one big program), but it is one reason why mainframes can scale to thousands of transactions per second and thousands of users. Each program is designed to do some work without further user interaction and then exit. At this point the user interacts with the screen that has been displayed (e.g. they edit the customer record), and only when they press the enter key (or some other key that is set up to alert the mainframe) is a program started to interpret the user's action. The mainframe can be doing other things (e.g. running programs for other users) while our user is reading the screen or typing things into the terminal. Note that to do this, whenever a different user runs our customer application, the mainframe allocates a different area of shared memory to that instance of the application.

In addition, the way we have designed this application program separates out the presentation of the screens and handling of keyboard input from the user (in the presentation program) from the business logic and database access (in the data access program). You can write other programs that can make use of the data access program to read, update, write and delete customer records. This is a standard approach and has enabled much reuse of existing CICS applications over several decades.

Now we have covered the basics of how a CICS mainframe platform works, let's examine what this means for integrating our core banking platform and credit card platform. We envisage that both of these have been implemented to run using CICS, and they may also be hosted on the same mainframe system – although they are likely to be in different logical partitions of the mainframe (or LPARs in IBM's mainframe terminology) – in effect their own virtual machines and which appear entirely separate to the applications running within each partition. Our key aims are to:

- Track what customers have which products and accounts
- Provide joined up servicing in branches and contact centres
- Enable a single Internet servicing platform across all products and accounts
- Enable a single mobile app across all products and accounts

We could provide for these aims in different ways. First, we could integrate the two platforms so we end up with one platform including a single datastore as shown in Figure 3.23.

When doing this, we would combine the records for customers from each original platform into one file, table or database. Given the fact each application is comprised of many programs we may find many programs can be kept untouched. Similarly, we may find the various elements (e.g. tables or files) in each datastore are mainly kept the same in the new combined datastore.

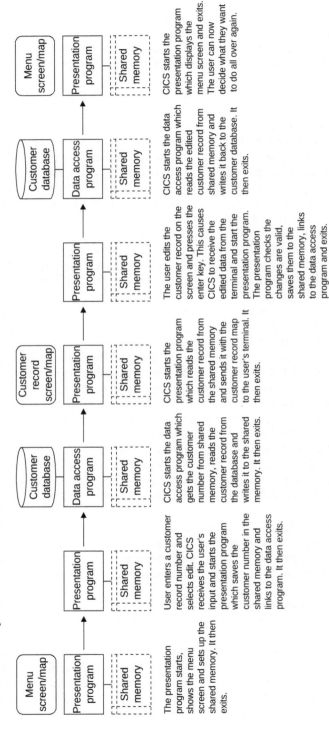

FIGURE 3.22   Sequence to edit a customer record.

Menu screen/map			

Presentation program → **Shared memory**

The presentation program starts, shows the menu screen and sets up the shared memory. It then exits.

Presentation program → **Shared memory**

User enters a customer record number and selects edit. CICS receives the user's input and starts the presentation program which saves the customer number in the shared memory and links to the data access program. It then exits.

Customer database

Data access program → **Shared memory**

CICS starts the data access program which gets the customer number from shared memory, reads the customer record from the database and writes it to the shared memory. It then exits.

Customer record screen/map

Presentation program → **Shared memory**

CICS starts the presentation program which reads the customer record from the shared memory and sends it with the customer record map to the user's terminal. It then exits.

Presentation program → **Shared memory**

The user edits the customer record on the screen and presses the enter key. This causes CICS to receive the edited data from the terminal and start the presentation program. The presentation program checks the changes are valid, saves them to the shared memory, links to the data access program and exits.

Customer database

Data access program → **Shared memory**

CICS starts the data access program which reads the edited customer record from shared memory and writes it back to the customer database. It then exits.

Menu screen/map			

Presentation program → **Shared memory**

CICS starts the presentation program which displays the menu screen and exits. The user can now decide what they want to do all over again.

FIGURE 3.23 Fully integrating the customer, core banking and credit card platforms.

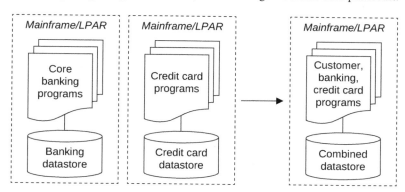

A less integrated approach is to install the core banking and credit card platforms in the same mainframe (and in the same logical partition), and write new CICS programs that provide the customer functionality and a joined-up way to navigate between the platforms, as shown in Figure 3.24.

We must set up a new customer application and associated datastore in this model and keep it synchronised with the two existing platforms. We envisage that the customer platform becomes the front end to the core banking and credit card platforms, by which we mean it's the first platform that a user in a branch or contact centre would access, and when servicing a customer would start by finding and reviewing that customer's record (or setting up a new record if it's a new customer). If the customer needs a banking service then the user can navigate to the core banking programs through menu choices provided by the customer platform, and if the customer needs a credit card service then similarly the user selects the menu choices provided by the customer platform. We may still need to have programs that check customer records in the banking and credit card datastores are synchronised with the customer datastore, particularly if we have, for example, a separate credit card business unit that uses just the credit card platform.

An even less integrated approach is to keep the two platforms running on separate mainframes (or separate logical partitions) and build a new customer platform, probably

FIGURE 3.24 Partial integration of the customer, core banking and credit card platforms.

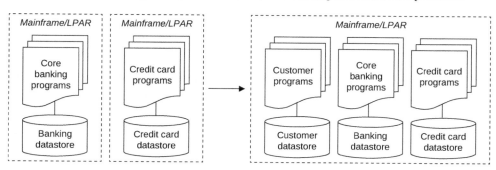

FIGURE 3.25   Minimal integration of the customer, core banking and credit card platforms.

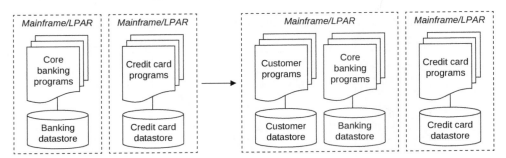

running on the same mainframe (or logical partition) as the core banking platform, with its own datastore, as shown in Figure 3.25.

The new customer programs can interact with the credit card platform running on the other mainframe (or logical partition) using the abilities of CICS to call programs running on remote platforms (such as the distributed program link and distributed transaction processing features, in IBM's terminology[9]). As in the previous approach, the customer platform may provide a navigational front end for access to core banking and credit card programs, and we may still need to have programs that check customer records in the banking and credit card datastores are synchronised with the customer datastore. This more segregated approach may be preferable where the bank has a separate credit card business operation and wants a stricter separation between the core banking and credit card platforms. We'd also envisage that there are fewer credit card functions available to banking staff with this approach and in fact there may be none – for example, this approach could be used just to enable banking staff to see if a banking customer has a credit card. We hope you can also envisage how this could be extended to handle many different product platforms – a large bank may have dozens of different platforms used to maintain different types of customer accounts.

It's worth considering what factors would be relevant when deciding between the integration approaches above. They include:

- Implementation cost and time: Broadly, the first approach would cost the most and take the longest time as it involves major changes to two existing platforms to combine them into a single platform. The third approach is probably the quickest and cheapest option.
- IT operating costs: It costs money to run mainframe computers, from the electricity they consume (probably the smallest element in their running costs), the cost of system administrators to manage them and the software license costs, which are typically charged on the basis of how much processing power each mainframe has, irrespective of whether it is used or not. Concentrating processing onto fewer mainframes normally allows for higher utilisation of available processing capacity, lower software license costs and fewer system administrators. So, we expect the three approaches discussed earlier are in order of increasing IT operating costs.

- Operational costs: Having a fully integrated platform may allow customer servicing to be consolidated and therefore result in a higher staff utilisation (particularly in contact centres). So, the first approach could offer lower operational costs.
- Customer experience: Tighter integration could well enable a better customer experience – as a customer, my bank knows what products I have with them and provides appropriate services to me. It can also enable the bank to make more relevant offers to me.
- User training and expertise: In reality, the bank may not be able to get the benefits of lower operational costs or a more joined-up customer experience with a more integrated platform because it isn't feasible to train all users on the bigger set of functions, or there may be regulatory or other reasons (e.g. separation of concerns to reduce internal fraud risks) why the bank has to have separate groups of users who perform different functions using the platform. In our experience it is necessary to provide an escalation process in all but the simplest banking institutions, with front-line customer service staff handing off to specific experts for some customer service processes.
- Agility: Having one bigger, integrated platform compared to relatively independent platforms could reduce the bank's agility to make changes. A bigger, more integrated platform is more complex, so designing and developing changes to the platform takes more time. The bank must test the whole platform before it can release a new version, and this takes more time if there is more functionality to test. Therefore, the bank's release cycles can be longer with a more integrated platform. The first approach discussed earlier may make the bank less agile than the third approach, which has a much lower level of integration and with which the bank could probably develop each platform separately, as long as the integration between the two platforms was maintained.
- Software ownership: The bank may not own the software that comprises the core banking platform or the credit card platform, and so may not have access to the source code for the software or the ability to change it. This may limit how much integration of the two platforms is possible.

All the previous approaches were based on users inside the bank accessing the platforms using green screen terminals, which was all that was available when CICS was launched. However, this is unlikely to be the case (or at least exclusively the case) in a modern bank. At a minimum, users can now access IBM mainframes using terminal emulator software running on their PCs. Such software may well just display what looks to be a green screen inside a window, and as far as the mainframe is concerned users are just using green screen terminals so no programs must be changed.

However, in the 1990s, IBM made it possible to run a web server on an IBM mainframe, as shown in Figure 3.26. The web server can access CICS programs on the local mainframe and use the CICS facilities to call CICS programs on other mainframes (e.g. to access the credit card platform).

Note that in practice there would be other components required between the web server and the existing CICS programs to do things like convert data entered by users into their web browsers into the format required by the various CICS programs (and back again) and to map webpages to CICS programs.

FIGURE 3.26 Accessing CICS programs via a web server using a browser.

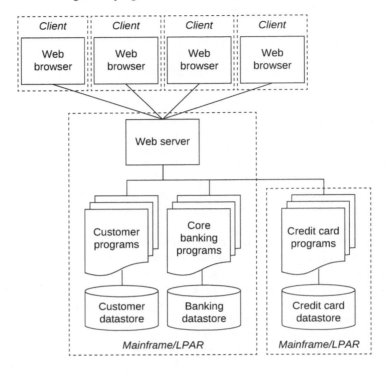

Probably more common is to run a web server and application server on another platform, which sits between the mainframes and users accessing the applications using web browsers (on PCs or other devices), as shown in Figure 3.27.

Here we have shown an additional database, the integration database, which we envisage being used to hold new data used by the programs running in the application server on the integration server. For example, the bank may enable users to customise what they see, such as the order in which accounts are shown, and the integration database would be used to store users' preferences.

The diagram in Figure 3.27 doesn't explain how the application server connects to the mainframes and the programs running on them. There are many choices with IBM mainframes and CICS.

First, it's possible for the programs running in the application server to emulate a set of green screen terminals, interpreting the data the mainframe sends to each terminal and formatting responses back to the mainframe so that it appears as though someone is using a terminal to respond. This technique is called terminal emulation and, more colloquially, screen scraping. There are at least three approaches that IBM provides to do this, including a plug-in component for programs using IBM's WebSphere Application Server called Host Application Transformation Services (HATS).

Second, programs running in the application server can make calls over the network to the IBM mainframes and receive responses back – what are generically called

FIGURE 3.27   Accessing CICS programs via a web server and an application server.

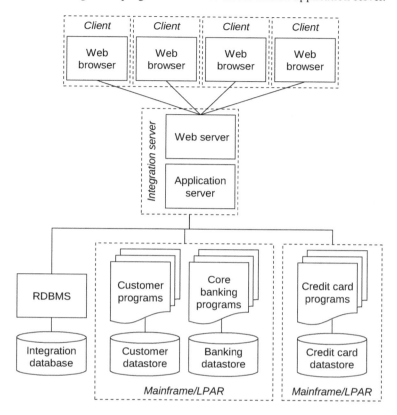

remote procedure calls. Again, there are several approaches to doing this, including using standard web services using a range of protocols (such as REST and SOAP over HTTP) and message formats (such as JSON and XML), remote procedure calls (using the ONC and DCE RPC protocols) and sending messages and receiving them back over message queues (using an IBM product called WebSphereMQ). We explore these approaches in later sections.

Third, IBM provides various plug-in components for a range of programming languages including Java (including connectors that can be used in a JEE application server), C and C# that enable an application to communicate across the network with mainframe CICS programs (which is, in fact, yet another way to make remote procedure calls). Such applications can even be written to run on an application server that is running on the mainframe, which can then provide any other type of integration method that a bank may need.

The summary is that there are many approaches available to building new applications that reuse existing mainframe programs. The need to provide Internet banking was often the driving force for such services, which leads us to the next topic.

3.10   Internet Banking

An Internet banking platform allows customers to access banking functionality using a web browser that connects to the bank across the World Wide Web using the Internet. Much like we saw in the previous section, it would almost certainly be built using a web server and application server with its own database for data not held anywhere else, as shown in Figure 3.28.

The application server would host one or more programs that comprise the Internet banking application. Let's consider why splitting the Internet banking application into multiple programs is probably preferable. Suppose there is one monolithic program that provides all the Internet banking functionality and communicates with the bank's other platforms. Every time a user connects to the Internet banking platform from their web browser, the application server runs a new copy of the Internet banking program to handle the interaction with that user. When they log off, that copy of the program ends.

FIGURE 3.28   Context of the Internet banking platform.

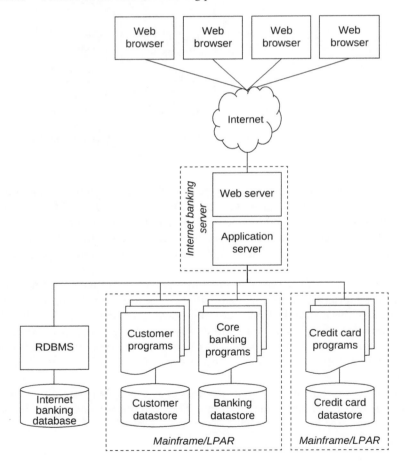

However, having such a single, big program to do everything can present some challenges. First, it probably wouldn't make the most efficient use of computing resources, as all the functionality has to be loaded every time a user logs on, even if they only want to check an account balance. This would require more computing resources to scale the platform. Second, maintenance of the program is more difficult because more developers are involved, as it covers a wide range of business domains and accesses multiple other platforms. Therefore, it is often better that the Internet banking application comprises several separate programs with well-defined interfaces. Such programs are often called components, and that is the term we will use going forward. An interface defines how a component and its functionality can be accessed. Each component can be maintained by a different team, as long as its interface either stays the same or, if it must change, the developers of other components that use the component with the changed interface are informed and change their components to work with the new interface. One approach to designing the components, and determining what component is responsible for what, is to have each component represent a business entity such as a customer or a bank account. Such components are usually called objects, and when an object runs it can be populated with details of such an entity. So, for example, a customer object could be populated with details of one of the bank's existing customers. Conceptually, we could build a simple Internet banking platform as illustrated in Figure 3.29 from the following range of components and objects:

- An Internet Banking component that receives requests from a customer using a web browser and is responsible for calling all the other objects and sending information back to the customer.
- A User object that represents a user of the Internet banking platform. One important role for this object is to take a set of credentials such as a username and password and confirm whether these are correct. This enables a user to log onto the Internet banking website.
- A Customer object that represents a customer. This holds details of the customer, such as name and address and what products and accounts the customer has with the bank. This may determine, for example, that a customer has some bank accounts and a credit card and to get this information it must interact with the customer platform. Note that a customer may be different from a user in that a customer could be a business for which there are multiple users.
- A Bank Account object that represents a bank account. This object interacts with the core banking platform in our example. It supplies information on the bank account such as the account number and transactions that have taken place.
- A Credit Card Account object that represents a credit card account. This object interacts with the credit card platform in our example.
- A Payment object that provides a list of payees and enables outbound payment instructions to be created and submitted. This object interacts with the core banking platform in our example.

Each of these is hosted on (i.e. runs within or on) an application server. As we have already mentioned, an application server provides lots of functions that the programs (including components and objects) it hosts can use, such as standard methods for communicating with other programs, components and objects either running in the same application server or across the network, for accessing datastores and for interacting with the webserver. It also controls the lifecycle of the programs, components and objects – the application server can control how many copies of each are running at one time and which copy is used by another program, component, object or the web server. Finally, an application server can run on multiple systems (i.e. more than one server) to increase scalability and resilience.

Let's see how we use this architecture. To start, a customer uses a web browser and enters the web address (formally, the Uniform Resource Locator, or URL) for the bank's Internet banking platform, such as https://onlinebanking.mybank.com/login.html, or clicks on a link on the bank's main website. This causes the browser to send an HTTPS request to onlinebanking.mybank.com asking for the login.html page. HTTPS (Secure Hypertext Transfer Protocol) is an Internet protocol used to communicate between browsers and web servers in which the communications are encrypted.

The bank has a firewall between its internal systems and the Internet, which we haven't shown in Figure 3.29. A firewall is a specialised set of network equipment that only allows certain network traffic in and out of the bank, to help prevent hacking of the bank's systems from the Internet. For example, a firewall may only allow HTTPS messages using TCP/IP port 443 (the normal port number used by HTTPS messages) into the bank. Also, the bank is highly likely to have more than one web server providing the online banking platform, for resilience and scalability. However, the bank only publishes a single URL for the platform and as far as customers are concerned, there is only one

FIGURE 3.29   Components comprising a simple Internet banking platform.

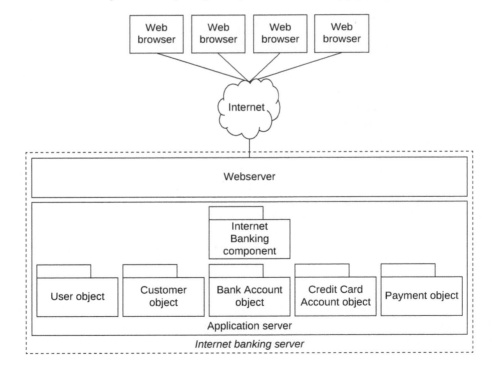

web address for the online banking platform. What is called a network load balancer receives requests for this URL and distributes them to different web servers. Again, we haven't shown this in the diagram.

Ultimately, one of the bank's Internet banking web servers receives the HTTPS request and, seeing that the request asks for the login.html page, it gathers the content for this page (it is likely to be based on a file that the web server accesses) and sends it back to the customer's browser which renders it for the customer to read. The user enters their login details into the login page presented by their browser and presses the submit button (or equivalent) to log in. This causes the browser to send another HTTPS request, containing the login details, back to the web server. Note that because the browser and webserver are communicating using HTTPS, all the messages they exchange are encrypted.

The web server knows from the address sent back with the user's login details that it should run a copy of the Internet Banking component and pass the details to it, and asks the application server to do this. The application server runs a copy of the Internet Banking component, passing to it the user's login details. The Internet Banking component then does several things:

- It creates a User object that it gets to authenticate the user and determine what customer the user is representing. We'll explore the authentication process in detail in Section 3.11.
- It creates a Customer object with the customer ID determined in the first step. The Customer object determines what products and accounts the customer has. It returns this information to the Internet Banking component.
- It creates a webpage containing the list of the customer's accounts and their balances, and a menu to give the user access to relevant services.
- It returns the webpage to the web server, which sends it back to the user's browser. There are various ways in which the web server and the application server can interact to create a webpage. We've assumed that the application server provides fully formed webpages to the web server for it to send. Another approach is for the web server to construct a webpage from a template, calling objects in the application server at various points during this to get the information to put on the page (somewhat like using the objects to fill in the blanks on a template).

From this page, the user can select an account and get a list of recent transactions. The user can also create a payment from the banking account(s) which would use the Payment object. Finally, they can also log off. Of course, a real Internet banking platform would have more functions, such as managing recurring and future payments and direct debits, access to soft copies of statements, reporting a card lost or stolen and a secure messaging service.

This is a short summary of what really happens. We're going to go into further detail to explain how each of the objects works. First, it's worth noting that we seem to have two types of components or objects – there is the Internet Banking component, which deals with processing the user's input (e.g. selecting an account), creating and calling the other objects to get the information it needs, sending the information it has collected for display as a webpage and keeping track of the user's Internet banking session for as long as they are logged on; and the other objects, which are single-focused, in that they represent one entity and don't deal directly with the user's input.

3.11   Customer Authentication

The first thing the Internet Banking component must do is verify that the user is autho-rised to log on, using the username and password supplied by the user which are stored in the Internet banking database. Therefore, the Internet Banking component creates a User object and then passes the username and password to it. The User object then checks the username and password and returns the result of the check to the Internet Banking object. This process is illustrated in Figure 3.30.

Let's look at how the User object checks the customer login details. No bank should store the actual customer passwords anywhere, so we would not expect the passwords of the bank's customers to be in the Internet banking database (or any other database or file) because it would be possible for a system administrator to gain access to the passwords. However, obviously the bank must be able to validate the login details. There are various approaches to this (see, for example, references 10 and 11), and we cover one approach to give an indication of the challenges involved in dealing with customer passwords. If you need to design or build such an approach, we believe you should take advice on this, given that information security standards evolve as weaknesses are exposed in the various algorithms and techniques that are used.

Let's assume each customer has a unique username assigned by the bank when they sign up for the Internet banking platform. The Internet banking database contains a table with a row for each user's username with information on the password for that user. We could consider encrypting the passwords using a secret key and decrypting them using the same key. However, this is not sufficient, as anyone who comes into possession of the secret key and a copy of the username/password table could decrypt all the passwords. Also, even without the secret key it would be possible to see if any users were using the same password, which reduces the security as well. To avoid the first problem, what is often done is to use what is called a hash function to convert each password (or to hash it) to a fixed-length, seemingly random string of characters called the hash value for that password. A hash function is an algorithm that is implemented using software, and it is irreversible, which means that it is not possible to calculate the original password from its hash value. It gives no clue about the length of the original passwords, as all the hash values it generates are the same length. Also, there should be a very, very small probability that passwords that are different will generate the same hash value, so that it is extraordinarily difficult to find a password that generates the same hash value as another password. Unfortunately, this was found not to be the case with two once common hash functions called MD5 and SHA-1, so these two should not be used. Conversely, the same passwords will always generate the same hash value, so even with a hash it is still possible to see if two people have the same password. Therein lies a weakness that hackers who have managed to get a list of hashed passwords (e.g. by hacking into a server where they can be accessed*) have exploited. It is human nature to use normal words for passwords, often with a number or symbol at one end, and hackers have created massive lists of hashed passwords by taking a dictionary and hashing every word in it, and also every

---

*For example, with various flavours of the UNIX operating system (until roughly before the mid-1990s), the file of usernames and hashed passwords was accessible to all users of the system. Various hacks of public websites have accessed files containing usernames and hashed passwords and used the dictionary approach to get the original passwords.

FIGURE 3.30   Checking a customer's Internet banking login details.

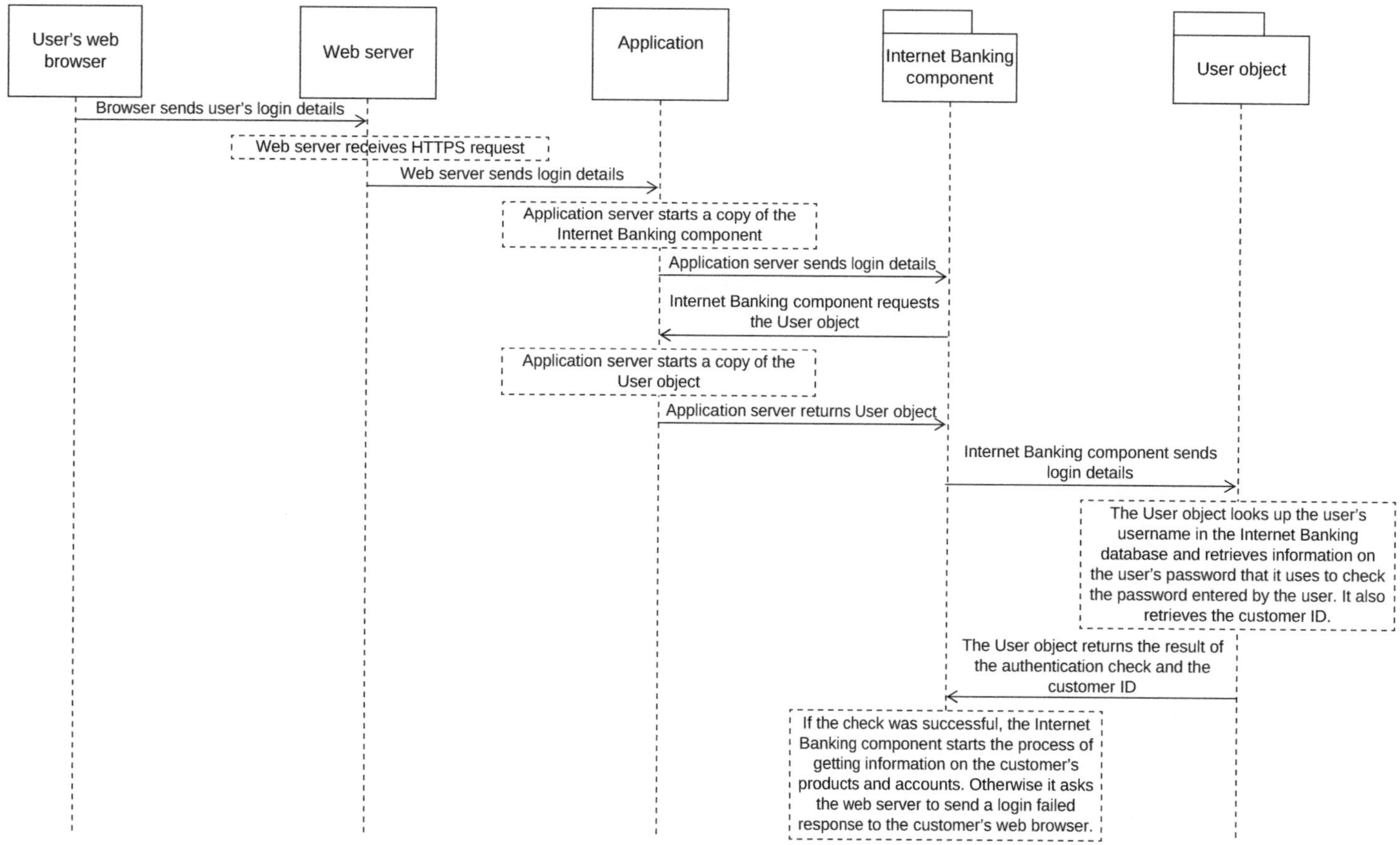

word plus one or more digits or symbols, plus every word with letters changed to digits (e.g. the letter l changed to the digit 1). So, to make this harder for hackers, passwords should be salted before they are hashed. Salting a password means adding a random string of characters (the salt) to it (either at the start or the end of the password or mixing it in some deterministic way with the password). The salt should be different for each user, so that even if two users have the same password, their salted, hashed passwords will be different. The salt must be kept with the hashed, salted password. So, the process of checking a user's password is to look up the salt and add it to the password entered by the user, then run this through the hash function. If the output is the same as the hashed, salted password, then the user has entered the correct password. This means that a hacker who has gotten a copy of the password table (including the salt for each password) can't use a pre-prepared dictionary of hashed passwords, but has to re-create the dictionary for every salt in the table, taking much longer.

To make it even harder, more can be done:

- First, pepper can be added to the salted passwords before they are hashed! This is another form of salting, and it means adding another random string of characters, this time the same for every password, but that is not stored anywhere in the table or even in the database. A hacker needs to get the pepper as well as the table to be able to try and discover the passwords. The pepper could be stored in a secure piece of infrastructure, called a hardware security module (HSM), that is tamperproof and that the User object calls to get the pepper.
- Second, the hashed and salted passwords can be hashed many times over. This could be, say, a thousand up to multiples of millions of times. This means that it takes longer for our User object to check a user's password because it must put the password entered by the user through the same process. In practice this can still be done within a few seconds so it is of little consequence to a user logging on, but it multiplies the time a hacker would take to create the password dictionary for a particular combination of salt and pepper. So, each row of the table containing username and password information must contain the user's username, the hashed, salted password, the salt for that password and the number of times the password has been hashed.
- Third, the table itself should be encrypted and access controlled (i.e. restricted to specific programs such as the User object) and logged. RDBMSs often have the capability to do this, sometimes in combination with a hardware security module for secure storage of the encryption key. Encrypting the table means that even if the hard drives used by the RDBMS are stolen, the data on them is unusable. The encryption can be transparent to the User object, so it doesn't have to do any extra processing to read the table.

Some consideration should also be given to being able to change the process for checking passwords in the future. We've already said the number of times a password is hashed should be stored in each row of the table, so this can be increased if necessary. It may also be advisable to be able to change the pepper value, so something that denotes which pepper value has been used for each customer password should also be stored in each row of the table, but not the actual pepper value itself. You may need to change the hashing algorithm completely, but it's generally not possible to rehash existing hashed passwords, and passwords can only be rehashed using the new algorithm when the customer logs in, so the old and new algorithms may have to co-exist. It would make sense to store on each record in the table something that indicates what algorithm was used (but probably not the actual name of the algorithm, which would help a hacker).

Now, we note some banks ask for two types of password – a password comprising letters, digits and symbols and two or three digits from a passcode comprising typically between four and six digits. Note that in this case the bank must either store the passcode without hashing it, because hash functions require the full original passcode to be entered, or the bank could store a hash value for every possible permutation of selected digits – for example, choosing three digits in order from a passcode comprising six distinct digits has 20 permutations. There are at least two reasons for using passcodes as well as passwords. First, it gives some protection against someone overseeing a user logging on (or recording the keystrokes on their computer) and reusing the passcode, because not all the digits of the passcode will have been captured. Second, it helps mitigate the impact of a particular type of denial of service attack. The first thing the User object will do with the digits from the passcode is check if these are correct. If they aren't correct, it won't bother checking the password, which is computationally expensive to do given the amount of hashing required as described in the previous paragraph. If it didn't do this, a hacker could flood the bank's Internet banking platform with username and password combinations, causing it to grind to a halt more quickly (and therefore denying the service to others) as the User object uses all the available processing capacity.

We also note some banks display a picture or phrase chosen by the user or some information about the user such as their date of birth during the login process. This can help reduce phishing attacks, in which a user is induced to enter their login details into a website that looks like the bank's Internet banking website, but is in fact set up to collect such login details. It helps the user determine if the website is indeed delivered by the bank. Obviously it's of limited use if it only appears after the user has logged in, so there would have to be a two-step process for logging in, probably displaying the picture, phrase or information after the user has entered their username but before the password, or (preferably) between passcode and password entry.*

Finally, in many markets there has been a move to the use of two-factor authentication to reduce the risk of password hacking. Two-factor authentication generally means that a user has a password (this is one of the two factors – something the user knows) and a device that takes part in the authentication (this is the other factor – something that the user has). Such devices usually take one of two forms. The first is the user's phone, to which the bank sends a text message containing a random code when they log on, which the user must enter to continue the logon process. Some banks also offer an automated service to call the user and say the code using a voice response unit. The second is a code-generation device which displays a passcode that typically changes every minute. RSA SecurID tokens are probably the best-known example of these devices and we have seen them used in many organisations to authenticate employees when they

---

*It's preferable not to do it just after the customer has entered their username because sometimes usernames are just email addresses, so in effect the picture, phrase or information would be easily accessible once a hacker knows a customer's email address. Similarly, usernames allocated by the bank may be predictable.

access the organisation's network or even specific platforms. HSBC issued devices like the one shown in Figure 3.31 to their customers in the UK.

Some authentication devices, such as the one shown in Figure 3.32, require the user to insert their debit card and enter the card's PIN. This generates a one-time code in response, which is a function that is part of the EMV standard for Chip and PIN cards. Also, there are smartphone apps that can be used to generate such codes and the Internet Engineering Task Force (IETF)'s RFC6238[12] defines the Time-based One-Time

FIGURE 3.31   Code generation device issued by HSBC.

FIGURE 3.32   EMV authentication device.

Password (TOTP) algorithm that is commonly used by such apps. We find that few banks issue devices to users, probably because of the expense of the devices and the management of them. Also, such devices tend to be less convenient for customers. We have seen many banks using text messaging. The User object in our Internet banking platform could be extended to handle whatever form of two-factor authentication is used.

3.12   Remote Procedure Calls

Following on from the previous section, we assume the User object confirmed that the user is authorised to log on and returns this confirmation to the Internet Banking object. In addition, we assume that the User object has also determined the customer represented by the user (which should also be stored in the Internet banking database) and has returned the customer ID to the Internet Banking object. This must create and access a Customer object to determine what products or accounts the customer has. The Customer object must communicate with the Customer platform shown in Figure 3.28 which is a set of CICS programs running on a mainframe. As we mentioned in Section 3.9, there are many ways that programs can call CICS programs. If we had been developing the Internet banking platform in the 1990s, we might have gone directly to the mainframe using terminal emulation (screen scraping – discussed in Section 3.9), remote procedure calls, or WebsphereMQ message queues. Let's look at remote procedure calls first.

A remote procedure call (RPC) is a way for one program to make a call to another program, wherever the two programs are running, such as on the same system or on different systems connected in some way by a network, and get a response back. It's a fundamental concept and requirement in a distributed environment, that is, one in which programs are being run on different systems and need to communicate with each other. The basic process is illustrated in Figure 3.33, in which the calling program (or client program) on computer A makes a remote procedure call, usually passing some information in the call, to an RPC client program also running on computer A that is a component of the RPC software. The RPC client program packages up the information, finds out where the server is running and sends the information across the network to it. An RPC server program on computer B listens for such messages, and when it receives the message

FIGURE 3.33   Basic remote procedure call.

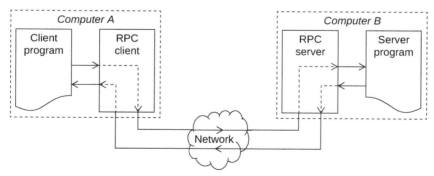

from the network, unpackages the information and passes it to the server program, which ultimately sends some information back (even if just an acknowledgement). Normally, between making the RPC and receiving the response back, the client program waits and does nothing else; such an RPC is termed synchronous. Some RPC implementations provide a means for the client program to keep working and be interrupted when the response comes back or for the client program to periodically check to see if a response has been returned – such RPC calls are termed asynchronous.

In fact, we've already seen some examples of RPCs. When an application interacts with an RDBMS on a different server, it is making some form of remote procedure call to the RDBMS.

There are many different implementations of RPCs with perhaps the Open Network Computing (ONC) and Distributed Computing Environment (DCE) implementations being the most well-known historical examples. ONC RPC was developed by Sun Microsystems (acquired by Oracle) and specified in the IETF's RFC5531.[13] DCE RPC was defined by the Open Software Foundation and it is maintained as a standard by The Open Group.[14] More modern implementations include Apache Thrift (originally developed by Facebook), Google's gRPC and Twitter's Finagle, and there are many others with specific purposes. Remote procedure calls are still very much a part of mainstream software and system development.

One addition to the process shown in Figure 3.33 is that some implementations also provide a means for the RPC service to find out where a server is located by having an RPC directory service, as shown in Figure 3.34. The process of making a remote procedure call is similar, but the RPC client on computer A can go and find out where the server program is located at the time the call is made by querying the RPC directory service. This would enable lots of copies of the server to be run simultaneously in order to service a lot of clients. Note that the RPC server on computer B has to inform the RPC directory service that it is running and the server program is available. The

FIGURE 3.34   RPC directory service.

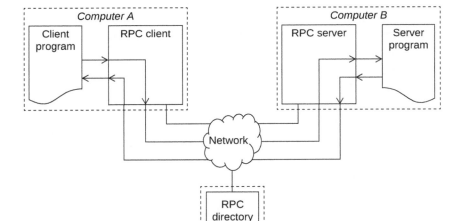

directory service can also be used to authenticate the programs that are making remote procedure calls – in other words, making sure that only approved programs can access specific RPCs.

So, in our Internet banking platform, the Customer object makes a remote procedure call to the Customer platform running on the mainframe, via an RPC adapter that is running on the application server, as shown in Figure 3.35. It sends the customer ID with the call. The CICS environment on the mainframe has an RPC server (called a server controller in IBM's terminology) which receives all remote procedure calls, and that starts another program (called an alias transaction) to process this specific request and work out what CICS program should be used. The alias transaction also populates the shared memory area that the CICS program accesses to get the customer ID and any other information sent with the call. In our example we have a CICS program called Product Enquiry that looks up the customer record in the database based on the customer ID sent by the Customer object. The Product Enquiry program is part of the mainframe-based Customer application. It populates the shared memory area with the information on that customer (i.e. what products they hold) and exits, causing control to return to the alias

FIGURE 3.35   Customer object using an RPC to a CICS program.

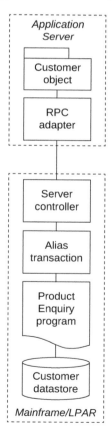

transaction, which sends the information back to the Customer object. Note that there may be other programs involved on the mainframe side (e.g. to decode and encode the data passed with the RPC and its response).

The Bank Account and Credit Card Account objects work in a similar way, making RPC calls to CICS mainframe programs. In our example the Payment object is a little different because it uses messaging to send a payment instruction rather than an RPC call, which we explore in Section 7.9.

An important consideration when using RPCs is what to do if there is a failure during the call. For example, if the client has started an RPC, and is waiting for a response and then there is a failure, the client cannot tell if either the RPC has been executed by the server but the response has not come back, or the RPC has not gotten to the server. One approach is for the client to make the same RPC again, assuming it doesn't matter if the server receives it more than once (a property of the server that is called idempotence). This is an important consideration for designers and developers of platforms that use RPCs to communicate with other platforms.

3.13   Distributed Objects and CORBA

It was natural to extend the idea of remote procedure calls, where one program calls across the network to a function in another program, to objects, where a program or an object can access an object running across the network. The technology industry released the first version of the Common Object Request Broker Architecture (CORBA) standard in 1991.[15] In this approach, two objects communicate as shown in Figure 3.36. Each computer has an object request broker (ORB) which is part of the implementation of the distributed object framework provided by a software vendor through which the calling program (or client) requests an object and communicates with the object provided by a server program.

With CORBA, our Internet banking platform may have used remote objects instead of objects in the same application server, as shown in Figure 3.37.

The potential advantage of this sort of architecture is that the bank can develop lots of different platforms that use the objects and their functionality, rather than this having to be developed every time. So, its branch platform, contact centre platform and Internet banking platforms could all be fairly lightweight applications that focus on the interaction with their users rather than integration with other platforms or the business

FIGURE 3.36   Communicating with a distributed object.

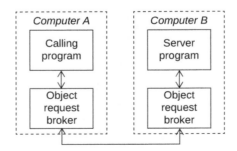

FIGURE 3.37   Internet banking platform using distributed objects.

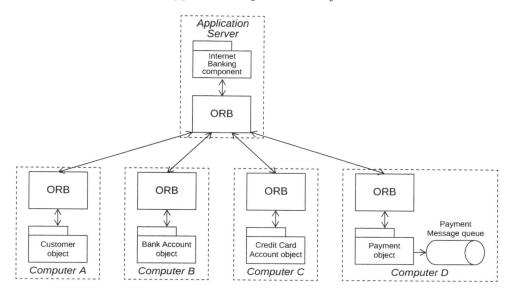

functionality of banking objects, and all of them use the distributed objects, which only have to be developed once.

We saw several implementations of CORBA in the banking industry in the late 1990s, and it may be that some of these are still being used today. We even started building a greenfield bank using CORBA and WebsphereMQ but ran into issues with poor performance and ultimately removed CORBA from the architecture. CORBA and the various implementations of it were criticised for overwhelming complexity (and the resulting challenges for designers and developers in actually using it), poor or non-existent interoperability between implementations, the cost of the software licences, lack of in-built support for security (i.e. only allowing specific users or programs to access objects), poor performance due to large amounts of uncompressed data being shipped across the network, lack of support for versioning (which made rolling out new versions of objects a major headache) and use of network protocols that enterprise firewalls generally blocked. The uptake of Java, XML and web services in effect killed it off and by around 2005 CORBA was essentially obsolete as far as mainstream software development was concerned. Microsoft also developed an approach to remote objects called DCOM (Distributed Component Object Model), which did not gain widespread enterprise usage. We'd be very surprised if anyone would build a bank using these technologies now or even use them for new developments in an established bank.

3.14   Services

Virtually any activity that someone does for someone else can be described as a service if we can define (e.g. write down) what is required to initiate the activity and what the potential outcomes of the activity are. For example, a teller in a bank branch can perform the service of accepting a cash deposit. To do this, I initiate the service by saying what I'd like to do and then handing some cash to the teller with details of my bank account (e.g. a completed paying-in slip). The teller takes my cash and performs the service and then tells me the outcome, which normally is that the balance of my bank account is increased by that amount of cash. I don't know (or care too much about) how the teller does this, but I expect they count the cash and increase the balance of my bank account by accessing the bank's core banking platform. There could be other outcomes: the cash could be forged and therefore the bank won't accept it, or the core banking platform could be unavailable so the teller can't record the deposit and returns the cash.

Obviously defining a service is really only of much use if the service is reusable, by which we mean that more than one person can initiate the service (e.g. any customer of the bank can make a deposit over the counter) *and* more than one person can simultaneously perform the service (e.g. the bank has lots of tellers who can accept deposits over the counter).

Performing a service may require other services. For example, my bank provides me with a domestic payment service: I can ask it to make a payment from my account to an account at another bank in the same country. This involves multiple organisations including my bank, the receiving bank and probably a payment scheme and a central bank. So what is a single service as far as I am concerned (making a payment) actually involves multiple services and organisations: my bank sends a payment message to the payment scheme, the payment scheme transmits the message to the recipient bank and settles the payment by asking the central bank to transfer the funds between the account of my bank and the account of the recipient bank at the central bank. In other words, a service can use other services to perform its activity.

Finally, a service can also be a collective noun in English. For example, my bank provides a teller service. This means I can go into a bank branch and ask a teller to perform several different services such as taking cheque deposits, withdrawing cash from my account, initiating the payment of a bill, requesting a new chequebook and so on. These are all different services, the full list of which comprises the bank's teller service.

You can think of a service in technology terms as a program that other programs can call using a well-defined mechanism (normally called an interface) in order to get it to do something. In other words, a service's interface defines what information must be passed to the service so that it can initiate its activity.

A service is reusable because generally more than one copy of it can be executed at the same time, and any other programs can call any copy of the service. Think of our example of tellers in a bank branch again – when I go into a bank branch, there is usually more than one teller and I can go to any of them. However, if all the tellers are busy I must wait until one comes free. With a service, it should be possible to run many copies of it simultaneously but ultimately there will be some limit dictated by the amount of computer processing capacity.

A service can call other services, as these are just programs with well-defined interfaces. A service may also be a collection of services – in which case it has (at least notionally) an interface for each individual service.

A program or service calling another service does not care or need to know how the service being called performs its activity, just like I didn't need to know how a teller accepts a cash deposit. Because of this, a service is usually described as a black box. What is vitally important, however, is the definition of the interface to a service.

You may ask how a service differs from an object. An object is intended to hold the information on a specific entity such as a customer or bank account and enable actions to be done to that entity (e.g. change the address of a customer or provide a list of transactions in a bank account). An object is typically intended to persist for some period such as during the session when a user is accessing a platform, interacting with the user for the duration of that session, maintaining information on the state of the object during the session and then saving its information safely (e.g. to a database) and ending. A service may be running for a long period of time and will service many users over that period, typically in single shots – as a user you send it some information and it does something with it then forgets about the request and goes on to service another request from another user, or you request some information from a service and it sends it back and then moves onto another request from another user. Services can maintain state information from one call to another, but for maximum scalability this is normally avoided. From a software perspective, objects tend to be strongly coupled to the programs that use them because an object is typically created (instantiated, in the terminology of object-oriented programming languages) and then ended by the program that uses it, with a strictly defined and typically synchronous interface that the program must adhere to. Services are more loosely coupled, typically existing independently of other programs and reacting to programs accessing them, with an interface that requires a specific message format and which is extensible,* often based on receiving a message and sending a message back – that is, asynchronous. In practice, the distinction between objects and services is not black and white, although, as we have already stated, distributed object platforms are legacy technology.[†] On the other hand, services technology in various forms is very much in use for existing and new platforms.

3.15 Web Services

Strictly speaking, according to W3C, the standards-setting body for the World Wide Web:

> A Web service is a software system designed to support interoperable machine-to-machine interaction over a network. It has an interface described in a machine-processable format (specifically WSDL). Other systems interact with the Web service in a manner prescribed by its description using SOAP-messages, typically conveyed using HTTP with an XML serialization in conjunction with other Web-related standards.[16] (© 2004 W3C® (MIT, ERCIM, Keio))

---

*By extensible, we mean, for example, that such message formats allow additional values to be put in the message, which the service will typically ignore if it does not understand them. This is another aspect that makes services loosely coupled.

[†]Note that this is a comment about distributed object platforms such as CORBA and DCOM. It is not a comment about object-oriented programming languages such as C++, C#, Java, Python, Scala, Swift and many others. Object-oriented programming languages are rightly widely used, for many different purposes.

According to this definition, a web service is a type of service, much like we have seen already, and which can be called across a network using a specific type of messaging called SOAP (which originally stood for Simple Object Access Protocol and can now also stand for Service Oriented Architecture Protocol[17]), which defines a message format and some aspects of how the messages must be handled. In common usage, the term web service is more loosely defined and typically refers to a service that can be called using messages sent using HTTP or HTTPS and with one of a variety of message formats, including formats commonly used on the World Wide Web, most commonly XML (eXtensible Markup Language) and JSON (JavaScript Object Notation).

Let's cover how we might design our Internet banking platform around the use of web services, as shown in Figure 3.38. In this diagram, the Internet banking platform comprises a web server and application server (as before), with an Internet Banking component hosted by the application server. Every time a user attempts to log in to the Internet banking platform, the application server starts a copy of the Internet Banking component dedicated to that user for the duration of their session.

The first thing the Internet Banking component does is make a web services call to the User service to validate the login details supplied by the user and get the customer ID for that user. We mentioned various formats that could be used for a web services call, and we will cover these in turn. In all cases, we assume that the call is made using HTTPS over the corporate IP network.

FIGURE 3.38   Internet banking platform using services exposed by other platforms.

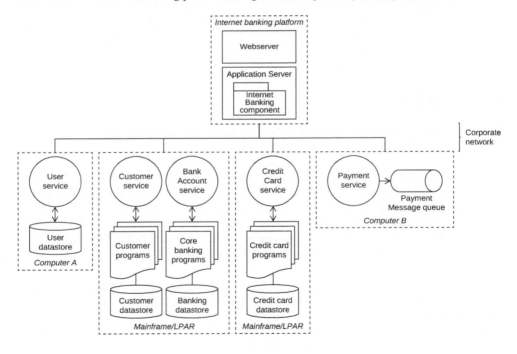

First, using SOAP, the message would look something like the following:

```
<?xml version="1.0"?>
<env:Envelope xmlns:env="http://www.w3.org/2003/05/soap-envelope/">
 <env:Header>
  <m:AuthenticateHeader
   xmlns:m="http://mybank.com/external/2018/06/auth-envelope"
   env:mustUnderstand="true">
   <m:requestID>bdf06ef8-37e9-4864-b7d4-c6a10efd0fa9</m:requestID>
   <m:expires>2020-06-20T14:56:51</m:expires>
   <m:version>0301</m:version>
  </m:AuthenticateHeader>
 </env:Header>
 <env:Body>
  <p:AuthenticateExternalUser
   xmlns:p="http://mybank.com/external/2018/06/auth-body">
   <p:username>4424194648</p:username>
   <p:password>FgBdnJvi8b</p:password>
  </p:AuthenticateExternalUser>
 </env:Body>
</env:Envelope>
```

The very first line of this message declares it to be an XML message, and like all SOAP messages it then contains an Envelope section. Inside the Envelope section is a Header section (optional for SOAP messages) and a Body section (mandatory). The header provides a unique ID for this specific request, a date and time at which the request expires (if the request was delayed beyond this time, the User service would not process it and would probably return some error message) and some version information (to indicate what type of authentication mechanism is being used). The body contains the actual username and password entered by the user. Note that, as this message is sent using HTTPS, it will be encrypted. However, further consideration could be given to securing the message exchange so that, for example, only authorised programs could call the User service. The message returned from the User service would look something like the following:

```
<?xml version="1.0"?>
<env:Envelope xmlns:env="http://www.w3.org/2003/05/soap-envelope/">
 <env:Header>
  <m:AuthenticateResponseHeader
   xmlns:m="http://mybank.com/external/2018/06/auth-envelope"
   env:mustUnderstand="true">
   <m:requestID>bdf06ef8-37e9-4864-b7d4-c6a10efd0fa9</m:requestID>
  </m:AuthenticateResponseHeader>
 </env:Header>
 <env:Body>
  <p:AuthenticateExternalUserResponse
   xmlns:p="http://mybank.com/external/2018/06/auth-body">
   <p.result>true</p.result>
   <p.customerID>519510405149</p.customerID>
   <p.token>de10efb3-4d0b-456d-b12c-ad07aba62e4f</p.token>
  </p:AuthenticateExternalUserResponse>
 </env:Body>
</env:Envelope>
```

The response header includes the same requestID so that the response can be matched to the request. The body of the response message includes the output of the check (true in this case, which means that the user has been successfully authenticated), the customer ID for this user and a token, which represents the login session for this user.

The calls could be made using XML that isn't compliant with SOAP, or what is sometimes referred to as POX (Plain Old XML). The request message could be like the following:

```xml
<?xml version="1.0"?>
<AuthenticateExternalUserRequest
 xmlns="http://mybank.com/external/2018/06/auth">
 <requestID>bdf06ef8-37e9-4864-b7d4-c6a10efd0fa9</requestID>
 <expires>2020-06-20T14:56:51</expires>
 <version>0301</version>
 <username>4424194648</username>
 <password>FgBdnJvi8b</password>
</AuthenticateExternalUserRequest>
```

The response would look like the following:

```xml
<?xml version="1.0"?>
<AuthenticateExternalUserResponse
 xmlns="http://mybank.com/external/2018/06/auth">
 <requestID>bdf06ef8-37e9-4864-b7d4-c6a10efd0fa9</requestID>
 <result>true</result>
 <customerID>519510405149</customerID>
 <token>de10efb3-4d0b-456d-b12c-ad07aba62e4f</token>
</AuthenticateExternalUserResponse>
```

A JSON request message would look like the following (note that we have added line breaks to make it more readable but the message could be just one long string):

```json
{AuthenticateExternalUserRequest:
{
requestID:"bdf06ef8-37e9-4864-b7d4-c6a10efd0fa9",
expires:"2020-06-20T14:56:51",
version:"0301",
username:"4424194648",
password:"FgBdnJvi8b"
}}
```

The response would look like the following:

```json
{AuthenticateExternalUserResponse:
{
requestID:"bdf06ef8-37e9-4864-b7d4-c6a10efd0fa9",
result:"true",
customerID:"519510405149",
token:"de10efb3-4d0b-456d-b12c-ad07aba62e4f"
}}
```

All the message formats are human-readable, and they range from being very verbose in the case of SOAP to relatively condensed in the case of JSON. For these relatively simple messages, there isn't much advantage in one format over the other.

SOAP not only defines a message format, but also how messages should be handled and routed and how the format of different types of messages can be defined. There are associated standards that cover topics such as securing SOAP messages, finding SOAP-based web services, making message delivery reliable and so on. This means that SOAP can form the basis of enterprise-scale integration approaches, and we believe many banks have indeed internally implemented services using SOAP.

On the other hand, JSON is just a simple data encapsulation format whose specification[18] is tiny in comparison to SOAP, and which says nothing about how messages should be processed or routed. XML is a more powerful data encapsulation format than JSON that is widely used, particularly where data needs to be defined accurately and robustly, but which also says nothing about message transmission.

Very large-scale websites have found that using XML-based formats requires too much processing power or network bandwidth and, for internal use at least, there appears to have been a move towards JSON and even more compact message formats such as Google's Protocol Buffers binary format. Google claims Protocol Buffers messages are 3 to 10 times smaller than XML messages and can be processed 20 to 100 times faster.

In Figure 3.38 the Customer, Bank Account and Credit Card Account services have all been implemented on the mainframe and call the CICS mainframe programs that comprise the Customer, Core Banking and Credit Card platforms respectively. The Payment service has been built separately. This provides two functions – supplying a list of payees for a specific customer, which it gets by calling the Bank Account service on the mainframe, and sending payment messages by putting them into the Payment Message queue (see Section 7.9 for more details).

3.16   RESTful Web Services

There has been a movement towards a specific type of web services, so-called RESTful web services. In this context, REST stands for Representational State Transfer and was defined by Roy Fielding in his PhD thesis.[19] REST is a technical term for an approach to accessing content and functionality (or more generically resources). It was a key concept Fielding developed during his work in the mid-1990s to formally define the architecture of the World Wide Web, uniform resource identifiers and version 1.1 of HTTP. A RESTful web service is a service that is accessed using the HTTP (or HTTPS) protocol, including the use of uniform resource identifiers (e.g. webpage addresses), that supports the various commands available in HTTP (e.g. GET, which is used, for example, by a browser in the HTTP request that it sends when it wants to get a webpage from a website) and that provides information on how to access linked resources in its responses (for example, a webpage often contains hyperlinks to other webpages).

There isn't a standard for RESTful web services, but there are widely accepted traits:

- Use of the HTTP/HTTPS commands (or verbs) including GET, PUT, POST and DELETE to indicate the intention of a message. This includes the notion that some commands are safe, in that they do not change the state of a resource (e.g. use of GET to get some information about a resource such as a customer from a web service is in effect reading some information, and not altering any information), whereas others are not safe in that they change the state of one or more resources (e.g. POST can result in a new resource such as a customer record being created, DELETE can delete a resource such as a customer record). In comparison, the HTTP/HTTPS command set is not really utilised with SOAP, POX or JSON messages as used in the previous section (SOAP messages usually use the POST command, irrespective of the purpose of the message).

- Use of the HTTP/HTTPS status codes. For example, when trying to navigate to a non-existent webpage, you may have seen a 404 Page Not Found error. This status code is defined in the HTTP/HTTPS standard and so with a RESTful web service, if a program tries to GET some information on a resource which does not exist (e.g. a program requests some information on a customer with a specific customer ID, but that customer record does not exist), the web service would return an HTTP/HTTPS 404 status code. On the other hand, a successful GET would normally result in an HTTP/HTTPS message with a 200 status code. For the SOAP, POX or JSON web services in the previous section, results of a request are communicated inside the body of the message with no standardisation in the case of POX or JSON messages (there is a defined mechanism for communicating an error in a SOAP response message).

- Use of uniform resource identifiers to navigate resources. For example, information on a specific customer could be located at https://customer.mybankinternal .com/customer/4424194648 where the 10-digit number at the end is the customer ID, and the customer's list of bank accounts could be accessed at https://customer .mybankinternal.com/customer/4424194648/bankaccounts.

- Use of hypertext links in response messages to indicate to the requester how it can navigate or act on the resource. For example, if a program asks to GET information on a specific customer, the response message should send the information and can include one or more relative URLs with an indication of what these are intended for. A request for information on a specific customer could return a result that gives the customer's name and other personal details, and provides hypertext links to related information such as the customer's default address, the list of the customer's bank accounts and so on. This promotes loose coupling, in that the program making the request does not have to know a specific address to access or act on a resource (although of course there must be some common understanding of how navigation should take place).

- RESTful web services are stateless, in that the server does not remember the context from one request to another. In other words, the requesting program must supply all the information in each request that the server needs to respond to that request. This means that RESTful web services can be easily scaled and made more resilient (e.g. if one server fails, any other server can process the next request).

- Use of any (reasonable) format for the body of the HTTP/HTTPS message, frequently XML or JSON.

In some respects, these traits are a pushback against the complexity and rigidity of SOAP, require less processing power and provide much greater scalability. So, if you were building a highly scalable public website (or online bank) that provided information on lots of resources to many users across the Internet you would almost certainly be considering RESTful web services. The UK's Open Banking Read-Write API specification[20] defines a mainly RESTful interface for banks to implement to give third-party service providers access to bank account information. Internally, RESTful web services, SOAP web services or other approaches may all be valid for different reasons and in different situations. We think that most large banks have embraced the use of web services in one form or another (or probably more than one form) as a means to integrate various platforms in order to provide Internet banking and other Internet services, mobile apps and many internal applications. Similarly, most modern third-party platforms provide some form of interface based around web services and are often architected internally to use web services.

3.17   Service-Oriented Architecture

We have talked a lot about different ways in which programs can communicate with each other across a network and as part of this we explained the concept of IT services that can be integrated to provide business platforms. For example, a simple Internet banking platform uses services that enable a user of the service to log on to access a set of bank accounts and make payments from those accounts. Having built such services, there was a natural desire to reuse them for other platforms and standardise how services should be built and accessed. This is one of the drivers for what is called service-oriented architecture (SOA), which typically provides a framework for building, deploying and accessing services. Another driver for service-oriented architecture is the need to integrate platforms that have been acquired either through mergers and acquisitions or to replace legacy platforms.

Many large banks have ended up with platforms built using a wide mixture of different technologies and several different integration approaches and technologies. In our experience, only start-up banks in their early years have the luxury of relatively homogeneous technology. Within 10 years of being launched, a start-up bank we worked for had at least three product platforms and at least five different integration technologies. Service-oriented architecture typically enables a bank to knit such diverse technology together.

The same drivers exist in many other industries, and as a result the concept of service-oriented architecture became the dominant concept in enterprise IT development at the start of the twenty-first century. Having said that, there is no widely adopted standard definition of a service-oriented architecture. In our view and others' views (see, for example, reference 21), it comprises four concepts:

1. **Application front ends:** These are the user interfaces that users, including customers, third parties and internal users, interact with – for example, an Internet banking website, a mobile banking app, the application used by customer service representatives in a contact centre, the branch application and so on. This concept also includes application programming interfaces (APIs) offered to third parties (e.g. the UK's open banking API) that provide a single programmatic front end to multiple services.

2. Services: These are the programs used by application front ends and other services, typically each representing a single business domain or that provide a technical service such as logging, security or message translation.

3. A service directory, repository or inventory: This is a register or catalogue of services that provides technical information that services and application front ends can use, for example, to locate specific services (e.g. determining the network address of a server on which a specific version of a service is hosted), and that can also supply human-readable information such as the service owner, the notional charge for use of a service for internal billing purposes, details of service levels and technical documentation about the service (see Section 9.4). In our experience, service directories are often incomplete and out of date and don't cover the whole enterprise.

4. A service bus (often called an enterprise service bus or ESB): This is typically a set of technologies that connects services to each other and to application front ends. The service bus may also provide technical services such as logging, security and message translation, and the service directory, and is the fundamental component of a full service-oriented architecture. Often the service bus internally uses a standard data format (typically based on XML) into which it translates incoming messages and from which it translates messages to services and programs that require a different format. ESBs often offer business process functionality, which conceptually allows business analysts to define and deploy process flows that use multiple services. For example, a customer applying for a loan online can result in a business process being initiated. Such a process runs on the ESB and in this case it uses services to determine the customer's credit rating, underwrite the loan application (including referring it for human review if necessary), create a new loan account, transfer the funds to the customer's current account and email the customer to tell them the funds have been transferred. There is a range of fully featured third-party ESB platforms and the sale of such platforms has been a highly active market for technology companies including IBM, Microsoft, MuleSoft, Oracle, Software AG and TIBCO. There are also open-source ESBs such as Apache Synapse and several others based around Java Enterprise Edition application servers. Finally, some enterprise resource planning platforms (e.g. from SAP and Workday) and core banking platforms (including SAP's banking platforms and Finastra's Fusion Essence) come with integrated service buses to facilitate integration with other platforms, to integrate the components from which they are built or to provide a way for a bank to build its own business processes using the platforms. Often large banks end up with several ESBs from different vendors, implemented by different organisations within the bank at different times.

In most implementations that we have seen, a bank (normally, its IT architecture function) sets standards for the technologies and solutions that should be used for each of these components, often further subdivided into different categories (e.g. application front ends delivered to customers over the Internet should be built using technologies x, y and z, internal application front ends should be built using technologies u, v and z, services must be built using programming languages a, b and c, and so on). This is often accompanied with governance (typically aimed at IT projects) to enforce use of the standards, to evolve the standards and to handle deviations from standards.

3.18 An Updated Model of Our Bank

So, let's look at our modern bank and how it might look given that it now supports Internet banking, branches, a contact centre and ATMs, having adopted a service-oriented architecture to integrate a number of operational platforms (a core banking platform, a customer platform and a credit card platform) and provide various user applications. This is illustrated in Figure 3.39. In this diagram we have four channels – ATMs, branches, contact centre and Internet. The ATMs are managed by the ATM management platform and send and receive card payment messages via the card payment switch (see Section 4.5 for more information). Typically, they do not use the enterprise service bus or the services accessible through it, although this could be possible given that modern ATMs are just PCs and, in our view, doing so could enable some innovative services to be offered via ATMs. The branch platform runs on PCs, directly communicating with equipment in the branch such as teller cash recyclers, and uses the enterprise service bus to access banking services, customer services, credit card services and payment services. The contact centre platform also runs on PCs, and directly communicates with the contact centre equipment such as the IP PBX. It also uses the enterprise service bus to access the various services. Finally the Internet banking platform provides web access to customers, and runs on an

FIGURE 3.39   A mainly service-oriented architecture for our bank.

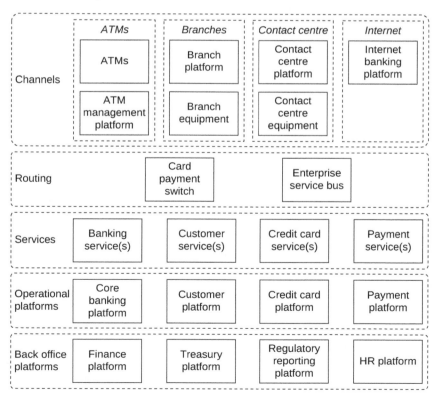

application server. It too uses the enterprise service bus to access banking and other services. We have assumed as well that the user authentication functionality required by the Internet banking platform is provided as another customer service.

Below the channels we have a notional routing layer, comprised primarily of the enterprise service bus which routes messages between the bank's channel applications and the services. We have also put the card payment switch in this layer because it too routes messages between a channel platform (i.e. the ATMs) and the core banking and credit card platforms. Note, however, it uses highly domain-specific messaging and direct connections to the platforms that use it. It does not use the enterprise service bus – which would be far too slow for the sub-second response times required for card payment messages.

Then we have a notional services layer, which represents a set of services offering standards-based interfaces (e.g. SOAP web services). These services access the underlying operational platforms – the core banking, customer and credit card platforms and the payment gateway (which we discuss in Section 7.9). The services may be built directly on the operational platforms (for example, using the web services capability provided by CICS on IBM mainframes), or may run on their own servers.

Finally, we have a set of back office platforms – finance, treasury, regulatory reporting and HR (human resources) platforms. These typically take direct feeds from the operational platforms and so do not take part in the service-oriented architecture. We explore finance, treasury and regulatory reporting platforms in Chapter 8.

In reality, in most banks we've seen the adoption of any particular service-oriented architecture is incomplete and there are likely to be applications directly accessing operational platforms as well as more modern applications using services. There is rarely a business case to re-engineer a legacy application to use more modern integration approaches.

3.19   Application Processing

Given that our bank has now grown to cover multiple channels and a range of banking products, we need to consider how customers' applications for products are handled. The process of opening a current account involves capturing information from the customer, verifying their identity, undertaking a credit check, determining what type (or types), if any, of current account can be offered to the customer and with what conditions (e.g. overdraft limit, monthly fees), capturing the customer's agreement to the terms and conditions, opening the account on whatever platform it will be hosted, issuing personalised stationery and plastic cards, setting up login details for the customer and educating the customer about the use of the account. This can all potentially be done in a single session and the customer could do it online using a browser, using a mobile app, in a branch, or over the phone, and ideally they should be able to start the application in one channel and continue it in another (e.g. if they run into difficulties). Opening a mortgage account is even more involved and can run over several weeks or months, from the initial fact finding through the offer of a mortgage in principle to the firm offer of a mortgage on a specific property and the transfer of funds for the purchase. For many products, the information that was captured and used to offer the product and the terms and conditions of the products need to be retained for the lifetime of the product, which could be decades in the case of a mortgage.

So, it's necessary to store the state of an application and the associated information so that it can be continued later or in a different channel. In addition, there needs to be a user interface for the application for each channel. This is where larger banks struggled, with product applications typically limited to a single channel, or if offered through more than one channel with little or no ability for a customer to shift channels in the middle of an application. However, in a modern bank built on services that can be reused across channels, it is significantly easier to offer application processes that can cross channels. Conceptually, this requires a datastore where the application state and information can be held for the duration of an application, a service for each product type, which accesses the datastore and channel-specific user interfaces. The service that handles an application for a specific product typically has to make a decision about some of the terms and conditions that will apply to the product being offered (e.g. interest rate for a loan, maximum loan-to-collateral value ratio, monthly credit limit for a credit card), or even if the product will be offered to the customer or if the application should be referred for review. In some cases, a sophisticated decision engine could be required, and some companies offer such decision engines as a service. Application processing typically also must go to third-party information sources to check the identity (e.g. the electoral roll or equivalent for individuals, to a register of companies or to a register of charities) and creditworthiness of the customer. There are also services that can check the appearance of an individual with their government-issued photo identification document, which we cover in Section 5.6.1.

3.20   Microservices

The imaginary bank we have been constructing in this chapter has, we hope, illustrated how technology in banking has developed over several decades. Legacy banks find themselves in the situation where there are some major platforms such as the core banking platform, the customer platform and so on, with a lot of technology from different eras that integrates with them to provide support for new channels and products and services. The platforms appear to be essentially monolithic – like big black boxes to most users – although we saw that in reality mainframe-based platforms are composed of many small programs running on the mainframe. Usually, these platforms also rely upon large databases that also appear to be monolithic. Not only is the whole technology estate complex, but each major platform in it is complex. Typically, each platform will have a team that is responsible for maintaining the software it is built from, building, testing and releasing new functionality. In addition, there will typically be a team responsible for the enterprise service bus (or *each* ESB) used in a service-oriented architecture, and a team responsible for the user interface used in each channel (e.g. the Internet banking platform). So, releasing a new banking product, for example, involves multiple teams – the core banking platform team, the enterprise service bus team, the Internet banking platform team, the branch platform team, the contact centre platform team and possibly others. If any one of these teams is late, the whole release gets delayed. Also, any change to a platform typically requires the whole platform to be tested to make sure the change hasn't impacted anything else on the platform. So even simple changes are a big deal, and therefore banks typically have set release windows when all the changes to a platform must take place. This was exacerbated in many large banks by the technology function being centralised into a large shared service organisation, serving many different business functions. Therefore, the business functions lost direct control over and responsibility for the implementation of technology change. We worked for one large international bank in which the business imposed huge sets of new requirements on the technology organisation, which were not given sufficient resources to implement them and subsequently failed to do so (despite some technology teams working 365 days a year), or did so badly, and were then blamed for non-delivery by the business functions. We saw similar issues arise where technology was outsourced in large banks, with breakdowns in relationships between the business functions and the outsourcers where the business functions blamed the outsourcers for poor quality deliveries or outrageous (but probably, in some cases, realistic) quotations for changes. The pendulum began to swing back to direct control of technology change by business functions in some banks with the establishment of web development teams co-located with the business functions and using agile delivery methodologies. Even so, deliveries were often slow and expensive because the web development teams had dependencies on many other technology teams across the bank.

However, between roughly 2010 and 2020, what seems like a revolution in software development and software architecture took place, namely the advent of the microservices approach. It was a reaction to the problems that arise when software and platforms get too big or complex and it builds on two things. The first is the take-up of agile methodologies that started around 2000 (although they had roots in the previous decade[22]) and gathered steam through the dot-com boom and which are now mainstream even in the largest banks, particularly for Internet and mobile development. Second, it reuses ideas from service-oriented architecture, particularly the notion of services with well-defined interfaces, but also rejects some aspects of it such as the notion of an enterprise service bus at the heart of integrating the services and platforms (and typically maintained by a technology team upon which everyone then depends).

The shortest definition of microservices we found is in Sam Newman's book *Building Microservices*:

Microservices are small, autonomous services that work together.[23]

Of course, this leaves a lot unsaid. What this approach really encompasses is building platforms out of services with well-defined functional boundaries that align to business contexts, rather than having platforms that have a monolithic code base covering many business areas. For example, there are many third-party core banking platforms available, some of which have a huge set of functions, and were in fact designed to be used as a bank in a box – they provided nearly all the functionality to operate a small (and in some cases not so small) bank. The problem with such monolithic platforms is that changing them becomes increasingly difficult – although they may well have been designed initially with well-ordered, structured code bases, over time code bases get overly complex (often because of the pressure to provide new functionality quickly with inadequate time to design it properly and because the code base is so large nobody has an overall view of how it is structured) and therefore fragile. Making even a simple change means the whole platform must be retested, so adding or changing functionality takes longer and longer and costs more and more. The microservices approach says that such platforms should be comprised of independent, self-contained services. For example, at the heart of core banking platform is a set of ledgers that record transactions in accounts. A microservice could be built to do just that, i.e. post transactions to ledgers. In fact, a (simple) core banking platform could comprise something like the following microservices:

- A service to create banking transactions and record them in the right accounts. For scalability, this service could be deployed multiple times so that different transactions could be recorded simultaneously.
- A service to create a bank account (or perhaps a different service to create each type of bank account).
- A service to process inbound payments.
- A service to receive payment instructions.
- A service to process immediate payment instructions.
- A service to execute the end-of-day process (which may in turn call other services that do things like calculate and post interest, calculate and post fees, process batch inbound payments, process batch outbound payments, post transactions to the finance platform, and so on).

Each service can be deployed on its own server, and there can be multiple copies of each service if it must be scaled up and for resilience. In fact, a key enabler of microservices was the development of what are called containers. A microservice is typically deployed in a container, which to the microservice looks like a server all to itself. However, one hardware server running a modern operating system can host multiple containers, which it keeps segregated. A microservice running in one container can communicate with other microservices across the network (even if they are running in different containers on the same server), but they have no other visibility of each other and can't look into each other's containers. Using the network for communication also means different microservices can be deployed either on the same server (in different containers) or on different servers, without any changes, therefore promoting scalability. Using containers means that a new version of one microservice can be deployed without interfering with other microservices – this is unlike a monolithic application where even just a small change can require the whole application to be reinstalled. Microservices also fit well with so-called devops processes that agile methodologies often use – rapid or continuous deployment of new functionality into production using automated tools – whereas this is more difficult with large monolithic applications. All these aspects open up opportunities for rapid deployment of changes, trying different versions of the same microservice simultaneously, scalability (with the possibility of scaling up just those services that need scaling up, not a whole monolithic application), resilience (with multiple copies of a microservice running, if one fails the others can keep going) and rapid deployment of changes (and easily falling back to previous versions if necessary).

Microservices often use messaging to communicate with each other, and one approach is for a microservice that has just updated some information (e.g. created a new customer record) to publish it as a message that any other service can read and do something with. For example, another microservice could read such messages and for each one create a welcome email and send it to the customer. In the future, we could add another service that also reads such messages and does something else (e.g. assign a relationship manager to each new customer), so such messaging promotes extensibility of our platform. In fact, by retaining all such messages we would naturally have a record of everything that happened and could replay events if necessary. This is the basis of what is called stream processing and is supported by products such as Apache Kafka. The lure of this approach compared to just putting everything in a database is that it not only promotes extensibility but also produces a complete history of events that took place that can be used for analysis purposes and to create different views of information easily. In fact, we were involved in building an omnichannel banking platform using this approach. The downside is that virtually the whole banking industry, and in our experience the finance teams in banks, are so used to data being presented in relational database management systems that asking them to define what reports they would like is often met with blank stares – they typically take whatever the finance platform gives them! There is an excellent and relatively accessible description of stream processing in Martin Kleppmann's book *Making Sense of Stream Processing*.[24]

Other benefits available from microservices include the ability to use the technology or set of technologies (such as programming language) that best fits the job each microservice is required to do, and the potential ability for the technology organisation to organise itself around business contexts and therefore align more strongly with business teams.

However, there are downsides. Using microservices at scale requires sophisticated tooling, discipline and rigorous development, testing, deployment and systems monitoring processes. We reflect how agile development was hijacked by some organisations and turned into meaning writing and deploying code quickly without documentation and insufficient testing – when in fact agile development requires just as much rigour, discipline and communication, if not more, as any other methodology. If your organisation can't manage agile development, it is unlikely to handle microservices well. Furthermore, in a legacy bank, it isn't going to be feasible to reengineer the whole of the technology estate to use microservices, so any use of microservices is likely to be limited to front-end development and still be heavily reliant on other teams that maintain legacy platforms. A microservices architecture is essentially a distributed system, and may have complex, unintended emergent behaviour that is hard to debug. Communication between microservices, across the network, is inherently anything between one (i.e. 10 times) and several orders of magnitude (100, 1,000, 10,000 or more times) slower than inter-process communication in a monolithic application running on one server, so microservices architectures do not always provide highly responsive platforms, and network communications are not completely reliable. Many of the benefits of microservices are also available from alternative, well-established approaches and the careful design of platforms and governance around how they are changed.

As is often the case with new paradigms in software development, there are evangelists for the microservices approach who say the old approaches, particularly service-oriented architecture, were disastrous and the new approach is applicable in all situations. In reality, the microservices approach contains some key learnings from earlier software engineering approaches that may be helpful. If you are looking to set up a neobank, then using a microservices approach would be completely reasonable and neobanks such as Monzo in the UK have done so, although some neobanks such as N26 in Germany and Volt Bank in Australia decided to use third-party core banking platforms. If you are looking to resolve complex legacy challenges in a large bank, your mileage with microservices may be more limited.

3.21   Modern Databases

When we look at an RDBMS and the various approaches to making it highly available (see Section 3.5), we can see that the RDBMS or the underlying storage system is really a single point of failure, which we mitigate with various approaches such as sophisticated redundant storage systems with high-speed or synchronous replication. In addition, the RDBMS can present constraints on how much we can scale a solution up (e.g. how many simultaneous users, how many transactions per second and so on) and the rate at which we can change the applications that use the RDBMS for several reasons:

1. The need to isolate transactions in the RDBMS can cause them to be done at least partially sequentially and this limits the rate of change to the data in the database.
2. Relational data models are good at minimising the duplication of data (because a properly implemented data model will be normalised), but in doing so they are not optimised for writing changes to the data or adding more data. This can limit the rate of changes to the data in the database.
3. The RDBMS can be swamped with read requests if the applications using it always access it to get data required to construct webpages. This can be mitigated by applications keeping local copies (in a cache) of frequently used data that changes infrequently, which in turn gives rise to a need to update such caches if the data in them does need to be changed. This adds complexity to the application software.
4. A single database presents a constraint on the speed at which changes and enhancements to the applications using the database can be made, because changes to the data model have to be tested and rolled out to the production platform, and there can be limited opportunities to do this during the course of a year.
5. Finally, there is a criticism of relational data models that they are ideal for representing the state at the current point in time (for example, the current balance of every account in a bank and the current addresses of customers) but relatively poor at holding a history of the state (because holding lots of historical records degrades the performance of RDBMSs). In reality, they can be designed to hold whatever information is required, but they do not do this as well as other types of datastores.

Enterprise-scale RDBMSs mitigate some of these challenges by providing various facilities for running multiple instances of the RDBMS which will support more simultaneous users, normally in tandem with storage system replication. RDBMS vendors may suggest that their products can scale almost infinitely but in practice the cost of commercial RDBMSs and the infrastructure to host them are likely to be significant.

We have also come across architectures in which the data is partitioned across more than one RDBMS because of scaling challenges. For example, although it wasn't a banking platform, we were involved in the implementation of a national platform for health care records, which would have held over 100 million health records. At the time, no RDBMS could have scaled up to the size of database required or handled the volume of queries, so it had been decided to partition the single database into two. The applications accessing the databases had to be aware of this and avoid creating records for the same person in both databases, and we also needed to ensure that the two databases remained a similar size to each other and handled a similar volume of queries and have a way to rebalance them if they diverged.

So, international and global websites tend not to use RDBMSs for managing the tremendous amounts of data they (and their users) generate. Instead, they use so-called NoSQL database management systems, which are based around several approaches to data storage and retrieval, as we explain next.

Key-value stores: These are almost a reversion to the indexed files technology developed in the 1950s and 1960s, in which a record is retrieved by using an index value (the key) that the database management system uses to locate the record (the value) in a data file. The value could potentially be anything of any size, including, for example, a file (unlike in a simple file-based database, where the records are often a fixed length or of a specific format). Given the ease with which the record can be located, a query can be extremely quick. Databases can readily be distributed across multiple servers (as they can allocate a range of key values to each server) to offer huge scalability. Apache Kafka, which, as we mentioned in Section 3.20, can be used for stream processing of event messages, is a key-value store.

Wide-column stores: These are conceptually an extension of key-value stores to two dimensions. So, a row in a table can be accessed by its key value (just like in a key-value store). However, the fields in that row are not fixed and don't have to be (and generally aren't) the same as the fields in other rows (in other words, there isn't a single set of columns that each row must follow). Each row contains several key-value pairs – the keys inside the row become the field names for that row, and the values are the values of those fields. This offers more flexible data storage than pure key-value stores but with similar advantages in terms of speed and scalability.

Document stores: These are essentially key-value stores but where the value is in a structured format (not necessarily fixed-length), for example information held in a JSON or XML file (both of which are standards for structuring data records – see Section 3.15 for examples of these). They offer similar advantages of speed and scalability as key-value stores and flexibility around data storage like wide-column stores. Where might this type of database be applicable in a bank? We envisage that loan underwriting (particularly for business loans) where a range of information, often in various formats (e.g. copies of financial accounts) needs to be held for the life of a loan in one area. We have seen the combination of an RDBMS for standardised data and a file store for documents used for such purposes and using a document store as a single repository may be preferable (all the information is in one place, for example). We could also keep a record of all interactions with each customer in a document store, along with copies of correspondence, records of chat sessions, audio and video call logs and so – a complete contact history that can be quickly adapted to new types of interaction and is highly scalable to millions of contact records.

Graph stores: Conceptually, graph stores hold information on entities (termed nodes and typically representing business entities, e.g. customers, accounts), the relationships between them (sometimes termed edges, e.g. a customer holds an account) and the properties of the entities/nodes (e.g. a customer's name) and of the relationships/edges (e.g. a customer may be the primary holder of an account). That may sound similar to a relational database, with the essential difference being that in a relational database the types of relationships between entities are built into the data model used to implement the database (remember that in our simple model for customers and accounts above, in the RDBMS we had a third table to hold the relationship between customers and accounts), whereas in a graph store any relationships between any entities can be dynamically stored along with the properties of those relationships without changing the data model. In effect, they enable us to dynamically relate entities in a way that sometimes better suits the complexities of the real world, and then exploit that information much more efficiently than with an RDBMS. Technically, they typically use fixed-length record files and key-value stores to hold the information. Graph stores have found applicability in the banking sector in analysing fraud as they can be used to rapidly identify common aspects and relationships across data sets. For example, payment card fraud has in the past involved shop workers skimming or copying cards when a customer purchases something, then using the details from the cards to make online purchases. The challenge is to look back through all affected cardholders' transactions to see which retailer locations they have in common and with a graph store this is simple, whereas with a relational database it would be a highly intensive activity.

We don't expect that NoSQL databases will replace RDBMSs, but they will find use in circumstances where they offer significantly better performance. We have seen various arguments that NoSQL databases don't offer ACID transactions – in our experience they can and do, but in some implementations (typically very large scale, where data is being replicated across sites or even around the world), a view of the data in one location may not be as up to date as in another location. The same challenge exists with replicating data held in RDBMSs, because of the laws of physics which limit how fast we can transmit data.

To complicate the picture further, you may come across NoSQL databases that provide a SQL interface, that is, can look like a relational database (often with some limitations), and SQL databases that offer NoSQL features.

One further development of databases is noteworthy: the development of in-memory databases, both SQL and NoSQL varieties. These offer significantly faster data access and have been promoted by some vendors as offering much faster batch processing times, e.g. to reduce the time taken to generate the end of month financial accounts in complex corporations (including banks). The risk of a purely in-memory database is that if the server on which it is running crashes, the data would probably be lost. Therefore, in reality, in-memory database technology is used to supplement traditional databases, so that when data is updated it is immediately written to permanent storage (i.e. to a traditional hard drive or solid-state hard drive), and data that is being analysed and not updated is held in memory for faster access.

3.22 Data Analysis and Reporting

Traditionally, there has been a separation between operational platforms, such as core banking platforms, credit card platforms and customer platforms, and platforms used for analysis and reporting. One reason is that we don't want to impact the performance of operational platforms by performing non-urgent analysis or running reports. There are other reasons.

First, operational and analytic databases hold different information. Operational databases record the state of a part of the business, e.g. what accounts a bank's customers have, what customers the bank has and their names and addresses. The databases for banking platforms also typically hold some historical information (e.g. the transactions on each account for the last two years), but in many cases historical information is not kept (e.g. a customer's previous addresses). However, databases used for analysis and reporting purposes need to retain historical information to make comparisons between different periods and look at trends over time.

Second, operational databases are both read (or queried) and written to all the time and therefore are designed for multiple simultaneous queries and updates, whereas databases used for analysis are only written to periodically with new data and then queried intensively the rest of the time, so are designed to respond quickly to queries. Put another way, operational databases are used to execute business processes whereas analytic databases are used to evaluate business processes that have already been executed. Because of the difference between how they are used, the database management systems on which they are based and how data is stored in them are different.

A note on naming: normally, the databases used to analyse data and run reports are called data marts.

3.22.1   Analytic Data Models

As we explained in Section 3.4, operational databases that are based on RDBMSs use normalised data schemas, which define the relationships between entities they hold (e.g. the relationship between customer and accounts is that a customer may have zero or more accounts and an account may have one or more customers) and minimise (or often aim to avoid altogether) any duplication of data. Data marts use what are called dimensional schemas. For example, a bank may want a report on the number of new accounts by type opened at each branch in the previous year. The report should provide a fact (the number of new accounts) by type of account (which is termed a dimension) per branch (which is also a dimension) for a specific period (last year, in this case, which is also a dimension). The data mart from which a user would extract the required report would contain a fact table, which usually holds many rows. Each row would hold an account type identifier, a branch identifier, a date identifier and the number of accounts of that type opened on that date in that branch. In fact, I may want to be able to filter on the employee who opened each account, so that would be yet another field in each row. So, the fact table will contain as many rows as there are lines in the most detailed report that the bank wishes to be able to produce. In addition, there are dimension tables that contain more information on the dimensions (or filters) the bank wishes to use for the report – in this case one containing branch information, one containing employee information, one containing product information and one containing date information. The fact table has foreign keys for each dimension that link it to the dimension tables. Dimension tables typically do not contain large amounts of data – for example, the branch table would contain a list of branches (including closed branches). This is illustrated in Figure 3.40, in which the fact table is at the centre of the diagram, with four dimension tables around it (clockwise from top left for branches, employees, dates and products). For brevity, we have only shown the first four rows in each table. The lines from the fact table to each dimension table indicate where the foreign key for each dimension in the fact table can be found in the corresponding dimension table. As mentioned, each row in the fact table indicates how many products (the value of the Count field) of a specific type (indicated by the Product_FK field) were opened by a particular employee (indicated by the Employee_FK field) in a branch (indicated by the Branch_FK field) on a specific data (indicated by the Date_FK field). So, the first row of data in the fact table shows that Lee Williams opened six retail instant access version 1 accounts in the Hammersmith branch on 13 July 2020.

FIGURE 3.40 Fact and dimension tables for branch sales reporting.

Primary_Key	Employee_ID	First_Name	Family_Name
1000000001	457362	Alex	Adams
1000000002	392875	Chris	Park
1000000003	110495	Lee	Williams
1000000004	837462	Sam	Polk

Primary_Key	Branch_ID	Name	Postcode
1000000001	1001	Hammersmith	W14 1AA
1000000002	1002	Vauxhall	SE1 1RS
1000000003	1003	Watford	WD18 1HX
1000000004	1004	Reading	RG1 1UB

Primary_Key	Branch_FK	Employee_FK	Product_FK	Date_FK	Count
1000000001	1000000001	1000000003	1000000002	1000000001	6
1000000002	1000000001	1000000003	1000000003	1000000001	1
1000000003	1000000001	1000000003	1000000004	1000000001	5
1000000004	1000000002	1000000002	1000000002	1000000001	12

Primary_Key	Date
1000000001	13/7/2020
1000000002	14/7/2020
1000000003	15/7/2020
1000000004	16/7/2020

Primary_Key	Type	Version	Status	Description
1000000001	RFTD	1	Unavailable	Retail fixed term deposit version 1
1000000002	RIAS	1	Available	Retail instant access version 1
1000000003	BIAS	1	Available	Business instant access version 1
1000000004	RFTD	2	Available	Retail fixed term deposit version 1

Such schemas are called star schemas, because the fact table is surrounded by several dimension tables, linked by primary key/foreign key relationships and it looks (vaguely) star shaped. Sometimes schemas are more complex, with the dimension tables having subsidiary tables, in which the schemas are sometimes called snowflake schemas (although they are also still often just called star schemas). Several variants of a report could be produced from the star schema shown in Figure 3.40. For example, one report could show the volume of all product openings per branch per month over the last year. A more detailed report could show the volume of each product opened per branch per month over the last year. Another report could look at the volume of openings of each type of product across all branches according to the day of the week, which may be useful to use for staffing purposes (e.g. branches may have less demand for business banking specialists on the weekend). What this schema couldn't do is provide reporting on what times of the day accounts are opened, because the data is not granular enough. Of course, the source systems for the data may record information on time of opening of each account, but this would have to be loaded into an amended or additional star schema in the data mart.

Another commonly used term in data analysis is data cube (or often just cube). Let us consider a simpler data schema for reporting on product sales where we just look at the number of each type of account opened per branch per day (in other words, we remove the employee dimension), as shown in Figure 3.41. Now we can envisage the fact table shown in this diagram as a large cube made up of lots of smaller cubes, with the three axes of the large cube (x, y and z or left-to-right, front-to-back and bottom-to-top) representing the date, branch and product, respectively, as shown in Figure 3.42.

In this diagram, each small cube contains the number of accounts opened that were of the type corresponding to the position on the z axis at a branch corresponding to the position on the y axis on the date shown on the x axis. So, for example, the cube labelled A would contain the number of retail fixed-term deposit (version 1) accounts, opened on 13 July 2020 at the Hammersmith branch. The cube labelled B would contain the number of business instant access (version 1) accounts opened at the Vauxhall branch on the same date. The cube labelled C (on top of the large cube) would contain the number of retail fixed-term deposit (version 2) accounts opened at the Watford branch on 14 July 2020. The large cube has a small cube for every possible combination of date, branch and product. As before, we have only shown the first four values for each dimension, whereas the cube would extend to cover all the values of the dimensions. The cube analogy also shows where the term *slicing the data* comes from. For example, we can take a vertical slice of the large cube shown in Figure 3.42 comprising the first row of small cubes (i.e. all those with the date of 13 July 2020). If we add up all the values in the small cubes in this slice, we get the total number of all accounts opened on that date across all branches.

Now, we could extend this visualisation to incorporate employees, but we would need to add another dimension to the cube, so it becomes a four-dimensional hyper-cube. Obviously, we can't easily picture this, but we hope the concept is clear. Typically, data cubes have many dimensions.

A data mart is likely to have many star schemas because there may be many different reports that are typically required. There is normally a lot of data that needs to get extracted from the operational databases, transformed to the right format for the data mart(s) that will consume it, and loaded into the data mart(s), and this process needs to take place efficiently with minimal impact on the operational platforms. The next section will explore approaches to this.

FIGURE 3.41 Star schema for simple branch sales reporting.

Primary_Key	Branch_ID	Name	Postcode
1000000001	1001	Hammersmith	W14 1AA
1000000002	1002	Vauxhall	SE1 1RS
1000000003	1003	Watford	WD18 1HX
1000000004	1004	Reading	RG1 1UB

Primary_Key	Branch_FK	Product_FK	Date_FK	Count
1000000001	1000000001	1000000002	1000000001	6
1000000002	1000000001	1000000003	1000000001	1
1000000003	1000000001	1000000004	1000000001	5
1000000004	1000000002	1000000002	1000000001	12

Primary_Key	Date
1000000001	13/7/2020
1000000002	14/7/2020
1000000003	15/7/2020
1000000004	16/7/2020

Primary_Key	Type	Version	Status	Description
1000000001	RFTD	1	Unavailable	Retail fixed term deposit version 1
1000000002	RIAS	1	Available	Retail instant access version 1
1000000003	BIAS	1	Available	Business instant access version 1
1000000004	RFTD	2	Available	Retail fixed term deposit version 1

FIGURE 3.42   A simple data cube.

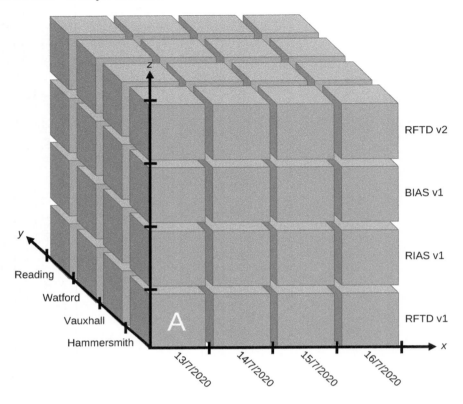

3.22.2   Data Analysis Architectures

Historically, providing daily and periodic reports in a bank would have been done as part of the daily batch processing run (along with all other processing, which was entirely done in batches) of the core banking platform. However, such reporting is limited to what data is kept in the core banking platform's database, and there might not be enough time in the daily batch window to produce some reports as they may require intensive processing. Because of these reasons and because of the advent of online banking platforms and ultimately real-time 24×7 banking, it became necessary to move reporting away from the core banking platform and other operational platforms. Of course, this means that the required data needs to be extracted from the operational platforms and ultimately loaded into a data mart (or, usually, more than one data mart).

Fortunately, the ability to mirror a database in real-time or near real-time as we described in Section 3.5 means that a bank can maintain a copy (or even multiple copies) of the core banking platform's database, take a snapshot of it at a particular point in time (say midnight) and then extract the required information from this snapshot. This is illustrated in Figure 3.43. In this diagram, step 1 is the ongoing real-time or near real-time copying of updates from the live operational banking database to a standby database

FIGURE 3.43 Process of loading a banking data mart.

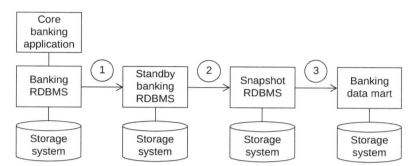

(which is there to provide a recovery capability if the primary database fails). Step 2 is the daily process of taking a snapshot of the standby database (the ability to take a snapshot is a feature provided by enterprise databases) to create a point-in-time copy of the banking database. Data is then extracted from the snapshot database in step 3, transformed and loaded into the banking data mart, typically using specialist ETL (extract, transform and load*) tools.

This approach is fine when the bank has only one operational platform, i.e. its core banking platform. In fact, some core banking platform vendors (and some third parties) sell ready-designed banking data marts that readily integrate with their core banking platforms, providing a standard set of reports and often the ability to customise and add reports.

However, consider the bank with the architecture we set out in Section 3.18, which had several operational platforms – a core banking platform, a credit card platform, a customer platform and a payment platform. The same approach of having a data mart for each operational platform could be used again, but this has the disadvantage that it does not allow reports combining information from across the operational platforms to be easily created. In reality, different departments in the bank will have different requirements on reporting from across the operational platforms, and the data marts should align with each department's requirements. Therefore, it is common for data from the operational platforms to be extracted into what is called an enterprise data warehouse, and from there into data marts that are aligned around business requirements, as shown in Figure 3.44. One debate among data warehouse specialists is whether the enterprise data warehouse should use a relational data model (as promoted by Bill Inmon with such an architecture termed a corporate information factory) or one that is based on star schemas (as promoted by Ralph Kimball with such a data warehouse termed a dimensional data warehouse).[25] In the latter approach, the data marts can be hosted within the data warehouse. We suspect that in practice some (if not many) banks use a hybrid approach.

*Sometimes the order of these steps is extract, load and transform (ELT), which means that data is extracted from one platform, loaded into a database such as the data warehouse and then transformed. This is because databases typically have lots of useful functionality and tools for transforming data, so it can make sense to do the transformation after loading the data into the target datastore.

FIGURE 3.44   Enterprise data warehouse architecture.

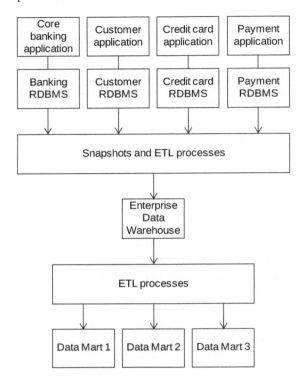

In both cases, however, the enterprise data warehouse usually contains the lowest level of data available from the operational platforms, so that future needs for analysis and reporting can be met without having to re-engineer the ETL processes to extract data from the operational platforms. Of course, the enterprise data warehouse will end up housing huge amounts of data.

Incidentally, the customer matching process we set out in Section 3.8 could use data from the enterprise data warehouse.

3.22.3   Operational Data stores

One challenge with the analysis and reporting architectures described in the previous section is the time (or latency) between operational events happening and them being included in analysis and reports – at a minimum the delay will be overnight if extracts are taken from the operational platforms overnight. For many purposes this is acceptable. However, a bank may want to monitor events in real time or near real time. Of course, the operational platforms can often provide alerts directly. However, an operational data store (ODS) can provide information on events and intraday trends across the operational platforms. The basic approach is that each operational platform sends a stream of events to an operational data store as shown in Figure 3.45, which loads them into its database and provides intraday reports. There are several ways in which the

FIGURE 3.45   Sending data to an operational data store.

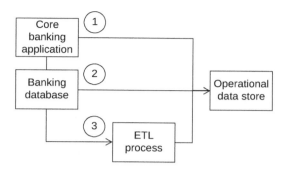

operational platforms can supply the event data – the applications themselves can send information on the event to the ODS (labelled 1 in the diagram) whenever an event that is of interest occurs. In this case, the core banking application shown in the diagram would have to be programmed or configured to do this. The second approach shown (labelled 2) is for the banking database to be set up with what are called triggers. This functionality is provided by RDBMSs, and allows them to be configured so that a stored procedure (see Section 3.4) is executed whenever a record is inserted into or deleted from a table or updated. The stored procedure can then send details of the event to the ODS. Finally (labelled 3), data could be extracted in batches from the banking database at frequent intervals, e.g. every five minutes, and loaded into the ODS. Note that there would also be feeds from the other operational platforms into the same ODS.

All of these approaches have limitations, including adding load and complexity onto the operational platforms, so designers of operational data stores typically have to consider what events will be monitored and with what latency (i.e. the time between an event happening and it being visible in the operational data store). We have seen this approach used to generate marketing events – for example, if a customer receives a large amount of money in their account, the bank may wish branch staff to be alerted within minutes, and for a message to be generated that appears if the customer logs onto Internet or mobile banking with an offer (e.g. to open a savings account). Note also that an ODS can also feed the enterprise data warehouse in place of or (more likely) as well as the operational platforms.

3.22.4   Big Data

The approaches we described in Sections 3.22.1 to 3.22.3 were enough for many banks, and probably still are. However, they do not satisfy all the potential needs of banks.

Storing all the data that a bank can collect (including transaction data, clickstream data from Internet and mobile banking services, unstructured data from customer interactions and correspondence, postings to sub-ledgers, invoices, and system access records) at the finest level of granularity for all time in an enterprise data warehouse is not feasible because the processing power required to extract, transform and load and then analyse such amounts of data and the costs of highly available infrastructure, scaling up the storage area network and software licenses for commercial database software would be prohibitive. In addition, data warehouses only store structured data that has typically come from operational relational databases, therefore excluding things like customer correspondence, in schemas that must be defined before the data can be loaded. So-called big data requires a different technological approach for it to be useable and amenable for analysis such as identifying fraud patterns and fraud attempts, measuring customer propensity and segmenting customers, analysing customer behaviour using the Internet banking and mobile banking services, credit risk scoring, compliance analysis and reporting, and modelling the impact of various scenarios on the bank's financial position. However, an open-source platform called Hadoop, which emerged from Google, and associated tools enable massive amounts of data to be processed across commodity servers and storage, therefore significantly reducing infrastructure and software costs compared to a traditional approach. The use of commodity servers means that cloud computing can also be used. The basic approach is that the data that a bank collects and generates is put into a data lake[*] with zero or minimal transformation. A data lake is really just a file system spread across any number of servers (potentially thousands or more) and so any data that can be stored in file, irrespective of the file format, can be put into a data lake[†] without having to transform it into a format or schema that must be defined in advance, which would be the case with a data warehouse. Of course, incoming data must be categorised in various ways and catalogued so that analysts using the data lake can find the type of data they are looking for, such as the source of the data, date and time information and the type of data. Even data from relational database tables can be extracted into files and stored in a data lake, where tools such as Apache Hive can allow it to be read using SQL as though it were still in a relational database.

With Hadoop, the file system that holds the data is usually configured to store multiple copies of each file, and to split files into chunks that are located on different servers. This means that if a server fails (and with thousands of servers, failures will occur regularly), there are other copies of the data; also, processing the same data for different

---

[*]James Dixon, CTO at Pentaho, is frequently credited as having come up with the term data lake in a post to his blog in October 2010 (see reference 26) in which he wrote:

> If you think of a data mart as a store of bottled water – cleansed and packaged and structured for easy consumption – the data lake is a large body of water in a more natural state. The contents of the data lake stream in from a source to fill the lake, and various users of the lake can come to examine, dive in, or take a sample.

One important point is the notion of business users (or at least business analysts) helping themselves to the contents of the lake without having to involve the technology function. Since then other terms have been coined, such as *data puddle* (a collection of data for use by a single project or for a single purpose – equivalent to a data mart but not in a dimensional schema), a *data pond* (a co-located collection of data puddles but still segregated into separate data puddles/marts), and a *data ocean* in which business users can access data from across the enterprise in a self-service manner without it even being pulled into a data lake. A *data swamp* is a data lake that hasn't attracted much business usage.

[†]We struggle to think what data that a bank has in electronic format to which this does not apply. However, for data to be more easily analysed, some formats would be better than others – so for example, digitised audio files of customer telephone calls would be harder to analyse than transcripts of such calls held as text files, and scans of documents would be harder to analyse than those documents converted to text files using optical character recognition.

purposes can be done simultaneously on different copies of the data held on different servers. Finally, analysis jobs can be run across all the servers, each using its local data, and then the outputs of these jobs combined. Thus data lakes based on Hadoop lend themselves to analysing huge amounts of repetitive, unstructured and structured data (e.g. clickstream data from websites, data from social media, sub-ledger postings from hundreds of entities in large international banks, transaction data from millions of card transactions, event messages emitted by microservices).

One aim of big data is to make data as widely available with as few access permissions as possible so that analysis can draw on the biggest data sets possible. This contrasts with enterprise data warehouses, where typically permission had to be sought from the each of the owning departments to access and use the data it held. Therefore, data entering a data lake goes through a process of what is termed democratisation so that it is freely available (to data and business analysts across the bank), which could include anonymising customer data, and where it cannot be made freely available for it to be categorised to note what restrictions it has on availability. Note that some departments may resist their data being made available to other departments without permission each time it is to be used (or at all), and therefore democratisation of data may meet with a large amount of resistance. We suspect small and medium-sized banks are better at data democratisation than large banks, which are more likely to have function-specific data lakes (sometimes termed data puddles) because each function (e.g. finance, procurement, HR) can still only access their own data. Of course, banks have a huge challenge to understand what data they have that can be made freely available and to what extent it should be desensitised.

3.22.5 *Operational Dashboards and Stream Processing*

In many parts of a bank it is important to monitor processes (and platforms) in real time or near real time. For example, contact centres need to monitor contact volumes so that action can be taken if they are rising to such an extent that contact response times would increase beyond acceptable service levels, payment inflows and outflows need to be monitored so that the bank doesn't run out of settlement reserves, card payment authorisations need to be monitored in case there is a rise in declined authorisations, unexpected volumes of higher-risk transactions (e.g. foreign ATM cash withdrawals) or delays in returning an authorisation, unusual patterns of system logins that could indicate a hacking attempt, and so on. Often operational platforms provide such alerts. However, correlating events across platforms and providing operational dashboards and measuring and displaying executive-level key performance indicators (KPIs) in near real time is much harder. Historically, executive KPIs, typically focused on financial metrics, were available at best overnight and in some cases had to wait until period closures (e.g. every month-end).

One area where such monitoring has routinely been done for many years is around the health of servers, systems and platforms. This is because infrastructure and software very often logs technical events as they happen, typically categorising them into notifications, warnings and errors and sending such logs to monitoring platforms if they are significant enough.* The technology function can monitor the health of the technology estate from the operational dashboards that the monitoring platforms display.

---

*There is a protocol called the Simple Network Management Protocol that was designed to collect information on infrastructure on IP-based networks.

Of course, the same idea could be used to create operational dashboards – in other words, get the operational platforms to send events of interest to a monitoring platform which displays relevant dashboards and monitors the position of key performance indicators. An ODS, which we covered in Section 3.22.3, could potentially be used as the source of data for near-real-time operational dashboards. However, something much more powerful comes out of the microservices approach that we discussed in Section 3.20. Each microservice is supposed to perform one role, and primarily communicate with other microservices using messages. For example, a microservice may open an account for a customer and, when it has done so, publish a message holding information on the account. This message could be read by another microservice that sends a confirmation email to the customer, and another service that generates a request for a letter to be sent to the customer. It could also be read by an operational dashboard service that displays information on how many accounts were opened in the last hour. Of course, a bank with hundreds of microservices would generate tremendous volumes of messages in its normal course of business. Consider, however, that these interservice messages are just repetitive pieces of data that are held on a filing system (often several copies to ensure that a message can't be lost). They form a data lake and can be analysed using Hadoop. This feels to us to be another major advantage of the microservices approach – the operational platforms, built out of microservices, naturally create the data lake that the bank can use for analysis, at scale.

3.23 Further Reading

Unfortunately, we have rarely found material on technology in banking apart from that published by software and infrastructure vendors, which was one of the reasons we decided to write this book. The following list provides further reading, mainly aimed at more technical readers. Only the book on SOA by Dirk Krafzig et al. has much banking-specific material.

Evans, E. (2003). *Domain Driven Design: Tackling Complexity in the Heart of Software.* Upper Saddle River, NJ: Addison-Wesley.
  An often-referenced book, particularly for the definition of the term bounded context, which is important in defining the scope of services (particularly microservices). It becomes apparent through reading this book that designing software well so that it meets business needs is not easy. Complexity of technology (many IT platforms are more complex than any man-made structure ever built) combined with the challenges of reaching common understanding and agreement in large organisations make large IT endeavours challenging, to say the least.
Inamdar, K., Holl, S., Salgueiro, G. et al. (2018). *Understanding Session Border Controllers: Comprehensive Guide to Designing, Deploying, Troubleshooting, and Maintaining Cisco Unified Border Element (CUBE) Solutions.* San Jose, CA: Cisco Press.
  This highly technical book provides a detailed description of the various offerings from Cisco that are used in VoIP implementations in office and contact centre environments. By providing real-world examples, it is a useful addition to the many RFC documents that define the various standards used in VoIP implementations. For the same reason we also studied the online documentation for the Genesys contact centre solutions at help.genesys.com.
Kleppmann, M. (2016). *Making Sense of Stream Processing: The Philosophy Behind Apache Kafka and Scalable Stream Data Platforms.* Sebastopol, CA: O'Reilly Media.

A well-reasoned explanation of a radically different approach to building systems that is based on a fundamental concept used in database management systems (the write ahead log), and explains in detail our conclusion in Section 3.22.5.

Krafzig, D., Banke, K., and Slama, D. (2004). *Enterprise SOA: Service-Oriented Architecture Best Practices*. Upper Saddle River, NJ: Prentice Hall. A pragmatic description of service-oriented architectures backed up with three fairly detailed financial services case studies (including a legacy banking environment at Credit Suisse and the greenfield UK bank Intelligent Finance). The book hints at the microservices approach that was to come a decade later. We worked on designing a new greenfield bank with one of the authors of this book at the turn of the millennium.

Martin, R.C. (2018). *Clean Architecture: A Craftsman's Guide to Software Structure and Design*. Boston, MA: Prentice-Hall.

The author, often referred to as Uncle Bob, provides an experienced view on what is and isn't important when designing and implementing software so that it is testable, maintainable and extensible. It is written in light of the service-oriented architecture and microservices approaches and makes clear that these approaches still require a set of principles for how software is designed and implemented. The autobiographical afterword, recapping Uncle Bob's career, is hugely enjoyable and will resonate with many people who have had a career in IT.

Newman, S. (2015). *Building Microservices*. Sebastopol, CA: O'Reilly Media. This covers the latest fashion in software architecture, which has been enabled by various containerisation technologies and the development of continuous deployment techniques and driven by the need for massively scalable highly available web applications. Some people would claim microservices architecture is just a further development of service-oriented architecture.

Richards, M. and Ford, N. (2020). *Fundamentals of Software Architecture*. Sebastopol, CA: O'Reilly Media.

A summary of different approaches to software architecture. It's fairly clear that the authors think service-oriented architecture was a disaster, which we find to be a fairly common view among our IT colleagues. In reality, it enabled integration on a massive scale in financial services, and probably most other industries, using the tooling and thinking that was current at the time.

Wakelin, P., Farrag, A., Hobson, S. et al. (2012). *Architect's Guide to IBM CICS on System z*. Poughkeepsie, NY: IBM Redbooks.

A technical overview of IBM CICS on IBM mainframes. A lot of the ideas that were incorporated into service-oriented architecture and microservices already existed decades before.

3.24   References

1. American Society of Mechanical Engineers (1984). The IBM 350 RAMAC disk file. https://www.asme.org/wwwasmeorg/media/resourcefiles/aboutasme/who%20we%20are/engineering%20history/landmarks/90-ibm-350-ramac-disk-file.pdf (accessed 22 May 2020).

2. Hyde, R. (2003). *Art of Assembly Language*. San Francisco, CA: No Starch Press.

3. Russell, A.L. (2011). Charles Bachman, an oral history conducted in 2011 by Andrew L. Russell. Hoboken, NJ: IEEE History Center. https://ethw.org/Oral-History:Charles_Bachman (accessed 22 May 2020).

4. Klein, B., Long, R.A., Blackman, K.R. et al. (2012). *An Introduction to IMS: Your Complete Guide to IBM Information Management System*. Second edition. Boston, MA: IBM Press.

5. IBM (2016). Fiducia & GAD IT AG: Bringing high-speed, low-cost, low-risk development to core banking systems. https://www.ibm.com/case-studies/t111146x01262w28 (accessed 14 June 2020).

6. Codd, E.F. (1970). A relational model of data for large shared data banks. *Communications of the ACM* 13 (6): 377–387. doi:10.1145/362384.362685.

7. Prosoft Engineering, Inc. (2017). How long do hard drives last? Lifespan and signs of failure. https://www.prosofteng.com/blog/how-long-do-hard-drives-last (accessed 22 May 2020).

8. IBM (2011). IBM archives: Chronological history of IBM – 1960s: 1968. https://www.ibm.com/ibm/history/history/year_1968.html (accessed 25 May 2020).

9. IBM (2020). CICS transaction server for z/OS Version 5 Release 5 Intercommuni-cation Guide. https://www.ibm.com/support/knowledgecenter/en/SSGMCP_5.5.0/pdf/intercommunication_pdf.pdf (accessed 25 May 2020).

10. Moriarty, K. ed., Kaliski, B., and Rusch, A. (2017). *PKCS #5: Password-Based Cryptography Specification Version 2.1*. RFC 8018, doi:10.17487/RFC8018. https://www.rfc-editor.org/info/rfc8018 (accessed 25 May 2020).

11. Open Web Application Security Project (2019). *Application Security Verification Standard* 4.0. https://owasp.org/www-project-application-security-verification-standard/ (accessed 25 May 2020).

12. M'Raihi, D., Machani, S., Pei, M. et al. (2011). *TOTP: Time-Based One-Time Password Algo-rithm*. RFC 6238, doi:10.17487/RFC6238. https://www.rfc-editor.org/info/rfc6238 (accessed 25 May 2020).

13. Thurlow, R. (2009). *RPC: Remote Procedure Call Protocol Specification Version 2*. RFC 5531, doi:10.17487/RFC5531. https://www.rfc-editor.org/info/rfc5531 (accessed 25 May 2020).

14. The Open Group (1997). *DCE 1.1: Remote Procedure Call*. https://publications.opengroup.org/c706 (accessed 25 May 2020).

15. Object Management Group. Common Object Request Broker Architecture. https://www.omg.com/spec/CORBA/1.0 (accessed 25 May 2020).

16. W3C (2004). Web services glossary – W3C Working Group Note (11 February). https://www.w3.org/TR/ws-gloss/ (accessed 25 May 2020).

17. W3C (2004). Web services architecture – W3C Working Group Note (11 February 2004). https://www.w3.org/TR/2004/ws-arch/ (accessed 25 May 2020).

18. ECMA-404 (2017). *The JSON Data Interchange Syntax*. Second edition. Geneva: ECMA International. http://www.ecma-international.org/publications/standards/Ecma-404.htm (accessed 25 May 2020).

19. Fielding, R.T. (2000). Architectural styles and the design of network-based software architec-tures. PhD thesis. *University of California*.

20. Open Banking (2019). API specifications. https://standards.openbanking.org.uk/api-specifications/ (accessed 5 July 2020).

21. Krafzig, D., Banke, K., and Slama, D. (2004). *Enterprise SOA: Service-Oriented Architecture Best Practices*. Upper Saddle River, NJ: Prentice Hall.

22. Varhol, P. (2015). To agility and beyond: The history – and legacy – of agile development. *Tech-Beacon* (26 August). https://techbeacon.com/app-dev-testing/agility-beyond-history-legacy-agile-development (accessed 5 July 2020).

23. Newman, S. (2015). *Building Microservices*. Sebastopol, CA: O'Reilly Media.

24. Kleppmann, M. (2016). *Making Sense of Stream Processing: The Philosophy Behind Apache Kafka and Scalable Stream Data Platforms*. Sebastopol, CA: O'Reilly Media.

25. Adamson, C. (2010). *Star Schema: The Complete Reference*. New York, NY: McGraw-Hill.

26. Dixon, J. (2010). Pentaho, Hadoop, and Data Lakes. https://jamesdixon.wordpress.com/2010/10/14/pentaho-hadoop-and-data-lakes/ (accessed 13 July 2020).

CHAPTER 4

Channels

4.1 Introduction

Before we explore this topic in detail, we should define what we mean by channels. A channel is simply any one of the various means that a bank employs to communicate with its customers, whether physical, such as a branch, or digital, such as the Internet.

In this section we look at the various channels available to banks, discuss the challenges and opportunities presented by each channel and, for the most important channels, the technology that supports them.

It wasn't so long ago that there really was only one channel over which your bank could engage with you, which was face to face. This could be a market stall, the local temple, your home, an office location or a branch, with the location depending upon the point in history and the type of bank. Customers would physically meet with their bankers to carry out their business, be that depositing money, withdrawing money, opening an account, taking out a loan or pretty much any other banking activity. The physical channel was the means through which a bank could interact with its customers. For many people, the local bank manager, or agent, really was their only way to engage with their bank.

As we noted in Chapter 2, some of the constraints imposed by the need for face-to-face interaction were overcome, to some extent, by the creation of branch networks during the Middle Ages. In fact, the concept of a branch bank has now been at the core of banking for so long that many modern banks still operate a branch model even in their core banking platforms. In the UK, for example, the sort code (part of the method of addressing a domestic payment) is a reference to a branch and some core banking platforms even have the concept of a branch built directly into the software, including the financial reporting. The branch network, as far as the technology platform is concerned, is the bank.

Although the branch concept still influences much of how banks operate, it is by no means the only channel that we use today. Banks now often support a diverse range of channels, many of them based upon advances in telecommunications, be that mobile banking, Internet banking or the telephone.

The use of telephones to provide basic banking services, such as account balance information, occurred as early as the second half of the 1950s, and the first telephone-only bank, First Direct, was launched in 1989. This first foray into the world of direct banking was destined to be followed by an explosion of other direct banking businesses and models as the array of telecommunications technologies exploded in the late twentieth and early twenty-first century. Since the 1990s, the explosive growth of the Internet and the more recent development of smartphones and tablets has extended the number of channels to what we know today.

Of course, the channels mentioned earlier only really cover those mediums that support two-way communications, where the transmission of data can be initiated from either end of the connection. One-way push channels have also existed for many years in the form of printed media, radio and television. These one-way channels are still an important means of raising awareness of a bank and its offerings and, while social media has captured much marketing expenditure, the traditional channels should not be underestimated.

In the modern era, the number of channels available, and the uses to which those channels have been put, have proliferated. Modern banks have a variety of ways in which they can engage customers and they need to deploy, manage and maintain those channels with skill and purpose.

4.2   Branches

Banks used to have branches for two reasons: first, they provided a place where customers could engage with members of the bank, e.g. to negotiate a loan or deposit some cash, and second, they could hold cash and other valuables safely. Also, customers were more likely to deposit their money (and other valuables) with a bank if it had a permanent establishment. Of course, in order to market the bank and to generate more business, having prominent and easily accessible branches was highly desirable, and growing a network of branches was also desirable, as more branches meant more customers. However, in the modern era, when most money is electronic and banking can be carried out over the Internet or by phone, the rationale for having branches has weakened, and customers' association with specific branches has also weakened – after all, if I open an account online, I don't feel an association with any particular branch, and in fact many banks don't associate customers with any specific branch any more. The result, as we saw in Chapter 2, is that the total number of bank branches in developed markets looks to have been declining since around 2010. In fact, we note that the redundancy of branches because of digitisation and the transformation to a cashless and chequeless society was already being forecast in the late 1960s.[1] Nonetheless, there is still demand for branch banking, including small business customers wanting to deposit cash takings and get notes and coins and retail customers wanting face-to-face service, particularly for more complex products such as mortgages. High-profile branches still provide a way for a bank to market itself. Governments are also concerned about financial inclusion, with physical cash still being of huge importance to some segments of society, including the least well-off, and so branch closures (and lack of ATMs) can come under political and regulatory scrutiny. A modern branch is a complex and expensive environment and, with the shift towards digital banking, is generally regarded as being under threat.

Unless regulators or governments intervene, established banks therefore have a choice about their branches – to close the ones that they deem to be economically unviable, retaining only those that are useful for marketing purposes or that generate enough revenue, or to reinvent them in order to make them economically viable. What is clear is that there is a need for the branch format to adapt if it is to stay relevant through the twenty-first century. In the UK, for example, there are a variety of banks that are developing alternatives to the staid old British bank branch. Metro Bank has led the way in trying to breathe new life into the branch, through enhanced customer service (such as seven-day opening), rapid account opening, instant printing of payment cards and chequebooks, safe deposit boxes (which had all but disappeared from all large UK banks by the time Metro Bank was launched), free coin counting machines (the other large UK banks discourage their customers from depositing coins) and the use of technology to support better customer engagement (tablets, for example, remove the barriers that a desktop PC and monitor place between staff and their customers). However, it would be a mistake to think that Metro Bank's branch technology is the key driver of its success. The customer-focused culture plays an equally important role in ensuring that customers' needs are met (in fact, internally Metro Bank aims to exceed customers' expectations) and it is the combination of culture, process and technology that really makes Metro Bank stand out to its customers.

Fully staffed branches are not the only model that banks are testing on the UK high street. Other banks are seeking to turn their branches more digital, by introducing technology to better support the customers' needs. A good example of this is NatWest's digital branch concept, which includes free Wi-Fi, video facilities, iPads and technical support staff.[2] Some banks are looking closer at creating engaging spaces, where customers can go to relax. Virgin Money, for example, launched banking branch lounges in 2012 where the focus was as much on relaxation as it was about banking.[3] The use of the word *lounge* brings to mind airport passenger lounges and, in reality, this is pretty close to how these branches felt inside. In an even more interesting development, three banks – Barclays, Lloyds and NatWest – announced the launch of shared mini branches, where all three banks would be able to serve their customers alongside each other in March 2019.[4]

The UK, of course, is not the only place that such innovation is occurring. In the United States, both JPMorgan Chase[5] and Bank of America[6] are aggressively pursuing innovative branch strategies. The former launched a branch in Harlem in 2019 that hosts community events covering topics such as financial management, job application and small business skills development. In 2017, the latter launched robo-branches in Minneapolis and Denver that are unmanned. In Thailand, the banks have, for many years, deployed different branch formats to appeal to customers at different points in the wealth spectrum – branches aimed at wealthier customers, for example, often have more space, more staff, more comfortable furnishings and better-quality refreshments. The branch, it would seem, is not dead, but it is evolving.

Which, if any, of these new branch models succeeds remains to be seen. However, one thing is absolutely true: for any of them to succeed, the key will be in the execution. The challenge in branch banking is to bring together the right technology, people and processes to support the bank in achieving its goals. Whereas many newer banks are focusing on digital-first strategies that are arguably simpler to implement, the branch requires an altogether more comprehensive approach that includes technology, comprehensive staff training, culture and an approach to branch locations that maximises the return on the cost of the property lease. In fact, location is the key consideration at Metro Bank when looking for a new branch (or what it prefers to call store) location – like all retailers, it considers footfall to be king.

4.3   Branch Technology

Historically, the accounts of a customer of a bank were held at that customer's branch, in large books called ledgers. When accounts were first computerised, the computers were located in different buildings from the branches and were not directly connected to the branches. Staff in each branch would input transaction data into a machine that recorded it onto paper tape (and later magnetic tape) which was then either physically transported to the computer centre or read by another machine that transmitted the data over a telephone line to the computer centre. Over time, branches got terminals that connected directly to the computer centre using telephone lines – and, in some banks, once computers were cheap and small enough, their own computers – the original branch platform holding information on the accounts at the branch where it was located. So within such a branch you would have an architecture with a number of green screen terminals wired directly to a minicomputer running the branch banking application, as shown in Figure 4.1.

The minicomputer would have a tape drive attached to it, which was used to copy information from its storage to be sent to the bank's central data centre for safekeeping, for consolidation into the accounts of the bank as a whole and to provide details of payments being made to other branches and banks (e.g. customers of this branch paying bills where the billers' accounts were at other branches or banks). Typically, a van would pick up the tape every day and at the same time deliver a tape of payments information (e.g. payments made at other banking institutions or other branches destined for the accounts at this branch). The tape drive could also be used for loading updated information (e.g. changes to branch numbers and addresses) and new software into the minicomputer (e.g. updates to the branch banking application).

FIGURE 4.1   Terminals connecting to a branch platform.

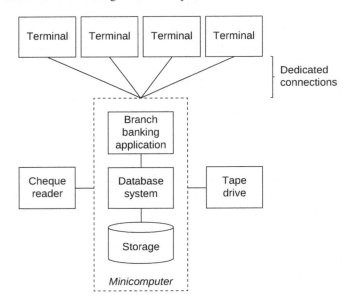

One other historical role of a branch was to process cheques drawn on the accounts at that branch, and in some countries it was the law (and may still be in some jurisdictions) that cheques had to be physically returned to the branch where the accounts were held. Of course, given that the accounts were being maintained at a branch, this was necessary so that the branch could validate each cheque and ensure that the funds were available to actually pay it. The cheque reader shown in Figure 4.1 can read the machine-readable text, known as an MICR (magnetic ink character recognition) code, on a cheque (typically giving details of the bank, branch and account the cheque is drawn on) which partially automates the entry of cheques into the branch banking platform. Someone in the branch would still have to check the signature and date and enter the amount written on the cheque into the branch banking application and see if there were sufficient available funds to honour the cheque. Typically, if the cheque was not validated (e.g. incorrectly written, incorrect signature) or the funds were not available, it then had to be returned to the bank that had first received it (i.e. the beneficiary's bank) so that they could alert the beneficiary that it had been returned and the funds would therefore not be paid into their account. If the cheque was successfully validated and could be honoured, then the bank would transfer the funds to the other bank.

Given that the accounts of a customer were held in their branch, if they went into a different branch the staff there would have to telephone the customer's branch to do things like check the customer's account balance and to update the balance if the customer wished to withdraw cash.

We also expect that in smaller or satellite branches there may have been a terminal with a dial-up connection via a modem connected to a telephone line to the minicomputer in a bigger branch, as shown in Figure 4.2.

Such a branch platform may well have also been used to control specialised passbook printers in the branch and maintain records of over-the-counter cash deposits and withdrawals so that the amount of cash in each teller's drawer was tracked (which would facilitate decisions relating to ordering in more physical cash or deciding when to send physical cash out of the branch).

Finally, the branch platform would have an end-of-day process including batch payment processing, reconciliation of over-the-counter cash transactions and cash held at the branch and production of branch activity reports (e.g. volume and value of transactions in the branch).

Over time, banks installed network connections to their branches. These were initially dial-up connections using modems and, over time, ISDN* or leased line

---

*ISDN (Integrated Services Digital Network) is a technology that telecommunications companies provide and that comes in two flavours. First, as a domestic or small business customer you could buy an ISDN line from your local telco – what is termed a Basic Rate Interface (BRI) service. An ISDN connection reuses the existing copper telephone wires from the exchange or street cabinet to the home or business and provides one or two channels that can be used to either make and receive calls or send and receive data at a guaranteed maximum rate of 64 kbit/s in each channel, and depending on which variant of ISDN is used, a 16kbit/s channel used to send and receive signalling information (e.g. CLI and DNIS information on a call using one of the other channels). This means that with an existing copper phone line you could get, for example, two phone lines or a phone line and a guaranteed-bandwidth Internet connection (albeit only 64 kbit/s). With the advent of ADSL ultimately offering up to 20 Mbit/s with the simultaneous ability to use the phone for voice calls over a copper telephone line, in some markets the take-up of this type of ISDN connection was minimal

FIGURE 4.2   Satellite branch with a terminal connecting to the main branch platform.

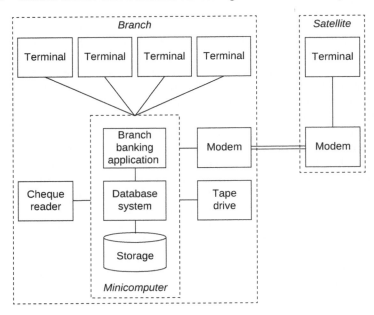

connections and then, most recently, broadband connections. This removed the need to ship tapes and ultimately removed the need for local branch platforms (and the costs associated with them) altogether. A modern banking institution will almost certainly maintain customers' accounts using a central core banking platform. Some institutions still associate customers to specific branches (e.g. because their relationship manager is located there), and end-of-day processing as it relates to a branch must still take place (e.g. cash reconciliation). All the functions of a branch platform could be provided by the core banking platform, or there could still be a dedicated branch platform, albeit run centrally.

With the centralisation of core banking platforms, the need to send cheques back to each branch disappeared (unless the law in that jurisdiction still required it) and banks established centralised cheque processing centres and could therefore remove cheque payment processing from branches other than physical receipt of cheques over the counter and printing of cheques and banker's drafts on demand. They may have kept cheque readers to keep the ability to capture account information to send with the cheque for processing, although we note that in many bank branches these have disappeared.

---

to non-existent. However, in some markets BRI ISDN was commonly used by some businesses, e.g. to connect bank branches to the bank's central data centre. However, BRI ISDN is likely to disappear because broadband connections provide more bandwidth and flexibility. Second, ISDN is also used in trunk lines – these are connections either between telephone exchanges or between telephone exchanges and corporate data networks that carry multiple channels, each channel being used for a voice call or for data transmission. You may still come across these to connect corporate networks across sites.

The functions required in a branch encompass:

- Managing tellers and their access to the bank's platforms.
- Keeping track of deposits into and withdrawals from cash drawers and cash recyclers, performing cash reconciliation and scheduling cash deliveries and pickups.
- Accepting cheques and sending them for centralised processing.
- Managing specialised printers and scanners in each branch.
- Handling appointments with customers, including maintaining diaries of branch staff.
- Identifying and verifying customers who enter the branch. Some banks use specialised equipment for scanning and verifying ID documents.
- Opening new products for customers.
- Updating customer information.

We can now set out what technology a modern branch would have in it, as shown in Figure 4.3. In this setup, we have four workstations for tellers, each equipped with a PC that has the thick client for the teller installed on it, and to which are directly connected (probably using a USB connection) a cash recycler, a card terminal and a passbook printer. The cash recycler is a specialised piece of equipment that verifies, counts and sorts banknotes that are put into it and also dispenses banknotes. It is under the control of the teller client, and automatically handles banknote counting and dispensing on behalf of the teller. It is also a security measure in that it is in effect a safe for the cash it is holding and it can be configured to dispense a maximum amount of money, so in the event of a hold-up the bank's cash loss is limited. The card terminal accepts Chip and PIN cards and has a keypad for customers to enter their card PIN in order to identify themselves. It too communicates with the teller client on the teller's PC. Finally, the specialised printer is used for printing banker's drafts, receipt slips and so on, and may also handle passbooks if the bank still uses them.

We've also shown two customer service desks, where customers can sit with a member of the branch staff and open accounts and perform other services. These comprise a PC with the customer service client installed, to which is connected (again via USB) a PIN entry keypad (with card reader), a camera and a specialised ID document scanner. These are all used for opening products. For example, say a new customer wants to open a current account. During the process of opening an account, equipment in the branch may be used as follows.

- *Scanning and checking the customer's official ID document(s):* The document scanner is a highly sophisticated machine that not only takes an image of the relevant documents, but can also verify certain security features in them (e.g. the presence of holograms). It, or the customer service client program, can read some of the customer's personal information using optical character recognition and load this automatically into a new customer record.
- *Taking a photo of the customer:* The camera is used to take a photo of the customer which can be stored on record and used in the future as another way to verify the customer's identity in a branch.
- *Capturing a PIN securely:* The PIN entry keypad can capture and set the PIN the customer wishes to use for their payment card(s). Alternatively, a PIN could be mailed to the customer.

FIGURE 4.3 Modern branch technology.

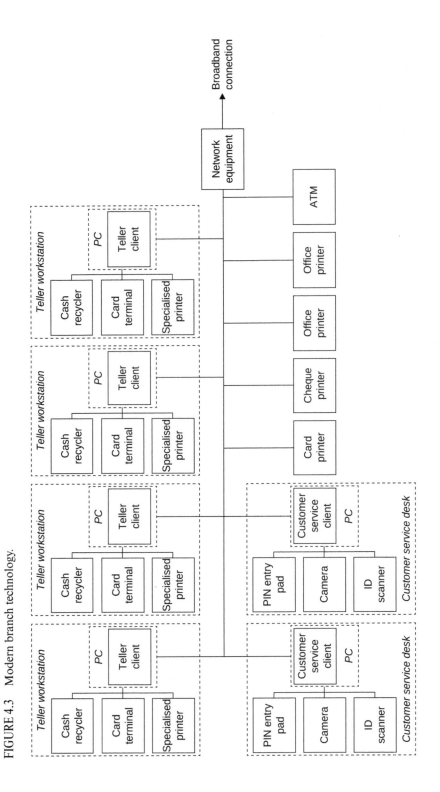

- *Printing chequebooks and plastic cards:* There's some shared specialised equipment in the branch – the card printer and the cheque printer that can produce new plastic cards and chequebooks. The card printer takes blank plastic cards, prints the front and back of them and embosses them with the card number, issue and expiry dates and cardholder names. It also writes the required information onto the magnetic stripe and chip and burns in the cardholder verification value on the signature strip. Alternatively, a chequebook and plastic card(s) could be produced centrally and mailed to the customer.

Finally, as you may expect, there are office printers and an ATM in the branch, and some networking equipment using a broadband connection to connect to the parent bank's network and through that to platforms in its data centre(s). There may be more than one set of networking equipment and dual broadband connections in case one fails.

As well as what we have shown in Figure 4.3, we'd expect the branch to contain cameras, with a video recorder and other security measures (e.g. a safe with tamper detection equipment). Some branches also have coin counting machines.

This would be a relatively expensive branch, given the specialised equipment we envisage it contains, and in reality there are few banking institutions that would have all of this equipment or have it all integrated to the same extent we have described here. For example, the teller cash recyclers could be standalone devices and the teller has to manually enter into the teller client how much cash they deposit with them and also manually type into the cash recycler how much cash to issue. Many banks do not use stationery that require specialised printers (such as passbooks or stationery which requires magnetic ink) anymore, and so regular office printers may be used to print documents.

4.4 Post

Postal banking products, where most account management can be carried out through the postal system, were at one time quite popular. In fact, National Savings and Investments, a UK-based business which still carries out a large amount of business through the postal system, has some 25 million customers (almost 40% of the UK population) as at July 2020.[7] However, modern postal banking products often use a variety of channels in order to provide the full range of services to customers and, frankly, broaden their appeal. Postal accounts typically have a very particular customer base, most of which is made up of people who have little engagement or interest in modern digital channels and, frankly, have much more patience than the rest of us. Postal propositions have some benefits (for the bank) over digital systems in that the channel is relatively hard work from a customer perspective and therefore discourages withdrawals – accounts that don't often see withdrawals tend to be referred to as sticky by bankers. To overcome the opposite issue – that is, barriers to customers making deposits – many postal savings accounts offer competitive rates of interest and regular deposit capabilities such as deposit by standing order. The additional benefit that postal products provide is that the platforms that support it can be fairly basic. There is no need for 24×7 uptime, teller functionality can be mainly manual, and staff can be trained to work around platform issues, all without any degradation to customer service. However, the minute that digital channels or contact centres enter the scene, much of this changes.

Historically, a customer would have addressed their letters to their branch, which would have received them in the post and responded to them as required as part of the normal activities in a branch. However, a modern-day bank is highly likely to have centralised handling of both incoming and outgoing post. A bank may well use different addresses for different categories of post, e.g. for cheques that are being deposited by post, for payment requests such as giro payments, for customer complaints, for general customer correspondence, for application forms, for business banking mandates and so on. Some post can be handled as it would be by tellers in a branch, with corresponding technology requirements. A modern bank would scan general correspondence and retain it electronically as part of the records corresponding to the customers that sent it. A workflow system could be used to route correspondence to the appropriate team or person for review and response. Some banks have used optical character recognition for processing application forms, although with customers encouraged to apply online, we expect the volume of such post has declined hugely.

Outgoing correspondence is often fulfilled (i.e. printed and posted) by third parties. The obvious example is monthly bank statements. To send these, typically a bank agrees on a template with the fulfilment provider and then will send it a file containing the required data (for each statement this would include the customer name and address, transaction data, marketing messages and so on). Core banking platforms often have the functionality to produce such files. The provider prints the data onto the relevant stationery, inserts it into an envelope and posts it. Banks encourage customers to go paperless, with statements available through the Internet banking service or mobile app, as this can significantly reduce the cost of running an account, particularly given the cost of postage.

4.5 Automated Teller Machines

Most people are familiar with the basic functions of automated teller machines (ATMs): a customer enters their card and can withdraw cash, check their balance, change their card PIN and perhaps carry out a small number of other actions. Originally a bank would have provided ATMs for the use of its own customers only, with very limited functionality such as dispensing a fixed amount of cash when a customer put a token into the machine – the ATM would retain the token so that it could not be used again. Such ATMs were not connected to any other platforms in the bank, and there would have been a manual process to get the list of transactions carried out at each ATM each day and record these on the corresponding accounts.

As well as cash withdrawals and balance enquiries, ATMs can support magnetic stripe, Chip and PIN, and contactless cards, authorisation by smartphone and Quick Response (QR) codes, account opening (with document scanning), video calling, biometric authentication and much, much more. ATM manufacturers are even deploying facial recognition capabilities.[8]

4.5.1 Basic Arrangement of a Bank's ATMs

With the increasing availability of telephone lines, ATMs could become more sophisticated. In the 1970s, ATMs were increasingly connected to other platforms in the bank with a setup as represented in Figure 4.4. Each customer was issued with an ATM card with a magnetic stripe.

In this representation, each of the bank's ATMs is connected to a telephone line. When a customer uses an ATM, the ATM dials the ATM host in the bank's data centre to verify the customer's ATM card and PIN and check the available balance on the corresponding customer account. Because core banking platforms typically processed account transactions and recalculated account balances only during the end-of-day process (i.e. they were batch-oriented), it was necessary for the ATM host to get the latest balances of all accounts that had an ATM card issued as soon as this was available from the core banking platform at the start of the day. Figure 4.5 shows the process that takes place when a customer withdraws cash at an ATM.

As well as this process, at the end of the day, the ATM host sends a file of all ATM cash withdrawals to the core banking platform for it to include in its end-of-day processing of transactions. The cash withdrawal process means the ATM can dial up the ATM switch just once to issue cash to a customer. Of course, the ATM could fail to dispense cash because it gets stuck or there is a physical failure. In this case, the ATM will log the transaction as failed (and the receipt provided to the customer should also state it has failed), and ultimately when the ATM's transaction log is reconciled with the core banking platform, this will get identified and the customer's account will be rectified.

The ATM management platform shown in Figure 4.4 can dial up each of the ATMs and download information from them (e.g. amount of cash remaining, transaction logs) and send instructions (e.g. to tell an ATM to take itself offline or bring itself back online) and upload changes to screens and software onto the ATMs. The ATM host may also communicate with the ATM management platform so that the ATM management platform can monitor the activity level of each ATM. In some implementations the ATM host and ATM management platform may be combined.

FIGURE 4.4   Basic arrangement of ATMs.

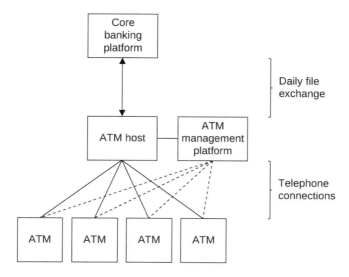

FIGURE 4.5   Historical process of withdrawing cash from an ATM.

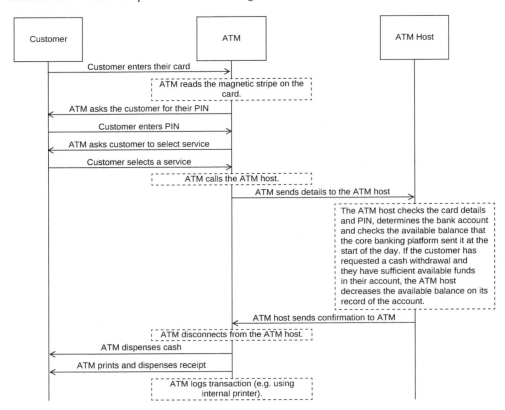

Dial-up phone line connections were replaced over time with network connections and ATMs have become more sophisticated, and whereas they were little more than terminals originally, modern ATMs can provide a much broader range of functions, including:

- Transfers between accounts held by the same customer
- Bill payments (either from a list of payees already set up by the customer or by scanning a bill)
- Cash and cheque deposits
- Allowing a customer to change their PIN
- Donations to charity
- Mobile network top-up
- Dispensing cash using a contactless card or without a card at all by entering a code or by scanning a QR code on a smartphone or piece of paper
- Video chats with a customer service representative
- Dispensing foreign currency

In a more modern bank, with an online core banking platform, the ATM host can now go directly to the core banking platform to get the latest available balance for an

FIGURE 4.6   Modern arrangement of a bank's ATMs.

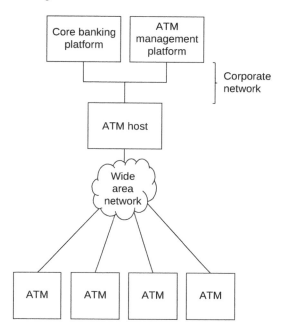

account and to update the available balance on the core banking platform immediately following a cash withdrawal. So, an updated arrangement for a bank's ATMs might be as shown in Figure 4.6.

There are several other ways in which the cash withdrawal process shown in Figure 4.5 would be different with modern ATMs. An ATM may present screens tailored to each specific customer. For example, a customer may have a preferred cash withdrawal amount and so an ATM could present this as the first option. The ATM could present marketing messages tailored to each customer. Modern ATMs read the chip inside Chip and PIN cards in preference to the magnetic stripe. Also, cash withdrawals are normally cleared as soon as they happen, and not at the end of the day. This means that ATMs do not have to send a list of all transactions at the end of the day.

4.5.2   ATM Hardware, Software and Message Formats

Internally, ATMs comprise a number of modules which normally include:

- ATM computer
- Screen (often a touchscreen)
- Encrypting PIN pad (which includes specialised cryptographic hardware for encrypting the PIN before it is transmitted to the ATM computer)
- Audio socket (intended for visually impaired users to get audio guidance using headphones)

- Motorised card reader that reads the chip in modern payment cards (also with the ability to read the magnetic stripe for cards without a chip and to retain cards that are left or notified as stolen or lost)
- Cash-dispensing unit (that also detects and withholds damaged notes and counts notes)
- Banknote storage cassette(s)
- Printer and receipt dispenser (for issuing receipts)
- Networking equipment for connecting to the bank's wide area network (some ATMs can connect via a mobile connection or a broadband Internet connection)
- Supervisor module (e.g. to allow the ATM to be reset, loaded with cash, etc.)

An ATM could also include other modules such as:

- Scanner (ranging from a barcode or QR code scanner to a cheque or document scanner)
- Envelope dispenser
- Motorised receptacle to receive deposits
- Deposit cassette to securely store deposits
- Contactless card reader
- Camera(s) (for video calling and security)
- Journal printer (for logging transactions)
- Biometric devices (e.g. fingerprint scanner)
- Battery power backup

Some ATMs even have modules to recycle banknotes, much like teller cash recyclers in bank branches. There are also security devices which may include a lock, sensors to detect attempts to move or penetrate the ATM, an alarm system and indelible ink in the banknote storage cassettes that is released if they are tampered with.

As we have already stated, ATMs were originally specialised terminals, with proprietary hardware and software. A modern ATM computer is highly likely to be built using standard PC hardware, running a variant of Microsoft Windows or, less commonly, Linux (in 2014 Robert Johnston, a marketing director at NCR, an ATM supplier, claimed that 95% of ATMs were running Windows XP[9]). In order to communicate with the other components inside the ATM and with the ATM management platform, there are various options for what software should be run on the PC.

First, for ATM computers based on the Microsoft Windows operating system there is a platform called XFS (eXtensions for Financial Services), which is defined by the European Committee for Standardization (CEN; see www.cen.eu) and illustrated in Figure 4.7.

This is predicated on the basis that the ATM is controlled by a Windows application written by the ATM manufacturer or supplier. This application will in turn communicate with the XFS Manager using the XFS application interface. CEN provides sample code for the XFS Manager. The XFS Manager in turn communicates with a number of service providers, which are also software components, using the XFS service provider interface. Each service provider represents a service that one of the modules inside the ATM provides (e.g. printing a receipt is a service) and communicates with that module. One module may have more than one service.

FIGURE 4.7   ATM based on the XFS platform.

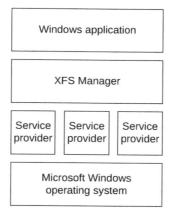

FIGURE 4.8   ATM based on the J/XFS platform.

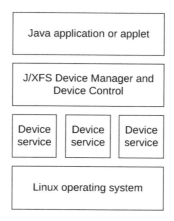

Second, there's a similar platform for ATM computers which is not restricted to Microsoft Windows, J/XFS, also defined by CEN, which will work on any computer that can run Java applications. So, for example, it could run on a Linux platform, as shown in Figure 4.8.

In this case, the ATM application written in Java uses the J/XFS platform to interact with the modules inside the ATM through device services (similar in concept to the service providers used by XFS). Some vendors claim that basing an ATM on Linux instead of Windows avoids the challenges in migrating to a new version of Windows when support ends for the version used by a bank's ATMs, although we note that security updates are also only available for releases of various Linux distributions for a certain number of years.

Finally, there is yet another approach that could potentially be used, using a standard called Xpeak (specified at www.xpeak.org). This defines standard XML message formats for different types of modules found inside an ATM. It isn't specific to any operating system, programming language or communication protocol so may offer different approaches to building an ATM than XFS or J/XFS, but probably with more work to be done to build a functioning ATM.

These standards are also used for other devices such as POS terminals and teller cash recyclers. The teller client program and the customer service client program we showed in our final example of a branch may use one of them.

The application running on an ATM also has to communicate with the ATM switch and ATM management platform. This was typically done using message formats that were proprietary to each ATM manufacturer such as NDC and NDC+ (used by ATMs supplied by NCR), DDC 911 and DDC 912 (used by ATMs supplied by Diebold), IBM ATM message formats and others. Other manufacturers of ATMs have configured their ATMs to use these message formats as well for easier integration into existing ATM estates. There is an initiative run by Nexo Standards to establish a modern standard for ATM messaging (see www.nexo-standards.org) based on the ISO 20022 financial message standard.

A bank or ATM operator may find itself with a heterogeneous set of ATMs using different messaging formats by having acquired them at different times and as a legacy of mergers and acquisitions. ATM switches will usually deal with any ATM message format, but the efficient management of a varied set of ATMs (e.g. ensuring that they are all using the same screen designs) may be more difficult. There are independent suppliers of ATM application software based on the XFS and J/XFS standards and of ATM management platforms that can work with a wide range of ATMs, which may provide a route to more efficient management of a mixed ATM estate.

4.5.3   ATM Networks

Starting in the 1980s, banks began networking their ATM networks* with other banks so that customers of a range of banks could use any of the ATMs provided by that group of banks. This resulted in the development of national ATM schemes such as LINK in the UK, PLUS in the US, Multibanco in Portugal, ServiRed in Spain, the Eurocheque ATM network in Germany and so on. Figure 4.9 shows how two banks would be connected to enable a customer of one bank to withdraw cash at an ATM of the other bank.

In this diagram, the box labelled ATM scheme switch represents a platform that is operated by the ATM scheme and connects the members of the scheme, including Bank A and Bank B as shown here. Note how we have replaced the ATM host in each of the banks shown here with an ATM switch – the two perform broadly the same functions, but the switch terminology is used because the ATM switch must switch (or route) each transaction message between the ATM and either the core banking platform (if a customer is using an ATM at their own bank) or the ATM scheme for that transaction (if a customer of another bank is using an ATM), which we will explain next.

Let's consider what happens if an account holder at Bank A uses their ATM card to withdraw cash from an ATM at the same bank. The ATM recognises that the card

---

*Note that when we talk about ATM networks, we mean networks of automated teller machines. The term ATM network can also mean a data network that uses a technique called asynchronous transfer mode, which is something entirely different.

FIGURE 4.9   Basic network of ATMs.

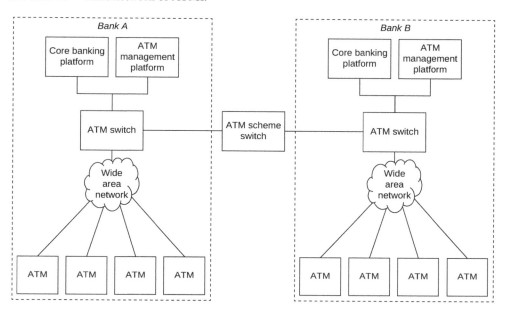

has been issued by Bank A by either looking at the first few digits of the card number, which are unique to the institution that issued the card, or by checking the information in the chip on the card. In this case it is called an *on-us* transaction and the ATM displays screens that are specific to customers of the bank and that may offer more features (e.g. access to several different accounts, transfers between them, deposits and so on). The ATM then sends a transaction message to Bank A's ATM switch. The ATM switch also recognises that this is an on-us transaction and checks and reduces the available balance on the bank's core banking platform and responds with a message back to the ATM, which issues the cash.

Now suppose a customer of Bank B inserts their card in an ATM at Bank A. The ATM they are using recognises that the card has not been issued by Bank A and that it is a card from a member of the ATM scheme. This means it can display appropriate screens, which tend to be mandated by the ATM scheme and are necessarily more generic and limited compared to what it would present to a customer of Bank A. Let's assume the cardholder asks to withdraw cash. The ATM then sends a message to Bank A's ATM switch to which it is connected with various details, including the card number, expiry date, PIN, cash withdrawal amount and so on. Bank A's ATM switch also checks the card number and determines that it is not issued by Bank A and that it is issued by another member of the ATM scheme. So, it reformats the message and sends it to the ATM scheme's switch. Note that it is normally necessary to reformat the message from the proprietary formats typically used by ATMs to the format mandated by the ATM scheme, which is usually based on a version of the ISO 8583 financial message standard (see Chapter 6). The ATM scheme's switch checks the message and determines which member should receive it. It sends the message to Bank B's ATM switch, which also checks that the message is valid and then checks with the core banking platform that the customer has enough available funds, that the card isn't stolen or lost and that the PIN is correct. Bank B's ATM switch then replies via the ATM scheme's switch to Bank A's ATM switch, which informs the ATM that the withdrawal is authorised. The ATM issues the cash.

As cash has been dispensed, Bank B must pay Bank A for the cash. The ATM scheme calculates the net position of each participating member, typically daily, and arranges settlement payments. It will also bill the members for use of the scheme and collect any fees that may be charged for one bank's cardholders using a different member's ATMs. Such fees are typically set by the scheme.

In Figure 4.9, we only showed two members of the ATM scheme. Most schemes would have many more members than this. In some countries, independent operators of ATMs have also arisen, often taking over ATMs that banks decided were too expensive to operate themselves and also installing ATMs in shops and other locations. In the UK Cardtronics and NoteMachine, two independent ATM operators, now operate more ATMs than the banks combined. In such markets, banks may no longer need to operate ATM networks, although they will often still have arrangements with an independent ATM operator to brand ATMs as their own. An ATM operator typically makes money from the fees for using its ATMs which are either charged directly to the cardholders who use those ATMs (by adding the fee to the amount debited from a cardholder's account so a cardholder would see an ATM cash withdrawal transaction for the amount of cash withdrawn plus the ATM operator fee) or collected from the cardholder's bank via the scheme.

This has resulted in national ATM environments that look like that shown in Figure 4.10. On the top left is a processor member. This organisation doesn't have ATMs of its own, and in the first instance provides authorisation services to other banks. For ATM cards, a bank such as Bank C shown here may use a processor because its own platforms can't maintain an intraday account balance, which is required to authorise ATM withdrawals (and also debit card purchases). So as part of its end-of-day (or start-of-day) process, Bank C sends all its account balances to the processor, who then maintains an intraday balance on the accounts and authorises ATM withdrawals. The processor needs its own online core platform as shown to do this. At the end of day, the processor (or the scheme) sends details of the transactions back to Bank C so it can update its own platform.

Sometimes banks still use a processor even though their own core banking platform is used to authorise ATM withdrawals (and debit card purchases), which is the case for Bank D shown in the diagram. Such a bank may still wish to use a processor as its own platform may not be available 24 hours a day (in which case the processor and Bank D would exchange account balances as in the case with Bank C) or because the processor also provides other functions such as card management (e.g. issuing cards, dealing with lost and stolen cards etc.), transaction fraud detection, customer services related to cards and scheme settlement. Bank D may have decided it doesn't want to invest in such platforms or processes and may not have or want to develop the expertise to operate them.

Banks, processors and ATM operators are likely to participate in more than one card scheme. For example, a bank or ATM operator may participate in a national ATM scheme (e.g. LINK in the UK) and also accept Mastercard, Visa and other international payment schemes' cards in its ATMs. The ATM switch at such a bank or ATM

FIGURE 4.10   National ATM network.

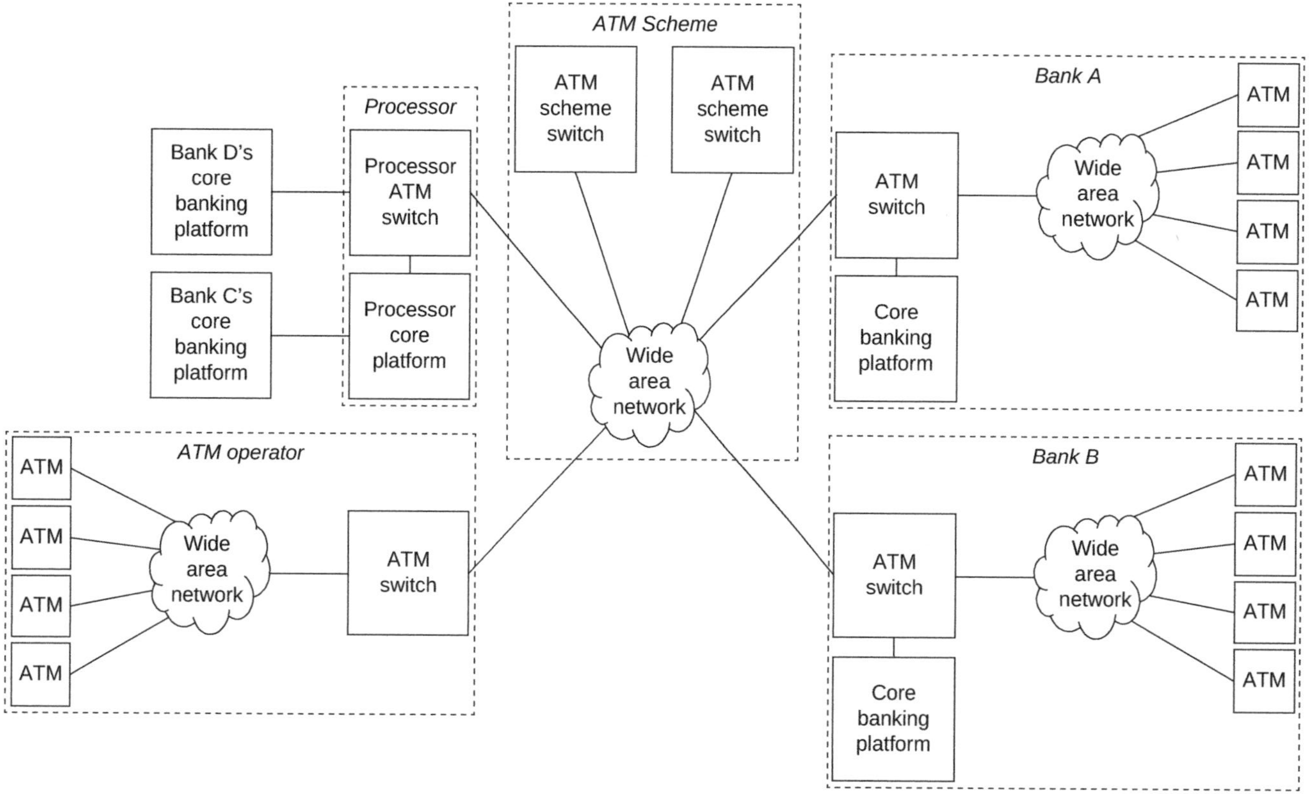

operator will be connected to each scheme network* and route transaction messages accordingly. The ATMs will also be programmed with the agreed screens to be used for each scheme. A processor will have to participate in all the schemes in which its bank customers participate.

ATM withdrawal cards have to a large extent been replaced with debit cards, and these now are typically Chip and PIN cards, which no longer rely on the magnetic stripe on the back of the card (although this remains in case there is a problem with the chip and for the dwindling occasions where Chip and PIN transactions are not supported), including in ATMs. Some ATMs even support contactless withdrawals up to the maximum amount allowed for a contactless transaction.

4.5.4   Considerations When Deploying ATMs

However, implementing and running an ATM network is not as simple as just plugging them in. Typically, ATM machines must be run on a separate physical or virtual network than the rest of the technology estate in order to protect the card data from snooping. ATMs also run an operating system (often a version of Microsoft Windows) which requires maintaining and upgrading, and the screens themselves need to be regularly changed as customer behaviour and the needs of the service provider vary. They must also be managed, monitored and re-stocked with both paper and ink (for receipts) and cash. Above and beyond these are the security requirements. Not only are they a consideration in siting an ATM (it requires a secure location in a robust wall), but security monitoring and alerting must also be thought through.

It should also be noted that consideration must be given in the implementation of any new ATM solution for the requirements laid down by the card schemes, payment card schemes (such as LINK in the UK), banking regulators and the Payment Card Industry Data Security Standards (PCI DSS).[10]

4.6   Telephony

Historically, it was possible to call your local bank branch if you needed to check on a payment or make some other enquiry. With your branch holding details of your account on its own server (or in its own paper ledgers before servers), this was in fact the only way other than visiting your branch to find out the current status of your account. However, with the centralisation of core banking platforms, it was also possible to centralise telephone services, and large banks embraced this in the 1980s and 1990s and set up large call centres to handle telephone enquiries, to the extent banks often made it impossible for a customers to call their local branch.

When we talk about telephone banking we specifically mean telephone calls, whether initiated on a land line or via a mobile phone, that are handled automatically by a voice response unit or manually by customer service agents in a call centre or contact centre, the distinction being that a call centre only handles telephone calls, whereas a contact

---

*Some schemes can also route to other schemes, so a bank could potentially just be connected to a national scheme that would route transactions through to Mastercard or Visa as required. The bank still has to be a member of all schemes to which the transactions it acquires are routed.

centre manages multiple contact methods, typically including telephone calls and any other contact method such as video calls, online chat, email and possibly even post.

4.7 Online Chat

Online chat (often just called chat) is the exchange of private text messages over the Internet (so therefore does not include public social media messaging). A primary consideration is how customers would be authenticated, and most banks therefore only provide chat-based servicing after a customer has logged onto the Internet banking website or a mobile banking app. Of course, it is also possible to provide a chat facility for general enquiries that wouldn't require a customer (or potential customer) to have logged on.

Although handling chat is a logical extension of the contact centre's responsibilities, consideration should also be given to implementing technology solutions to handle more common queries. There is now a large range of commercially available chatbots (or bots, as they are sometimes called) that can be implemented to address the majority of more common queries. Many of these chatbots use text matching and complex decision trees to attempt to understand what the customer might want, and more sophisticated versions use artificial intelligence and natural language understanding to support more sophisticated and nuanced communication.[11]

However, for those elements of chat that will require human interactions, a key consideration for a bank that is looking to add chat handling to an established contact centre is the impact on staffing and the skills staff will require. This might appear to be an odd question because, on the face of it, adding chat is straightforward from a technology perspective. However, many banks have spent decades recruiting contact centre staff for their ability to talk and interact with customers, not for their written skills. Writing clear, coherent sentences quickly and with few errors is a different skill from talking and responding to chat messages is not as stimulating as talking to customers. It is important that a bank finds staff with the right skills before launching such a service.

4.8 Video Calling

This is another area that started to gain traction as advances in technology, particularly bandwidth and latency improvements, made it more viable. While still not very common, a number of high street banks have experimented with video. In the UK, Barclays[12] and NatWest[13] deployed video banking solutions and in the US, Pioneer Federal Credit Union, in southwestern Idaho, started video calling through its ATMs in 2015[14]. Implementing video calling, like chat, does generate some additional issues for the bank. First, there must be a means of authenticating customers, and possibilities include using video-equipped ATMs (where the customer uses their payment card and PIN to authenticate themself) and through the bank's mobile app or Internet banking website after a customer has logged on. However, as with chat-based solutions, there is also a problem to overcome on the staffing front. In a telephone-only contact centre, neither the environment, nor the staff manning it, can be seen. With a video solution, this clearly changes. The surroundings visible in a video call should demonstrate a professional working environment – although some video calling platforms can partially address this through obscuring the background or even changing it completely. Also, the staff handling video calls must be happy to be on video and present themselves in a way that best represents the business.

4.9   Handling Telephone, Chat and Video Contacts

In this section we look initially at the technology that was used to handle telephone calls and then at modern multimedia contact handling, including telephone calls, chat and video calls.

4.9.1   The Call Centre Platform

Figure 4.11 represents a simple model of the system architecture used to handle telephone calls in a call centre, and we have also shown the bank's core banking platform on the same network. This is the sort of architecture used in the 1990s and 2000s.

In this diagram, when a customer calls their bank, the phone call is transmitted over the PSTN (public switched telephone network) which is shown as a cloud. Telephone lines (shown as double lines in the diagram) come from the PSTN into the call centre's telephone system (originally known as a PBX or private branch exchange). Inside the bank, its telephones are connected to the PBX, also using dedicated phone lines (for simplicity, the bank's telephones are not shown in the diagram). The primary functions

FIGURE 4.11   Historical call centre architecture.

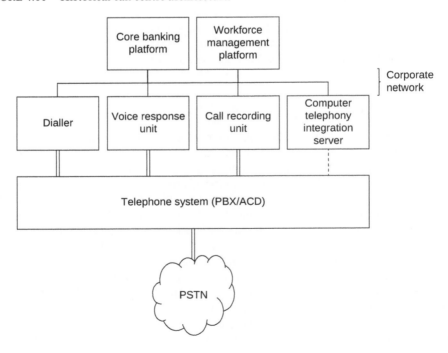

of the PBX are to enable calls between telephones inside the bank and also to enable bank staff to make and receive external calls. More internal telephone lines connect the bank's PBX to the dialler (used to automate the placing of outbound calls), voice response unit (used to provide automated telephone servicing to customers) and call recording unit (used to record calls for quality checking and to provide an audit trail). These platforms are also on the bank's corporate network, shown as a single solid line in this diagram, which connects to the other platforms in the bank.

The computer telephony integration (CTI) server is connected to the PBX via a dedicated physical connection, shown as a dashed line in Figure 4.11. This may be what is termed a serial or RS232 connection, a type of short-range connection for computer equipment first introduced in 1960. The PBX informs the CTI server about the status of every call it is handling (such as when an inbound call arrives) and the CTI server can send commands to the PBX to tell it to do things like terminate a call or route it to a specific internal extension. More modern PBXs may connect directly to the network and communicate with the CTI server across the network (although even in the late 1990s we were using new PBXs and CTI servers that connected using RS232 connections).

Next, we're going to cover how a call is handled using the equipment shown in Figure 4.11, describing what each one does in more detail, starting with how the telephone network routes a call to the call centre.

4.9.2   The Intelligent Network

Historically, any organisation would have published a geographic number for its call centre, i.e. a number with a dialling code (or what is also called a telephone area code) that belonged to a specific area, where the call centre was located. This is because telephone calls were routed strictly according to their dialling codes, at first using human operators who knew what each dialling code meant (and who would know how to set up a long-distance call) and then with electromechanical equipment that could automatically route calls based on dialling codes. This meant that every dialling code was associated with an actual exchange, so if you had a phone line, its corresponding phone number would have the dialling code from the local exchange to which it was connected.

In 1966, the US phone company AT&T, at that time the monopoly provider of phone services in the US, launched toll-free numbers (with a dialling code of 800) which were free for the caller. Initially these were only available for calls within the same state, and in 1967 the service was extended so that such calls could be made between different US states.[15] The system wasn't particularly intelligent, as specific sets of 800 numbers (dictated by the next three digits of the number) were associated with specific geographic dialling codes. In the 1980s the system was improved so that an 800 number could be located anywhere. This was possible because in the intervening years the telephone network had been computerised so that when a call was made to a non-geographic number (e.g. a toll-free number beginning 800) the network would look up in a database which geographic number the call should actually be sent to and then route the call there.

Many countries followed suit with numbers that had dialling codes that weren't limited to specific areas, often using the 800 dialling code (or a national equivalent) as one that is free for callers and often with other numbers that charged callers various amounts, from the same amount as geographic numbers to premium amounts. Mobile phone numbers are the ultimate example of this – a mobile phone number incorporates a dialling code, but it isn't associated with any specific location, or often even a specific mobile network operator where number portability is available.

To put it a different way, telephone numbers no longer have to be associated with a specific exchange based on their dialling code. When you make a phone call, the telephone network determines how to physically route your call by looking up where it should route the call to. This can change dynamically (e.g. if you call a mobile phone from a fixed line, the mobile phone could be located anywhere in the world).

Such capability – the ability to look up the routing for a phone number – is a function of what is called the Intelligent Network, which is defined in standards issued by the International Telecommunications Union.[16] In essence, the standards set out an architecture for public telephone systems which separates the basic telephone service (i.e. the lines, exchanges and so-called trunk lines that connect exchanges) from the control of phone calls that run over the basic telephone service. So, when you dial a number, the Intelligent Network first of all looks up the number you dialled to see how it should route the call – it will also check you have enough credit to make such a call.

Having the logic that routes calls separated out from the basic telephone system has meant telecommunication companies have been able to provide many different types of services, not only to the general public but also to companies, including those that operate call centres.

For example, what it means for call centre operation is that an organisation can have its call centre spread across multiple locations, and have calls routed in "intelligent" ways to each location. For example, the Intelligent Network could be programmed to route each call to a different call centre location in turn, or between certain times route to one location and then another location (e.g. in a different time zone) outside these times. Or, the organisation operating the multi-site call centre can provide information on agent availability at each location to the Intelligent Network so that calls are routed only to locations where agents are available – and this can be done in real time.

Note that every fixed (as opposed to mobile) phone line is still usually associated with a geographic number, and it is the Intelligent Network that decides where a phone call to any number (either geographic or non-geographic, such as a toll-free number) is routed. Although this has improved over time, calls to non-geographic numbers from a different country may not always work and so banks often publish both a non-geographic number plus a geographic number for each service. Both numbers are often seen on the back of debit and credit cards for reporting lost and stolen cards.

The Intelligent Network can also be used to give the impression that a bank has a local telephone number. For example, it could route calls on a local number (e.g. supposedly the number of a local branch) to a call centre at a completely different location.

4.9.3   Handling a Call in the Call Centre

Let's walk through how an incoming telephone call is handled. The customer calls the bank on one of its customer service numbers. The public telephone network determines where to route the call and sends it to the PBX or telephone system at the bank's call centre (or to one of its call centres).

Once the call arrives at a call centre location, the PBX at that location then decides how to deal with the call. The public telephone system not only routes the call to the PBX, but also passes some information to the PBX about the call, including information about the number that the call was routed to (this function is called the Dialled Number Information Service or DNIS for short) and the caller's number if they have not withheld their number (this is called the Caller ID or Calling Line Identification or CLI for short*). There are various ways to do this and a small number of standards in use around the world such as SS7 (Signalling System 7^{17}), but we will not go into them in this book. The PBX can then use the DNIS and CLI information to decide how to handle the call.

The bank may have several customer service telephone numbers. For example, it may have one for regular retail customers, another for its premium retail customers, another for small business customers, another for new retail customers applying for an account, a general enquiries number and so on. The DNIS information passed to the PBX allows the PBX to determine what number the caller called, and therefore what type of customer is probably calling or for what reason. Telling the PBX what inbound number the call was routed to, i.e. the DNIS, may seem odd, but in reality the PBX could have several inbound numbers which share the same set of telephone lines into the PBX. In other words, when the PBX receives a call, it can't tell which of the inbound numbers the call is intended for, unless the telephone network tells it – that is the purpose of the DNIS. The DNIS is typically the geographic number that the call was routed to (and not the non-geographic number the customer dialled).

For a call to the regular retail customer service number, the PBX may well be set up to route the call to a voice response unit (VRU). The VRU may offer some servicing functionality such as enabling customers to check their account balance and to initiate payments to payees that they have already set up. So, the VRU will normally check the identity of the caller by asking them to enter their customer number using the keypad of their phone, and then asking them for a PIN. The VRU will then ask what service the caller wants. For a balance enquiry, the VRU has to get the current balance from the core banking platform and then read it back to the caller.

If this caller wants to speak to a customer service representative, typically they will select that option when offered it by the VRU which will then send the call back to the telephone system, which will put the call into a queue waiting for the next available representative.

The telephone system queues each call until a customer service agent becomes free, at which point it sends the call to that agent. This queueing functionality was historically called automated call distribution and could be provided by the PBX or in some cases was provided by another system attached to the PBX, typically called an Automated Call Distributor (or ACD). The ACD functionality or unit enables a bank to set up different queues for different purposes (e.g. one queue for regular customers, one for premium customers, various queues for specialised services such as handling deaths, product applications, etc.). When an agent becomes available, the ACD routes a caller to that agent from one of the queues, depending on what skills the agent has (this aspect of the ACD functionality is often termed skills-based routing) or to what services or queue(s) the agent has been assigned. Therefore, the ACD must keep track of which agents are working, and what skills or expertise each one of them has. In addition, different types of calls or

---

*You may also see this referred to as ANI (Automatic Number Identification). However, there is a difference in how CLI and ANI are defined, with ANI including the class of service (e.g. regular telephone call placed by the caller or one placed by the operator on the caller's behalf) and the caller's number for billing purposes. We will only use CLI.

customers can be given different priorities. For example, the bank may have a policy that calls from premium customers are answered more quickly than from regular customers, so the ACD has to factor this in when deciding what call to put through to an agent.

The staffing of contact centres is a skill and for larger contact centres relies upon a workforce management platform. This platform holds details of all the contact centre agents and their skills, and details of all the queues set up on the ACD. It also collects and uses information on previous call volumes and durations (in contact centres, the average call duration is referred to as the average handle time, or AHT) in order to determine how many contact centre agents are needed at any point in time in order to be able to answer calls quickly enough. It will then create rosters for the contact centre agents which show the times each agent will be on duty and when they are expected to be at work.

Tracking and maintaining agent skills is not only important so that customers receive appropriate service from knowledgeable agents, but also when the contact centre is providing services that are regulated. For example, only suitably certified agents may be allowed to handle mortgage applications and queries, so such calls must only be routed to those agents.

Contact centres measure their performance in various ways. Most have targets for the percentage of calls answered within a certain period, for example 90% of calls answered within 30 seconds. The targets may vary according to the type of caller or service – typically each queue in the ACD will have its own target. Again, the ACD and workforce management platform must be informed about these targets so they can route calls and schedule agents appropriately.

4.9.4   Workforce Scheduling

The workforce management platform in a contact centre uses an area of mathematics called queueing theory to work out how many contact centre agents should be working in order to achieve a desired service level, i.e. a percentage of calls answered within a certain period such as 90% of calls answered in 20 seconds. Agner Krarup Erlang published his first paper on this topic in 1909,[18] followed by various other papers that established formulas for, among other things, the number of telephone lines required to connect a telephone exchange to the rest of the telephone network based on the number of telephone subscribers connected to that exchange waiting a specified average period for a line to come free. The same so-called Erlang C formula is used to calculate how many agents are needed to achieve a service level based on the number of calls and average call handle time. The calculations are more complicated when agents are servicing multiple queues and different agents have different skill levels, and modern workforce management platforms use various modelling techniques to determine staffing levels required, but at the heart of these models are the Erlang formulae and their underlying statistical mathematics.

4.9.5   Computer Telephony Integration

In Figure 4.11, we show a computer telephony integration (CTI) server. We haven't touched on this directly. However, it's a vital system for tracking and communicating information about each phone call. When a call arrives at the PBX, certain information such as DNIS and CLI is passed by the PSTN to the PBX at the same time as the call.

The PBX passes the fact a call has arrived to the CTI server, alongside the information that came with the call and a unique identifier (i.e. a unique number) for that call. Then, whenever the status of the call changes (e.g. it is routed to the VRU or put on an ACD queue or sent to an agent), the PBX tells this to the CTI server. Bear in mind that whenever a call is in progress, it is flowing through the PBX, so the PBX is aware of what endpoints (e.g. a telephone set, a line to the VRU, etc.) the call is connected to. It also knows if the caller hangs up. What the CTI server also knows is what internal telephone lines connected to the PBX are associated with what network addresses. So, when, for example, the PBX routes a call to an agent, the CTI server knows the address of the PC that that agent is using (typically because the agent has signed into an application on the PC that communicates with the CTI server). The CTI server can then tell the application on the agent's PC information about the call (normally including the CLI and DNIS).

The primary functions of the CTI server are to provide a way for information on telephone calls that are in progress to be passed around to the different recipients of that call (e.g. an agent, the VRU and so on), and updated as the call progresses, and to provide a facility for applications to take control of the agent's telephone extension, e.g. to dial a number, to transfer the call, to hang up the call and so on. This is enabled by having a piece of software provided by the CTI server vendor on the agent's PC that integrates with the applications on the agent's PC and sends messages to and receives messages from the CTI server over the network. The CTI server in turn can send instructions to the PBX (e.g. to hang up a call, transfer a call, etc.).

Given that the CTI server can send instructions to the PBX, it was an obvious step to develop functionality on the CTI server to take control of call routing. Originally, the PBX would make the initial decision about where to route an incoming call and then further decisions would be made by the PBX, the ACD, the VRU, agents themselves and so on. Having the CTI server control call routing meant that it could be all controlled from one place and often with a lot more flexibility and ease of maintenance than when it was done by the PBX and other proprietary systems in the call centre. In addition, CTI server functionality was developed to communicate with the Intelligent Network and work in tandem with other call centre sites across the bank so that the Intelligent Network could route incoming calls to whatever call centre had the highest availability at a specific time (for example). So, this means a bank could have multiple call centres at different locations, all perhaps using different PBXs (often the case as a legacy of mergers and acquisitions), and the CTI servers could be used to combine the call centres virtually into one big call centre. This provides resilience (e.g. an outage of one site leaves the other sites to handle the calls), better utilisation of agents (according to the statistics behind workforce management, the larger the pool of agents, the higher the utilisation for the same quality of service), more flexibility and lower cost in dealing with multiple time zones and peaks outside normal working hours, and so on.

4.9.6 *Interactive Voice Response*

In Section 4.9.3 we covered the basic role of a voice response unit or VRU. The functionality this provides is usually called interactive voice response (IVR), and sometimes the VRU is called an IVR platform. This area of functionality, like everything else, has developed over the years. Telephone banking in the 1990s often included an IVR service that customers could use for basic account servicing using a touchtone telephone. When you press a button on the phone during a call it makes a tone – or more precisely two simultaneous tones at different frequencies (e.g. pressing 1 results in simultaneous tones at 697 Hz and 1209 Hz). The standard for such tones is called Dual-Tone Multi-Frequency (DTMF) and is set out in an ITU standard.[19] The VRU can identify the two tones and therefore determine what key was pressed on your phone. DTMF is still very much in use today – your smartphone will send such tones when you press keys on the keypad during a phone call. Such touchtone IVR applications are typically designed as a decision tree based on a series of *if this, then that* scenarios.

Since then many organisations have implemented IVR that recognises spoken words and phrases. However, users tend to find such platforms to be mediocre at working out what they have said, and users also tend to be unsure about how to ask succinctly for what they want. In some ways, less is more, with good old DTMF selection being more accurate and faster, but probably more limited.

Historically, VRUs were highly proprietary computers that were programmed using proprietary languages. However, as in many areas, standards have arisen for programming them, with VoiceXML the prevalent language used to specify the operation of a VRU. A sample VoiceXML script is shown below:

```
<vxml version="2.1" xmlns="http://www.w3.org/2001/vxml">
  <form>
    <block>
      <prompt>
        Welcome
      </prompt>
    </block>
  </form>
</vxml>
```

All this script does is announce *Welcome* to the caller. In effect a VRU interprets VoiceXML scripts in order to play messages to the caller and accept voice and DTMF input back – much like a web browser interprets HTML scripts in order to display information in a browser and accept keyboard and mouse input back. So, you may now see a VRU referred to as a voice browser.

IVR is an area that in many ways has been supplanted by Internet and mobile banking and new banks would probably provide little, if any, IVR functionality. The decision to use IVR was and still can be a contentious one. Existing banks may have made major investments in IVR in the past and have a sizable segment of customers who still use the capability and many large banks rely upon callers being routed through such platforms, with basic servicing functionality (balance enquiries, for example). However, many customers hate the experience of IVR, on the basis that if they have gone to the bother of calling the bank it is because they actually wanted to talk to someone.

Nonetheless, there is one area of IVR functionality which is hard to achieve by other means and that is to handle the authentication part of a call from a customer. Suppose a customer calls their bank and speaks directly to a contact centre agent. The agent has to identify the customer and authenticate them, i.e. check that the customer is actually who they say they are. In this scenario, the agent may ask the customer for some personal pieces of information such as date of birth, place of birth, two characters from a password or answers to other security questions that the customer has already set up. The agent therefore gets to know some of the customer's security information. Some banks use IVR to collect and check such information. This means that no human agents normally become aware of customers' security information – although we would expect there to be a means to fall back to manual authentication for customers who can't use IVR.

Some banks have implemented voice recognition (for example, HSBC launched a service in 2016 in the UK[20]) as a way of checking the identity of a caller. This had promise for improving the customer experience, as it could remove the need for the customer to remember their user ID or password. However, the technology is not infallible. In May 2017, the BBC published a report on an investigation that had been carried out by two non-identical twins, where one had managed to access the other's bank account.[21] In practice, voice recognition provides a score that gives the probability that the person speaking is actually the customer they claim to be, but it does not provide certainty.

After the customer has been authenticated by the VRU, they will be routed to a human agent, whose PC screen will automatically show information on that customer. In that way, the agent doesn't even have to search for the customer, and is only given access to the record of a customer who has successfully authenticated themself using IVR and been routed through to that agent, therefore further improving information security. We used a different approach recently in which customers initiated calls from the bank's mobile app, which they had signed into already. As these were Voice over IP calls (which we will explain shortly), the app could securely pass the customer ID to the bank at the initiation of the call, and given we had no requirements for IVR we did not implement a VRU.

4.9.7   Visual IVR

Visual IVR refers to a technology that can be used to take the scripts created for the VRU and convert them into webpages or a mobile app. This is made easier if the scripts are written in VoiceXML. For example, an IVR menu such as *press 1 to hear your balance, press 2 to make a payment, press 3 to transfer money between your accounts, press 4 to speak to a customer service representative* could be shown on a webpage as a simple list with four entries:

1. Your account balance
2. Make a payment
3. Transfer money between your accounts
4. Speak to a customer service representative

The user would be taken to another webpage by clicking any of the items on the list.

We think this technology could have been relatively appealing when banks were looking to set up websites after having invested in telephone banking platforms or even to quickly launch mobile apps, but in reality probably came too late for most banks. Implementing it is also not simply a matter of taking all the VRU scripts and loading them into a visual IVR application – there is work to be done to change spoken scripts to text such as changing "hear" to "see", authenticating users, dealing with the request to speak to a customer service representative (you could call the user back or start an online chat session, for example) and coordinating with the bank's other platforms. IVR applications also aren't as functionally rich as banking websites, which typically offer things like the ability to download statements and view several months of transaction history that VRUs just can't. So, we think that in a bank you are unlikely to either come across visual IVR technology or find a need to implement it.

4.9.8   Call Recording

It is normal for all calls to be recorded, using a call recording unit. Again, at one time this would have been done by a specialised proprietary computer able to handle telephone calls, with lots of storage to hold the recordings. As well as the recording of a call, the call recording unit stores the date and time of the call, something that identifies the agent that handled the call, and other information that allows the call recording to be quickly retrieved (e.g. the customer number). This gives the bank a record of every call in case there is a dispute or complaint. It also enables contact centre management to review calls to see if agents are servicing customers correctly and according to the standards and policies the bank has for handling calls. The call recording unit can also get information on each call from the CTI server, and store this information along with the call recording to enable easier retrieval of recordings, for example in the case of a complaint from a customer about their treatment – the CTI server may have passed a customer number to the call recorder that enabled all the calls relating to that customer to be retrieved.

Call recorders typically provide another feature, which is often called quality management. In a call centre, this means assessing the quality of phone calls and determining if agents are servicing customers correctly. Typically, call centre management will review a sample of every agent's calls in a set period and then determine if agents need specific training (either as a team or as individuals). It may be important, particularly in a regulated environment, that agents are including certain things in a call, for example alerting callers to specific terms and conditions, and the call recorder allows management to check compliance with such a policy. Agents may be given the ability to flag calls they have taken, for example because they felt they were not able to service the customer properly or the caller was abusive or the agent felt there is a fraud risk. The call centre management can then review such a call with the agent who flagged it.

Call recording has to take into account any requirements to flag certain portions of a call as sensitive or not record those portions at all. For example, in most situations payment card information should not be recorded as it could be accessed later and misused. In such cases, if a call flow requires payment card information to be taken, the agent should be able to suspend recording or even redact the data later. The CTI client or a call recording control application on the agent's PC could be used to do this.

Call recording technology has developed to the point where the tone of the voices on the call and the language the speakers use can be interpreted, and the sentiment of the speakers analysed and compared across thousands of calls. This could be used to determine what behaviours improve the perception of customer service and also replace at least some of the manual quality monitoring that call centre supervisors and managers perform.

4.9.9   Diallers

Most of what we have written has been from the perspective of a call centre handling inbound calls. However, call centres often also need to make calls. Perhaps the primary example in a bank is for collections, where contacting customers to pursue overdue loan payments is a typical activity. A dialler takes a list of telephone numbers and starts calling them. It also knows what agents are available (e.g. because the agents have an application on their desktop that communicates with the dialler to say when they are available to take a call). If a call is answered by a human (and not an answering machine, fax machine or modem – the last two of which are pretty rare these days), the dialler automatically routes the call to an available agent (in effect, it transfers the call to the agent's phone). The dialler will send some information on the call from the call list it was loaded with (e.g. a customer reference) to the agent's PC – either directly to the application on the agent's PC or by using the CTI server to pass the information with the call – so that the application on the agent's PC can show it to the agent.

The fundamental challenge with diallers is to match the number of successful calls (i.e. those answered by a human) to the number of available agents. A conservative approach is to allow the dialler to make only as many calls as there are agents available. This is so-called progressive dialling, and it has the benefit of being able to assign a call to an available agent before the call is actually answered, so the agent can review the call or customer details in advance of having to introduce themself to the person who answers the call. However, the majority (often significantly more than 50%) of calls are not successful, i.e. do not get answered. So, with this approach, agents will be underutilised. Predictive dialling takes a more aggressive approach: the dialler will attempt to predict the percentage of successful calls so that the number of successful calls matches the number of agents. This isn't guaranteed, so there will be occasions when more calls are successful than the number of agents available to handle them. The dialler can do one of several things when this happens, including hanging up, playing a message to the person who answered the call asking them to wait or saying nothing (i.e. being a silent caller). If all agents become busy, the dialler may decide to drop all calls that it is currently dialling, even if they haven't been answered. This is of course a contentious area, because of the potential for the bank to be seen as making nuisance calls. Often regulators and governments have set standards or legislated in this area, typically banning dropped calls or limiting the percentage of dropped calls.

Diallers were originally yet another proprietary computer system with telephone lines connecting them to the PBX or even directly to the PSTN. Over time, with the opening up of PBX systems to external control (e.g. via the CTI server), diallers no longer had to have telephone lines coming into them, but could control the PBX to make calls and then route them to agents when they became available.

4.9.10   Modern Contact Centre Technology

So far, we have described a call centre with its own technology platforms based on what would have been implemented in the 1990s and the first decade of the twenty-first century. These are all expensive pieces of infrastructure that have to be operated and maintained at the same location as the contact centre and tend to be specialised and proprietary computers as they need to handle telephone lines (in the case of the PBX, VRU, ACD and call recorder). Not only would they require a large up-front capital expenditure, but they often had expensive license fees, typically per agent or per telephone line. They were programmed using proprietary tools and languages. Quite often (particularly in the case of PBXs) they lacked features or had limitations. Once a bank had purchased such equipment, it would be locked into that vendor or set of vendors both financially and technically. However, a new bank establishing a contact centre would not purchase such equipment, for several reasons. If nothing else, banks now need to handle not only phone calls, but also instant messaging, video calls, email, social media, and so on – although in our experience banks pick and choose which of these they support for customer interaction. Although it would be hard to avoid having to deal with customers over the phone, we once built a bank where initially all contact was via messaging from the app on our customers' smartphones (although given that the initial customers were friends and family, you could actually call the COO directly if you had an issue). In addition, much of the telephony equipment has been superseded by the use of Voice over IP telephony (even if customers are still calling in using old-fashioned telephone lines). In fact, we suspect that in many markets it would be hard, if not impossible, to buy a traditional PBX. Enterprise-level Voice over IP telephony is standards based and "open", i.e. supposedly interoperable across vendors. The functionality is available in the cloud, in other words remotely and off the bank's own premises, from specialist providers as well as the major telecommunications companies, often on usage-based pricing terms. So, there would be minimal capital expenditure – although there are always costs, even if only internal, to set up and configure the functionality.

The architecture of a modern contact centre is fundamentally different, as illustrated in Figure 4.12. For now, we'll assume the contact centre technology is still hosted by the bank itself and isn't in the cloud. So, what's different? Two things are immediately obvious: the PBX has been replaced by a PSTN gateway and an IP PBX, and there are no telephone lines anywhere except between the PSTN and the PSTN gateway. All calls run over the local data network connecting the various platforms. All telephone sets are connected to the same local network and don't have a direct connection to the IP PBX – the telephone sets are either VoIP sets or (increasingly rarely) old-fashioned telephone sets with an adapter that enables them to be plugged into the corporate network.

Note that suppliers of these platforms tend to use very different names for them and split the functions between them differently from what we have shown in Figure 4.12. You may find, for example, that a supplier offers an IP PBX combined with a PSTN gateway (probably named something different) and also a contact centre platform (which could contain skills-based routing, contact queuing, workforce management and dialler functionality). Another supplier may put all these functions in one platform.

We will go into some detail about Voice over IP (VoIP). Note IP stands for Internet Protocol, the standard messaging protocol used by all data flows across the Internet and in virtually all corporate networks as well – data centres using mainframes may use older communication protocols (although we suspect this is increasingly rare). VoIP is a generic name for transmitting voice calls over IP-based networks, including the Internet and corporate networks, and now is also used for video calls, text messaging and other media types. Although most VoIP implementations normally use a number of standards, which we will dip into shortly, there are many choices to be made (thankfully, normally completely hidden from users).

For example, one choice is the method of converting an analogue voice call to a digital stream that can be transmitted across a network (and also the conversion in reverse at the other end). The software that does this is called a codec (for coder/decoder). There has been a lot of research into the optimum algorithms for digitising speech and there are a number of algorithms in use today – different algorithms typically require different amounts of network bandwidth, offer different levels of quality and require different levels of processing power to encode and decode.

Another choice to be made is how to address a call – in other words, what should you use as the equivalent of a phone number for VoIP calls so that the recipient can be reached? One possibility is to use the recipient's email address, and another is to use their phone number, as these both tend to be pieces of information that can identify a single individual or a business. Of course, for a bank, if a customer is calling using their telephone then the bank has to be contactable using a phone number, even if the call actually takes place using VoIP. Also, the bank could enable VoIP calls to be initiated through its smartphone app, in which case the customer doesn't have to know any address for the bank.

Another aspect is how to find out the actual location of the recipient and where they are on the local network or the Internet. In practice, the recipient has to update a server with their address on the local network or the Internet, and when someone wishes to call them, the process of placing a VoIP call will determine what server to use to check the recipient's location, then ask that server for their location and route the VoIP call to that address. This is one of the functions of an IP PBX – it maintains information on how to route a call to each possible recipient registered with the PBX. So, a contact centre agent has to inform the IP PBX that they are logged on and ready to take calls, which they would do either through their VoIP phone or through the computer application they are using.

You may well have used various smartphone and computer apps for consumer VoIP calls, such as Facebook Messenger, Facetime, Skype, Telegram, WeChat, WhatsApp and so on. These typically use different approaches (probably all of which are proprietary to some extent) from the various aspects of VoIP calls and are often fenced in, in that you can't break out of one app into another (e.g. use Skype to call someone who answers using WhatsApp). There is typically one exception – they do in some cases allow you to call old-fashioned telephone numbers (often this is chargeable). They typically require you to ask each of your contacts to allow calls from you and to make calls to you and maintain a list of those contacts, so how the apps actually address a VoIP call is hidden from you.

Now we focus on a customer calling their bank from an old-fashioned fixed telephone line to a contact centre that is based on standards-based VoIP. So, the customer calls their bank. The Intelligent Network decides how it is going to route the call. As we discussed before, the bank could have more than one contact centre site, and the Intelligent Network may need to decide to which of the sites it should route the call. Ultimately, the call arrives at the PSTN gateway shown in Figure 4.12. This converts the call to a VoIP call. At this point, as far as the customer is concerned, the call is ringing – no one has answered it yet and as far as the PSTN is concerned, it has routed the call to the intended destination but it hasn't been picked up yet. The PSTN tells the PSTN gateway the CLI and DNIS of the call (much like it would have told a PBX). The PSTN gateway then communicates with the IP PBX over the bank's network, in effect telling the IP PBX that a call has arrived destined for the phone number given by the DNIS information. In our example, the network protocol used by the PSTN gateway to do this (and to manage the call) is the Session Initiation Protocol (SIP). Another protocol that could be used is H.323.

FIGURE 4.12   Modern contact centre architecture.

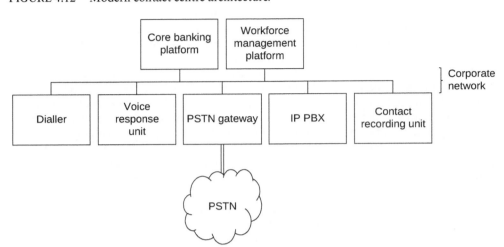

4.9.11   Session Initiation Protocol and Handling a VoIP Call

Session Initiation Protocol (SIP) is a standard Internet protocol, defined by the Internet Engineering Task Force (IETF) in RFC3261[22] with various extensions to it in later RFC* documents. Two computers exchange SIP messages across a network in order to set up, maintain and end a VoIP session (and also other forms of media such as video, text chat and so on). The messages are in human-readable text, like other standard Internet protocols. So, in our example of a customer calling the bank, the PSTN gateway has received the call and now must ask the IP PBX to route the call to an appropriate endpoint. So, there is an exchange of messages as shown in Figure 4.13.

Note that in the terminology of RFC3621, the IP PBX is a proxy server which inspects, modifies and routes SIP messages. The first message from the PSTN gateway to the IP PBX, labelled INVITE in Figure 4.13, would have content like the following:

```
INVITE sip:+441234555222@callcentrepbx.mybank.com;user=phone SIP/2.0
Via: SIP/2.0/UDP pstngateway.mybank.com:5060;branch=z9hG4bKR4R3OM6aPNtDUXFv
Max-Forwards: 70
From: <sip:+441923222333@callcentrepbx.mybank.com;user=phone>;tag=EdXdohH4L7
82gHeD
To: <sip:+441234555222@callcentrepbx.mybank.com;user=phone>
Call-ID: NPBFwVdv5unmX55L@pstngateway.mybank.com
CSeq: 70152 INVITE
Contact: <sip:pstngateway@mybank.com>
Content-Type: application/sdp
Content-Length: 183
v=0
```

*RFC stands for Request for Comments, and is the name used on the documents (collectively called RFCs) that specify standards and other technical information relating to the Internet (see https://ietf.org/standards/rfcs/ for more information).

FIGURE 4.13   SIP messages to establish a VoIP call.

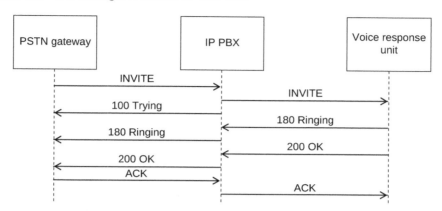

```
o=PSTN 1582733280917 1582733280917 IN IP4 pstngateway.mybank.com
s=
c=IN IP4 pstngateway.mybank.com
t=0 0
m=audio 11014 RTP/AVP 8 0 18 96
a=rtpmap:96 telephone-event/8000
a=fmtp:96 0-15
```

This message has two sections – a header comprising 10 lines and then the body of the message. If you've ever examined a full Internet email message, you'll have seen something similar – a series of header lines (although most email programs don't display these normally, some do allow you to see the full message source) and then the body of the message itself. The very first line of the header is in effect the PSTN gateway telling the IP PBX that it has received an inbound phone call to the number of the contact centre (+44 1234 555222 – this would be the geographic number of the contact centre, not the Intelligent Network number that the customer may have dialled) and inviting the PBX to deal with it. The following lines give more details of the call, including several unique identifiers for the call that the PSTN gateway has assigned so that it can keep track of it. It also contains the caller's number (+44 1923 222333), which has been supplied by the PSTN to the PSTN gateway. The PSTN gateway's network address (pstngateway.mybank.com) and the IP PBX's network address (callcentrepbx.mybank.com) are also shown. The last two lines in the header of the message, beginning with Content-Type and Content-Length, tell the PBX that the body of the message that follows is in the Session Description Protocol (SDP) format and give the size of the message body in characters. SDP is another Internet standard protocol, defined in IETF's RFC 4566 document.[23]

The body of the message states the encoding and transmission methods the PSTN gateway is capable of using, set out in the line stating m=audio 11014 RTP/AVP 8 0 18 96. This says the PSTN gateway can handle audio communication exchanged over the network using RTP (Real-time Transport Protocol, another standard defined in the IETF's RFC 3550[24]), using the RTP Profile for Audio and Video Conferences with Minimal Control (RTP/AVP – yet another standard, this time defined in the IETF's RFC 3551[25]) with payload format numbers 8, 0, 18 and 96. The RTP/AVP profile defines that the RTP messages will be sent using UDP (User Datagram Protocol, one of the basic protocols for sending data across an IP network), and the gateway has requested that RTP messages should be sent to its UDP port number 11014. The first three payload format numbers relate to different codecs that could be used – in effect the PSTN gateway is telling the recipient of the call what codecs it has the ability to use (in order of preference from most to least preferred). The RTP/AVP profile defines payload format 8 as audio encoded (i.e. converted from an analogue input to a digital stream) using a standard named G.711 (defined by the International Telecommunications Union[26]) with A-law pulse code modulation (sometimes abbreviated as PCMA), payload format 0 as G.711 with μ-law pulse code modulation (sometimes abbreviated as PCMU) and payload format 18 as G.729.[27] The final payload format number, 96, has a different meaning. The RTP/AVP standard defines this payload format number as "dynamic", which means it should be defined in the SDP message, and the very next line in the message says this represents a "telephone event" format, which is used for DTMF tones. This format is defined in the IETF's RFC 4733.[28] In a normal phone call, DTMF tones are just sent over the same audio connection that the people on the call use (which is why you can hear them) but in a VoIP call they are often sent separately as some audio codecs do not code and decode them correctly.

At this stage, these audio formats are being offered by the PSTN gateway, and there is a protocol for how the recipient should respond to such an offer which is set out in yet another IETF standard, RFC 5939. Normally the recipient should respond by saying which of the offered formats it is capable of using, and given that this is all internal to our bank, it is highly likely that the VRU will have been set up to support the same formats, and will respond saying it will support all of them for this call.

We actually simplified this message by removing all optional lines which if you were to examine a real SIP INVITE message you may well see. It's worth pointing out that the PSTN gateway doesn't know where to route the call – it is a relatively unintelligent server whose primary function is to convert between PSTN calls and VoIP calls and ask a different server – which in our architecture is the IP PBX – to work out how to route them.

So, the IP PBX receives the INVITE message from the PSTN gateway. Its job is to determine where to route the call based on the destination number. It holds an address book, which it uses to look up the destination number specified in the message (+44 1234 555222) and which is associated with the network address of the voice response unit in its address book (because whoever set up the contact centre configured this). It then creates a new INVITE message, copying many of the same details, and sends it to the VRU.

There is then an exchange of messages between the VRU and PSTN gateway going via the IP PBX which results in an agreement on the audio formats to be used, and the ports the RTP channel will use on the PSTN gateway and the VRU. Once the PSTN gateway receives the 200 OK message from the IP PBX and sends an ACK message back, the call will stop ringing and the PSTN gateway will start sending RTP messages directly to the VRU. Once the VRU receives the ACK message, it too will start sending RTP messages to the PSTN gateway, and the caller will be connected to the VRU. Note that the RTP messages do not flow via the IP PBX.

Now, there is another communication channel that is established at the same time as the RTP channel. This is for sending RTP Control Protocol (RTCP) messages between the PSTN gateway and the VRU. RTCP is defined in the same IETF RFC document as RTP – RFC 3550 – and is used to exchange information on the quality of the communication that is using RTP, such as the time taken for an RTP message to traverse the network. The PSTN gateway and VRU could use such information to swap to a less network-intensive codec (out of the codecs agreed by the two at the start of the call), for example. The PSTN gateway specified that it wanted to receive RTP messages on port 11014 (we picked this port number randomly for this example). By default, RTCP messages will be sent to the port one higher than the corresponding RTP channel, so the PSTN gateway is expecting to receive them on port 11015. The specification of RTCP is actually more complex than RTP and we aren't going to go into it any further here.

So once the call has been established, there are actually three network channels in use, as illustrated in Figure 4.14. This diagram shows the port numbers that we have covered so far. We haven't covered what port numbers the VRU decided it wanted to receive RTP and RTCP messages on, but this would have been specified in its response to the INVITE message. The port numbers it uses are very likely to be different from the ones on the PSTN gateway (it would be pure chance they were the same). In addition, we have assumed the PSTN gateway is using the same ports to send RTP and RTCP messages as it uses to receive them (11014 and 11015 respectively). This is not mandatory but is recommended by the IETF in RFC4961.[29] SIP messages are normally received on port 5060 (but do not have to be sent from that port), and we have assumed that the PSTN gateway, as the initiator of SIP messages for the call, will have sent the INVITE message to port 5060 on the IP PBX, which in turn will have forwarded the message to port 5060 on the VRU. There may be hundreds of calls in progress at any time, and the PSTN gateway and VRU are likely to use different ports for the RTP messages for each call (and also for the corresponding RTCP messages) so that the calls remain strictly segregated. Using different ports also enables the servers to be scaled up to support hundreds or even thousands of simultaneous contacts, as different processes can service each port and these processes can run on different CPUs within the same server. It would even be possible to use more than one server for any of the contact centre platforms with very little additional effort.

If we assume the caller does everything they need to do using the VRU, the next thing that will happen is that either the VRU or the caller will end the call. This will result in more SIP messages going via the IP PBX to cleanly terminate the call. However, let's assume the caller needs to speak to a contact centre agent, and so the VRU needs to be

FIGURE 4.14   Network channels during a VoIP call.

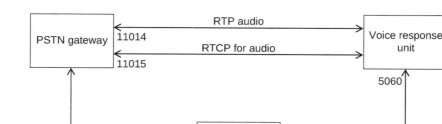

able to transfer the call to a queue from where it can be picked up by an agent. However, we haven't got an ACD in our VoIP contact centre! In practice, the IP PBX or the VRU could provide the ACD functionality, including the ability to play music and keep the caller updated about their position in the queue. If the VRU provides the functionality, the call does not need to be transferred and the fact that the call is now in a queue may be completely unknown to the PSTN gateway and the IP PBX. However, we think it is better practice for the VRU to inform the IP PBX (using SIP messages) that the call should be transferred to a queue, and for the IP PBX to work out where this queue is located, even if it is still on the VRU. This means the IP PBX will continue to be aware and in control of what is happening to the call. Similarly, the IP PBX is aware of what agents are online and connected, so it will know when it can transfer the call to an agent. With this arrangement, contact centre managers can get a full picture of calls from the IP PBX rather than having to check each platform.

We have one further comment to make about SIP: in reality, its name – Session *Initiation* Protocol – is misleading, as it is used to not only initiate communication sessions but also to manage them (e.g. to transfer between recipients) and to end sessions.

We have gone into some detail about how just one audio call is handled in a modern contact centre. We are sure it's clear that this is a technically complex and rich area with many standards and protocols in use. As well as those we have mentioned, there are more standards for dealing with other types of media including video calls and text messaging and for encrypting and authenticating VoIP communications. There are also more RFC documents that clarify or provide further guidance on how to use SIP, SDP, RTP, RTCP and other associated protocols. All in all, the standards documentation runs to several thousand pages and has been built up over something like 20 years. In fact there are so many RFC documents relating to SIP that there is even an RFC document that sets out to explain what each one covers – RFC 5411[30] – although this is now incomplete, given further developments in SIP standards.

However, we haven't yet finished with our modern contact centre and there are other functions we need to describe.

4.9.12 Contact Recording with VoIP

In our example of an inbound call from the PSTN, after some negotiation the audio was routed directly between the PSTN gateway and the VRU, and if transferred to a contact centre agent, between the PSTN gateway and the agent's headset. Most banking contact centres will want to record the call. In our legacy call centre, this was done by, in effect, tapping into the phone line through the PBX (in principle joining another pair of wires to the pair carrying the phone call through the PBX) and having another phone line connecting from the tap to a call recording unit. In our modern IP-based contact centre we could scan the network for all RTP messages and save them, but this would present a challenge to reconstruct any single call – the various tags and unique IDs in SIP messages would help here and we are aware that some vendors have used this approach. If the messages were being encrypted it would potentially be impossible to reconstruct any call. There is another IETF standard for recording calls and other media called the Session Recording Protocol, which is defined in RFC 7866.[31] The basic approach is for at least one of the computers that are involved in exchanging RTP messages to send copies of all the messages it sends and receives to a call recording server.

FIGURE 4.15   Network channels used while recording a VoIP call.

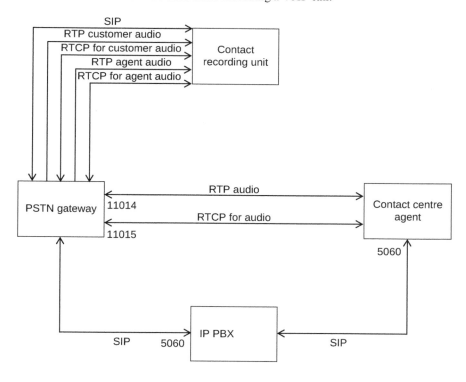

There are, as is often the case with such standards, various ways of implementing session recording. The PSTN gateway is involved in all external calls and could make copies of the media traffic sent using RTP messages. This is perhaps the simplest solution building on what we have described so far, and this is what some vendors do. This would result in flows of RTP messages as shown in Figure 4.15.

Note that the PSTN gateway could simplify the flows to and from the contact recording unit – for example, it could combine the two audio channels (from the customer and from the agent) into a single audio channel. It could also recode the audio to a single audio codec so all recordings on the contact recording unit are in the same format. Note also how the RTP messages only flow from the PSTN gateway to the contact recording unit and not in the other direction, because the contact recording unit doesn't generate any audio – it just needs to receive it so it can record it.

The obvious question with this approach to contact recording is how the contact recording unit can log things like the customer ID with a contact recording to make it easy to find a set of contact recordings (e.g. for a single customer). There is indeed a mechanism to do this. The SIP messages sent between the various platforms involved in the contact can also include additional data on the call (termed metadata in the various IETF RFC documents that cover this, such as RFC 7865[32]), including any information any of the call participants send. So, in our scenario of an audio call, once the VRU has identified the customer, it sends a SIP message to the IP PBX with metadata including the customer ID. The IP PBX then includes this information in SIP messages it sends to the PSTN gateway, which can then include it in its SIP messages to the contact recording unit.

4.9.13   Computer Telephony Integration with VoIP Calls

In our modern contact centre we haven't included a computer telephony integration server. In a legacy call centre, its function is to keep track of information on each call and supply this to each platform that is involved with the call, as well as receive updates and commands from those platforms (such as customer ID from the VRU and instruction to end the call from the agent's desktop). This was necessary because the call was carried over telephone lines, while the information relating to that call and maintained by the CTI server was carried over the bank's data network. The CTI server was the only platform that could see the status of each call and take commands to handle the call from applications because it connected directly to the PBX and was also connected to the bank's data network. However, in our modern VoIP contact centre, the IP PBX inherently maintains all routing information on each contact (including calls, video calls and so on), controls the routing of those contacts and is located on the bank's data network. Unlike a legacy PBX, however, the contacts do not themselves flow through the IP PBX.

In practice, we note that some vendors of VoIP contact centre platforms still provide CTI modules, and they do this for two reasons. First, VoIP contact centre platforms are being supplied to call centres where it is still necessary to connect to legacy telephone equipment (such as VRUs or call recorders) or interface with legacy business applications. Second, our example modern contact centre was using SIP messaging to route data typically supplied by the CTI server to the agent desktop, because we assumed the agent desktop and the agent phone or headset were connected. This may not be the case – the agent may be using a standalone VoIP phone and a separate desktop running a core banking platform client. In order for the core banking platform client to be aware of the ongoing contact and data such as the customer ID for that contact, there would have to be some mechanism for getting the data to the core banking platform client. A CTI module that interfaces with the IP PBX could do this. The CTI functionality could also be built directly into the IP PBX.

4.9.14   SIP Trunking and Contact Centre Platforms in the Cloud

So far our scenario has involved receiving calls over the public switched telephone network into a PSTN gateway, where they get converted to and from VoIP calls which are transmitted over the bank's internal network. In many countries there is an alternative, more modern mechanism for connecting to the telephone network – using what are called SIP trunks. Basically, SIP trunking means phone calls arrive as VoIP calls over the Internet, so there is no need for any phone lines to connect to the PSTN, just an Internet connection. In effect, the telco that provides the SIP trunks has already converted calls to VoIP. Modern telcos transmit IP-based traffic across their networks without changing it anyway, so this approach actually removes the decoding stage that converts a VoIP call running across a telco's IP network back to an old-fashioned PSTN call running over a telephone line only then to be converted back to a VoIP call by the PSTN gateway. The use of SIP trunks is likely to become the dominant method of connecting corporate telephone networks to the PSTN, and in some countries the PSTN will, to all intents and purposes, be replaced with an IP-based network with only domestic and small business telephone lines that are still running over copper wires, remaining on the old technology. Copper lines will disappear over time as fibre is laid or strung all the way to such properties and phone calls then run over the fibre connection (as VoIP calls).

So, with SIP trunks, the PSTN gateway is no longer required. However, it is still necessary to protect the bank's network from being flooded with spam SIP calls. This is because anyone connected to the Internet could start bombarding the bank with SIP calls at essentially no cost (much like spam email is free for the sender). For regular Internet traffic (e.g. for web browsing) this is done with a firewall, and for connections with SIP trunks, the equivalent device is called a Session Border Controller.

Now that physical telephone lines are no longer needed, the contact centre platforms can be hosted anywhere with a fast enough Internet connection – so using a cloud service is possible. So now our contact centre architecture looks like the diagram in Figure 4.16.

FIGURE 4.16   Contact centre platforms in the cloud.

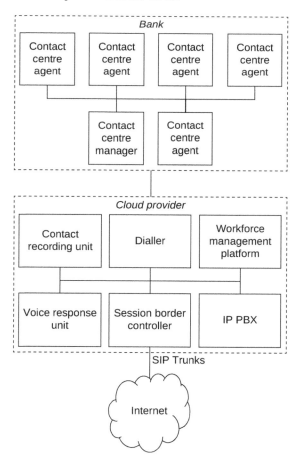

In this diagram calls are made over SIP trunks from and to the PSTN. SIP and RTP traffic also flows between the cloud provider and the contact centre agents. Note that different suppliers of cloud-based VoIP platforms combine different functions into the same server (often the IP PBX) and use different names for the various servers compared to what we have used here. It can be difficult to compare offerings from different suppliers because of this. There are also open-source VoIP platforms available.

4.9.15   Other Contact Media Types

We described a VoIP audio call in the previous scenario and described how audio was coded and decoded and sent via RTP messages. SIP, SDP, RTP, RTCP and associated protocols were actually designed to handle a range of media types. Let's suppose our bank is accepting video calls over the Internet. In practice, we expect it would do so via its own smartphone app in order to ensure that it can secure the call by encrypting the communication and authenticating the caller, to control what protocols are used for the call (including how the video is encoded) and to ensure that the customer has a compatible smartphone. Alternatively, a bank could offer the facility through its Internet banking service, although it would rely on a customer accessing it from a PC or other device that has a camera, speaker and microphone, or through ATMs that have video calling capability.

First, let's cover how the video call is made secure. Given the video call is going across the Internet, it must be encrypted so that eavesdroppers can't access the communication and authenticated so that the caller and the bank can verify each other's identity. To do this, rather than use unencrypted SIP messages, the first thing the caller's smartphone app will do is establish a Transport Layer Security (TLS) session with the bank's Session Border Controller and use this to exchange SIP messages – the combination of these two is called SIPS (Secure Session Initiation Protocol). This is in effect the same thing that a web browser does when it connects using HTTPS (i.e. HTTP over TLS) instead of HTTP. As well as defining the audio and video to be used in the video call, the SIP messages will also be used to define how the RTP messages carrying the audio and video streams and the RTCP messages will be encrypted (turning them into SRTP and SRTCP messages, respectively).

Second, let's look at how a video call is specified in the SIP messages. Remember from our earlier audio call example that the SDP message body of the INVITE message contained a line stating that the call included audio m=audio 11014 RTP/AVP 8 0 18 96. For a video call, the INVITE message would also include a line for audio, which would look something like m=audio 11014 RTP/SAVP 8 0 18 in which RTP/SAVP denotes the secure RTP/AVP profile (and which uses the same payload formats as RTP/AVP), and we have dropped what was profile number 96 at the end, as DTMF is unlikely to be used in a video call. Further down it would also include some lines specifying the video codecs it can use, for example:

```
m=video 11016 RTP/SAVP 97 96
a=rtpmap:97 H264/90000
a=rtpmap:96 H263-2000/90000
```

This is saying the video can be encoded using H.264[33] or H.263-2000[34], which are both video coding standards defined by the ITU. In reality, we may expect to see several more video encoding profiles in such a message which would have different trade-offs between quality, resolution, bandwidth requirements and processing power requirements. There may well be other lines giving further parameters for each of these video encoding methods, which would also tailor the resolution, quality, bandwidth requirements and processing power requirements. Once the call is established, the audio and video are exchanged in SRTP messages.

Finally, it's worth noting that video calls coming from the bank's smartphone app would be routed directly over the Internet to a Session Border Controller at the bank. They would be unlikely to pass over SIP trunks which are intended for telephony.

So, we've covered how a VoIP call can be set up with both audio and video media streams. In addition, there are a small number of other media types that can be used, namely:

text – one potential use of this is for subtitles that are synchronised with a video stream, and in general the exchange of text-based information such as chat sessions, using RTP.

message – this can be used for instant messaging, with the text messages sent using the Message Session Relay Protocol (MSRP, which is different from RTP) defined in RFC 4975.[35] Note that instant messaging smartphone apps are virtually all proprietary, do not interoperate and may well use different protocols.

application – this allows for any type of information to be exchanged (the implication of the name is that the information is application-specific). It has been used to supplement the other media types to provide error handling and retransmission of RTP messages that were lost in transit and for screen sharing, including providing mouse or pointer and keyboard input. Screen sharing may be useful in a banking environment for helping customers complete applications or talking them through how to use online banking or a banking app, although there are implications for information security.

We have also seen some suppliers of VoIP platforms and software define their own media types, including one for screen sharing (e.g. during conference calls).

So, it would be possible to use the same contact centre platforms to support a range of contact types including audio calls, video calls, chat sessions and screen sharing. The contact recording unit can be sent copies of all the RTP messages involved in such sessions and it could retain a full history of the interaction with customers. Of course, there are implications for organising and managing customer service representatives as the range of contact types increases.

4.9.16   A Modern Contact Centre

Let's look at what we end up with in our modern multimedia contact centre, as shown in Figure 4.17. In this setup, we've shown four video workstations (used by customer service representatives who can take all types of contacts including video calls) and four

FIGURE 4.17   A modern multimedia contact centre.

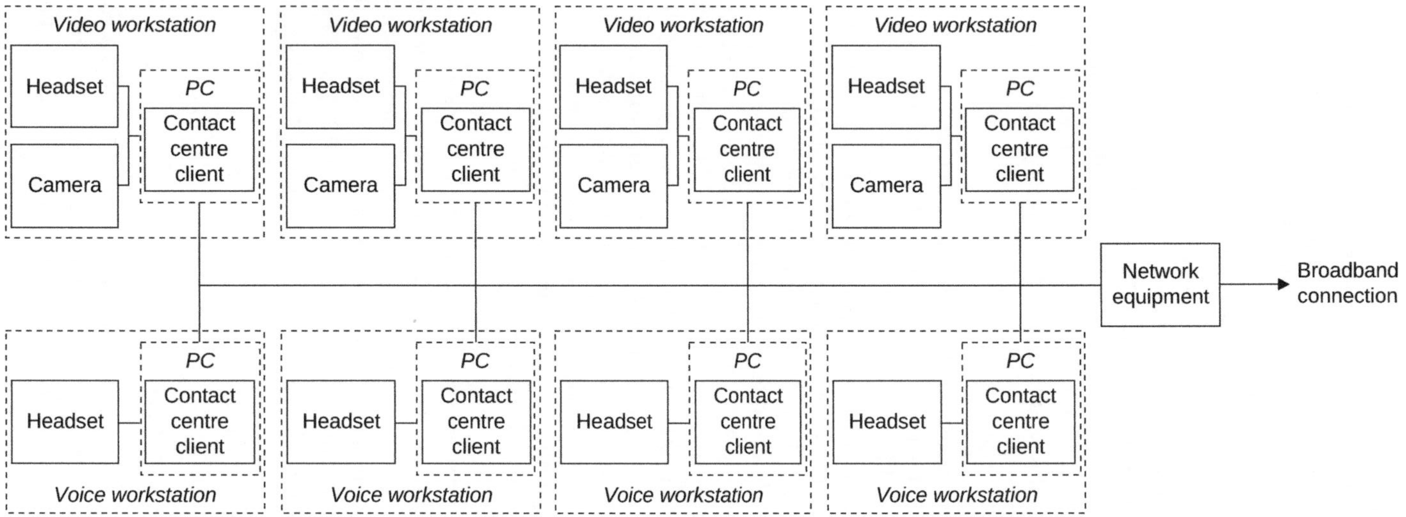

voice workstations (used by customer service representatives who can take all types of contacts except video calls). In reality you may well have many more workstations than this. Each workstation has a PC with a contact centre (thick) client installed on it. This performs two functions – it handles the VoIP contact and it provides access to the bank's platforms so the user can service the customer. The contact centre is connected to the rest of the bank's network (assuming it is in a different location) and to the contact centre technology provider over a broadband connection.

4.9.17   H.323

We mentioned that H.323 is another protocol that could be used instead of SIP for managing VoIP calls. Like SIP, there is a very large set of standards documents that cover the usage of H.323,[36] and these are published by the ITU. At one time, H.323 was the leading protocol used to manage video conferencing in enterprises and was also used for VoIP calling within enterprises. However, we believe SIP has become, and will remain, the predominant standard used for enterprise VoIP. There are various different strengths and weaknesses of both these protocols and we aren't going to go into them in this book. However, VoIP calls established by both protocols use RTP as the protocol for actually transmitting the voice data (and data for other media types) between call participants.

4.9.18   Contact Handling Considerations

Compliance (i.e. adherence to regulation and law) is one of those areas that has become increasingly important. While its relevance was accepted, to some extent, prior to the banking crisis of 2008, regulators now demand evidence that banks have integrated compliance into their operations. In a contact centre context, contact recording is an important feature for compliance so that issues can be investigated and the performance of agents can be proactively reviewed. In addition, delivery of compliance training and recording its completion by contact centre agents is also in effect required.

The launch of a range of modern banks, from Metro Bank to Monzo in the UK, N26 across Europe, and the likes of (the now defunct) Moven, in the US, has highlighted how important culture is. Culture covers how a bank does its business, how it engages its customers, how it engages its staff and many other aspects of how it operates. In an increasingly digital world, the contact centre is often the only time customers really experience a bank's corporate culture and it is therefore key to ensure this comes across in every interaction. This is where contact recording can be useful in ensuring consistency and quality in every customer interaction, and enthusing contact centre staff is vital. We feel that neobanks have an advantage here – they can build their desired culture from the start, and there can be direct contact between customer-facing staff and senior management so that a one-team culture prevails.

Any good contact centre facility should have been designed to make the space pleasant for the staff, limit how easily sound travels and reduce the impact of any background noises. It must also be secure. Consideration needs to be given to who has access to the contact centre, what might be overheard and how fraudsters and fraud can be prevented; such efforts often include running reference and credit checks on new recruits, and inside the contact centre banning mobile phones and paper and limiting access to email and the Internet.

Location can play an important role in the decision-making process for a new contact centre. It has a direct impact on costs such as salaries and rent, as well as local development incentives and regeneration scheme benefits. Location also affects the availability of skills and, importantly, languages and accents. In some areas there are laws dictating the need to provide services in certain languages (in Welsh, for example, in Wales), but the accent can have a significant role to play, not just in customers' ability to understand what is being said, but in perceptions of the contact centre by customers. It may not be what everybody wants to read, but customers' perceptions of a contact centre may have a direct relationship with the accent that they hear.

Core systems availability – if the contact centre is available on a 24×7 basis, then the bank's platforms (including contact centre platforms) must mirror this. Similarly, if the bank provides more than one way for customers to access their accounts, then these must be synchronised with data available to the contact centre agents. There are few things worse, from a customer perspective, than realising that they are looking at data online that is different than the data that the contact centre sees, and where there are differences in the timeliness of transaction and balance information, there could be an opportunity for fraud or it could impact vulnerable customers.

4.10   Text Messaging

Short message service (SMS) messaging – short text messages originally sent between mobile phones using a feature of mobile networks – has been used by banks almost since it became available on mobile phones in 1992.[37] Uses include customer authentication (provision of a one-time code to enable login to Internet banking, for example), notification of various transactions occurring on customer accounts and checking that transactions are not fraudulent. Due to the relatively simple use cases, SMS-based messaging is simple to set up and requires very limited human intervention, but is limited by the restricted format and by the costs associated with texting (for example, the cost per text to a bank typically starts at a small number of pence or cents, and reduces with volume). Some banks use app-based messaging instead of SMS, probably to reduce the cost. We suspect that usage of SMS will decline as in-app messaging takes over. Even M-Pesa, one of the original champions of SMS-based payment services (see Section 4.13), moved to a policy of app-based use over SMS.

From a technology perspective, various suppliers provide a means for banks to send and receive texts. They typically use either a protocol specifically for SMS text messaging, called the Short Message Peer-to-Peer (SMPP) protocol[38] that can be used over the Internet (with suitable encryption) or using a leased line to the SMS provider, or a RESTful interface over the Internet (see Section 3.16) to which the bank's platform will post the details of a message to be sent to a customer (along with their mobile number). The same service can send responses from customers back to the bank (either using the same SMPP connection or to a web server at the bank if using a RESTful interface). If available, the service may allow the bank to send messages with a text address (e.g. the name of the bank) rather than a mobile phone number. There are similar RESTful Internet interfaces for messaging apps, and it may be possible to find a provider who can handle a mixture of SMS and messaging apps. It is possible to run a chat session using SMS or a messaging app; it could be handled via the bank's contact centre like online chat.

4.11   Internet

The Internet and mobile seem to have become the primary channels between banks and their customers. In fact, the growth of Internet and mobile banking have even been cited as the primary reason why banks are seeing a decline in use of their branches.[39] The Internet banking platform typically provides customers with a feature-rich capability that enables balance checking, transactional analysis, creation of new payees and payments, statement downloading and, increasingly, account opening. Often customers can change many of their profile details as well.

While the data shows that increasing Internet usage typically coincides with a drop-off in branch use, there is a question of cause and effect here. The Internet does, clearly, make some elements of banking much easier to manage remotely, but there is also a good argument that the big banks are investing heavily in pushing the custom from branches towards the cheaper Internet and mobile channels. Either way, Internet banking is a key consideration for many established banks but not necessarily so for new start-ups. Many newer banking business models, such as Monzo and Starling in the UK, Moven in the US, and 86 400 in Australia eschewed Internet banking in favour of mobile-only solutions.

Section 3.10 covers the technology used to support Internet banking.

4.12   Email

Despite email being widely available for as long as the Internet has been available, usage for communication between banks and retail customers often feels like it is treated as another one-way push channel such as broadcast advertising and print media, although it has the advantage that messages can be tailored to each customer. We are unaware of any mass retail banking service that will accept instructions or requests via Internet email, limiting inbound customer correspondence to general enquiries and complaints and using outbound email for marketing and some alerts and notifications. This is because Internet email was historically not secure and in 2020 still lacked some security features. Historically, emails were sent across the Internet unencrypted, so anyone who used a packet sniffer on a Wi-Fi or wired network could read email traffic. Most email services encrypt emails between the client (e.g. the mail app on a PC, tablet or smartphone) and the email server (in both direction) and often between each other, but there is still no definite guarantee that outbound emails are encrypted after the email server forwards them to the recipient or that inbound emails are encrypted before they reach the final email server. Even if an email happens to be encrypted along its whole route, each server on the route decrypts and re-encrypts the email, so anyone hacking into (or who has access to) an email server en route could access it. Also, email services themselves usually have access to the emails.*

Of course, banks often provide a secure messaging facility as part of their Internet banking or mobile banking services. These do not use the Internet email protocol. Such a facility could be handled by the same contact centre that supports telephony, chat and other multimedia contacts.

---

*There are some premium email services such as ProtonMail which cannot access the content of emails after they receive them because they are encrypted on their servers, with decryption only possible by the end-recipient.

For relationship-managed services including premier banking and business banking, Internet email is used more often, but most banks will typically only allow this to be used for more administrative matters (e.g. arranging a face-to-face appointment).

One final consideration for this channel is that beyond the implementation of the email platform itself there is also the need for a degree of integration with any customer relationship management (CRM) platform to ensure that customer queries and complaints are logged to the right customer and can be managed.

4.13   Mobile

Mobile banking is the current star of banking channels. The first smartphone to see significant market success, the original Apple iPhone, was released to the public only in 2007. The huge success of the smartphone, less from its ability to support telephone calls than its support for apps, has led to a revolution in the way we run our lives, and banking is no exception to this.

Although Apple gets a lot of credit for driving the revolution in mobile phones, its innovation was not the first to enable mobile banking. That credit lies elsewhere. There may be other claimants to being the first user of mobile phones to support banking transactions but arguably the first real success was M-Pesa, a money transfer service launched commercially in Kenya in 2007 by Safaricom, as we noted in Chapter 2. M-Pesa has seen significant ongoing success over more than a decade of operations, with its Kenyan customer base now exceeding 25 million[40] and its global base, outside of Kenya, at over 13 million[41]. While it is now primarily app-driven, M-Pesa owes its original success to the use of SMS.

There is no denying that mobile banking is now huge business; for example, according to analysts at CACI[42] in 2019 mobile apps were used by more than half of UK banking customers to manage their account. A quick search of the Internet, though, reveals that other countries claim higher penetration than this. For example, in 2018, a report by Global Data claimed that in India the proportion of current account holders using mobile banking was approaching 60%.[43]

There are several reasons why mobile banking is popular. From a customer's perspective it provides a simple and easy way to manage their finances wherever they can get a reasonable mobile phone signal. Through the eyes of a financial services provider it provides a higher level of security than Internet sites through the inbuilt capabilities in our smartphones (such as biometric authentication), is easy to deploy to a high volume of customers through the various app stores (albeit potentially requiring at least two different flavours of app to support the two prevalent smartphone operating systems) and significantly reduces usage of more conventional (and manpower-heavy) channels such as the branch and contact centre.[44]

There are basically three approaches to providing a mobile banking app, which are the same whether the devices being targeted are smartphones or tablets and irrespective of what operating system they use.

First, it's perfectly possible to offer a website that is tailored to the web browser and touchscreen on a smartphone or tablet. Using what is called responsive design it is even possible to have a single website that tailors itself to the screen format and user entry method (e.g. keyboard and mouse or touchscreen with on-screen keyboard), so that it can be used for Internet banking on a PC, tablet or smartphone. With this approach the architecture looks exactly the same as shown in Figure 3.37, although the Internet banking component and the webpages have to be more sophisticated so that webpages are appropriately sized and formatted. In reality, banks will probably want to do this anyway, because some customers will access Internet banking from web browsers on smartphones, tablets and PCs. Relatively recently, with the availability of what are called service workers with modern web browsers, so-called progressive web apps delivered through a web browser can offer some of the facilities of native apps including being able to send notifications, having an app icon and being usable when the device is offline. In effect the website is partly installed on the device, running in the background, using a service worker provided by the device's web browser.

The next step is to provide an app that wraps the bank's website. This is a so-called hybrid approach, in which the user starts the app, which may have a built-in logon screen, from which point it displays webpages served by the bank's Internet banking website, normally using the device's built-in web browsing capability. If a bank wants to have a presence in the Apple or Google app store and be able to market that it has a banking app, this can be done relatively quickly using this approach. It also makes sense, because banking apps typically present details of accounts and transactions that are maintained by the bank and not stored or copied locally to the mobile device – in other words, the device has to be online anyway in order to provide the banking service. In our experience, many banks did indeed take this approach (and probably still do). Apache Cordova is an open-source cross-platform development environment that can be used to produce hybrid apps, and a commercial version, Adobe PhoneGap, is also available.

The final step is to provide a native app. The app is responsible for retrieving data from the bank (typically using some form of web services call) and then formatting it and presenting it to the user. This has at least two advantages. First, the amount of data retrieved from the bank can be very small relative to the amount of data involved in receiving fully formed webpages, so the app is more responsive to users and consumes less mobile data. Second, the user interface itself can take full advantage of features of the operating system and provide more functionality, such as providing notifications, using the device's fingerprint reader for logging in, video calling, and offline functionality (e.g. providing account balances and transactions from when the app was last used). The primary disadvantages are that the bank has to have the capability to develop, test and support an app, and normally it has to do this for at least two device operating systems – Google's Android and Apple's iOS/iPadOS and multiple versions thereof – and the approaches to developing native mobile apps are still in a state of flux as the operating systems and the features available on mobile devices develop.[45] There are cross-platform development environments such as Appcelerator's Titanium, Drifty's Ionic, Facebook's React Native, Google's Flutter and Microsoft's Xamarin that can be used to develop an app that can be compiled for each platform, although there is some debate about the pros and cons of these compared to developing apps for both platforms side by side (see e.g. reference[46]). Some cross-platform development environments also provide a path from hybrid apps to native apps, allowing embedded webpages to be progressively replaced with native functionality.

Banks also have another option for Internet banking and mobile apps, with a number of third-party digital banking platforms that provide banking functionality that can be customised to a bank's specific requirements around look and feel and integrated with its underlying business platforms. Examples include Backbase Digital Banking, Crealogix's range of digital banking products, Finastra's Fusion Digital Channels, Oracle Banking Digital Experience, Sandstone Technology's Digital Banking and Temenos's Infinity and Quantum (originally Kony DBX) – although we note that what is available and the names of the products change frequently. The advantage of such products is that they can potentially rapidly provide a large amount of functionality across retail, SME and corporate banking that encompasses servicing and origination across multiple channels and cross-channel integration, and they can often be hosted in the cloud rather than on premises, avoiding up-front capital expenditure on infrastructure. The disadvantages are that they may not offer the specific functionality, look and feel or support for banking products required by a bank, and the potential implementation and licensing costs may be high. For some banks that do not want to build their own digital platforms or do not have access to the expertise to do so, such products may be interesting.

4.14   Social Media

At the risk of stating the obvious, social media is extremely popular with the general public. For whatever reason, people share many of their most intimate moments and thoughts with a cast of thousands through Facebook, Twitter, Instagram, Snapchat, WeChat, Weibo and many other social media platforms. This presents both an opportunity and a problem to any marketer, regardless of their industry. The opportunity is clear – the audience for a well-placed advert is massive. However, the problem it poses is that identification of specific individuals on social media is difficult, meaning that it is extremely hard to identify and engage with just customers. When they are ranting about poor service or failed systems on every social media platform they engage with, that is a real problem! Like many consumers, we have observed that marketing departments (and not customer service departments) tend to monitor social media and they are much more sensitive to criticism and can often force the rapid resolution of issues on behalf of customers.

Potentially, social media platforms may be interested in offering a channel to banks through which they can offer their banking services – on the basis that keeping a customer on the social media site or app is better than losing them to another website or app. With the advent of open banking in the EU and UK, they could even build such interfaces to banking services themselves. Whether customers would value this or get concerned about offering their financial data up to social media platforms remains to be seen.

Many social media platforms incorporate private messaging services. These are walled gardens, i.e. they use proprietary protocols and don't interoperate. Banks have to choose which ones they will support and for what purposes. There are various interfaces that they can use to receive and send private messages, and these could be integrated into a bank's contact centre platform.

4.15   Marketing

Historically, marketing was either through advertisements (on billboards, in printed media and on broadcast media) with coarse targeting and little direct feedback on its effectiveness or through direct mail and telephone campaigns which could be targeted at specific individuals. In the latter case, banks could purchase lists of potential new customers from third parties or they could generate their own lists from their customer records. With the advent of computers, generating lists from existing customer data could be done using more sophisticated analysis.

A general view of the technology required to support such analysis and manage marketing campaigns is illustrated in Figure 4.18. This builds on the architecture for our bank that we developed in Chapter 3, in which the bank has various core platforms and an Internet banking platform, all of which have their own databases. Daily extracts of new and changed data are taken from these databases (which are shown at the top of the diagram), using extract, transform and load (ETL) tools (not shown on the diagram). These tools load the data into what is called a data warehouse, which is usually a type of relational database management system (RDBMS; see Chapter 3) and which usually has specially designed schemas that enable very fast searching of data attributes. The data warehouse may be used for many purposes, such as identifying patterns of fraudulent behaviour, reporting on trends across the customer base and product set, and for identifying groups of customers for marketing purposes. A variety of specialised data analysis tools would be used to support these types of analyses, often used by an expert team

FIGURE 4.18   Traditional marketing architecture.

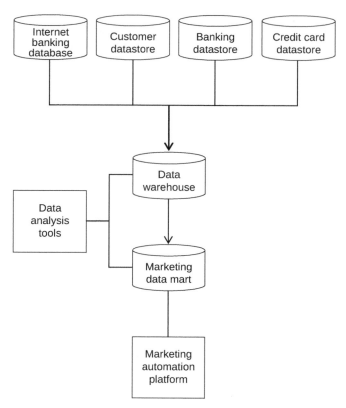

within the bank. Marketing data identified from this analysis would be loaded into a marketing data mart (which could just be a segregated area within the data warehouse, or a separate database), where it could be further analysed and sliced and diced into target customer groups, campaign lists and so on. A marketing automation platform can be used to manage campaigns including generating mailshots and lists of telephone numbers for telephone campaigns, and it may also provide marketing messages on demand to operational platforms – for example, the Internet banking platform could ask the marketing automation platform for a marketing prompt after a customer logs on. Marketing automation platforms also typically support many campaign management features such as the ability to test campaigns, A/B campaigns and so on.

With the advent of the World Wide Web, followed by social media, the ability to track individuals and target them has become even more sophisticated, and banks have to decide how much they want to use such abilities while respecting legal requirements such as the EU's General Data Protection Regulation (GDPR).

4.16   Cross-channel Considerations and Implications

4.16.1   Consistency

The ultimate goal for many banks is to create a true omnichannel experience for the customer, where a customer can interface with the bank over any channel, and also swap between channels, and get a consistent, joined-up experience. We have already noted how the introduction of online ATMs forced banks to maintain an intraday available balance across channels (i.e. the branch and ATM), which was subsequently exacerbated by the introduction of debit cards and then Internet banking. In effect, banks are forced to have real-time banking capability, even if in many cases their systems of record still fundamentally process in batches. Also, many people have experienced the frustration of starting an application for a product in one channel (e.g. the Internet channel), running into problems and then having to restart the whole process (e.g. over the telephone or in a branch) with the bank's customer service agent completely unaware of information previously provided by the customer. Given the different heritages of channels in large legacy banks, they find this problem difficult to solve. Neobanks can design for this from the start, by logging all customer interactions in a uniform way and making the history of such interactions available to all customer service staff.

4.16.2   Operational Availability and Resilience

Historically, core platforms were able to have downtime for maintenance and end-of-day processing outside of the branch network opening hours, although this window was smaller in places where the bank had multiple time zones in a single geography to contend with. The implementation of telephone contact centres often didn't change this much as they tended to operate on only marginally longer opening hours than the branch network. However, the Internet is always on and that means that customers expect to be able to use the Internet and mobile banking services at any time, and they also expect to be able to withdraw cash from ATMs at any time. Daily downtime is no longer acceptable, and this places obvious requirements on banking platforms. Note in particular how moving from batch-oriented processing to real-time processing immediately means that failures must be minimised. For example, with batch processing, if a system fails, the batch is typically restarted on a standby system (in effect, the clock is turned back to an earlier point in the batch cycle). Of course, with a real-time system, the clock cannot be turned back and no transactions that have already taken place (such as outbound payments) can be replayed.

We explored how banking platforms can be made highly available in Chapter 3. Historically, robustness was often created by the use of server farms and clusters, where multiple servers would serve a single purpose, with resilience provided by multi-site implementations that would switch over to the second site if the first should fail. This was, of course, expensive, and banks had to determine how much they would invest in such approaches. In the era of microservices and cloud computing, high availability is much easier and less costly to achieve. With containerised, self-healing systems that are capable of spinning up new services automatically, it is now possible to build services that are extremely reliable at little incremental cost. Netflix has produced one of the most highly available services on the face of the planet and is famous for doing so, not just for its levels of uptime but for the approach that it took to achieving it. In around 2011, Netflix developed the concept of chaos engineering,[47] which is a method of purposely seeking to force running services to fail and then seeing whether the system can automatically cope with the failure. This approach went as far as developing the Chaos Monkey, a service whose role it is to force other services to randomly fail. Chaos Monkey runs within Netflix's live environment and forces its software engineers to build for both robustness and resilience at every step of the development process. Taking it a step further, Netflix has since developed a whole suite of tools, the Simian Army, that all have different roles in testing Netflix's services, from dropping entire data centres within the cloud that host Netflix services (Chaos Kong) to randomly introducing latency (Latency Monkey).[48]

It should be noted that even the best-designed banking platforms occasionally experience unscheduled outages (often, it seems, as a result of software errors or human errors when updating a platform) or need some form of maintenance or upgrade for which they must be taken offline. Also, during end-of-day processing there may be some restrictions on what banking services can be performed. In these cases, designing the channel platforms to cope gracefully and, if appropriate, informing customers in advance are typical approaches adopted by banks.

4.16.3   Security

When banks only had branch networks and physical cash was the primary medium of exchange, security was primarily concerned with physical security. Now, with ATMs and telephone, Internet and mobile banking (as well as open banking interfaces) the attack perimeter is much broader and as well as attacks on banks' property (including branches, ATMs, data centres and operational centres), anyone connected to the Internet could mount an attack from anywhere in the world. Cyber-attacks on businesses and governments receive a lot of press, and they are very concerning for banks, but they are also not the most frequently successful form of attack carried out against banks. Card fraud, authorised push payment fraud and money laundering are much more commonly carried out than any form of successful cyber-attack (see Chapters 5, 6 and 7 for more information).

In terms of financial loss, fraud is a massive overhead for the banking industry. Every channel operated by a bank must help protect against this by appropriate use of identification and verification technologies both during the account origination process as well as at every login. We cover eKYC in Section 5.6.1 but banks must also consider robust security on user devices, including the potential for advanced biometric identification (not just fingerprints, but also gesture recognition, for example).[49]

Any business operating in financial services (or pretty much any industry, for that matter) should seek to develop a comprehensive approach to security across each of the commonly accepted security control categories:

- Administrative controls – This covers policies and processes, including the development of security policies, standards and guidelines, screening and training of staff and implementation of change controls.
- Physical controls – This includes managing physical access to the environment, locking down computer hardware and monitoring (and alerting) of physical spaces.
- Technical controls – This includes controlling access to IT systems (through identity and access management systems and role-based access control), enforcement of password and other security policies, implementation of security devices and software such as firewalls, antivirus software, intrusion prevention and intrusion detection systems, SIEM (Security Information and Event Management) and encryption of data in transit and at rest.

This list only hints at the level of work required to implement and manage an appropriately secure environment. However, the ramifications of not doing so can be severe.[50]

4.16.4   Heterogeneity of Endpoints

Banks used to be in complete control of their channels, with the biggest challenge coming when a bank's ATM supplier changed the message format used by its ATMs (as IBM did in the 1970s). However, the proliferation of online channels has also brought a proliferation of endpoints over which no bank has control, other than to decide whether to support them or not. For example, a customer can use any version of any web browser (such as Chrome, Edge, Firefox, Opera, Safari, and several others) with virtually any screen resolution. Although there are only two predominant mobile operating systems, Apple's iOS/iPadOS and Google's Android, there are many different versions of them. For example, Google released Android 11 in September 2020. There were 14 codenamed versions prior to Android 11 (plus three versions with no codename), and some of these had multiple sub-versions. So, for example, Android KitKat came in versions from 4.4 to 4.4.4.

However, there are limits to how far one can go in order to accommodate this vast diversity of platforms and versions. Trying to support too many flavours of client software is an expensive enterprise and quickly moves into the law of diminishing returns. The simple answer is to target a certain percentage of the market. For example, according to statcounter, supporting just six flavours of Android in May 2020 would cover about 80% of all Android users.[51] In many cases once a bank's app is functioning on one version there is a high degree of likelihood that it will work on some or all of the others, but it must be tested. Testing can range in sophistication from the extremely simple (buying a bunch of representative smartphones) to using cloud testing solutions or even outsourcing to third-party testing specialists.

4.16.5 *Accessibility*

Being the interface through which customers are engaged, making channels accessible is an important consideration. This is not only good practice; in many places it is the law. Consideration should be given to language and disability as part of any good interface design.

Accessibility comes in many flavours but is typically addressed as one of the outputs of the dual disciplines of user experience and user interface design (UX and UI, respectively, often combined as UX/UI). These two disciplines are often confused. The user interface is the design of the interface between the consumer and the channel. It could include the elements of the screen that engage the customer, or the voice used in an IVR session or the presentation of chat responses. On the other hand, user experience covers the entire customer experience when engaging through a channel and might cover the flow or order of screens or perhaps the speed of getting to where the customer wants to go. These two disciplines are related but different and require separate consideration. When they are executed well they can give every customer, regardless of their needs, a great experience.

4.17   References

1. O'Brien, J.A. (1968). *The Impact of Computers on Banking*. Boston, MA: Bankers Publishing Company.
2. Finextra (2019). NatWest opens new 'digital branch'. https://www.finextra.com/pressarticle/77373/natwest-opens-new-digital-branch (accessed 28 June 2020).
3. Manchester Evening News (2011). Virgin Money to launch first lounge style branch in Manchester. https://www.manchestereveningnews.co.uk/business/business-news/virgin-money-to-launch-first-lounge-879357 (accessed 28 June 2020).
4. RBS (2019). NatWest, Lloyds Bank and Barclays pilot UK's first business banking hubs (12 March). https://www.rbs.com/rbs/news/2019/03/natwest--lloyds-bank-and-barclays-pilot-uks-first-business-banki.html (accessed 28 June 2020).
5. JPMorgan Chase & Co. (2019). Chase opens first-of-its kind branch in the heart of Harlem. https://mediachase.com/news/chase-opens-first-of-its-kind-branch-in-the-heart-of-harlem.htm (accessed 28 June 2020).
6. Future Branches. Here's how Bank of America is reinventing high street banking with tellerless 'robo-branches'. https://futurebranches.wbresearch.com/blog/bank-of-america-reinventing-high-street-banking-with-tellerless-robo-branches (accessed 28 June 2020).
7. National Savings and Investments (2020). One of the UK's largest savings organisations. https://nsandi-corporate.com/ (accessed 9 July 2020).
8. CashEssentials (2019). CaixaBank introduces ATM facial recognition technology (26 February). https://cashessentials.org/news/caixabank-introduces-atm-facial-recognition-technology/ (accessed 9 July 2020).

9. Summers, N. (2014). ATMs face deadline to upgrade from Windows XP. Bloomberg (17 January). https://www.bloomberg.com/news/articles/2014-01-16/atms-face-deadline-to-upgrade-from-windows-xp (accessed 22 May 2020).

10. PCI Security Standards Council. https://www.pcisecuritystandards.org/ (accessed 9 July 2020).

11. Amazon. Amazon Lex. https://aws.amazon.com/lex/ (accessed 9 July 2020).

12. Barclays. Barclays video banking. https://www.barclays.co.uk/ways-to-bank/video-banking/ (accessed 9 July 2020).

13. NatWest. Banking with NatWest. Discover video banking. https://www.cnet.com/news/hackers-siphon-off-31-million-from-british-bank-accounts/ (accessed 9 July 2020).

14. The Financial Brand (2018). The next big mobile banking breakthrough: Two-way interactive video. https://thefinancialbrand.com/70010/mobile-video-banking/ (accessed 28 June 2020).

15. Michigan Bell (1966). What's INWATS? *Traverse City Record-Eagle* (13 April), p. 28. https://newspaperarchive.com/traverse-city-record-eagle-apr-13-1966-p-28/ (accessed 22 May 2020).

16. ITU-T Q.1200 (1997). *General Series Intelligent Network Recommendation Structure*. Geneva: International Telecommunications Union. https://www.itu.int/rec/T-REC-Q.1200 (accessed 22 May 2020).

17. ITU-T Q.700 (1993). *Introduction to CCITT Signalling System No. 7*. Geneva: International Telecommunications Union. https://www.itu.int/rec/T-REC-Q.700 (accessed 22 May 2020).

18. Erlang, A.K. (1909). Sandsynlighedsregning og Telefonsamtaler (Probability calculation and telephone conversations). *Nyt tidsskrift for matematik* 20 (B): 33–39.

19. ITU-T Q.23 (1988). *Technical Features of Push-button Telephone Sets*. Geneva: International Telecommunications Union. https://www.itu.int/rec/T-REC-Q.23 (accessed 22 May 2020).

20. Peyton, A. (2016). HSBC launching voice recognition and touch security services in UK. *Fintech Futures* (19 February). https://www.fintechfutures.com/2016/02/hsbc-launching-voice-recognition-and-touch-security-services-in-uk/ (accessed 9 July 2020).

21. Simmons, D. (2017). BBC fools HSBC voice recognition security system. *BBC News* (19 May). https://www.bbc.co.uk/news/technology-39965545 (accessed 28 June 2020).

22. Rosenberg, J., Schulzrinne, H., Camarillo, G. et al. (2002). *SIP: Session Initiation Protocol*. RFC3261, doi:10.17487/RFC3261. https://www.rfc-editor.org/info/rfc3261 (accessed 22 May 2020).

23. Handley, M., Jacobson, V., and Perkins, C. (2006). *SDP: Session Description Protocol*. RFC 4566, doi:10.17487/RFC4566. https://www.rfc-editor.org/info/rfc4566 (accessed 25 May 2020).

24. Schulzrinne, H., Casner, S., Frederick, R. et al. (2003). *RTP: A Transport Protocol for Real-Time Applications*. RFC 3550, doi:10.17487/RFC3550. https://www.rfc-editor.org/info/rfc3550 (accessed 25 May 2020).

25. Schulzrinne, H. and Casner, S. (2003). *RTP Profile for Audio and Video Conferences with Minimal Control*. RFC 3551, doi:10.17487/RFC3551. https://www.rfc-editor.org/info/rfc3551 (accessed 25 May 2020).

26. ITU-T G.711 (1988). *Pulse Code Modulation (PCM) of Voice Frequencies*. Geneva: International Telecommunications Union. https://www.itu.int/rec/T-REC-G.711 (accessed 25 May 2020).

27. ITU-T G.729 (2012). *Coding of Speech at 8 kbit/s Using Conjugate-structure Algebraic-code-excited Linear Prediction (CS-ACELP)*. Geneva: International Telecommunications Union. https://www.itu.int/rec/T-REC-G.729 (accessed 25 May 2020).

28. Schulzrinne, H. and Taylor, T. (2006). *RTP Payload for DTMF Digits, Telephony Tones, and Telephony Signals*. RFC 4733, doi:10.17487/RFC4733. https://www.rfc-editor.org/info/rfc4733 (accessed 25 May 2020).

29. Wing, D. (2007). *Symmetric RTP/RTP Control Protocol (RTCP)*. RFC 4961, doi:10.17487/RFC4961. https://www.rfc-editor.org/info/rfc4961 (accessed 25 May 2020).

30. Rosenberg, J. (2009). *A Hitchhiker's Guide to the Session Initiation Protocol (SIP)*. RFC 5411, doi:10.17487/RFC5411. https://www.rfc-editor.org/info/rfc5411 (accessed 25 May 2020).

31. Portman, L., Lum, H. ed., Eckel, C. et al. (2016). *Session Recording Protocol*. RFC 7866, doi:10.17487/RFC7866. https://www.rfc-editor.org/info/rfc7866 (accessed 25 May 2020).

32. Ravindranath, R., Ravindran, P., and Kyzivat, P. (2016). *Session Initiation Protocol (SIP) Recording Metadata*. RFC 7865, doi:10.17487/RFC7865. https://www.rfc-editor.org/info/rfc7865 (accessed 25 May 2020).

33. ITU-T H.264. (2019). *Advanced Video Coding for Generic Audiovisual Services*. Geneva: International Telecommunications Union. https://www.itu.int/rec/T-REC-H.264 (accessed 25 May 2020).

34. ITU-T H.263 (2005). *Video Coding for Low Bit Rate Communication*. Geneva: International Telecommunications Union. https://www.itu.int/rec/T-REC-H.263 (accessed 25 May 2020).

35. Campbell, B., Mahy, R., and Jennings, C. ed. (2007). *The Message Session Relay Protocol (MSRP)*. RFC 4975, doi:10.17487/RFC4975. https://www.rfc-editor.org/info/rfc4975 (accessed 25 May 2020).

36. ITU-T H.323 (2009). *Packet-based Multimedia Communications Systems*. Geneva: International Telecommunications Union. https://www.itu.int/rec/T-REC-H.323 (accessed 25 May 2020).

37. Stewart, A. (2020). Texting. *Encyclopedia Britannica* (4 March). https://www.britannica.com/technology/text-messaging (accessed 8 July 2020).

38. SMS Forum (2003). Short message peer to peer protocol specification v5.0 (19 February). https://smpp.org/smppv50.pdf (accessed 8 July 2020).

39. Bennett, O. (2020). Bank branches: Why are they closing and what is the impact? House of Commons Library Briefing Paper CBP 8740 (2 January). https://researchbriefings.files.parliament.uk/documents/CBP-8740/CBP-8740.pdf (accessed 9 July 2020).

40. Reuters (2019). M-Pesa has completely changed Kenyans' access to financial services, this is how… *CNBCAFRICA* (3 April). https://www.cnbcafrica.com/east-africa/2019/04/03/m-pesa-has-completely-changed-kenyans-access-to-financial-services-this-is-how/ (accessed 28 June 2020).

41. Alushula, P. (2019). M-Pesa users outside Kenya hit 13.4 million. *Business Daily* (29 January). https://www.businessdailyafrica.com/corporate/companies/M-Pesa-users-outside-Kenya-hit-13-4-million/4003102-4956208-16s8a9/index.html (accessed 28 June 2020).

42. CACI (2019). The Growth of Digital Banking Report. https://pages.caci.co.uk/rs/752-EBZ-498/images/caci-future-growth-digital-banking-report-2019.pdf (accessed 28 June 2020).

43. GlobalData (2018). Global mobile banking usage highest in India, while Sweden sees fastest growth, says GlobalData (25 April). https://www.globaldata.com/global-mobile-banking-usage-highest-india-sweden-sees-fastest-growth-says-globaldata/ (accessed 28 June 2020).

44. Bennett. Bank branches.

45. Lewis, S. and Dunn, M. (2019). *Native Mobile Development*. Sebastopol, CA: O'Reilly Media.

46. Peal, G. (2018). React Native at Airbnb. Medium (19 June). https://medium.com/airbnb-engineering/react-native-at-airbnb-f95aa460be1c (accessed 28 May 2020).

47. Netflix (2011). The Netflix Simian Army. *The Netflix Tech Blog* (19 July). https://netflixtechblog.com/the-netflix-simian-army-16e57fbab116 (accessed 28 June 2020).

48. Wikipedia. Chaos engineering. https://en.wikipedia.org/wiki/Chaos_engineering (accessed 28 June 2020).

49. Hitachi (2019). Hitachi's new hand gesture biometric technology raises the bar for computer security (10 September). https://www.hitachi.eu/en/press/hitachis-new-hand-gesture-biometric-technology-raises-bar-computer-security (accessed 9 July 2020).

50. Collins, K. (2015). Hackers siphon off $31 million from British bank accounts. CNET (14 October). https://www.cnet.com/news/hackers-siphon-off-31-million-from-british-bank-accounts/ (accessed 9 July 2020).

51. Statcounter (2020). Mobile & tablet Android version market share worldwide. https://gs.statcounter.com/android-version-market-share/mobile-tablet/worldwide (accessed 28 June 2020).

CHAPTER 5

Banking Operations

The area of banking that tends to catch most of the headlines today is the channels, where bank meets customer. To be fair, historically, the branch counter was rarely regarded as all that exciting, but somehow the digital channels in particular and the associated reduction of bank branches have achieved a level of recognition that no prior channel has ever reached and are now the aspects of a bank that everyone talks about, particularly when that comes to new entrant banks.[1]

However, the real work of the bank is primarily carried out in the areas of operations. This is the core of the bank. Forget the glamour of the digital interface, or the back office (including finance which plays an important role but doesn't make the bank tick on a daily basis), the engine room of the bank is actually the area of banking operations. Why? Well, because that's where a lot of the functions that will either build customer loyalty or ensure that the bank doesn't become the next front-page catastrophe reside. It is the operations function that most often resolves many of the issues that technology cannot yet fully address, or steps in where the technology solution throws an exception. This bit of the bank, that ceaselessly drives the ongoing success of the business, is (unfortunately) often overlooked, but building an understanding of it is key to the successful delivery of a modern banking business.

This chapter covers most of the areas shown in the Banking operations layer of the model of a bank that we introduced in Chapter 1, focusing on drawing out those areas that we regard as most complex, interesting or requiring most discussion. Within this chapter we therefore focus primarily on the areas of payment operations, cash management, credit operations, collections and recoveries, and fraud services.

5.1 Contact Centre

We cover the contact centre in more detail in Chapter 4, but in terms of management oversight it typically sits within the sphere of operations. Contact centre staff don't just talk to customers to address their questions; they are often required to identify and resolve issues, mollify angry customers and fend off fraudsters.

The effectiveness of the contact centre is heavily dependent upon the quality of its people and the training they receive, backed up by telephony and customer relationship management platforms.

5.2   Payment Operations

The payment operations team is arguably one of the most important functions in terms of the day-to-day activities of a banking business. Payments are critical to the activities of most customers and it is imperative that they run smoothly and that any issues are identified and addressed efficiently. Typically, the activities that would usually be undertaken by the payment operations team include originating payments, tracking payments, resolving issues with payments and performing reconciliations of different types of payments.

First, on some occasions the payment operations team will be asked to set up a payment on behalf of a customer. Such payment origination used to be a significant part of the activities of payment operations, but with the arrival of the Internet and, later, mobile banking, along with the international standardisation of account numbering – all of which grant customers the ability to easily set up their own payments – this function has been on the wane. For an international payment, particularly for an unusual destination, it could be necessary to manually work out the routing, including which correspondent banking relationships to use. Most payments typically start out being processed automatically, but when the payment platform is unable to process a payment the payment instruction will end up in a queue for the attention of the payment operations team. Another aspect of payment origination is the review of large or unusual payments, potentially getting further confirmation from the initiating customers about such payments.

Second, the payment operations team is often asked to track payments. Although many payments are now instant, there are still plenty of payment schemes (and circumstances) that are not, and this can often result in customer queries relating to where their payment is. This is particularly true for international payments, where a payment can still take several days to reach the intended recipient. The payment operations team is responsible for attempting to track down missing and delayed payments and, if required, resolving any issues that may be delaying them or, at least, providing the contact centre with details on where the payment has reached in the network so that the customer can be informed. The team may also have to provide evidence that the payment has been made or contact the bank where it is held up and get that bank to resolve the issue.

Third, the payment operations team has to resolve issues with incoming and outgoing payments. This could be with one-off payments, but issues regularly occur with direct debits and standing orders. For outbound payments, as well as payments going astray en route as described earlier, there could also be inbound and outbound payments that match sanctioned entities or jurisdictions or trigger money-laundering alerts (see Section 5.2.2). These usually have to be manually reviewed to determine whether the match is correct or a false positive. Inbound payments may have invalid account numbers on them or other inconsistencies in the payment data that mean they can't be credited directly to customer accounts. Under such circumstances, the payment platform will send a payment to a queue for manual review and it inevitably falls to a person in the payment operations team to review each such payment. The value of inbound payments that can't be credited to customer accounts would normally be credited to a suspense account while each payment is analysed, and a decision made on what to do with it. Depending on which stage of the payment process a faulty outbound payment gets to will determine whether the customer's account has already been debited and if the value is credited to a suspense account at the paying bank or has already been transferred to a payment scheme or correspondent bank. Payment platforms usually have a range of queues in which to hold different categories of failed or stuck payments.

When it comes to managing direct debits and standing orders there can be issues at both ends of the payment chain. For example, if the account that is receiving a standing order payment has been closed, the funds should be returned to the sender. For the bank which holds an account that is receiving a direct debit there exists a large number of exception codes that can explain why a sender has failed to send (e.g. account closed and lack of funds) that the receiving business needs to understand so that it can decide how to respond. Often this results in queries from the receiving business to its bank and the payment operations team may be asked to help. We cover the direct debit process in more detail in Chapter 7.

When implementing a new payment platform, consideration should be given to how to manage (i.e. queue) payments when they can't immediately be applied to an account. Normally this would be through applying the payment value to a suspense account while the payment data is analysed, and a decision made regarding what to do with it. All the banking and payment platforms that we have seen have a variety of queues to hold all kinds of failed or stuck payments. When implementing a third-party banking or payment platform it's important for the payment operations team to know what queues have been configured and how to manage them. We have seen cases in the past of banks not realising that some of the queues existed and for payments to disappear into them for weeks or months!

Finally, payment reconciliation, which (as covered in Chapter 7) is fundamental to the business of banking and payments. The payment operations team is responsible for ensuring that the bank's records of all payments is consistent with that of the outside world, including the payment schemes, the clearing banks used by the bank (if any) and at correspondent banks. This is not always as simple as it might seem, as payments can go missing, become duplicated or just get delayed and, unless a customer queries it, reconciliations might be the first place an issue is identified.

Of course, all of these capabilities need to be supported by technology, and the more effective that technology is, the more efficient the payment operations team can be. We cover payment technology in Chapter 7. Smaller banks that rely upon third parties for payment processing (including payment aggregators and clearing banks) may face additional constraints (e.g. reduced time windows in which payments can be sent or received, maximum values for payments, delays in sending or receiving payments, reduced visibility of settlement positions, or little visibility of technical issues and unplanned outages), and tend to have less leverage with payment schemes. We were surprised when setting up a bank in the UK how much variation there was in the service levels, functionality and visibility provided by the small number of clearing banks and aggregators, often because they were reliant upon legacy technology that had various constraints. For this reason it is important to understand what technology these parties are running, what messaging protocols and standards they adhere to, what constraints are imposed (and why) and what data is made available and when it is made available.

Beyond the boundaries of a bank's own payment systems, it is also important that the payment operations team has access to partner or supplier systems where required, e.g. in order to check the status of payments and resolve any issues. This is particularly the case where a bank is using the services of an aggregator or intermediary or clearing bank rather than connecting directly to payment schemes' networks.

5.3   Cash Management

Many areas of banking businesses are fully digital and do not handle physical cash, but where a bank maintains ATMs or a teller line, for example, there is often a need for a dedicated cash management function. It should be noted that in this context cash management is the literal management of physical cash as opposed to the cash management function found in treasury functions (see Chapter 8 for more details).

It is, of course, important that the amount of cash a bank has on hand, in every location, tallies with the amounts in the bank's records. For example, some core banking platforms track the amount of cash in each teller's cash drawer and this should be reconciled with the actual amount at the end of a teller's shift. As well as reconciliation activities like this, a bank's cash management activities include logistics, i.e. managing the supply and collection of cash across its estate, and, if offered as a service, across its commercial customers. This can include ensuring that sufficient levels of each denomination of banknote and coin are available, ordering more cash from the central bank (or whoever supplies it), removing damaged and obsolete banknotes and coins from circulation and liaising with secure delivery and collection services. Note that governments or regulators have been known to focus on the availability of certain denominations of banknote, either to foster financial inclusion or to reduce money laundering, and this may require ATMs to be stocked with certain denominations. In some markets, specialist third parties provide services to collect, count, recycle and deliver cash from banks and commercial customers, including stocking ATMs. Such services, in tandem with banks, can credit the value of physical cash to the accounts of commercial customers from which it has been collected within hours, before it has actually arrived at the bank.

Obviously, security of cash and bank staff that handle it are important and appropriate security measures should be taken, including the use of security cameras and control over and monitoring of access to secure areas where cash is handled.

5.4   Credit Operations

The focus of credit operations is to ensure that the organisation's lending operations maintain an acceptable level of risk given the choice of product and the institution's risk appetite. What this means, in effect, is that lending decisions are appropriately managed and vetted to ensure that when the business lends money it understands the associated risks and manages them appropriately. Of course, giving the money out is only part of the process and credit operations are also closely involved in ensuring that money lent out eventually comes back with interest.

Historically, the credit operations team was almost solely responsible for manually processing credit decisions, but often this responsibility has been moved to more automated, systemised processing. However, there are still plenty of exceptions that occur during this process (including where customers feel that they have been inappropriately turned down and subsequently complain) and the credit operations team needs to step in.

5.4.1 Retail Credit Application Process

To date, the most effective way of gathering the data required to support the making of a retail customer credit decision has been through the use of credit bureaus (variously referred to as a consumer reporting agency in the US, credit reporting body in Australia, credit information company in India and a host of other names around the world), examples of which include Equifax and Experian, both of which provide credit reference services in many countries. However, the recent introduction of open banking and open data are starting to influence this by enabling banking businesses to draw on a wider dataset to support their decision making. For example, open banking enables a customer to share the details of their bank account, including all transactions, so that a lender can understand the customer's financial status and ability to repay in detail. Open data, for example, might allow a lender to understand footfall on a given street to support a decision on whether to lend to a retailer which wishes to expand its business (see Chapter 10 for more details).

Figure 5.1 provides an overview of a typical unsecured lending application decisioning process. It should be noted that this process will vary from institution to institution and also by the type of loan that the customer is applying for. For example, if the customer is seeking a secured loan, such as a car loan or mortgage then the process will also include an assessment of the value of the security (the car or house) and, in the case of the car, any anticipated depreciation.

5.4.2 Small Business Credit Application Process

Credit decisioning for businesses tends to be split into at least three sub-groups, sometimes more. These sub-groups are: sole traders, where loan decisions are often assessed against the individual rather than the business; small to medium enterprises (SMEs) which will be discussed here; and corporates, who typically (though not always) have data available to the lender through credit rating agencies or business data providers such as Dunn & Bradstreet, Moody's and Standard & Poor's.

Due to the small scale and limited amount of publicly available data on small businesses, this category can be the hardest to assess and the process has historically relied upon a good deal of manual data gathering and manual decisioning within the lender. However, things are changing and there are now more tools on the market to support the decisioning process, including plug-ins to accounting solutions so small businesses can share data directly with lenders[2] and open banking[3].

The decisioning process is not fundamentally different from our example retail credit decision as shown in Figure 5.1, in that many of the same steps still need to be completed. For example, the loan application will still require the applicant business to identify how much it wishes to borrow, over how long and how it will repay it. However, there are a number of the steps that are quite different in respect to the data and processes contained within the steps.

First, the know your customer (KYC) process for a business is quite different. As described in more detail in Section 5.6.1.2, the KYC process requires that the business is identified and that key staff (such as directors) and the ultimate beneficial owners are all also identified.

FIGURE 5.1   Example retail credit decisioning process.

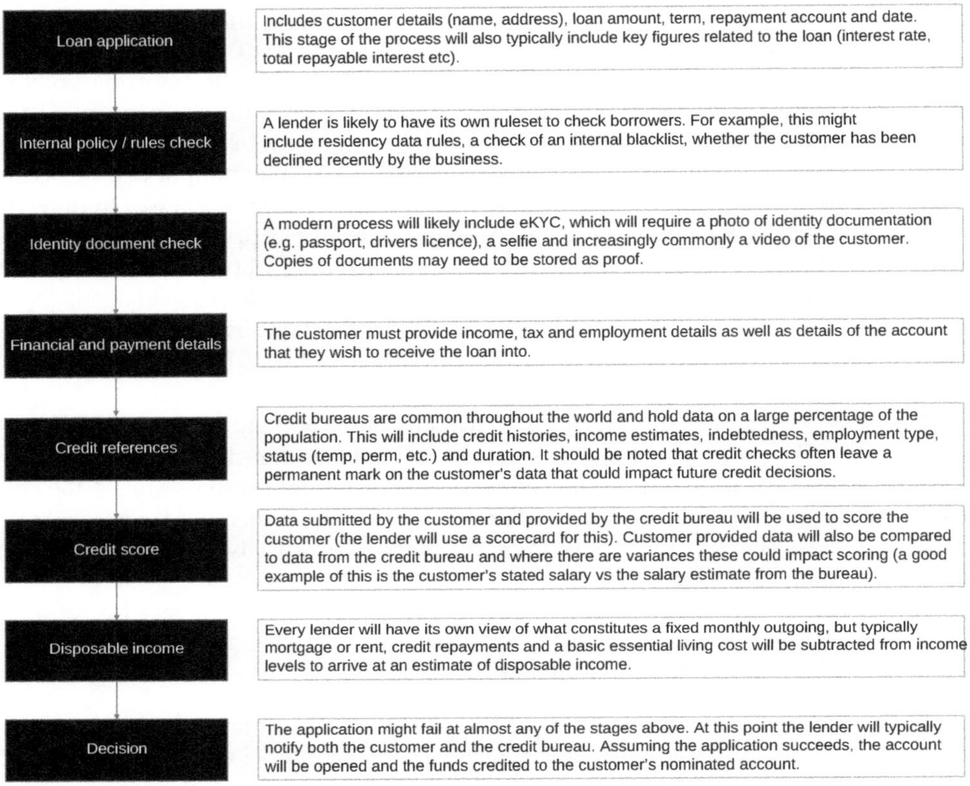

Loan application	Includes customer details (name, address), loan amount, term, repayment account and date. This stage of the process will also typically include key figures related to the loan (interest rate, total repayable interest etc).
Internal policy / rules check	A lender is likely to have its own ruleset to check borrowers. For example, this might include residency data rules, a check of an internal blacklist, whether the customer has been declined recently by the business.
Identity document check	A modern process will likely include eKYC, which will require a photo of identity documentation (e.g. passport, drivers licence), a selfie and increasingly commonly a video of the customer. Copies of documents may need to be stored as proof.
Financial and payment details	The customer must provide income, tax and employment details as well as details of the account that they wish to receive the loan into.
Credit references	Credit bureaus are common throughout the world and hold data on a large percentage of the population. This will include credit histories, income estimates, indebtedness, employment type, status (temp, perm, etc.) and duration. It should be noted that credit checks often leave a permanent mark on the customer's data that could impact future credit decisions.
Credit score	Data submitted by the customer and provided by the credit bureau will be used to score the customer (the lender will use a scorecard for this). Customer provided data will also be compared to data from the credit bureau and where there are variances these could impact scoring (a good example of this is the customer's stated salary vs the salary estimate from the bureau).
Disposable income	Every lender will have its own view of what constitutes a fixed monthly outgoing, but typically mortgage or rent, credit repayments and a basic essential living cost will be subtracted from income levels to arrive at an estimate of disposable income.
Decision	The application might fail at almost any of the stages above. At this point the lender will typically notify both the customer and the credit bureau. Assuming the application succeeds, the account will be opened and the funds credited to the customer's nominated account.

Second, the data gathered will be different. Depending upon the specifics of the lender's decisioning criteria it is likely that it will require access to financial information (cashflow, profitability, several prior years of financial accounts), business data (size of firm, number of employees, location), any creditors (and possibly credit terms) and debtors (including terms and values outstanding).

Third, depending upon the purpose of the loan there may be additional data required relating to the specifics of the loan. For example, if the business customer is seeking invoice financing, the lender is likely to need to understand the payment terms, historical performance and also the creditworthiness and reliability of the debtors.

As already noted, publicly available data relating to individual small businesses is often very limited, so the information required can only be gathered directly from the business. Much of the business data we refer to will come in a variety of formats, as it comes from the applicant business's own systems and often requires manual interpretation before it can be entered into the lender's decisioning process. The manual processes, smaller average size of loans (compared to corporates), limited track record of many small businesses and low survival rate of small businesses (in the UK, for example, about 10% of small businesses 'die' each year)[4] help explain why small business lending has historically not been regarded as particularly attractive for banks.

5.5   Collections and Recoveries

It is an inevitable fact of life that some loans go bad. In a small percentage of cases this is down to outright fraud or misrepresentation but often, even where the lender is prudent and the customer is responsible, things just don't work out and the customer becomes unable to repay the loan. Any business that provides lending services must acknowledge that irrespective of how carefully the credit origination process is managed, it will also have to have a process in place to manage the loan when things don't work out as expected. The term collections and recoveries (also referred to as arrears management) covers the processes that are used from the point a loan starts to falter (i.e. it becomes delinquent) through to the end of the process. The terms are often used together, but actually apply to very different elements of the process.

Once a repayment on a loan is overdue (and it is said to be *in collection*) the lender will attempt to recover any outstanding payments and return the loan to a position where the customer is making scheduled repayments (which may include agreeing a new repayment schedule). The period that a loan is in collection is often subdivided into phases based on how many days overdue the last repayment is. A typical process might include 30, 60 and 90 days past due. In the early phases of delinquency a customer's credit record may remain unimpacted, but as they move past 30 days the lender is likely to apply fines, press harder for payment and also notify credit agencies The chasing of past-due repayments is normally undertaken by the collections team inside a lender.

Managing a loan that has become delinquent is a sensitive operation. In most regulatory jurisdictions there are regulations on how lenders must treat retail customers that are in arrears, and penalties for those organisations that break the regulations.

From a technology perspective, there are a number of considerations that must be addressed during the collections process:

- Loan repayment tracking and alerting. The first step in the process is to identify when a loan becomes delinquent. In the first instance this is typically when a loan payment is not made, but there are times when a customer realises that they cannot make a payment and will proactively contact the lender. The credit operations and compliance teams must define a suitable process for handling the customer's situation from this point onwards.
- Re-scheduling. If a loan repayment fails, and is a direct debit, then it may be possible to automatically re-schedule a payment or re-try. This capability is dependent upon the features of the local payments scheme(s). Alternatively, a customer can make a one-off payment to make good.
- If the customer decides to make a one-time payment it is possible that they may want to do so on a payment card. Most responsible organisations won't allow a credit card to be used (moving debt from a lower-interest loan to a higher interest credit card is normally not in the customer's best interests), but debit card payments may be permitted.
- In the event that none of the above work, then the credit operations team will need to engage with the customer to come up with a repayment plan that works for them. A modern organisation's collections plan should be guided by principles, so that each individual customer has consistent outcomes, but with steps individualised to their

own circumstances. From a technical perspective this will cause some difficulties, as it means that a lender's platforms must be flexible enough to accommodate that variation. In particular, they must be able to accommodate variations in values of payments, interest rate calculations and potentially even payment holidays.

- Management of a customer relationship through a collections process is arguably more sensitive than day-to-day customer management. A lender's customer relationship management (CRM) platform must support the process and be able to provide an audited log of all calls, in chronological order, that is immutable.

Once a delinquent loan passes the 90-day point (or whatever period the lender sets out in its lending policy), the lender is likely to give up on attempting to collect on it and put it into recovery. In most cases a loan that has entered into recovery will be sold to a third-party recovery agency and the remainder of the outstanding debt written off, by the lender, from its books.

At the point the loan enters into the recoveries process one of the key differences that determines how it is resolved is whether the loan is secured (such as with an asset-backed loan) or unsecured. If the loan is a secured debt, then the collateral will likely be recovered by the recovery agency and sold. Once the lender's and recovery agency's costs have been recovered, any remaining funds will be returned to the customer. If the loan is unsecured, the recovery agency will seek to recover as much as it can from the debtor, initially through direct engagement with the customer, but also through the courts if that is feasible.

Most credit bureaus have a reciprocal clause in their contracts that requires lenders to notify them when loans start to go bad. This data is used to inform the customer's credit rating but can also be pooled with other data relating to that customer from other organisations so that the customer's overall financial health can be assessed. As we progress through the coming years it is highly likely that this data will be used more and more dynamically to monitor the financial health of a customer and identify when they are beginning to struggle to service their debts long in advance of any default.

However, the data is also very valuable to the lender, as it can be fed into credit underwriting (to be used for modelling and to improve future credit decisioning processes), risk (to help assess and manage the business's own risk) and finance (where it is used for reporting and to support P&L expectations.)

From a technology perspective the delivery of a lending solution must therefore accommodate not only the loan origination and payment process, but also all of the unhappy path outcomes and the various decisions on the way down that path. For instance, what if a customer starts to repay the loan after 65 days of being overdue? How does that impact the outstanding repayments? Are interest or fines due and, if so, are they added to the outstanding loan value?

5.6   Fraud Services

There are many ways to defraud a bank. While certain types of fraud are more newsworthy than others, fraud can take place over every channel the business operates. In fact, there are even fraudsters that specialise in particular forms of financial crime, such as card fraud.[5] Some examples of the varieties of routes fraudsters can take in order to open an account or extract money include:

- Physical. When Metro Bank was launched in the UK it immediately came under attack from financial criminals. The most obvious of these was one particular group of fraudsters. The group met down the road from the branch (we could see them) and would send one of their party up to open an account, typically with a passport for identification purposes. Each time they went through the account opening process it would become clear at some point that something was amiss and the customer adviser would send the person away, whereupon they would then meet with their accomplices and discuss what had occurred. We could see this happening a little further up the road. Once the discussion had been completed, and a course of action agreed, another member of their party would walk up the road, enter the bank and try an alternative approach to get past the point where the last fraudster had failed.
- Contact Centre. When banks suffer significant IT outages, they are often inundated by calls to their contact centres. Here, the staff do their best to support the customers, but the sheer volume of calls, combined with the impact on bank customers' everyday lives, presents an opportunity for fraudsters. Bank staff are, rightly, keen to support impacted customers in getting access to their money, and the fraudsters know this. Recent bank system outages have led to many stories of fraudsters calling contact centres and successfully gaining access to customer funds and accounts.[6]
- Customers. Customers are regularly taken in by fraudsters pretending to be from their bank and asking them to provide key data about their account or to move money to 'protect it' (the latter being known as authorised push payment fraud). These attacks occur over email, telephone and even door-to-door. As with contact centre fraud, this attack is more successful in times of stress for the customers, such as when the bank is suffering an IT failure.[7]
- Cyber. There are a wide range of attacks that fraudsters attempt in the digital arena. These attacks can be made against Internet banking platforms as well as digital apps and they range from using stolen identities to open accounts through to man-in-the-middle attacks on genuine customers.

These examples cover just a fraction of the types of fraud attacks that are regularly attempted within the banking industry. We have only scratched the surface on authorised push payment fraud[8] and there are many other forms of financial crime, such as money laundering, card fraud and more. For more information on fraud, please refer to Chapters 6 and 7, which cover fraud in cards and payments.

In order to fight fraudsters, the fraud team in a modern bank has a broad range of tools at its disposal. However, having the tools available is only part of the battle. They must be deployed effectively and then monitored on an ongoing basis in order to limit fraud over a prolonged period. Fraudsters are always looking for new ways to break the banks, so the bank's approach must also be able to adapt over time. It should be noted that while fraud can be limited, nobody has yet found a way to remove it entirely from a retail banking environment. Banks are well aware of this, which is why the press claim that many of them avoid revealing data relating to fraud in their businesses[9] – their concern is that by releasing fraud data they will put off current or future customers.

In the following sections we look at the key opportunities that banks have to spot and foil fraud.

5.6.1   Know Your Customer

Know your customer (KYC) checks are a key element of all banks' onboarding process (the process of taking on a new customer) for both retail and business customers, and undertaking them is usually a regulatory and a legal requirement[10] but is also fundamentally good practice. Not only do KYC checks limit the risks to the bank, but they also limit the broader risks to the industry and the general population in relation to crime and terrorist funding activities.

5.6.1.1   Personal KYC

This form of KYC is typically used for individual or joint personal accounts or where a small business is owned and run by a single person. The primary objective here is to confirm that the customer is who they claim to be. Until recently this would be a relatively straightforward and manual process but was prone to error and abuse. A customer would take an identification document containing a photograph, such as a passport, identity card or drivers' licence, and some recent bills (with their address on them) to the local bank branch. There, a customer service advisor or maybe even the bank manager would run through an onboarding process prior to opening any type of account. Identification of the customer would be the responsibility of the bank representative and it would be up to them to judge whether the customer documentation was valid and whether the customer was actually who they claimed to be. In the time of local branch banking it was quite common for the bank staff to know the prospective customer personally, thus making identification somewhat easier. These days, with the ongoing growth of the population and the reduction in bank branch numbers, technology is being used more frequently to address weaknesses and automate processes. There are a number of ways that technology can support the KYC process.

There are electronic document readers that can be deployed into bank branches to support document-checking processes.[11] Quite frankly, most people on high street (including branch staff) wouldn't be able to tell a genuine foreign passport from a good-quality counterfeit, so technology can be used to confirm whether a document is what it claims to be, is valid, and has not been altered in any way.

Whether the document is checked by hand or electronically, the evidence should be recorded as part of the customer record on the bank's CRM platform. The facility to store an image and any staff notes should be designed into the platform to allow the compliance team to check it later (either as part of a spot check or following up on an incident).

There is now a large (and growing) range of providers of digital document checking software providers (so-called eKYC services) that can take an image of the document (typically provided by the customer using their smartphone camera) and a photograph of the customer (again taken by the customer). The software will then use those two images first to confirm the validity of the identity document and that it has not been tampered with, and second to confirm that the photograph of the prospective customer matches that on the identity document. These systems are becoming ever more sophisticated, including the addition of capabilities to check that the photograph of the customer is actually a real photograph (or even a video).

As of 2020, there were many providers of eKYC services who were capable of operating on a global level. Examples included IDnow,[12] Jumio,[13] and Onfido,[14] and there were others. Many of these providers, although not all, could carry out verification of identity documents originating from a large range of countries.

If a bank has a requirement that is limited to a single country or select group of countries, then it is possible that it could use local or national digital identification schemes available in countries as varied as Estonia to Oman.[15] Many countries now have compulsory national identity card schemes and they may support the online identification of inhabitants of that country without needing to use an international eKYC service.

There are a number of implications of choosing eKYC:

1. The process is heavily dependent upon the customer. Photos and videos of the customer and their documentation need the right lighting conditions, minimal reflection and the customer's face to be clearly visible. Consequently, it is very common for a customer to be required to re-take a photograph or video, and even then the new photograph or video may not match the requirements of the eKYC system. This can be very frustrating and at this point the bank's customer services must be ready to step in and assist the customer.

2. No solution is foolproof and eKYC services cannot spot all fraud. While this may be alarming, it should be noted that there is no perfect solution. In fact, one might argue that manual processes are more prone to error and risk of internal fraud.

3. False negatives do occur and so a bank must be prepared for customer queries and complaints about the process. This may require that the bank's customer service team be able to override a machine-generated result. This process needs to be subject to controls to minimise the risk of internal fraud and the bypassing of the eKYC process.

4. The eKYC software will sometimes throw an exception when it cannot come to an absolute conclusion (perhaps there are issues with the optical character recognition reading of the identity document). In the first instance this will result in someone from the eKYC service checking the result, which can take some time to complete. The eKYC service will occasionally pass cases back, perhaps because it cannot be certain enough of the outcome, to the bank for review and approval. In such circumstances it will come to the operations team to make a decision on the validity of the evidence.

Points (1), (3) and (4) require the operations team to be able to see the document images and photographs that relate to the account and the outcome of the KYC validation service. This functionality needs to be available in the customer relationship management platform, along with the means for the reviewer to make and record their decision. There must be a means for the compliance team to engage in the process and review selected cases to ensure that the process is being followed correctly and consistently applied.

Whatever the outcome of the eKYC process, it should be recorded in an auditable format. Should there ever be a reason to question the identity of the customer (for example, as part of a fraud event review), or if the bank's compliance team carries out a spot check, there may be a need to refer back to it and prove that an appropriate process was followed and that the outcome achieved was correct.

When designing a take-on process a bank should bear in mind the fourth point above. Delays at this stage are common and it cannot be assumed that the onboarding process will flow seamlessly. A bank could consider inserting a pause in the take-on process to accommodate delays. Even the best digital onboarding processes do not proceed straight through all of the time and it is the management of customer expectations or working through the exceptions that can make a business stand out from the crowd.

5.6.1.2 Business KYC

Business KYC, by its very nature, is somewhat more complicated than personal KYC. It should be noted that business KYC is typically carried out not just on businesses but on any entity where multiple people are engaged in owning or running it, such as charities and partnerships. When carrying out a KYC process to onboard a new business account the bank will need to identify:

- The business – The bank will need to ensure that the business is a valid business entity, registered (where available) with appropriate authorities. In the UK, for example, Companies House holds records of many of the different types of business entities, although not all. For example, a sole trader does not need to register their business at Companies House, and charities are registered with the Charity Commission.
- The representative – The bank will need to understand who it is that is opening the account on behalf of the business and whether they have the authority to do so.
- Any mandate holder –Anyone who will have a role in the operational management of the account on behalf of the customer business will need to be identified.
- The directors of the business – All directors of the business will need to be identified.
- Any ultimate beneficial owners (UBOs) of the business – Typically a UBO is any-body that has a significant financial interest in the business. The rules on this vary, but there is normally a need to identify all entities that have greater than a certain percentage ownership in the business (even where this is through other companies), where that percentage is dependent upon the prevailing law and regulations and the bank's appetite.

In some countries confirming details about a business, its directors and ownership is relatively straightforward (unless the company has a complex group or ownership structure). For instance, in the UK a search of Companies House will confirm the name and activities of the business, its directors and any relevant documentation (e.g. articles of association, financial accounts, and so on). However, in many countries this process can be far from straightforward. Where records do exist, there are now software solutions that can make these searches easier to undertake.

Examples of businesses that can provide company data include Companies House (in the UK only, with similar public registries in many other developed countries), Bureau van Dijk (375 million companies worldwide, according to its website in mid-2020[16]), DueDil, Dun & Bradstreet and IHS Markit. There are, of course, many more compa-nies that provide company data globally. It is important when contemplating working with any of these parties to consider geographic scope, data elements available, interface specification, how regularly the data is updated and cost per search. As an example, in the UK it is possible to access a lot of basic company data from Companies House for free.

Any company that provides such data should offer it online from a database that is updated regularly. Company data changes so frequently that it is impossible to be up to date unless accessing a database that is updated on a regular basis, and, because the future relationship will be based on these initial steps, it is important that the data being used is current.

In all KYC cases discussed previously, customer identity documentation is being used, which is of value to criminals and must therefore be adequately protected. The storage of copies of these images must be secure and all access must be logged. Periodically the compliance function should review the KYC process, a sample of documents stored and the access logs for the document store.

5.6.2   *Politically Exposed Persons and Sanctioned Entities*

5.6.2.1   Identification

A politically exposed person (PEP) is typically an individual who works in a relatively high-profile role and could be regarded as a potential target for blackmail or bribery. Normally this group includes politicians and their families, but people in some other roles, such as senior individuals in religious groups or government-owned organisations, could equally be on the list. There is nothing wrong with taking a PEP onto the books of a business (they have to be able to bank somewhere, after all), but when a PEP is identified as a customer, or potential customer, of a banking business then enhanced due diligence of that customer must typically be concluded (such as the establishment of their source of funds and their income level) before an account can be opened for them. The accounts that they open must also be flagged and tracked more closely than other accounts to ensure that there is never any hint of bribery or blackmail-related activity (not that there should be on any account). For example, if a PEP's account indicates that they appear to have income beyond their declared means this should be flagged and investigated.[17]

In the event that suspicious activity should ever occur on the account of a PEP, it is the responsibility of the bank to notify the relevant authorities.

Obviously, any list of PEPs is subject to change. As politicians are elected (or unelected), lists of PEPs are updated and, to reflect that fact, it is the responsibility of the banking business to ensure that they keep up to date with these revised lists. Consequently, most banking businesses check published lists of PEPs on a periodic basis and update their customer accounts to reflect any changes.

Some providers of PEP screening services will even classify the types of PEP, for example identifying if they are a head of state or national government at one end of the scale, down to a more minor official at the other end.

Sanctions, on the other hand, are used by governments to place pressure on individuals, organisations or even entire countries by denying them access to financial services. Sometimes this is specifically to achieve a political goal (such as targeting high-level representatives of other governments) and sometimes it is aimed at attempting to deny specific individuals access to funds so that they are unable to use those funds for illegal activities (such as terrorism and drug smuggling). Sometimes it is both of these at the same time! These lists are created and maintained by many governments and supra-national organisations (such as the EU and UN) and they vary in content from list to list with different jurisdictions having different views on the applicability of such lists.

At a minimum, a bank should ensure that it complies with the sanctions lists applicable in its countries of operation, but consideration should also be given to including global or multinational sanctions lists such as those published by the UN, as well as any checklists issued by or applicable in any other jurisdictions in which the bank operates. Of course, a bank should consider whether it wishes to follow the sanctions lists of significant powers such as China, Russia and the United States, even if it does not operate within their jurisdictions.

Fortunately, it is pretty easy to put in place technology platforms to identify when a person is on a PEP or sanctions list. Sanctions lists are published by governments and supranational organisations. They can either be downloaded directly (in which case it is necessary to periodically check for any changes) or procured from third-party organisations that provide additional services such as notifying their bank customers when a list is updated and checking a bank's data for matches with entries on the lists. PEP lists are less easy to acquire but are available through commercial organisations such as ComplyAdvantage and LexisNexis in the UK. There are plenty of other organisations that can provide this data, including those that offer data specific to different locales.

However, getting access to the lists is the easy part. Matching the lists to the details given by the customer or prospective customer is where things become trickier. Many commercial list providers also offer matching services that attempt to verify whether a customer, or potential customer, is on a list. In such cases they often provide the ability to configure how closely two names need to match in order for them to be identified as a potential *hit* and an alert raised.

If an organisation decides to code a matching algorithm of its own, then it should be aware that it is not as straightforward as it might appear. For example, is *Boris Johnson* the same person as *Boris de Pfeffel Johnson* or even *Alexander Boris de Pfeffel Johnson*? What if the customer's identification document says *Borris Johnson*? There are enough variants of names, including the use of initials, to make matching very difficult and this is before considering the variations that occur in some names when they are translated into other alphabets.

This is where fuzzy logic comes to the fore. Fuzzy logic is used by computer systems in order to compare two data sets and identify how likely they are to be variants of the same thing. When using fuzzy logic to match names it is very useful to understand how the algorithm is assessing the variation in spelling. Typically one might expect fuzzy logic to assess at least the following types of variation: character insertion (addition of a new letter into a string), character deletion (removal of a character from a string) and character replacement (substitution of one character for another). Of course, consideration does not stop there, as thought must also be given to how much variation one is prepared to accept (e.g. one character, two, or more) and how likely a substitution is to occur (s for z, likelihood of a variance in short words compared to longer words or characters next to each other on a keyboard).

Implementing fuzzy matching requires careful consideration. There are in excess of seven billion people in the world and only a finite number of names, particularly surnames. As an example, according to forebears.io,[18] the sixteenth most common surname in the world in 2020 is Nguyen, a Vietnamese name by origin. We picked this because Nguyen is, today, a reasonably well-travelled surname. There are almost 25 million Nguyens in the world, with 37,000 in Australia, 400,000 in the US, almost 2,000 in Japan, and almost 24 million who are residents of Vietnam. Due to the popularity of the surname alone there are likely to be a large number of entries for Nguyen on PEP lists and also probably several on sanctions lists. Fuzzy matching logic that is too broad may result in excessive numbers of false positives.

A high number of false positives can result in a range of problems. It could mean that either a large team of people is needed to manually check matches or a large number of potentially high-quality customers will be declined. If the latter, the reputation of the business is at stake. If the former, this defeats the whole point of automating the process in the first place.

In our experience the compliance team should carry out a comprehensive assessment of the proposed matching solution before a solution is selected. Further testing should also be carried out prior to deployment.

It should be noted that no PEP or sanctions matching system (manual or automatic) is ever completely error proof. Some people will slip through the net and it is then the responsibility of the monitoring systems to identify them when their account behaviour becomes suspicious.

Any string-matching solution, whether built in-house* or procured from a third party, should include the following additional capabilities:

- Fuzzy logic configuration – the ability to tune the tolerance applied in a fuzzy logic matching algorithm to meet the needs of the business.
- Age matching – matching on the age of the person, including the ability to apply a fuzzy element to it (match on age +/– one year, for example).
- Matching of numbers from identity documents. Sanctions lists often include passport and national identity numbers and this could be a good cross-check option.

It should be noted that state actors on sanctions lists may have alternative options for gaining access to financial services other than opening an account in their own name. For example, it is very common for them to use businesses[21] to open accounts and hold money on their behalf. Additionally, sanctions targets relatively commonly have multiple identities and identity documents with different names, dates of birth and other personal details, and can attempt to use these to open accounts. Where known, these additional identities will be included·in the sanctions list as well. However, this is where the vigilance

---

*If you are particularly interested in understanding the logic associated with fuzzy matching, it is worth looking up Levenshtein distance, which is a measurement of the difference between two sequences (or strings) of characters. It was set out by the Soviet mathematician Vladimir Levenshtein in his paper of 1965 (see reference 19) and is used as the basis of many modern fuzzy matching algorithms, including many spellchecking applications. See reference 20 for a good article.

and professional curiosity of the operations and compliance teams will be of benefit to the business.

5.6.2.2   Ongoing Screening

Everybody's circumstances change from time to time and this is as true of PEPs and sanctions targets as it is of the rest of the population. Leaders step down or get voted out of power, and even sanctioned individuals become reconciled with the state that issued the sanction (after all, what is the point of issuing a sanction if it isn't intended to make the target re-think their position?).

Consequently, it is important that PEP and sanctions lists are kept up to date and that regular re-screening of customers is carried out to identify whether their status has changed. If the status of an individual has changed, in either direction, then an appropriate response should be taken.

Many PEP and sanctions list checking businesses provide two services that can support this, namely notifications when new PEP and sanctions lists become available and regular re-scanning of names previously checked with them (and notification if a change in status is identified).

Without a subscription to such services, it will be necessary to implement processes to update sanctions and PEP data and re-scan the customer database for changes to customers' statuses.

5.6.2.3   Managing PEPs and Sanctions

If a customer, or potential customer, is identified as a sanctioned individual on a sanctions list that is applicable to a banking business's jurisdiction, then the law is usually straightforward – it cannot do business with them.

PEPs, though, are an altogether different subject. There is nothing to stop a banking business from doing business with a PEP, but it must have the right controls in place. The biggest risk that PEPs face is bribery and corruption. This is more prevalent in some parts of the world than others, but it occurs everywhere. Therefore, it is important to manage PEPs. Typically, such measures might include:

- A PEP must go through an enhanced due diligence process so that the host bank understands their financial status and income levels.
- A PEP must have a flag applied to their accounts such that they can be tracked and monitored.
- PEP accounts must be monitored for suspicious activity. This is a little different from how one might normally characterise suspicious activity. Banks must be constantly on the alert to the risk of bribery and therefore PEP accounts must be closely monitored for any activity that looks out of the ordinary. Consider also that PEPs, as exposed individuals, are also more likely to be blackmailed. In the event that a PEP's account starts to behave in a manner that is out of the ordinary (such as movements of money that are inconsistent with the PEP's stated wealth or income bracket), the Money Laundering Reporting Officer (MLRO) must be notified immediately.
- A PEP's account must also be monitored for access by staff working for the banking business. As noted previously, PEPs are exposed to the risks of blackmail and if criminals can get an associate employed by a banking business there is a risk that they could access information related to PEPs. For this reason, all staff access to

PEP-flagged accounts must be monitored (as, really, should it for all accounts, but PEP account access should be actively monitored, and action taken if an alert is raised). Ideally, access by staff to PEP accounts should be available to privileged accounts only, but, either way, all access to the account should be tracked.

When a banking business identifies attempts at fraud, money laundering or terrorist financing, they must avoid letting the individuals involved know that they are suspected. Doing so is called tipping off and is an offence in its own right – more about this in Section 5.2.9.1.

Fortunately, this isn't usually the case with PEPs or sanctioned individuals. In both cases the individual is likely to be well aware that they are on a list, so there should be no issues with being open with them about their status (unless local laws or regulation dictate otherwise).

5.6.3 Adverse Media Checks

Although some members of the media are known to enjoy publishing scurrilous stories about celebrities, politicians and royalty, there is a large segment that provides a very valuable service to society – that of reporting real crimes and other wrongdoings. These articles can be very useful to the fraud and compliance teams in the banking industry.

While identification of PEPs and sanctions targets is a regulatory and/or legal requirement, adverse media checks are largely about risks to the reputation and ethics of a banking business. Avoiding doing business with individuals who have been reported as being involved with bribery or corruption, for example, helps banks maintain a high moral standing and avoid the risk of reputational damage. To a large extent, whether a bank deals with individuals who match with adverse media checks is a business decision, but one that should be taken seriously.

Many PEP and sanctions data providers also offer adverse media checks that can be run at the same time. A match is reported in the same way that a PEP or sanctions match is reported, but it is then up to the business to decide how it wishes to address the situation. If such an individual is taken on as a customer then it should decide whether additional monitoring or security on the account is required. Adverse media checks are often configurable to enable the business to decide what forms of reported activity are relevant to them. Configuration might include switches for financial crime, violence, drugs, sexual offences and fraud, for example. This allows the business to determine under what circumstances it might be prepared to work with a potential customer.

5.6.4 Immigration Checklists

In some countries there is also a need to determine whether a potential customer is on an immigration checklist. In the UK, for example, these lists are maintained by CIFAS[22] and the list must be checked before an applicant can be given a current account product. These are often accessible digitally, enabling banks to check the customer details quickly and easily. If a name is found on the checklist then the bank must investigate and, if the match is proven, take appropriate action (such as deny the customer an account).

Clearly, being on an immigration checklist does not make one a fraudster. However, an immigration checklist check is often carried out alongside KYC, PEP and sanctions checks and is therefore included here for completeness.

5.6.5   Fraud Databases

Fraud databases exist in many countries around the world. In the UK, for example, one of the most comprehensive sources, the National Fraud Database, is hosted by CIFAS[23] and includes data relating to thousands of fraud cases. The fraud database can be used as a reference to identify and stop fraudsters before they can open an account or access other services and should be searched in much the same way that PEP and sanctions searches are carried out. Such databases are often managed on the basis of reciprocity – organisations that use the database are also expected to report cases of fraud back to the database-hosting entity so that it is kept current.

5.6.6   High-Risk Countries

Beyond checking specific individual credentials, any banking business should give consideration to the level of risk associated with taking on customers from different jurisdictions. Not every country around the world operates at the same high levels of standards regarding prevention of money laundering, corruption and bribery, and detection, and prosecution of those involved in them and there are some countries that have very poor track records. There are a number of sources that should be considered when trying to determine which countries one wishes to operate within or take on customers from and what additional measures should be taken when onboarding customers from certain jurisdictions.

The first place to start is to look at the lists of high-risk countries provided by the Financial Action Task Force (FATF),[24] an intergovernmental body with representation from across the globe, but it is also necessary to identify what other lists are applicable to the local jurisdiction. For the EU, for example, the European Commission also provides a list.[25]

If a banking business wishes to operate within, or take customers on from, an identified high-risk location it will need to develop enhanced due diligence measures that go above and beyond the standard KYC, PEP and sanctions checks discussed earlier. It may have to present these measures to relevant regulators and convince them that it can manage the additional risk of working with those locales.

Above and beyond high-risk states are those countries that are generally regarded as pariah states where any engagement is looked upon dimly throughout much of the rest of the globe. At the time of going to press there are a small number of states that might be regarded in this category, with Iran and North Korea as the leading candidates.[26]

5.6.7   Ongoing Monitoring

No onboarding process is risk free. There will always be some fraudsters who manage to make their way through the process. Additionally, fraudsters do not always attack via the most obvious routes; they might attempt to take over a genuine customer's accounts, corrupt customers or even blackmail or fool them into making transactions that they would not ordinarily. Consequently, banking businesses must constantly monitor their accounts for suspicious activity.

When monitoring an account there are a broad range of activities that might be deemed to be suspicious and the risk and compliance teams should define those that are relevant to the specific area of business. However, consideration should be given, as a minimum, to the following:

- *Logon.* Monitoring customer logon events can provide important clues even before any activity occurs within the customer account. For example, is the customer logging on from the same Internet address as normal? Is it the same locale and the same device? Are they holding or using the device in the same way that they usually do (gesture recognition)? Variations from normal behaviours could indicate that something is amiss and raise alerts within the monitoring systems. However, a variance from the norm does not necessarily indicate that something is wrong. A degree of triangulation may be necessary. So, for example, if the logon is from a previously unused location and the customer attempts to create a new payee and high-value payment during that session, that might be regarded as highly suspicious and require further security before it can be approved. It should be noted that there is a growing stable of software providers that are able to provide biometric toolsets that can assess not only basic biometrics (such as iris and fingerprint) but can also assess gestures (e.g. pressure on the screen, how the hand moves and so on)[27] to determine a level of confidence that the person on the other end of the Internet connection is who they claim to be.
- *Access times.* What time does the customer usually use their banking app or access the Internet banking service? Are they logging on in the middle of the night or at a time they never usually log on?
- *Access frequency.* When was the last time the customer logged on to their account? Has it been dormant for an extended period? The creation of sleeper accounts is a common ploy among fraudsters. Dormant accounts rarely attract much attention from banks, but if they suddenly awaken after an extended period of dormancy then the bank should take note.
- *Password resets.* Has the customer just had their password reset? If so, then an attempt to set up a new payee (particularly if they don't often set up payees) or an attempt to send a material sum of money may be regarded as suspicious.
- *Is the account behaving normally?* Appropriate monitoring on an account over an extended period makes it possible to recognise patterns in a customer's usage of their account (such as types and amount of payment, where they make payments and so on). This can be used as a baseline to identify behavioural changes that might indicate the need to take action to protect the account and the customer.

5.6.8 Transaction Monitoring and Anti-Money Laundering

Historically, the banking industry has struggled to maintain effective transaction monitoring across the industry, and still does. Individual banks might have effective mechanisms (though in many cases there is doubt even as to the veracity of that assumption[28]) but the industry as a whole is pretty ineffective. This is particularly true when it comes to organised crime moving large sums between many banks in different jurisdictions. For example, the UN believes that between 2% and 5% of GDP each year is money laundering.[29]

The inability of the global banking industry to act effectively as a whole is, of course, not always due to technical, logistical or even management failures. Banks operating in markets where local high-profile politicians are targeted for sanctions can find themselves in a difficult position – do they enforce the sanction and risk localised consequences or fail to enforce the sanction and suffer the consequences in the country where the sanctions list originated?

Additionally, as not all banks are quite as upstanding as one might hope, there are always ways for criminals and sanctioned individuals to get money into the banking system. The challenge is for banks to identify these occasions and act appropriately, but that is easier said than done when money is held in other names, shell companies or the like.

Either way, this does not excuse banks from failing to appropriately track and monitor both accounts and payments on their own platforms; it merely emphasises how hard the problem is to effectively tackle.

Transaction monitoring comes in many forms:

- Sanctions screening – ensuring that payments are not being sent to, or received from, sanctioned individuals. Sanctions screening is not only relevant when an account is being created, but also when a new payment is set up. Wherever possible new payments, particularly international payments, should be sanctions screened (both outgoing and incoming payments). It should be noted, though, that many domestic payment schemes don't provide sufficient data within the payment data to properly identify the sender or recipient and careful analysis of the data available from the local payment scheme should be undertaken before attempting to build a sanctions solution. A poorly constructed sanctions screening solution can be highly inefficient due to all the false positives that might need to be investigated or, if it misses many matches, give a false impression of security to senior management.

- PEP monitoring – monitoring PEP accounts to determine whether there is any indication of inappropriate behaviour. Of course, with PEPs the objective is to spot any behaviour that might indicate either bribery or blackmail-related activities.

- Terrorist and criminal financing and money laundering – criminals use bank accounts for a variety of different reasons. Opening of the accounts can be carried out by representatives of the organisation, members of the general public or by apparently reputable businesses. Often the only way to identify that the account is suspicious is through the behaviour of that account. Are large quantities of cash being paid in? Are large payments being made overseas? Are there no regular smaller outgoings or is there a suspiciously large number of lower-value transactions? Of course, any one of these previous statements can also be the activities of a perfectly reputable member of society or business so monitoring for terrorist financing or money laundering requires a degree of triangulation as well as observant bank staff (both branch and back office).

- More general suspicious activity – suspicious activity can take many forms. It could be very small amounts being moved across large number of accounts, or larger amounts moving in ways that raise concerns. Sometimes it is moved by money mules (often younger people who are paid to open accounts and move money in return for a financial reward – often these people don't understand what they are doing or why they are doing it, they merely follow instructions from their handler[30]). Suspicious activity is often identified through event correlation, where a bank identifies a number of suspect transactions, such as card payments, and then looks for a common root. For a great example of this, the reader should look at the story of how the British start-up bank Monzo identified a significant breach at Ticketmaster in 2018, long before Ticketmaster or its bank realised that anything was wrong.[31]

- Fraud monitoring –monitoring for crimes in action. For example, authorised push payment fraud, where a vulnerable target is convinced by a fraudster to send some or all of their funds to a different account, is a worryingly common event. While there are some industry-wide attempts to address specific forms of attacks on bank customers (Confirmation of Payee in the UK is one such attempt[32]), this will not end such attacks. To protect their customers, banks must be vigilant and be prepared to put in place extra controls where a customer appears to be carrying out any activity that is out of character. This is also true for payments, which we cover in more detail in Chapters 6 and 7.

In the event that an issue is identified, the system must be capable of flagging the account and implementing whatever countermeasures the fraud and compliance teams (guided by regulation) have determined is appropriate. However, it should be noted that it is illegal in many countries to allow the owner of a suspect account to know that they are being investigated, as discussed in Section 5.6.10.

5.6.9   Reporting Suspicious Activity

When suspicious activity is identified at an account, or broader, level, the financial institution is obliged to report it to the relevant authorities. Most jurisdictions provide clear guidelines on what and how to report suspicious activity and even use a common language to describe the report, a Suspicious Activity Report (SAR). This is normally completed by the Money Laundering Reporting Officer (MLRO) team and submitted to the relevant authorities.

The storage of the report, and any supporting evidence, must be secured in a locked-down area of the network. From a technology perspective, the secure area is pretty much the only deliverable required to support SARs.

5.6.10   Tipping Off

When identifying, addressing and reporting suspicious activity a banking business should be careful to avoid tipping off. Tipping off is a serious offence and is one that can easily be committed by not giving due consideration to how a particular circumstance should be addressed.

Simply put, tipping off is the act of warning someone that a potential financial crime that they are involved with has been noticed. The exact offence of tipping off varies by jurisdiction. However, it usually becomes relevant to a banking business when suspicious activity is identified. As soon as suspicious activity becomes apparent the organisation should raise a SAR (see Section 5.2.9), but how it handles the situation then becomes a matter of local tipping-off law. A natural response to suspicious activity might be to freeze the account and suspend any further incoming payments. However, that might be construed as tipping off.

5.7   References

1. Barton, C. (2020). List of UK challenger banks, digital banks and banking apps. Finder (27 April). https://www.finder.com/uk/digital-banking/challenger-banks-list (accessed 9 July 2020).

2. CRiskCo. Credit risk analysis and management platform. https://www.criskco.com/ (accessed 29 July 2020).
3. Conroy, M. (2019). The benefits of Open Banking for SMEs. UK Finance. https://www.ukfinance.org.uk/news-and-insight/blogs/benefits-open-banking-smes (accessed 29 July 2020).
4. Office for National Statistics (2018). Business demography, UK: 2017. https://www.ons.gov.uk/businessindustryandtrade/business/activitysizeandlocation/bulletins/businessdemography/2017 (accessed 29 July 2020).
5. Lusthaus, J. (2018). *Industry of Anonymity, Inside the Business of Cybercrime.* Cambridge, MA: Harvard University Press.
6. Peachey, K. (2018). TSB admits 1,300 accounts hit by fraud amid IT meltdown. *BBC News* (6 June). https://www.bbc.co.uk/news/business-44385710 (accessed 10 July 2020).
7. Which? I think I may have given a fraudster my bank details. https://www.which.co.uk/consumer-rights/advice/i-think-i-may-have-given-a-fraudster-my-bank-details (accessed 10 July 2020).
8. Rutherford, S. (2017). What is authorised push payment fraud? FICO (5 December). https://www.fico.com/blogs/what-authorised-push-payment-fraud (accessed 10 July 2020).
9. Jones, R. (2006) Banks hiding online fraud, say police. *The Guardian* (5 December). https://www.theguardian.com/money/2006/dec/05/accounts.business1 (accessed 10 July 2020).
10. The Financial Conduct Authority (2020). Money laundering and terrorist financing (17 June). https://www.fca.org.uk/firms/financial-crime/money-laundering-terrorist-financing (accessed 10 July 2020).
11. Capita. ID verification. https://www.capitaworkforcemanagement.co.uk/hardware/id-verification/ (accessed 10 July 2020).
12. IDnow. The fastest way to verify your customer's identity. https://www.idnow.io/ (accessed 10 July 2020).
13. Jumio. Loved by users, loathed by fraudsters. https://www.jumio.com/loved-loathed (accessed 10 July 2020).
14. Onfido. Digital identity. Made human. https://onfido.com/ (accessed 10 July 2020).
15. Thales. National ID cards: 2016–20 facts and trends (3 June). https://www.thalesgroup.com/en/markets/digital-identity-and-security/government/identity/2016-national-id-card-trends (accessed 8 July 2020).
16. Bureau Van Dijk. https://www.bvdinfo.com/en-gb/ (accessed 8 July 2020).
17. The Financial Conduct Authority (2017). Guidance on the treatment of politically exposed persons (PEPs) under the Money Laundering. *Terrorist Financing and Transfer of Funds (Information on the Payer) Regulations* 2017 (March) https://www.fca.org.uk/publication/guidance-consultation/gc17-02.pdf (accessed 29 July 2020).
18. Forebears. https://forebears.io/ (accessed 9 July 2020).
19. Levenshtein, V.I. (1966). Binary codes capable of correcting deletions, insertions, and reversals. *Soviet Physics Doklady* 10 (8): 707–710.
20. Babar, N. (2018). The Levenshtein Distance Algorithm. DZone (2 October). https://dzone.com/articles/the-levenshtein-algorithm-1 (accessed 9 July 2020).
21. Bullough, O. (2018). How Britain let Russia hide its dirty money. *The Guardian* (25 May). https://www.theguardian.com/news/2018/may/25/how-britain-let-russia-hide-its-dirty-money (accessed 10 July 2020).
22. CIFAS. CIFAS: Leaders in fraud prevention. https://www.cifas.org.uk/ (accessed 10 July 2020).

23. Ibid.
24. FATF. https://www.fatf-gafi.org/ (accessed 10 July 2020).
25. European Commission. European Commission adopts new list of third countries with weak anti-money laundering and terrorist financing regimes (13 February). https://ec.europa.eu/commission/presscorner/detail/en/IP_19_781 (accessed 10 July 2020).
26. FATF (2020). High-risk and other monitored jurisdictions. https://www.fatf-gafi.org/countries/#high-risk (accessed 10 July 2020).
27. Hitachi (2019). Hitachi's new hand gesture biometric technology raises the bar for computer security (10 September). https://www.hitachi.eu/en/press/hitachis-new-hand-gesture-biometric-technology-raises-bar-computer-security (accessed 10 July 2020).
28. Fruth, J. (2018). Anti-money laundering controls failing to detect terrorists, cartels, and sanctioned states. Reuters (14 March). https://www.reuters.com/article/bc-finreg-laundering-detecting/anti-money-laundering-controls-failing-to-detect-terrorists-cartels-and-sanctioned-states-idUSKCN1GP2NV (accessed 10 July 2020).
29. United Nations Office on Drugs and Crime. Money-laundering and globalization. https://www.unodc.org/unodc/en/money-laundering/globalization.html (accessed 10 July 2020).
30. Hughes, B. (2019). Money mules – What are they and could you fall victim? The Money Advice Service (12 February). https://www.moneyadviceservice.org.uk/blog/money-mules-what-are-they-and-could-you-fall-victim (accessed 10 July 2020).
31. Vernier, N. (2018). Protecting customers from the Ticketmaster breach: Monzo's story. Monzo (28 June). https://monzo.com/blog/2018/06/28/ticketmaster-breach (accessed 10 July 2020).
32. Pay.UK. Confirmation of payee. https://www.wearepay.uk/confirmation-of-payee/ (accessed 10 July 2020).

CHAPTER 6

Card Payments

Payment cards are a part of a broader range of plastic card products that are used for a variety of retail and commercial applications. The types of cards that use similar technologies are extensive, including everything from basic stored-value cards (like gift vouchers) through to bank-issued debit and credit cards.

For a payment product that has existed since the 1950s, cards have taken a long time to reach general acceptance globally, and even now there are some countries, including developed countries, where card acceptance is far from universal. The reasons for this could include cultural resistance, with ongoing reliance on and trust in cash, or lack of infrastructure, or merchant reticence or inability to invest in the infrastructure required or to pay the fees for card payments.

6.1 Types of Card

As noted above, there are a broad variety of payment cards issued around the world. However, in our experience, there are four common types.

6.1.1 Debit Cards

A debit card is directly linked to a bank account and when it is used the available balance of the account is reduced. For many people debit cards are a safe and easy option, as they are typically linked to the current account where they have their salary paid and there is little risk that a customer will build up a debit balance that he or she can't then repay, although they can empty their account and make the wait until the next payday distressing.

6.1.2 Prepaid Cards

A prepaid card functions in a similar way to a debit card in that it is associated with an account and when used to pay for goods or services the balance of the account is reduced. However, the account tends to be an e-money account rather than a fully functional account at a bank, with one of the key differences being that it must always be in credit. An e-money account is an account that is not operated by a bank and is typically not

230

subject to depositor protection schemes (although the e-money business must hold all client funds in a ring-fenced account) and, under certain circumstances, may also not be associated with a specific person (e.g. in the case of a gift card). Typically, with a prepaid card the account cannot go overdrawn and offline transactions are not allowed. In some cases pre-authorisation (where an amount on the account is locked on behalf of a merchant for later payment) is not available. The issuer may restrict what type of retailers the card can be used at. Confusingly, some issuers offer what they call prepaid cards which the card scheme categorises as debit cards and such cards often carry the label *Debit*.

6.1.3   Credit Cards

Credit cards work differently from the previous two types of cards in that the user builds up a balance of short-term debt that is owed to the card issuer, up to the credit limit set by the issuer. Within a set time from receiving their periodic (typically monthly) statement, the account holder must pay any amount between a set minimum amount and the total balance outstanding. Interest is charged, usually if the account holder does not pay off the full amount of the outstanding balance. Such products are often referred to as revolving credit products because the amount that is lent changes on a periodic cycle (i.e. typically monthly) over an indefinite period (unlike a loan, which normally must be paid off within a fixed term).

6.1.4   Charge Cards

Charge cards (e.g. the original American Express and Diners Club cards) work similarly to credit cards, but the account holder has to pay off the whole balance by the statement payment date. They often have higher credit limits than credit cards (and some were advertised as having no credit limit) and were historically associated with corporate expenses such as travel and entertainment. They are also occasionally called delayed debit cards.[1]

6.1.5   Other Payment Cards

Of note are public transport payment cards, with perhaps Hong Kong's Octopus as one that is the most well-known for extending its acceptance from transport to many retailers for small payments. Such cards are usually contactless smartcards (see Section 2.5.13) with a stored value application that means they can be used without needing an authorisation from whatever accounting platform maintains the associated accounts. This ensures a very fast response at turnstiles when entering or exiting a station, tram or bus.

Fuel cards, used for purchases of fuel and related goods at filling stations, are another category of payment card with a distinct function. Additional information is collected by the merchant and passed to the issuer such as vehicle registration and mileage, volume of fuel purchased, and tax included in the payment amount. This can make it easier for companies, the main users of such cards, to control and account for fuel and related expenses.

Store cards are similar to credit cards in that the cardholder can make purchases up to the credit limit of their account and then has to pay off at least a minimum amount after each statement. They differ from credit cards in that a store card is only useable in the stores of the retailer that issued it. In some cases, the distinction has disappeared, as some retailers have converted their store cards to scheme-branded credit cards (or sold the accounts to a credit card issuer) that are accepted everywhere the scheme's cards are accepted.

6.2   Information on a Payment Card

There are various pieces of information on a payment card. Some are visible because they are printed or embossed on the card while others are only recorded in the magnetic stripe or the chip.

The long number across the front of the card is the primary account number (PAN). It is commonly 16 digits long but may vary from 10 to 19 digits.* The format of the PAN is specified in the standard ISO/IEC 7812-1[3] and comprises the Issuer Identification Number (IIN), which is the first eight digits of the PAN, the account number and usually a final check digit. The check digit is compared against the value calculated by using the Luhn algorithm on all the other digits of the PAN. This guards against errors when manually entering a card number, such as mistyping a digit or transposing two digits (except 9 and 0).

The first digit of the IIN denotes the sector in which the card issuer operates. For example, 1 is allocated to airlines, 2 to airlines and financial services institutions, 3 to travel and entertainment, 4 and 5 to banking and financial services and 6 to merchandising (e.g. retailer loyalty cards) and financial services. The IIN was historically also called the BIN (Bank Identification Number) and a set of BINs is called a BIN range. In practice an issuer may have more than one BIN or more than one BIN range because of the volume of cards it issues or because it has different types of cards, and often a certain BIN range will represent a specific type of card from one issuer (e.g. debit card, credit card and so on). For example, BIN 372550 is the Starwood preferred guest hotel loyalty credit card.

As well as the PAN, a payment card may show a four-digit start date, a four-digit expiry date, the cardholder's name (up to 26 characters) and other information (e.g. bank account details if it is a debit card). On the back of the card, the signature strip often contains the last four digits of the PAN (to protect against a signature strip being physically transplanted from a different card) and the three-digit CVV2 (Card Verification Value 2, which we cover in Section 6.6.3.2). On some cards (e.g. American Express) the CVV2 comprises four digits and is printed on the front to the right and above the PAN.

The magnetic stripe on a payment card actually has up to three tracks that hold varying amounts of data. Track 1 holds most of the information printed on the card, apart from the start date and CVV2 value (for the reason we explain in Section 6.6.3.2), plus additional information such as the three-digit Card Verification Value (CVV) and optionally a PIN Verification Value (PVV) or equivalent which can be used to validate the PIN

---

*Historically, a PAN could be from 8 to 19 digits, but with the increase in the length of the IIN from 6 to 8 digits, the minimum length of the PAN was increased. See reference 2.

associated with the card. Track 2 normally repeats track 1, but without the cardholder name, and track 3 holds a range of information specific to the payment card scheme. The chip provides similar information as the magnetic stripe but can also compute dynamic values for use in improving authorisation security, which we cover in Section 6.6.3.2.

6.3   How a Card Payment Works

Several parties take part in a card payment.

First, there is the cardholder – the individual who is using a card to make a payment. This is often the same person who owns the account associated with the card (and who is termed the *primary cardholder*). As debit cards are associated with a bank account, there may be more than one owner of the account and each may have their own debit card. With credit and charge cards it is often possible for cards that debit the same account to be issued to relatives and friends of the primary cardholder. As we already mentioned, the account associated with a gift card may not be formally associated with the cardholder.

Second, there is the issuer of the card – typically a bank, e-money business or payment card company. This is the financial institution that has provided the card to the cardholder, authorises transactions and manages the balance of the account.

Third, there is the merchant – the business that is accepting the card as a means of payment for goods or services. The schemes typically categorise each merchant into a specific category such as Airlines and air carriers, Department stores and Dry cleaners, with each category assigned a Merchant Category Code (MCC). So, for example, Veterinary Services has the code 0742.[4] There is a standard, ISO 18245, for such codes.[5]

Fourth, acquirers process transactions submitted by merchants. Each merchant will have a contract with an acquirer for this service. An acquirer has to also have a contract with each card payment scheme for which it acquires transactions. Historically, acquirers could only acquire transactions for one card payment scheme, but now acquirers can acquire transactions for multiple schemes. Acquirers were historically banks, but now are equally likely to be specialist payment service providers.

Note that the issuers and acquirers are sometimes collectively called members of the scheme.

Finally, there is the card payment scheme such as American Express, Mastercard, UnionPay and Visa. The scheme sets the rules for how payments can be made using the cards issued with its brand, as well as rules on many aspects such as the technical details of each card, the design of each card, how refunds are handled, how payment transactions must be routed and so on – such rulebooks run to hundreds of pages and there can be variations between different countries and regions. Historically each scheme routed its own card payment transactions between acquirers and issuers, although in some regions and countries transactions can be routed across different networks. The scheme also ensures settlement between its members and sometimes steps in to authorise a payment if the issuer is offline.

Now that we have explained the parties that are involved in a card payment transaction, before showing the transaction flow it is necessary to explain that historically (and still often today) a card payment involves two steps. The first is what is called authorisation, which takes place at the point of sale. The second step is clearing and settlement which is initiated, after the purchase has taken place, by the merchant sending details of a completed card payment to its acquirer, who then submits it for payment via the scheme to the card issuer.

Originally, to purchase something using a charge or credit card (before there were debit cards or prepaid cards), you would present your card to the merchant at the point of sale, who would then write out a transaction voucher (a small booklet comprising at least three sheets of paper, all but the last of which were carbon-backed) setting out the amount of the purchase. The merchant would then put the voucher and your card into a simple manual machine – an imprinter (colloquially referred to as a zip-zap machine) – that pressed the embossed information on your credit card into the voucher. The machine typically also had a metal plate in it embossed with the details of the merchant, which were also impressed into the voucher. Then you would sign the voucher and the merchant would check your signature against the card and that the card was still in date, and give you one of the sheets from the voucher. Merchants were also supposed to verify that the card was not stolen by checking that the card was not listed in a book distributed by the relevant card payment scheme. Later on (typically at the end of the day) the merchant would send one of the paper copies from the voucher to its acquirer who would then submit it for clearing and settlement via the card scheme, and a handful of days later the payment would be debited from your account. Also, to combat fraud an authorisation process was set up. If a purchase was above a certain amount (typically set by merchant category), the retailer had to telephone its acquirer to get the transaction authorised. The acquirer would contact the issuer to check that there were sufficient funds in the cardholder's account to cover the payment and to confirm that the payment card being used was not stolen or blocked. The issuer would then give the acquirer an authorisation number for the transaction that the retailer would write on the transaction voucher. Authorisation gives an assurance (but not a guarantee) to the merchant that it will be paid. Therefore, historically a credit card purchase was a two-step process – an authorisation (which was not always required) followed by the actual payment transaction.

Obviously, a paper-based process like this was not particularly scalable or efficient, so in the early 1970s platforms were set up by the various card schemes to automate the transmission of transaction information between acquirers and issuers. Eventually electronic point of sale card readers were rolled out to merchants, which connected to the acquirers by telephone and ultimately across the Internet.

Figure 6.1 shows how a successful authorisation takes place, with the return of an authorisation code from the issuer of the card to the merchant. Of course, a payment could be declined for various reasons ranging from a lack of funds in the cardholder's account, limits on how much the cardholder can spend in a single transaction, an invalid PIN entered by the cardholder, transactions not permitted for the category of retailer, the card has been temporarily blocked by the cardholder (or the issuer), the issuer's platform is unavailable and suspected fraud. If a bona fide card payment is declined it is possible that the issuing bank will receive a phone call from the cardholder to ask why. A payment can also be referred, although in our experience this appears to be rare, and the merchant would typically have to contact its acquirer by telephone if this happens. Finally, in some cases the issuer may send back a partial authorisation, which provides authorisation up to a certain amount (typically the available funds in the cardholders' account), with the cardholder expected to make up the rest with some other payment means such as cash.

FIGURE 6.1   The successful authorisation of a card payment.

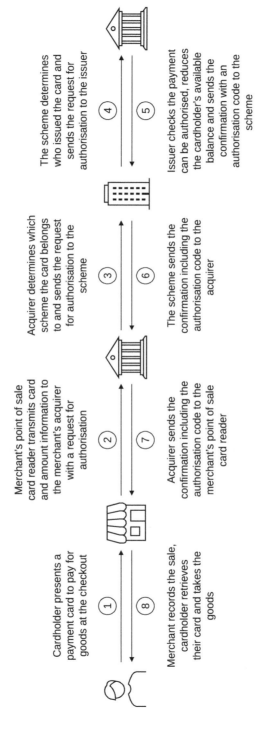

Cardholder presents a payment card to pay for goods at the checkout

①

Merchant records the sale, cardholder retrieves their card and takes the goods

⑧

Merchant's point of sale card reader transmits card and amount information to the merchant's acquirer with a request for authorisation

②

Acquirer sends the confirmation including the authorisation code to the merchant's point of sale card reader

⑦

Acquirer determines which scheme the card belongs to and sends the request for authorisation to the scheme

③

The scheme sends the confirmation including the authorisation code to the acquirer

⑥

The scheme determines who issued the card and sends the request for authorisation to the issuer

④

Issuer checks the payment can be authorised, reduces the cardholder's available balance and sends the confirmation with an authorisation code to the scheme

⑤

FIGURE 6.2   Clearing and settlement of card payments.

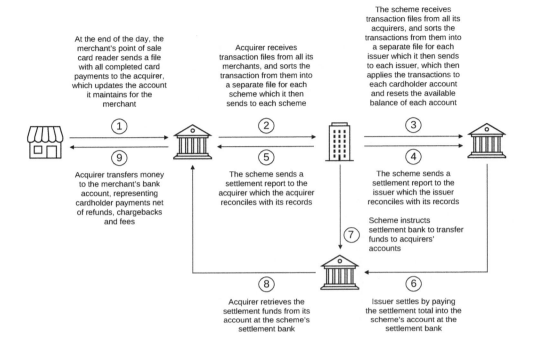

Once the payment is authorised as set out above, the actual flow of funds from the issuer to the acquirer and then to the merchant needs to take place, which is the second step in the card payment process and is illustrated in Figure 6.2. The merchant has to send a transaction copy to the acquirer – sometimes called banking the transaction. This was originally one of the copies from the transaction voucher used in the imprinter or zip-zap machine but is now sent electronically in a file with all the other transactions on that day from the merchant's point of sale platform (or card reader) to the acquirer. The acquirer collates all these files from its merchants and creates a file for each card payment scheme (e.g. Mastercard, Visa, etc.) of all the transactions it has acquired for that scheme on that day. It sends the relevant file to each payment scheme. The scheme receives all these files from its acquirers and does something similar – it creates a new set of files, one for each of its card issuers, containing the transactions received from the acquirers, and sends these to the issuers. This is the clearing process – the determination of who is responsible for paying each transaction. The issuer posts the transactions to its cardholders' accounts. The scheme also works out the net settlement position of all the issuers and acquirers – in other words, how much each is owed or owes in total for that day's transactions. Those owing money must pay it into the scheme's account at the settlement bank (which can be a commercial bank rather than a central bank) within a small number of hours. The scheme instructs the settlement bank to make the transfers to the accounts of the members that are owed money. Each acquirer then distributes the payments to its merchants.

Note that the sequence of the steps shown in Figure 6.2 from step 3 onwards may vary, and some steps may be combined (e.g. steps 3 and 4). For simplicity, we have only shown one acquirer and one issuer in the diagram, but all the scheme's issuers and acquirers take part in this process. Also, because transactions can also flow from issuers to acquirers (e.g. chargebacks), in reality the scheme receives inbound transaction files from acquirers *and issuers* in step 2 and sends out outbound transaction files to issuers *and acquirers* in step 3. Finally, in some schemes issuers have to fund a settlement account in advance so step 6 would be replaced with a transfer from the issuer's account at the settlement bank to the scheme's settlement account rather than an interbank payment by the issuer to the settlement bank – although the latter may still be necessary if the issuer had not advanced enough funds to cover the settlement.

Note how the flow of money is not instantaneous. From a timing perspective, the critical part of the process is the authorisation – the merchant wants a very fast response (within seconds) while the customer is at the point of sale. With traditional acquirers the merchant receives the actual sale proceeds at least a day later, and in some cases several days later. Some acquirers may advance funds to merchants sooner than this, with instant settlement sometimes offered,[6] although in reality this is made possible because the acquirer is paying the merchant in advance of actually receiving the funds. From a cardholder perspective, the available balance of their card account is reduced immediately once the authorisation is confirmed by their card issuer, but the actual transaction that debits their account takes place typically overnight.

As well as the clearing and settlement of card transactions, the scheme also charges fees for its service and collects interchange fees. Interchange is a fee that acquirers pay to card issuers; they were originally set up to encourage banks to issue credit cards and theoretically compensate them for the costs in doing so. They typically vary by the type of merchant, nominally representing that transactions at different types of merchants have different risk profiles to the card issuers (e.g. are more or less likely to be fraudulent). They have been the subject of much regulatory scrutiny and legal action to limit them in some markets.[7] So, a merchant pays a fee for every card payment transaction – comprising the scheme's processing fee, the interchange fee that goes to the issuer and a fee charged by the acquirer for its services.

You may ask why there should still be two steps in the card payment process. When what were originally credit card schemes implemented computers and networks to automate and digitise credit card payments, they replicated the two steps from the manual process described earlier. Because there are two message flows involved in a payment, this two-step process is often referred to as dual-message processing. However, ATM schemes, which from their start used online electronic messaging, often supported a single request/response message pair for a cash withdrawal[8] – the combination of an authorisation request and a successful response provides the information required by the scheme to clear and settle the payment transaction. In other words, the ATM operator does not submit a transaction copy for the cash its ATM dispensed. Obviously, this is a simpler process than dual-message processing. Another reason why ATMs often used single-message processing for cash withdrawals is because an ATM dispenses cash immediately once it receives the authorisation from the issuer, so the ATM operator (which is in effect the acquirer) immediately pays the cardholder. This is different from a purchase at a merchant, where the acquirer typically only pays the merchant after it has been paid via the card payment scheme. Therefore, ATM withdrawals have a different risk profile and cashflow impact on ATM operators compared to the risk profile and cashflow impact on acquirers of card payments to merchants. Single-message processing ensures that the ATM operator submits the payment clearing information to the scheme at the same time the cash is withdrawn, and settlement could potentially take place more than once a day. A natural extension of ATM schemes was to support debit card payments in merchants equipped with a card reader, with a cardholder entering their PIN for authentication, so debit card schemes also often supported single-message processing – and in fact this is sometimes referred to as *single-message debit* processing.

Because of the different histories of credit, debit and ATM payments it is normal for a scheme to support both dual-message and single-message processing and to translate messages between the two message formats[9] given that different issuers and acquirers will often only support one type of processing.

Even in markets that use dual-message processing for point of sale payments, some acquirers simplify the process for their merchants by removing the need for the merchants to send a transaction copy for each payment at the end of the day. In effect, the acquirer generates these itself and sends them to the scheme.

Schemes such as Mastercard and Visa in which a card payment involves a cardholder, a merchant, an acquirer and an issuer are termed *four-party* schemes. However, some of these parties are combined in other schemes. For example, American Express historically was the only issuer of its cards and also the only acquirer of transactions involving its cards, and as a result it was termed a *closed-loop* scheme or *three-party* scheme. However, American Express has, from time to time, made arrangements with other banking institutions to issue cards branded as American Express and now permits acquirers to acquire transactions on its behalf.

There is often another party involved in a card payment: an issuer may use a *card processor* to manage its card accounts, and the processor acts on behalf of the issuer in card payment authorisations and clearing. However, the card issuer still has to make settlement payments to the scheme and maintain its relationship with its cardholders.

6.4   Card Payment Networks

For payments to be handled electronically, a card payment scheme has to connect the acquirers and issuers to a network across which payment messages flow. In addition, acquirers must connect to their merchants. This is illustrated in Figure 6.3. A scheme can have multiple acquirers (represented by Acquirer A and Acquirer B in the diagram), and multiple issuers (represented by Bank C and Bank D in the diagram). Each acquirer has a merchant acquiring platform, which maintains an account for each of its merchants, holding details of each merchant's payment transactions. Each issuer has what is shown as an accounting platform – for debit cards this would normally be a core banking platform and for credit cards a credit card platform; some issuers may have both.

So, replaying the card payment scenario illustrated in Figure 6.1, a customer pays for something with their credit card at a merchant, who inserts the customer's credit card into a card reader and enters the amount to be paid. The cardholder enters their PIN, and the card reader sends an authorisation request message to the merchant's acquirer, typically via a dial-up telephone connection, over the public switched telephone network (PSTN), or over a fixed connection for larger merchants. Modern card readers also often have the

FIGURE 6.3 A simple card payment network.

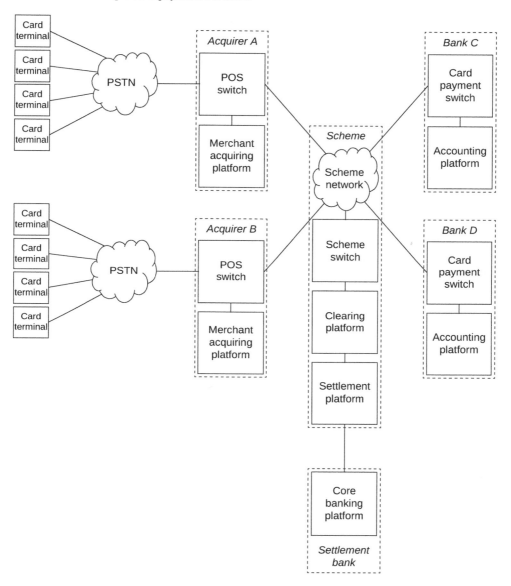

ability to connect via the Internet (including over mobile networks). The acquirer has a POS (point of sale) switch which receives the authorisation request message, determines what payment scheme the card is with (based on the card number) and sends the authorisation message (reformatted in line with the scheme rules) to the scheme. The scheme's switch receives the message, determines the issuer of the card (again from the card number) and sends the message to the card issuer – in our case, Bank C. Note that in reality the scheme is likely to have more than one switch to ensure very high availability – schemes aim to be always available and the scheme switch architecture may well be designed to be up to 99.999% available over a year. Bank C's card payment switch receives the message and checks the available balance and status of the card account with the accounting platform in order to determine if it should authorise the transaction. It sends an authorisation response message containing an authorisation code, via the scheme, to the acquirer, which sends it back to the card reader at the merchant. We would expect the scheme to have at least two switches for maximum resilience, and the issuers and acquirers may well have at least two switches each for the same reason.

Figure 6.3 also shows the platforms involved in the clearing and settlement process described in Section 6.2. A scheme uses its clearing platform to process all the inbound transaction files and create the outbound transaction files and settlement reports. Note that this platform will check that each transaction record is correctly formatted and contains records for cards that use the scheme. There is, of course, a chance that not all transaction records will be accepted, so it creates a report per network member of rejected transactions (which is typically included in the settlement report). The scheme's clearing platform also calculates the net settlement position of each member. The scheme uses its settlement platform to monitor transactions in its settlement account at the settlement bank and to instruct the settlement bank to make the transfers from its account to each member's settlement account. Each acquirer uses the settlement report it receives to update the account of each merchant held on its merchant acquiring platform, which calculates the amount it should pay each merchant.

The scheme would also likely have a billing platform to calculate its fees and the interchange fees and may incorporate them into the settlement reports and settle transactions net of these fees. Acquirers may simply add their own fee to these fees and debit them from each merchant's account, or they may use different fee structures depending on the commercial model they are using (for example, some acquirers charge a set percentage for all debit and credit card transactions). Typically, the merchant acquiring platform used by an acquirer would calculate the fees for each merchant.

The simple card payment network illustrated in Figure 6.3 became more complicated with the emergence of card processors (e.g. FirstData and TSYS) and organisations involved in taking payments over the Internet (including Internet Payment Service Providers). A corresponding picture of today's environment, albeit still simplified, could look like the diagram in Figure 6.4.

Starting from the left-hand side, we now have online retailers who connect via a third-party Internet Payment Service Provider (IPSP) to Acquirer A. IPSPs met the demand from online retailers for readily usable card payment acquiring functionality they could integrate into their websites (and more recently smartphone apps), when acquirers typically didn't offer such a facility. Many IPSPs have been acquired by acquirers (and schemes) – for example, Acquirer B in this diagram has its own Internet payment platform that online retailers can integrate into their websites and smartphone apps. We now have retailers with card terminals integrated into their point of sale platforms, so card payment transactions also originate from these platforms and not just standalone card terminals. Bank C could be a debit card issuer, in which case its accounting platform will be the core banking platform which maintains its customer's current accounts, or a credit card issuer, in which case its accounting platform will be a credit card platform, or even a prepaid card issuer, in which case the accounting platform

FIGURE 6.4   A more complex card payment network.

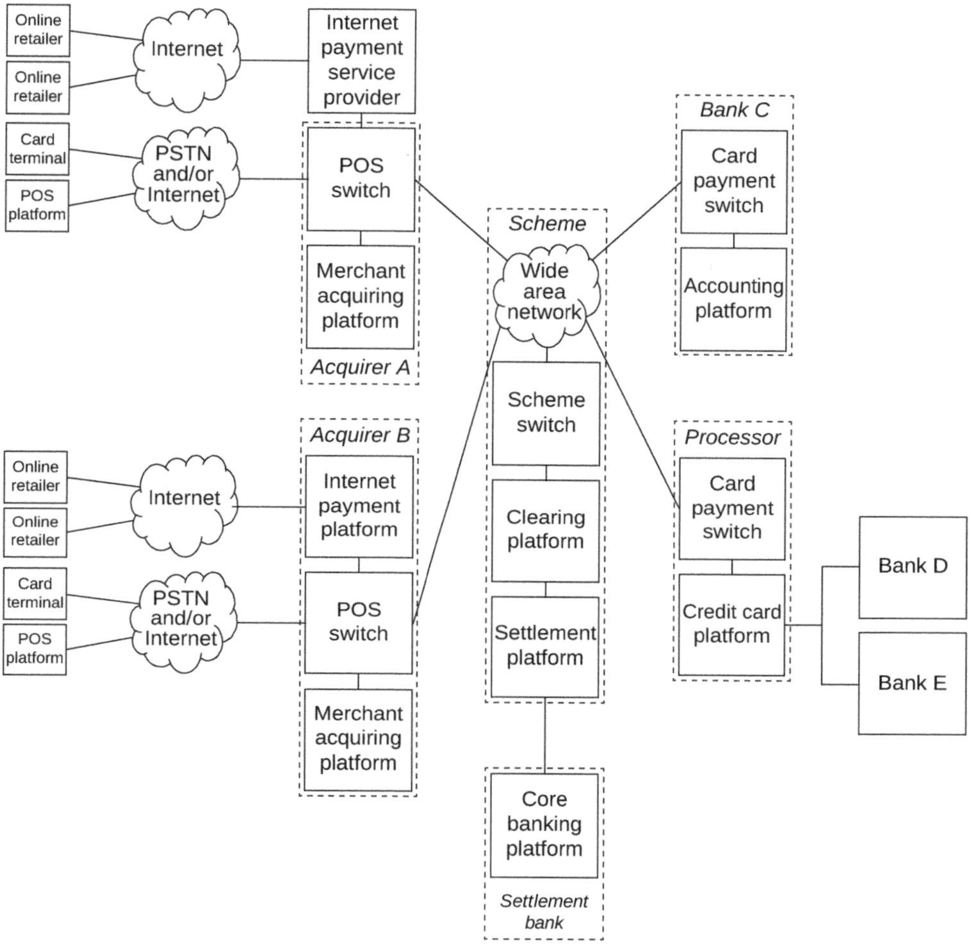

could be a simple core banking platform. On the right-hand side we show a processor that is processing credit card transactions and maintaining credit card accounts on behalf of Bank D and Bank E.

So far, we haven't considered using a card at an ATM. Figure 6.5 shows a simplified card payment network with ATMs. As in previous examples, we have a mixture of members, including an ATM operator (top left), a bank that issues debit cards and credit cards and runs its own ATM network (Bank A, top right), a processor (bottom right) that in this case switches debit card payments for Bank B and processes debit card balances for Bank C (see Section 4.5.3) and a merchant acquirer that provides card payment services to online retailers and physical retailers (via card terminals and direct point of sale platform integration). The processor may also be processing credit card accounts for Bank B, Bank C and other banks. Note that any of the organisations shown here may also be

FIGURE 6.5   A card payment network with ATMs.

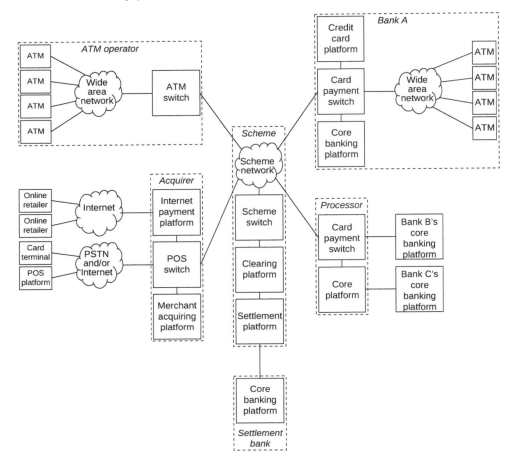

connecting to other schemes (e.g. a national ATM scheme and various international card payment schemes) and the card scheme shown here may also have gateways connecting it to other schemes. Any card transaction could be routed in one of several different ways. Note how the functions of an ATM switch, credit card switch and debit card switch have been incorporated into a card payment switch at Bank A. This is to be expected, given that these all function in essentially the same way. However, a bank may wish to keep them separate so that it has more switching capacity, for resilience (if they were all combined, a failure of the platform would result in all the services being lost) or because it has inherited separate platforms that are cheaper to operate and maintain separately.

The messages sent across a card payment network have different message type numbers for each type of transaction. For example, in Visa's network a message type number of 0100 is used for dual-message authorisation requests (sent by an acquirer to Visa) to which issuers would provide their response using 0110 messages. Similarly, a message type of 0200 is used for single-message authorisation requests, with a 0220 message type sent in response. The message types and basic format of card payment messages are defined in ISO 8583,[10] although how the messages are decoded and the data they hold can vary significantly between different schemes. We won't go into more detail about the various message types or formats in this book.

Finally, note that in the diagrams in this section we have only shown one card payment scheme. In reality, acquirers are likely to connect to more than one scheme and route transactions appropriately. Schemes also connect to each other in some markets, enabling transactions for one card payment scheme to be acquired through another before being routed through a gateway to the right scheme. It's even possible in some markets for an acquirer to route one scheme's transactions entirely through a different scheme if the issuer participates in both – one reason being that regulators may have forced this to happen to promote competition among card payment schemes.

6.5 Other Types of Card Transactions

We described in Section 6.2 how a card payment takes place at the point of sale in a merchant, with a successful authorisation followed by clearing and settlement of the payment. However, there are a number of variants of card transactions designed to support specific scenarios.

6.5.1 Pre-authorisations

A pre-authorisation (often referred to as a *pre-auth*) is typically taken to ensure that a cardholder can pay for something in the future if they are required to do so. It is only available to certain categories of merchants (as set by each card payment scheme), typically including hotels, vehicle rental companies and automated fuel dispensers, where the cardholder may incur costs in the future (such as incidental purchases in a hotel or damage to a rental vehicle). When a pre-authorisation is taken the amount is put on hold on the cardholder account. This hold is released either after a set period of time (which varies by merchant category) or when the transaction is completed (e.g. when the customer checks out of a hotel, returns the rental vehicle or after filling up their vehicle at a fuel dispenser), or if the merchant releases the hold. Not all card accounts will accept pre-authorisations (e.g. prepaid card accounts often do not accept pre-authorisations).

6.5.2 Offline Payments

Given the near ubiquity of networks, card schemes encourage merchants to make online transactions, but there are occasions when it is not possible for the merchant to make a connection to its acquirer in order to authorise a transaction. Probably the best example of this is in-flight purchases. In such cases, once the card has been presented and the card and PIN or signature validated, the merchant must assume that the card is not blocked, lost or stolen and submit the transaction once a connection is available. Clearly there are risks in this process (the card could have been cancelled, for example) and the merchant needs to decide whether the risk of taking an offline transaction is worth the upside of making a sale.

6.5.3   Card-Not-Present Transactions

Card-not-present transactions, often abbreviated to CNP transactions, are a very common form of transaction. Any online purchase is a CNP transaction. There are clearly risks associated with accepting payments when the merchant cannot see the customer or physically check their card, the most obvious being that the purchaser could be using the details of someone else's card. The card payment schemes have undertaken several major initiatives to reduce CNP fraud, with perhaps 3-D Secure for online transactions the most well-known, which we cover in Section 6.6.3.2.

6.5.4   PIN-based Authorisation

There are at least three scenarios in which a cardholder must enter a PIN to validate a card transaction. First, and probably most common, is if the card is an EMV smartcard (see Section 2.5.13). Second, even if it is not a smartcard, the issuer or card payment scheme may require cards of that type to be used with PIN validation. Third, the merchant may only be accepting cards that require a PIN to be entered (in much the same way that an ATM only accepts transactions after a PIN has been entered), although in practice the schemes have all sorts of rules about acceptance that often work to prevent merchants from only accepting certain types of card. Historically, in some markets, the last two of these scenarios often used single-message processing because they were typically using card payment networks that had originally connected ATMs (e.g. the Pulse and Star networks in the US).

6.5.5   Reversals, Refunds and Chargebacks

The term *reversal* is often used to denote the return of funds to a cardholder after a payment transaction, although we prefer to use it only for authorisation reversals. Consider a purchase at a merchant that is using dual-message processing. Suppose the merchant has got authorisation for a payment, but for whatever reason the cardholder decides not to complete the purchase or the merchant is unable to complete the purchase (for example, it may find that it is out of stock of the item being purchased). Historically, if this happened the merchant or cardholder would simply tear up the whole transaction voucher and no funds would be debited from the cardholder's account. With dual-message processing the merchant could simply not send in the transaction copy message. However, this means that the cardholder's available balance is still reduced by the value of the authorisation. To remove the impact of the authorisation on the cardholder's available balance the merchant should issue a reversal. Reversals are also used for cancelling a transaction when it is in progress (e.g. by pressing the cancel button on the point of sale card reader), or if there is an error during the authorisation process.

The term reversal is sometimes used (in our view, mistakenly) for a refund in which the merchant refunds a cardholder, probably because the cardholder is returning faulty goods. These are correctly termed refunds, and they are different from reversals. A merchant can initiate a refund very much like a purchase, although with a point of sale terminal a special merchant card (typically held by a store manager) has to be used at the point of sale, or some other form of manager approval given, so that refunds can be controlled.

Finally, a chargeback is initiated by an issuer on behalf of a cardholder in cases where a cardholder believes they are due a refund by the merchant but the merchant has refused to refund them. In effect the cardholder and merchant are in dispute. A chargeback is normally resolved between the issuer and the acquirer, but if an acceptable resolution cannot be found then a final ruling is made by the scheme. Chargebacks are also used for reclaiming fraudulent transactions, which we cover in Section 6.6.5.2.

6.5.6   Advice Messages

A participant in a card payment network can send advice messages to other participants. For example, an issuer may advise the scheme that its systems will be offline for a certain period and that it may not be able to authorise payments or process other transactions (see Section 6.6.3.1 for what the scheme does when an issuer is unavailable). If a card payment is captured offline (e.g. using the old-fashioned method of taking an imprint of the card using a zip-zap machine or on an aeroplane), the scheme may send an authorisation advice message to the issuer when it eventually processes the transaction.

6.6   Managing Payment Cards

The simplicity of making a card payment, be that in person at a shop or remotely over the Internet, belies the level of complexity of a payment card operation in a bank or other institution. As we described earlier, a card payment itself requires the engagement of a number of parties. An issuer of payment cards (irrespective of their type) must be able to process applications from customers, have cards manufactured and distributed to customers, issue statements, collect interbank payments to credit card accounts, provide support to customers for a wide range of issues, manage fraud, process card payment authorisations, reconcile settlement reports with the actual card payments, run arrears management processes for delinquent credit and charge card accounts, operate loyalty schemes, update platforms in line with changes mandated by card payment schemes and so on. However, there is a long history of successful outsourcing of functions in card operations, including outsourcing all card operations. One of the reasons for this is that card payments, and the major card schemes, are global and the basic card products, transaction flows and processing of card payments are essentially the same globally. Thus, outsourcers have been able to reuse their experience (and platforms) across markets and build large, international businesses.

Whether an organisation chooses to outsource its cards programme or build its own solution, it must be aware of the various elements that come together to make an effective cards capability. In Figure 6.6 we set out the capabilities that are required in a card issuer operation. This would be applicable for all types of cards that we set out in Section 6.1, although additional functions would be required for charge and credit cards (such as arrears management). We then cover each of the areas in the following sections.

The model in Figure 6.6 will change as technologies change. In fact, it is perfectly possible that the whole idea of payment cards becomes obsolete in the near future, although whether this changes much of the model in Figure 6.6, or just what we hold in our hands, remains to be seen. We touch on this in Chapter 10.

FIGURE 6.6 Card issuer capability model.

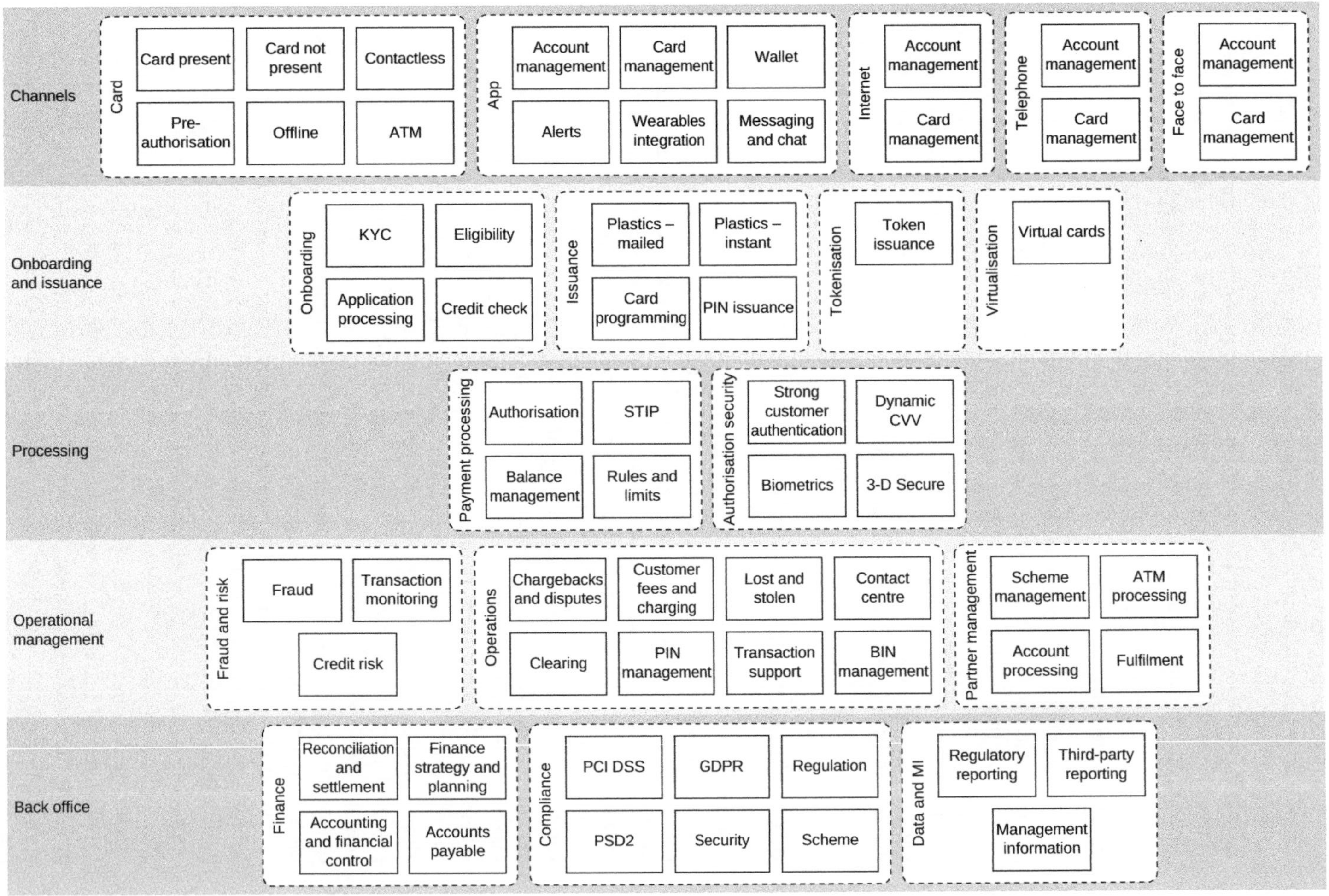

Channels				
Card	**App**	**Internet**	**Telephone**	**Face to face**
Card present / Pre-authorisation / Card not present / Offline / Contactless / ATM	Account management / Alerts / Card management / Wearables integration / Wallet / Messaging and chat	Account management / Card management	Account management / Card management	Account management / Card management

Onboarding and issuance		
Onboarding	**Issuance**	**Tokenisation**
KYC / Application processing / Eligibility / Credit check	Plastics – mailed / Card programming / Plastics – instant / PIN issuance	Token issuance
	Virtualisation	
	Virtual cards	

Processing	
Payment processing	**Authorisation security**
Authorisation / Balance management / STIP / Rules and limits	Strong customer authentication / Biometrics / Dynamic CVV / 3-D Secure

Operational management	
Operations	**Partner management**
Chargebacks and disputes / Clearing / Customer fees and charging / PIN management / Contact centre / BIN management / Lost and stolen / Transaction support	Scheme management / Account processing / ATM processing / Fulfilment
Fraud and risk	
Fraud / Credit risk / Transaction monitoring	

Back office	
Finance	**Data and MI**
Reconciliation and settlement / Accounting and financial control / Finance strategy and planning / Accounts payable	Regulatory reporting / Third-party reporting / Management information
Compliance	
PCI DSS / PSD2 / GDPR / Security / Regulation / Scheme	

6.6.1 Channels

The channels that we have included in Figure 6.6 are those that are most pertinent to a modern cards business. It is still common for there to be an Internet channel for customers to manage their accounts online. Telephone servicing is also still very common, although it may be limited to just reporting lost and stolen cards. Some card operations also provide alerts via SMS text messages to customers. Face-to-face interaction is often applicable where a card issuer has a physical presence, for example at a branch of a bank or a customer service desk at a retailer that issues cards.

However, many issuers are now focused on making their smartphone app the main interaction channel for their customers. The functionality available in an app usually includes the same services available through the Internet channel, i.e. account servicing and card management (e.g. temporarily blocking a card) plus the ability to associate the smartphone with a card (the wallet function shown in Figure 6.6) so that the smartphone can be used instead of the card for contactless payments. One new function, championed by the wave of fintech businesses in the past few years, is the instant notification of payments through alerts produced by the app. Customers can instantly see what their card is being used for (a useful anti-fraud measure) as well as being able to see their historical transactions and current balance.

Another recent development is the integration of cards with wearables, enabling cards to be stored and used on a wearable device, such as a smartwatch or ring. While this has yet to reach the market penetration that smartphone payments have, the use of wearables for payments is rising.[11]

6.6.2 Onboarding and Issuance

Onboarding processes vary depending on the type of payment card being issued. They can be minimal for gift cards, which are often purchased at a retailer and activated by the retailer at the point of sale. Some issuers encourage the end recipient of a gift card to register so they can check the card balance, and some may offer limited reloading of the card and other services. However, prepaid cards that are expected to be used like debit cards will typically involve the cardholder registering before being issued a card and this may include customer due diligence (KYC or eKYC, PEP and sanctions checks) and eligibility checks (such as age, income or location). A debit card is normally issued when a bank account is opened and the customer due diligence and eligibility checks for the bank account are used to determine whether a card can be issued.

The key question from a customer's perspective will be 'When do I get my card?' and this, unfortunately, is where digital processes become constrained by the physical world. While a virtual card can be issued for use with a smartphone wallet, most cardholders will also need a physical card to make in-person payments and use ATMs. There are really only two options here, which are either to use a specialist card printing operation to print, program and mail the card to the customer, or to print and program it on-site within the bank. This second option is only useful for issuers that have a branch network. However, this brings added processes to monitor and replenish card stocks and keep them secure. Irrespective of how a physical card is delivered to the cardholder, the PIN for a card also needs to be issued. Traditionally this was mailed out separately to the customer, but in-app options that allow the cardholder to set their own PIN are widely used and are significantly cheaper and potentially more secure than mailed PINs.

Tokenisation is used for two distinct, but closely related, activities. First, mobile payment brands such as Apple Pay, Fitbit Pay, Google Pay and Samsung Pay that enable contactless and online card payments to be made using a device such as a smartphone do not store the card number (or, strictly speaking, its Primary Account Number, or PAN) on the smartphone. Instead, when a cardholder registers their card with one of these brands, the brand requests a token from the card scheme that can be used instead of the PAN. The card scheme in turn asks the card issuer to authorise the issue of such a token. In some schemes issuers may use their own trusted token provider or provide their own tokens. Second, some merchants request a token so that they can take repeat payments from a customer's card account without having to hold the PAN. Tokens can be set up for one-time or multiple uses, including a limit on the total number of uses and are unique to each combination of merchant or mobile payment brand and card.

6.6.3   Processing

Modern card payment schemes provide an efficient, automated, process for the authorisation of card payments which, from a cardholder perspective, makes the vast majority of card payments near instant and reasonably frictionless.

However, despite the near-instantaneous nature of a card transaction the process of authorisation is not as straightforward as one might imagine. Beyond the basic balance checking (i.e. checking that the cardholder has a sufficient balance to make the payment) there are often other rules, some of which are set by the payment scheme and some by the issuer, and which often depend on the card product being used for the transaction (e.g. an issuer will normally categorise a gold credit card as a different card product or programme from its regular credit card). For example, for ATM cash withdrawals issuers often place limits on the amount that can be withdrawn and the number and the total amount of withdrawals per day (which may vary by location, e.g. international withdrawals may be more limited, or blocked if the cardholder has not informed the issuer in advance), for some debit cards transaction values and volumes are limited, and for debit or prepaid cards issued to teenagers there may be restrictions on what merchant categories they can be used at as well as transaction volume and value limits. Furthermore, issuers may evaluate the risk of a transaction being fraudulent (more on this in Section 6.6.5.1). There can be several balances that have to be maintained for each account associated with a payment card – the available balance being the primary one, with transaction value and volume limits for different periods (potentially for purchases, ATM withdrawals and different merchant categories) also widely used.

6.6.3.1   Stand-in Processing

Cards are now so entrenched in our everyday lives that we struggle to cope without them, even for short periods of time. Historically, network connections and processing platforms were not as reliable as they are today. Even today, many issuers have platforms that may be unavailable for several hours over the course of a year, when they are taken offline for routine maintenance or fail unexpectedly. Card payment schemes have dealt with this by insisting issuers make use of a facility called stand-in processing (STIP). In its original form, this meant that if an issuer's platform did not respond to an authorisation request routed via the scheme within a set period, the scheme would make a decision about whether to authorise the transaction. A scheme would agree with each of its issuers what limits would be placed on transactions when they were subject to STIP, possibly varying by merchant category, with transactions above this amount declined. In some schemes an issuer can opt to use a third party – normally a specialist card account processor – to provide the STIP service. Schemes insist on issuers having a STIP service on standby because it maintains a high level of acceptance of a scheme's cards and therefore minimises reputational risk to the scheme.

For example, a scheme's rules may stipulate that in the event the issuer's platform does not respond to an authorisation request within a set time period, the scheme will authorise the transaction. However, the issuer and scheme normally agree periodically on the number and value of transactions the scheme can approve if it stands in. So, the scheme might approve three transactions of up to £100 each or a maximum of £250 in total per card, after which it will decline all further transactions for that card. When the issuer comes back online, the scheme sends advice messages to the issuer detailing what transactions it has approved and declined, so the issuer can update the available balances of its cardholders' accounts. For issuers, setting the STIP thresholds is a compromise between maintaining a better level of service for its cardholders and the potential increase in fraud and credit risk. Also, a scheme's rules often allow the scheme to penalise an issuer if the percentage of transactions it fails to respond to goes above a threshold but can take STIPed transactions into account when calculating this statistic.

6.6.3.2 Authorisation Security

As an easy, and ubiquitous, means of paying for goods and services, card payments have always attracted fraud. The industry has responded with various countermeasures, including security features on cards such as holograms and tamper-proof signature strips, online authorisations, the use of smartcards with PIN authentication and two-factor authentication for online payments.

However, while fraud could be regarded as a huge issue for card payment services, and indeed it is regularly presented as such in the press, it is not so prevalent, even in countries with less advanced card security features, that it renders card schemes or issuing unprofitable.

As an example, one need only look at European card fraud. The European Central Bank's (ECB) fifth report on card fraud, published in September 2018,[12] reviewed card fraud over the period from 2012 to 2016 involving cards issued in the Single European Payments Area. In summary, in 2016 payment card fraud was valued at €1.8 billion, 73% of which involved card-not-present transactions, 19% point of sale transactions and 8% at ATMs. However, the total amount represented only 0.041% of the total value of card payment transactions in the same period. So, as we can see, the biggest fraud risk was with CNP transactions, of which online purchases are by far the biggest constituent. This is why European regulators were keen to push through initiatives such as Strong Customer Authentication (SCA) to reduce these forms of fraud.[13]

Point of sale payments, on the other hand, are now typically made with a smartcard reader or a Near Field Communication (NFC) (contactless) device. Probably the biggest risk is of a cardholder inadvertently giving away their PIN and then having their card stolen – various modifications of ATMs have been made by fraudsters to collect both the PIN and card.

To fight card fraud there are several technologies and techniques available to card issuers, some of which are mandated by schemes and regulators.

Original magnetic stripe cards had several security features, many of which are also still present on smartcards. We have already mentioned a tamper-proof signature strip and a hologram. Some card issuers also printed a photograph of the cardholder on the back of the card. We were once told that the Visa flag logo (as in use up to 2006) contained the text *VISA* repeated multiple times in very small print around it but with one occurrence of the word misspelt and that this was used as one check to see if a card was copied or unauthorised. The magnetic stripe data contained the card's PAN and expiry dates that were also embossed on the front of the card and also a card verification value* (CVV, sometimes referred to as CVV1 for reasons that will become apparent shortly) that was calculated from the PAN and other card data and an encryption key held by the issuer and the scheme. The CVV was there to stop visible card data (e.g. from receipts and transaction vouchers) being used to clone the card, as the CVV could not be calculated without knowledge of the encryption key and so the magnetic stripe data on a cloned card would be incorrect. Obviously, it does not prevent a magnetic card being swiped and the data, including the CVV, being captured that way. That is where CVV2 comes in. CVV2 is either the last three digits of the code shown on the signature strip of the card or four digits displayed near the PAN on the front of the card and is virtually universally required for card-not-present transactions. This code is calculated differently from the CVV and is not present in the magnetic stripe data. Therefore, merely swiping the magnetic stripe of a card does not give you all the data required for a CNP transaction. Note that merchants and acquirers are not permitted to retain the CVV2 value, to help reduce losses from card data stolen from them. Confusingly, CVV2 is often (albeit mistakenly) just called CVV.

Some issuers have gone one step further, with a dynamic CVV2 value that changes periodically and that is shown on a small display on the back of their cards.[14] The downsides of this are the extra cost of such cards and the potentially limited life of their embedded battery (although some cards can recharge their battery when inserted into a point of sale card reader). Rather than using a special card, we think a dynamic CVV2 value could be generated using the issuer's app, although we have not seen this done anywhere yet. Of course, thought must be given to how STIP would function for CNP transactions using cards that have a dynamic CVV2.

Another approach to reducing CNP fraud is to provide single-use temporary virtual card details (e.g. temporary values of the PAN, CVV2 and expiry date) for a cardholder to use when they make an online or telephone payment. The card can be used for a single purchase and is then replaced with a new virtual card for the next transaction.[15] Such *virtual cards* could be made available through the issuer's smartphone app, and some issuers have also provided virtual cards via their Internet servicing website. In reality, an issuer offering virtual cards has to recycle the PANs they issue, because they can only use a certain range (determined by the scheme). However, the combination of temporary

---

*Like many terms in the card payments world, there are many scheme-specific names for this such as card authentication value, card security code, card validation code, card validation number and so on.

CVV2 and expiry date (which can be set to the end of the current month) increases the frequency with which such PANs can be reused.

A relatively common step in an online checkout process is 3-D Secure (or, in full, *Three-Domain Secure*), the protocol for which was developed by EMV and was first launched by Visa in 2001. It is branded differently by each card payment scheme, such as American Express SafeKey, JCB J/Secure, Mastercard SecureCode or Identity Check and Verified by Visa. In its initial incarnation, the 3-D Secure process asked the cardholder to enter their password into a webpage provided by the card issuer that appears during the checkout sequence at an online merchant. It was widely disliked by online merchants for adding *friction* to the checkout process and for the number of dropouts as cardholders couldn't remember their password or typed it in incorrectly. Version two of the protocol, issued in 2016, enables more frequent usage of a risk-based approach, so that cardholders are not asked for a password unless the issuer determines that the potential transaction has a higher than normal risk of being fraudulent, in which case the issuer can use two-factor authentication, where the issuer texts the cardholder with a code to enter or asks for the cardholder to authenticate themselves using the issuer's app on their smartphone. These are examples of Strong Customer Authentication (SCA) methods which were made mandatory for online card transactions in the UK, for example, from September 2021.[16] An issuer could even use a biometric method with 3-D Secure by, for example, checking the cardholder's fingerprint using their smartphone fingerprint scanner or validating an image of the cardholder taken using their smartphone camera.

Some schemes offer an address verification service that enables an online merchant to verify the numeric details of a billing address supplied by the customer (e.g. house number and numbers in the postcode) with the issuer as part of the authorisation process.

At the point of sale, the use of Chip and PIN cards has significantly reduced fraud, although the widespread acceptance of contactless payments means that stolen cards can still be attractive for small-scale and short-term fraud. However, biometric authentication is also available for point of sale transactions, with one card manufacturer, Thales, embedding a fingerprint scanner in a payment card. The cardholder has to place their finger on the scanner on the card for the chip in the card to respond to a point of sale card reader or in a contactless transaction.[17] It remains to be seen whether the additional cost of such cards will outweigh the level of risk in card-present transactions. They can also remove the need to enter a PIN at the point of sale, so they could improve the card-present checkout process for merchants and cardholders.

6.6.4   Outsourcing of Processing

There are various options for the outsourcing of processing.

It is very common for prepaid card account processing to be outsourced to specialist processors. Such cards are branded by the merchant whose shops they can be used in, but they are issued by the processor. The payment scheme (if any) associated with the cards and the local regulator will normally regard the processor as the issuer of the cards. Using such processors is a common practice for fintech start-ups (or neobanks), because they do not have to have a licence to operate, as they draw on the licence of the prepaid card processor, and can focus on customer service and the added features of the accounts. This is probably not a sustainable model for a start-up given the annual fee it has to pay to the processor for each card or account, but it does enable it to launch its business more quickly. Another key consideration when using such a processor is the security of the cardholders' funds – for example, in the UK, prepaid card processors are regulated, but as electronic money institutions (often referred to as e-money businesses) and not as banks, which means each cardholder's funds are not covered by the UK's depositor protection scheme. Note, though, that UK-regulated e-money businesses must hold all cardholder funds in a designated ring-fenced account at a bank.

It became common to outsource credit card authorisations and account processing from the 1990s onwards, with organisations such as equensWorldline, Fiserv, Network International and TSYS offering such services in various markets. With such outsourcing, from scheme and regulator perspectives the issuer remains the bank or organisation that brands the cards, but at a minimum the processor responds to authorisation and other messages sent via the card scheme, processes clearing and settlement files, applies transactions to card accounts and creates the reports used to produce account statements. Over time, processors expanded the services they offered, and in some markets it was (and is) possible to outsource a whole credit card operation including application processing and customer onboarding, card production and distribution, customer services (including telephone and Internet servicing and the mobile app) and statement printing and mailing to a processor. The issuer usually remains responsible for settling with the scheme and owns the credit, fraud and settlement risks.

Outsourcing of debit card processing is more complex than with other types of payment cards. In a time when only card transactions (including ATM withdrawals) could reduce the available balance of an account during the course of the day, outsourcing of debit card processing was relatively straightforward. Issuers that outsourced debit card processing typically did so because their own platforms were not available online, being purely batch-oriented, or were offline for significant periods each day (e.g. when they were doing end-of-day processing). Typically, the issuer would send the processor a file containing the balance of each account as part of its end-of-day processing. The processor would then process card payment authorisations for the next 24 hours, reducing the available balance of an account whenever it approved an authorisation for a debit card associated with that account. The processor would then send the issuer all the cleared transactions for that day, for the issuer to include in its end-of-day processing and apply to the actual balance of each account. The issuer would then send a new file containing the account balances to the processor, and the cycle would then restart. In practice, this exchange of files still takes time and there can be a period, usually during the issuer's end-of-day processing, when the available balances and actual balances are not correctly aligned. In other words, the available balance maintained by the processor could be more than the actual balance maintained by the issuer if payments made by cheque or other means (e.g. an over-the-counter cash withdrawal in a bank branch) have come out of the account. This issue has been exacerbated by immediate payment schemes (see Chapter 7), in which funds are paid out of an account as soon as the payment instruction is sent rather than clearing overnight. This has forced issuers to have real-time, online account balance maintenance capability, even if they have outsourced their debit card processing – in which case the processor will ask the issuer for real-time balance information every time a debit card is used but will still perform other checks such as whether the card is blocked.

Of course, the associated card payment scheme must be aware of the outsourcing of processing because it has to be told where to route transaction messages, and in fact the role of a processor is typically formally established by schemes.

One other type of outsourcing of processing is the outsourcing of ATMs. Independent ATM operators in some markets will operate ATMs, the network used by the ATMs and ATM transaction acquiring on behalf of organisations that do not wish to do this in-house. Even if these are not outsourced, there are specialist organisations that will restock ATMs with bank notes and paper for receipts and collect deposits made via ATMs.

6.6.5 Operational Management

6.6.5.1 Fraud and Transaction Monitoring

As noted previously the card schemes are working hard to fight fraud, implementing countermeasures to address specific attack vectors. Chip and PIN, for example, has significantly reduced point of sale fraud, but wherever a countermeasure achieves success criminals will always seek other opportunities. At present, as is clearly demonstrated by the ECB fraud data, CNP fraud is their major attack vector.

Fraud is a major concern when offering payment cards. Payment card fraud typically falls into four categories,[18] of which we have already covered two, namely skimming and cloning of cards, and card theft, both of which result in fraudulent transactions. The other categories are card data theft, with the Payment Card Industry Data Security Standards (PCI DSS) the most important initiative to reduce this (see Section 6.6.6.2), and identity theft, which typically takes the forms of an account being opened in the name of another person by using data and documentation stolen from that person or taking over the identity of an existing customer and diverting correspondence and contacts away from that customer.

Given the standardisation of card payments, issuers use pan-industry standard approaches to combat transaction fraud, many of which we covered in Section 6.6.3.2. However, beyond these authorisation-based countermeasures, transaction monitoring and risk analysis are other widely used approaches to tackling both transaction and identity fraud.

Transaction monitoring involves creating a database containing data on failed and successful transactions, customers, acquirers and merchants and using this to identify trends and patterns. For example, one area of analysis is to determine patterns of fraud. Such analysis can be used to assign to each authorisation request a risk score (i.e. the probability of its being fraudulent), and then using this risk score in the decision whether to approve the authorisation request. We have seen neural network technology used in this area, where a neural network learns from historical authorisation requests and records of fraudulent transactions and is then used to generate a risk score on in-flight authorisation requests. Analysis can also reveal patterns in customer and merchant behaviour (e.g. a high level of chargebacks for non-delivery by a merchant). Periodic reports on authorisation request outcomes by card programme or segments such as customer region or merchant location can reveal information on fraud or even the card operation itself.

We mentioned 3-D Secure in Section 6.6.3.2, in which the issuer can make a risk assessment of whether to ask the cardholder to enter further verification. The risk assessment can include data that may not be present in the authorisation request message, such as the IP address of the device the customer is using for the online purchase and the customer's email address. This data could then also be used in the risk scoring of the authorisation request.

Analysis and profiling of each customer's transaction patterns can be used to identify unusual transactions and behaviour, which may be useful in limiting or even detecting an attempt to take over a customer's account.

6.6.5.2 Liability and Chargebacks

Liability for fraudulent transactions in a card payment scheme is a complex subject, involving rules set by each scheme and, often, regulations and law in the jurisdiction (or jurisdictions) involved in a card transaction. When there has been a fraudulent transaction, often detected by the cardholder when they see a transaction on their account that they do not recognise, the liability for the transaction – that is, who pays for it – will vary depending on many factors and we can only provide a summary and general view here that almost certainly does not apply in all cases or jurisdictions.

We now work through a scenario in which a cardholder has noticed a transaction they do not recognise and notifies their card issuer of it. It is common for law, regulations or accepted industry practice to limit the liability of a cardholder to misuse of their card or card details unless the cardholder has been negligent. Therefore, the issuer will normally seek to establish whether the transaction was made by the cardholder or not. For card-present transactions, if the transaction was made using a Chip and PIN card with PIN authentication, then the issuer will determine that the cardholder is indeed responsible for the transaction and will be liable to pay for it. This is on the basis that the cardholder must either have forgotten the transaction or that they have been negligent and allowed a third party to use their card and PIN. Note that, although a Chip and PIN card does not encrypt the card data it sends to a card reader,* it also holds an encryption key that cannot be read by a card reader and that the chip in the card uses (with a random or unpredictable number supplied by the card reader) to generate a one-time code for each transaction that is included in the authorisation request. Thus, a Chip and PIN card cannot be cloned because the encryption key cannot be extracted from it.[†]

Suppose the transaction was a card-present transaction but did not use Chip and PIN, either using the magnetic stripe or a manual imprinter with signature authentication. Liability for the transaction in this case may fall to the issuer or the acquirer (in which case, usually the merchant) depending on the rules of the scheme and the evidence that is available. Although issuers are the default owners of the risk, they will look to shift it to the merchant,[20] e.g. by getting it to prove that the correct authorisation process was followed.

---

*Cards sign the data (i.e. compute a number based on the card data and the encryption key) passed to card readers – similar in concept to the CVV and CVV2 values. Some cards create a dynamic signature value, similar in concept to the dynamic CVV discussed in Section 6.6.3.2.

†Research published in 2014 (see reference 19) showed that weaknesses in the process of generating the unpredictable number used to create the one-time code could be used to emulate a Chip and PIN card with a PIN chosen by the fraudster in a device (e.g. card reader or ATM) using a weak unpredictable number generation algorithm. Dynamic signing of the card data by the chip may rule out this attack, as would the better implementation of unpredictable number generation in more modern equipment.

For card-not-present transactions, successful verification using 3-D Secure with a password or other verification method has a similar impact on liability as Chip and PIN purchases with a valid PIN, i.e. the cardholder will be liable. Given that issuers can risk-assess a CNP transaction to determine if the cardholder should enter a password or use some other verification method, if the issuer determines this is not necessary, the liability is likely to remain with the issuer. Without 3-D Secure the merchant may have to prove delivery of the goods or service to the cardholder to avoid liability – a successful authorisation does not, on its own, remove the liability from the merchant.

In order for an issuer to claim back the funds for a fraudulent transaction from an acquirer (and, in turn, a merchant), it would issue a chargeback message. The merchant can dispute the chargeback, using a process set out by the scheme. Ultimately the scheme will arbitrate.

We make two observations about card transaction fraud. First, note that in all our examples the scheme does not take liability. Second, there has been a general shift in the liability for transactions to cardholders with the roll-out of Chip and PIN cards with PIN verification and 3-D Secure.

The other common reason an issuer raises a chargeback is when a cardholder has not received the goods or service they purchased or they are defective in some way, and the merchant and cardholder are in dispute about rectifying the situation. This is also a complex and potentially subjective area, which could involve merchant or cardholder fraud, or could simply be due to a misunderstanding between the merchant and the cardholder or could indeed be because of faulty goods or poor service.

There are yet more reasons for chargebacks. A cardholder could be billed twice for the same goods or service, either because of a technical error at the merchant, acquirer or scheme (there could also be a technical issue at the issuer, but the issuer should rectify this itself), or a clerical error at the merchant. A cardholder may dispute a regular payment taken after they cancelled an agreement or subscription with a merchant, typically because of a clerical error at the merchant. The issuer may automatically generate a chargeback where a merchant has not obtained authorisation for a purchase and the cardholder does not have sufficient funds to pay for the purchase or the card itself is no longer valid (which could indicate that the merchant had kept the details on file or the cardholder had used it either by mistake or fraudulently).

An issuer will assign a chargeback reason code to each chargeback it raises, giving an indication of its view of the cause for the chargeback. However, this can be subjective given all the root causes for disputed transactions.

When the chargeback is processed, the acquirer will automatically debit the merchant's account for the amount of the chargeback plus a chargeback processing fee (typically set by the scheme and paid to the issuer) and the issuer will refund the cardholder's account. At this point the merchant has to decide whether to dispute the chargeback or not. If the merchant disputes the chargeback, it must present evidence that shows the chargeback is invalid, and the evidence will be assessed by the merchant's acquirer, the scheme and the issuer. If the chargeback is determined to be invalid the merchant will be refunded for the transaction, but typically not the chargeback processing fee. However, with some schemes the cardholder can request a second chargeback and the process will take place again.

6.6.5.3 Partner Management

Partner management covers the management of all third parties that an issuer has engaged with in order to manufacture and operate their payment cards. Clearly the exact partner landscape will depend upon which elements the issuer organisation has outsourced as well as the local third-party supplier landscape. As with all outsourcing by regulated entities the local regulator will expect there are well-managed contracts in place, with experienced staff responsible for managing the suppliers.

Outsourcing of various capabilities required for a card payment operation is perhaps one of the most commonly used forms of outsourcing across financial services and, in terms of the outsource providers, is also one of the most mature and efficient. First, most issuers, in our experience, outsource fulfilment, which usually encompasses the printing, programming and distribution of plastic cards and the printing and mailing of statements. Second, many choose to use third-party processors for credit card and prepaid card processing. In fact, we think the scale that third-party processors have in some markets means that in those markets it should always be cheaper to outsource credit card processing, although we note that the cost of such services is a function of the procurement process. However, some issuers may choose not to outsource processing because they value the control they have over developing new features and services more highly or because they deem the risk or cost of migrating to an outsource processor to be too great.

Managing the relationship with the scheme (or schemes) includes ensuring that updates to rules and processing issued regularly by the scheme are reviewed and implemented where required. Of course, outsourcing processing can remove a lot of the work involved in implementing scheme processing changes. Also, a scheme will monitor the performance of its issuers (and acquirers), and it is necessary to review the reports it produces and react accordingly (e.g. by adjusting aspects of the operations). Each card programme operated by the issuer (e.g. regular credit card, gold credit card, regular debit card, teenage debit card, etc.) needs to be monitored (the responsibility of the BIN management function in the operations team), as schemes will also monitor an issuer's performance at this level.

6.6.6 Back Office

6.6.6.1 Finance

Finance covers at least three major areas. First, there is the operational aspect of finance in a card operation, i.e. settlement of transactions (and the associated reconciliation). This process is described in Section 6.3. Second, finance performs a strategy and planning role, providing insight into the financial performance of the business and forecasting and planning its future performance. Third, there are the standard finance activities of accounting, financial control (including statutory reporting) and accounts payable (including payroll). Finance may also be responsible for regulatory reporting.

6.6.6.2 Compliance

While some of the same regulatory and data management rules and regulations that apply in banking apply in a card-issuing environment, there are some specific obligations that a participant must meet.

First, a card issuer must comply with the rules of the scheme or scheme(s) in which it participates, and can be penalised for not doing so or for failing to meet performance targets (e.g. number of successful authorisations) set by the scheme. Scheme rulebooks can be substantial, and the rules can vary according to each card programme the scheme implements.

Second, the Payment Card Industry Data Security Standard (PCI DSS)[21] is an information security standard that applies to participants of all of the major card schemes.* It is maintained by the PCI Security Standards Council, which was established in 2006 by American Express, Discover, JCB International, Mastercard and Visa. The same organisation produces security standards that cover devices that are used for entering card PINs and software for processing card payments. Implementing the PCI DSS is onerous and intrusive.

Legal requirements abound around the world. Countries in the EU implemented the Payment Services Directive (EU) 2015/2366, commonly referred to as PSD2, with different aspects of it coming into effect in January 2018 and on various dates thereafter.[22] Strong Customer Authentication (SCA) is one such requirement (see Section 6.6.3.2).

6.7   References

1. European Central Bank (2020). All glossary entries. https://www.ecb.europa.eu/home/glossary/html/glossd.en.html (accessed 23 July 2020).
2. ANSI (2016). Announcing major changes to the Issuer Identification Number (IIN) Standard. https://www.ansi.org/news_publications/news_story?articleid=da7bcb04-0654-4e03-af54-0e55d50b93a8 (accessed 1 August 2020).
3. ISO/IEC 7812 (2017). *Identification cards – Identification of issuers*. Geneva, Switzerland: International Organization for Standardization.
4. Mastercard (2018). Quick reference booklet – Merchant edition. https://www.mastercard.us/content/dam/mccom/en-us/documents/rules/quick-reference-booklet-merchant-edition.pdf (accessed 2 August 2020).
5. ISO 18245 (2003). *Retail financial services – Merchant category codes*. Geneva, Switzerland: International Organization for Standardization.
6. PYMNTS.com (2019). Instant settlement: Disbursements next big thing. https://www.pymnts.com/digital-payments/2019/ingo-money-instant-settlement-merchant-sales/ (accessed 11 July 2020).
7. Shearman & Sterling (2020). UK Supreme Court gives important judgment in the Visa/Mastercard 'interchange fee' litigation (23 June). https://www.shearman.com/perspectives/2020/06/uk-supreme-court-gives-important-judgment-in-the-visa-mastercard-interchange-fee-litigation (accessed 11 July 2020).
8. Gifford, D. and Spector, A. (1985). The Cirrus banking network. *Communications of the ACM* 28 (8): 798–807.
9. Ibid.

---

*We remember that there used to be some doubt that PCI DSS applied to card issuers or to banks that issued payment cards. Later PCI DSS versions make clear that it does.

10. ISO 8583-1:2003 (2003). *Financial transaction card originated messages – Interchange message specifications – Part 1: Messages, data elements and code values*. Geneva, Switzerland: International Organization for Standardization.

11. Statista (2019). *Distribution of payment transactions via wearables across selected countries in Europe in* 2019. https://www.statista.com/statistics/1080078/use-of-wearable-technology-for-pos-payments-in-europe-by-country/ (accessed 11 July 2020).

12. ECB (2018). *Fifth report on card fraud*, September 2018. https://www.ecb.europa.eu/pub/cardfraud/html/ecb.cardfraudreport201809.en.html (accessed 11 July 2020).

13. Financial Conduct Authority (2019). Strong Customer Authentication (13 August). https://www.fca.org.uk/consumers/strong-customer-authentication (accessed 11 July 2020).

14. Segal, B. (2019). Will dynamic CVVs become the ultimate in credit card security? Creditcards.com (5 September). https://www.creditcards.com/credit-card-news/dynamic-cvv-credit-card-security/ (accessed 11 July 2020).

15. Braileanu, R. (2018). Introducing disposable virtual cards. Revolut (22 March). https://blog.revolut.com/introducing-disposable-virtual-cards/ (accessed 11 July 2020).

16. Financial Conduct Authority. Strong Customer Authentication.

17. Thales. EMV card with fingerprint biometrics – Introducing the biometric payment card. https://www.thalesgroup.com/en/markets/digital-identity-and-security/banking-payment/cards/emv-biometric-card (accessed 11 July 2020).

18. The Money Advice Service (2018). What is credit card fraud and how can I prevent it? https://www.moneyadviceservice.org.uk/blog/what-is-credit-card-fraud-how-prevent-it (accessed 11 July 2020).

19. Bond, M., Choudary, O., Murdoch, S.J. et al. (2014). Chip and Skim: cloning EMV cards with the pre-play attack. *Proceedings of the* 2014 *IEEE Symposium on Security and Privacy*, San Jose, CA, US (18–21 May 2014). Washington DC, US: IEEE Computer Society. doi:10.1109/SP.2014.11.

20. Pinsent Masons (2005). Identity theft and credit card fraud (30 March). https://www.pinsentmasons.com/out-law/guides/identity-theft-and-credit-card-fraud (accessed 25 July 2020) (accessed 11 July 2020).

21. PCI Security Standards Council. https://www.pcisecuritystandards.org/ (accessed 11 July 2020).

22. European Commission (2015). Payment services (PSD 2) – Directive (EU) 2015/2366 (accessed 11 July 2020).

CHAPTER 7

Payments

7.1 Introduction

Payments are the lifeblood of banking. The ability to move money from one bank account to another is fundamental to the modern world, global commerce, and the day-to-day lives of the general population in most parts of the world. If there was any doubt about the importance of payments to our everyday lives, a look at published data should dispel it very quickly. For example, *UK Finance* published a report in June 2019 looking at the different types of payments and their usage in the UK.[1] Working on the assumption that around 50 million people in the UK make payments, the data contained within that report implies that on average each person makes almost 60 payments per month, or about two per day. Of these, over 45% are card payments, almost 30% are cash and just over 10% are direct debits (for those not familiar with direct debits, we cover these in more detail later in this chapter).

High-profile banking technology failures around the globe, such as at Royal Bank of Scotland[2] and Commonwealth Bank of Australia[3], have highlighted just how critical these payments capabilities are. It shouldn't be assumed that banking technology failures are the preserve of the legacy banks, either. Monzo[4] and Starling[5], two UK neobanks, have also had payment-related failures. In every case the response from customers has been both immediate and vocal. Failures to process payments cause customers substantial issues – they can't buy fuel or food, bills don't get paid and cash can't be withdrawn from ATMs. We are now in a position where the people suffer that discomfort immediately, even when they still have cash in their wallet or purse. Payments are now a part of the fabric of our everyday lives.

As highlighted in Chapter 2, banking and financial services continue to evolve and, arguably, payment technology has seen the most rapid development, evidenced by the rise of fintech organisations focused on this area (e.g. PayPal, Ripple, Stripe and TransferWise), the involvement of big tech organisations (witness Amazon Pay, Apple Pay and Google Pay) and the rollout of new national and international payment initiatives such as Faster Payments in the UK (and similar schemes around the globe), the New Payments Platform in Australia, SEPA credit transfers and direct debits across Europe and SWIFT Global Payments Innovation (gpi) for tracking international payments.

Before looking at the technology that underpins payments, and how it works, it is first beneficial to understand the kinds of payments that commonly exist and are available to consumers.

7.2   Cash

Cash is arguably the oldest payment method still in use today. Yes, barter systems still exist (even in very modern countries),[6] and commodities can be used as a means of exchanging value,[7] but cash is globally recognised and understood even if its underlying value is sometimes questionable.

The simplest of all modern forms of payment, cash is typically issued by an institution that has been authorised by the government, often the central bank (e.g. the Reserve Bank of Australia, Banco Central do Brasil and the Bank of Japan issue banknotes in Australia, Brazil and Japan respectively). In the EU both the European Central Bank (ECB) and the national banks in the Eurozone can issue Euro banknotes, although in practice only the national banks do so, but under the supervision of the ECB.[8] In the UK, banknotes are issued by the Bank of England, three commercial banks in Scotland (Bank of Scotland, Clydesdale Bank and Royal Bank of Scotland) and four commercial banks in Northern Ireland (Bank of Ireland, Danske Bank, First Trust Bank and Ulster Bank). The Bank of England supervises note issuance by commercial banks and the value of the banknotes they issue must be backed up with assets held by the Bank of England.[9] In the US, the Federal Reserve issues banknotes, although the Department of the Treasury also issued banknotes until 1971.[10]

As we covered in Chapter 2, many nations used to underpin the value of cash using a gold standard, in which the issuing institution promised that it would substitute the cash for an equivalent value in gold if the cash is presented to it. For a variety of reasons countries moved away from gold standards before the end of the twentieth century and governments now work on the basis of issuing fiat money – money that has value because the issuer says that it does.

The legal status of cash as a form of payment varies depending on the applicable laws in a jurisdiction. Cash is often described as *legal tender*, which the Bank of England defines as:

> *[Legal tender] means that if you offer to fully pay off a debt to someone in legal tender, they can't sue you for failing to repay.*[11]

The US and other countries have similar definitions. Legal tender does not always include all forms or amounts of cash. For example, in the UK, Bank of England banknotes valued at £5 and above (which is all of the ones in current circulation) are legal tender in England and Wales but not Scotland and Northern Ireland, according to the Currency and Bank Notes Act 1954. Furthermore, not even banknotes issued by Scottish banks are legal tender in Scotland, and therefore no banknotes are legal tender in Scotland.[12] Coins (which are issued by the Royal Mint in the UK) are counted as legal tender everywhere in the UK, but only for payments up to 20p for 1p and 2p coins, up to £5 for 5p and 10p coins, up to £10 for 20p and 50p coins and an unlimited amount for £1 and £2 coins.[13] Similarly, Canada has tiered limits on when its coins are legal tender as set out in Bill C-41, *An Act to amend the Royal Canadian Mint Act and the Currency Act.*[14]

Legal tender must be accepted if it is offered as a means of paying off a debt, but it does not have to be accepted if the transaction has not already occurred. So, if you offered to buy a hot dog in the US with a $100 bill, the shopkeeper could decline to accept that bill as payment, even though it is legal tender. However, if you visit a café and have already eaten your hot dog and then present a $100 bill to the café owner in order to pay your bill, it must be accepted.

Cash is a popular medium of exchange and, in many countries throughout the world, is still the most common means of payment by volume of transactions. For example, in the UK in 2018, cash was used for about one in three payments, and the volume of debit card transactions only overtook the volume of cash transactions for the first time in 2017.[15]

One could be forgiven for believing that cash is on the verge of extinction given the rise in electronic payments using payment cards, mobile phones (M-Pesa, for example), smartphones, and digital payments (such as Amazon Pay, PayPal and QR, for example). In fact, this isn't the case. Cash is still in demand, both as a means of supporting transactions and as a store of value, particularly during periods of low inflation and low (or even negative) interest rates. Even in some of the most technologically advanced banking nations the volume and value of cash in circulation is still growing. For example, in the Eurozone the volume of banknotes in circulation nearly doubled from 12.9 billion at the start of 2010 to more than 24.1 billion at the end of 2019, with the value of those banknotes rising from €784 billion to €1.29 trillion.[16] In the UK, the number of banknotes in circulation increased from 2.6 billion in February 2010 to 4.0 billion in February 2020, with the value increasing from £47 billion to nearly £70 billion.[17] In the US the number of banknotes in circulation rose from 28.5 billion at the start of 2010 to 44.9 billion at the end of 2019, with the value doubling from $888 billion to $1.76 trillion.[18] In fact, between 2013 and 2017 every major economy except Brazil, Russia, Norway and Sweden saw the amount of cash in circulation grow.[19]

For the consumer, using cash is simple enough, but it can cause some logistical headaches for banks. For example, managing levels of cash, including holding appropriate levels of each denomination at every physical outlet, be that a branch or an ATM, requires a sophisticated stock management system or lots of people carrying out daily reconciliations. In modern banks, both the ATMs and the teller systems include stock reporting capabilities that can be integrated into bank systems to manage stock levels, which makes stock management much simpler. Going a step further, for banks that wish to add an extra level of sophistication, both ATMs and teller systems[20] that are capable of cash recycling (taking deposits and using the cash to automatically replenish the stock available for withdrawals) have existed for some time. The systems are highly accurate, although, in our experience, mechanical reliability can be variable, particularly if coins are also recycled.

When dealing with cash, security is always a concern, both in terms of theft by third parties and by staff. Cash is a favourite target of criminals, primarily because it is essentially untraceable. Any bank stocking cash will therefore have to consider carefully how it stores its cash, how it transports it and how it discourages criminals from attempting to steal it. An example of the implementation of secure cash management is Metro Bank in the UK. When we started to build the teller lines in Metro Bank we were told by experts that the open plan stores (as Metro Bank calls it branches), with no glass or security screens on the teller line, meant that we would be an easy target for bank robbers. In fact, this couldn't have been further from the truth. We implemented several features to secure the cash in the teller line. The first was the use of teller cash recyclers (TCRs), which protect against internal fraud by only dispensing cash when a withdrawal is booked on a customer's account (as the TCRs were integrated with the core banking platform), and also automate accounting and reconciliation of cash because they reliably keep track of their stock of cash. Additionally, even if the bank is held up, the store staff can only force the TCRs to release a relatively small amount of cash on demand. Second, each Metro Bank store contains numerous cameras. Technology doesn't just help secure the teller line, it also defends the ATMs (which have tamper monitoring and alarm systems), the safe (which has vibration monitors), the front doors (security alarms and more cameras) and so on. Finally, the open plan store layout, with large windows, and often located on a corner plot, was designed to encourage customers to enter but has the additional benefit that a hold-up of a store would be highly visible from outside.

Although cash is still very popular with the general public, supporting it in branches and ATMs is not as simple as it might seem. However, with a bit of careful thought and the use of the right technology, a modern bank can manage cash far more efficiently and securely than it used to be able to do.

7.3   Cheques

The humble cheque has been a mainstay of banking for hundreds of years. As identified in Chapter 2, the oldest known remaining cheque from England dates from 1659 and they were obviously used before then. A key feature of a cheque is that no details of the recipient's bank account are required to make a payment, but the processing of a cheque is a relatively complicated operation, comparable to the recipient's bank pulling the funds from the payer's bank; the process is described in Section 7.3.2. This contrasts with a giro payment or direct credit, in which the payer gives their bank an instruction to make a payment to a specific account, and is comparable to a push payment from the payer's bank to the recipient's bank.

In the modern era there are many good arguments for why the cheque is no longer needed, but it has proved to be remarkably resilient. In 2009, the Payments Council in the UK declared that cheques would be scrapped in 2018.[21] There were many objections to this news, including from charities representing older people and the Federation of Small Businesses, and in 2011 the council backtracked on its previous position and stated that cheques would continue for as long as they were needed. In fact, in recognition of the fact that cheques remained popular, the UK went on to introduce digital cheque scanning (using customers' smartphones) to enable more efficient processing of cheques. In other countries, cheques have either disappeared completely or are only used in very small numbers. For example, cheques were no longer processed after the end of 2001 in the Netherlands,[22] and Danish banks stopped clearing cheques between each other from 1 January 2017, although each bank continued to accept cheques it had issued.[23]

To put the continued use of cheques in perspective, it appears that in all markets cheque usage is declining, but at quite different rates and from different peak levels of usage. Table 7.1 shows data on cheque usage in Australia, India, the UK and the US[24–30] in the year the volume peaked (apart from Australia, where it is the first year for which data is available) and for the latest available year. All four countries use cheque imaging, although in India it is only a cheque truncation service (i.e. customers still submit paper cheques to their banks, which image them and submit the images into the cheque clearing process). The US is notable for the high per capita usage of cheques and although there

TABLE 7.1   Cheque usage in four countries.

Country	Australia	India	UK	US
Peak year	2002	2008	1990	1995
Volume of cheques (million)	601	1,461	4,000	49,500
Per capita usage	31	1.2	70.0	186.7
Total value (billion)	$2,045	₹133,961	Not available	Not available
Latest year	2019	2020	2019	2018
Volume of cheques (million)	54.5	1,036	258	16,000
Per capita usage	2.2	0.8	3.8	48.9
Total value (billion)	$546	₹79,175	£394	$26,200
Compounded annual rate of decline of cheque volumes	13.2%	2.8%	9.0%	4.8%

has been a significant decline in volumes, it is still remarkable. Across the globe cheque usage is declining, but it would seem that there is still a way to go before it disappears from general usage.

7.3.1   Types of Cheques

There are predominantly two types of cheques. The first, and most common, is a personal or business cheque that is paid using the funds in the account of the person or business who writes the cheque. Depending on local law and regulation, such a cheque can be written and used in various ways that affect whether it can be exchanged for cash (an open cheque) or can only be paid into a bank account (a crossed cheque), whether the recipient can endorse it so that a third party can deposit or cash it (an order cheque), and whether the bank will reserve funds in the payer's account and effectively guarantee it (a certified cheque). The second type of cheque, which is processed in exactly the same way, has various names such as a banker's draft, bank cheque, teller cheque or counter cheque and is paid out of the issuing bank's own funds. The disadvantage of the first type is that when it comes to cashing the cheque or paying it into the recipient's bank account, the account on which it is drawn may have insufficient funds in it and the cheque may not be paid. A banker's draft gives the recipient more certainty about the payment, as it will be honoured (as long as the issuing bank remains solvent). A personal or business cheque certified by the issuing bank can serve the same purpose as a banker's draft, but they are not used in every country.

With modern payment schemes able to securely transfer large sums of cash on the same day there is less rationale for using banker's drafts. It is unlikely that a new bank would ever want to issue such artefacts, but it may have to be able to handle all types of cheques deposited by its customers.

7.3.2   Clearing and Settlement of Cheques

Historically, processing of paper cheques took several days because the paper had to be physically moved from the recipient bank to the paying bank. A paper-based cheque process takes place broadly as follows (using the timings from the UK's paper-based cheque clearing process, which are based on working days i.e. Monday to Friday except bank holidays):

1. On day 1, a cheque is deposited at the recipient's bank – typically this requires the customer to deposit the cheque over the counter or use a paying-in machine or ATM. The cheque is registered at the receiving bank, bundled with all other cheques received, and sent to the recipient bank's clearing centre at the end of the day to arrive in time for the next step on the next working day.

2. When the cheque arrives at the clearing centre it is sorted based on the sort code or routing number on the cheque – i.e. the payer's bank or bank branch. In addition, for each cheque the sort code or routing number, account number, cheque serial number and amount are recorded. Cheques for the same sort code or routing number are bundled together. The recipient bank works out the total value of the cheques owed to it by each issuing bank. This step is sometimes called out-clearing and usually takes place on day 2.

3. All the bundles for the paying bank, including the cheque in this example, are sent to the exchange centre and each bank picks up its bundles of cheques from the exchange centre and takes them to its clearing centre. This takes place overnight between days 2 and 3.

4. At the paying bank's clearing centre, each cheque is validated and the corresponding bank account debited. Of course, some cheques are refused, e.g. if the payer's account has insufficient funds or the cheque is invalid in some way, such as the signature being wrong (although one of us was shocked to find out early in his career when visiting a bank's clearing centre in the UK that the signature was only checked if the value of the cheque was above a fairly high minimum). These are returned to the recipient's bank via the exchange centre. The paying bank works out how much it owes each recipient bank. This step is sometimes called in-clearing and takes place on day 3.

5. The recipient bank and the issuing bank agree on their net position with each other, taking into account the cheques that have gone both ways between them and returned cheques, and settle with each other (i.e. one bank transfers funds to the other's account at the central bank). This can take place after in-clearing has finished on day 3. Note that the paying bank would not include the value of returned cheques in its settlement calculation.

6. When the recipient's account is credited varies from country to country and from system to system. In the UK, for example, the paper-based cheque clearing scheme defined that funds accrued interest from day 2 and were available for withdrawal on day 4 (although the cheque could still bounce up to day 6, after which the banks all guaranteed the recipient's funds would be secure). In effect, the UK banks took on some of the operational risk of cheque processing in order to guarantee value and payment timescales to their customers.

We have put the shortest realistic timetable in these steps, which were generally achieved in the UK. When cheques had to be returned to individual branches for validation and debiting of the accounts, in the time before centralised core banking platforms, the time taken could be longer. Also, banks that didn't participate in clearing had to submit their cheques to a clearing bank, typically adding another day at the start, and receive the funds a day later. In other countries, such as Australia, India and the US, greater distances and, in some cases, greater volumes present huge logistical challenges for fast paper-based clearing.

Of course, with the use of technology, the clearing process can be improved. We already mentioned the use of machine-readable printing in Chapter 2, and automation of sorting also required standardisation of cheque sizes and paper quality. Another improvement is for the recipient bank to create a data file with details of all the cheques for each paying bank, and then transmit these files to the paying banks. Each paying bank still receives the paper cheques and can simply reconcile them against the recipient bank's file, as well as validating each cheque.

Another improvement is for banks to exchange images of cheques, which removes the need to transport cheques to and from an exchange centre, and an obvious next step is for banks just to exchange data on each cheque (with or without an image). In the UK, this required a change in law to end the requirement for physical cheques to be exchanged and for images to have legal validity.

The final improvement step is to enable customers to take images themselves of cheques they receive, which is now common in countries that still have sizable volumes of cheques. All these improvements changed the clearing period to next day in the UK – a customer can take an image of a cheque using their smartphone and submit it via their banking app before their bank's cut-off time, and the funds are available in their account by no later than the end of the next working day.

7.3.3 Cheque Fraud

Fraud occurs right across the payments landscape and, unfortunately, cheques are no exception. The UK's Cheque and Credit Clearing Company, which manages the cheque clearing process in the UK, classifies cheque fraud in three categories,[31] namely counterfeiting, forgery and fraudulent alteration of cheques. Counterfeiting of cheques encompasses false cheques created to look like genuine cheques drawn on a valid account. Forgery of cheques encompasses using genuine cheques but forging the signature(s) on the cheques. Fraudulent alteration of cheques encompasses altering a genuine cheque that has been made out by the account holder so that it can be paid into a different account or for a different amount. Probably the best defences against all these types of fraud are the use of security features on cheques, which are mandated in some countries, and educating customers about keeping chequebooks safe, how to write cheques to minimise fraudulent alteration, and the potential risks when accepting cheques as payment.

7.3.4 Considerations for Cheque Management in a New Bank

There is no escaping that, despite the volumes still currently in use in some countries, cheques are declining in popularity. The obvious question for a new bank is whether they should be supported – either not at all or accepting cheques or issuing cheques or both. A decision about whether or how to support cheques has to take into account the go-to-market strategy of the bank, how the bank will participate in cheque clearing, how it will detect and manage fraud, how it will accept cheques, how it will manage and physically issue cheques, and the customer service implications of its approach.

To issue or accept cheques or do both, the bank will either have to join the local cheque clearing scheme and implement cheque clearing processes or engage with a clearing bank that provides cheque clearing services for third parties. Using a clearing bank will require integration of the bank's and clearing bank's systems, which must be secure – this may be as simple as file transfers between the parties.

Issuing of cheques requires the implementation of the processes and system functionality to manage the printing and issuance of chequebooks, to identify and resolve fraud cases, and to take part in clearing to some extent.

Cheque printing may be regulated, given cheque standardisation and security features, and we expect that most new banks would outsource the printing of blank cheques to specialist third-party printers. The third-party printer may need to be suitably accredited; for example, in the UK it must be a member of the Cheque Printer Accreditation Scheme (CPAS).[32] Personalisation of cheques (with a customer's account details, name, and branch details, for example) can be done in-house and may require specialised printers (e.g. ones that can print using magnetic ink – see Section 2.6.1), although many banks also use the same third-party printer to do this. While the printing of cheques and binding them into a chequebook is a relatively simple process, given that there is confidential customer data on every cheque printed the process of transmitting that data to a third-party printer must therefore be secure (as should the printer's processes and systems). Schemes such as the CPAS will require members to uphold certain standards and so a bank's compliance team will need to understand these standards and ensure that the third-party printer meets the standards.

When issuing cheques, there will need to be processes to identify and resolve issues of fraud. For example, cheques drawn on customers' accounts must be validated to confirm the availability of funds and that the signatures are valid. A third-party clearing bank may be able to check that a cheque has not been altered or forged without any integration with the issuing bank's systems but for it to check availability of funds and signatures, some integration will be required or the issuing bank will have to take some part in clearing in order to do this itself.

While the issuance of cheques is something about which a bank can have an open perspective, the acceptance of cheques provides less latitude for debate. Any customer, at any time, could receive a cheque and to find out that they can't deposit it with their chosen bank would immediately cause an issue. A bank doesn't have to support the depositing of cheques but to choose not to is a significant decision. If image-based clearing is available locally, then implementing a mobile app cheque scanning solution should be considered – it reduces manual effort and significantly speeds the process up. If an image-based solution is not possible, or the bank's target customer base requires physical depositing of cheques, then consideration should be given to finding a partner to accept cheques on the bank's behalf. Of course, there must still be a process for receiving the outcome of cheque clearing and feeding the account updates back into the core banking platform. Image-based solutions should encompass appropriate technologies to check for tampering and forgery at the point at which the scanned image is uploaded to the bank from the customer's device.

As well as these considerations, thought must be given to implementing customer support processes and staff to field customer queries relating to cheques and also compliance processes to oversee the relevant elements of cheque payments.

7.4   Direct Credits

We briefly describe direct credits, sometimes called giro payments or direct deposits, because they form the basis of many electronic payment schemes. A direct credit is initiated by a payer, who instructs their bank to make a payment to a specific account, either at the same bank or another bank. The payer's bank debits the payer's account, sends a notice to the recipient bank of the payment and transfers the funds to the recipient bank's account at the settlement bank – usually the central bank. At one level, the recipient bank is only passively involved in the payment process, apart from that it has to check that it has received the funds and then credit the recipient's account. Of course, this process relies on the payer having knowledge of the recipient's bank account details. The paying bank can check up front whether the payer has sufficient funds in their account to make the payment and validate the request, therefore avoiding the complexity of dealing with returned payments that is a feature of the cheque clearing process. However, there is still the challenge of dealing with payments in cases where the recipient's account details are incorrect.

In some countries, such as Germany, giro payments were and are widely used, thus removing a lot of the need for cheque payments. A key part of the process in such countries is that utilities and other companies send customers a pre-completed, standardised giro form with their statements, which a customer then completes with their own bank and account details and gives to their bank for payment. This reduces the problem of the wrong recipient account details being used.

The UK does not provide a good historical example of giro payments – although there was a system of giro transfers, called Bank Giro Credits, these were instructions to credit a recipient's account, but did not provide any means of capturing the payer's account details or authorisation to make a payment from their account and were typically paid with cash or a cheque.

7.5   Clearing and Settlement

Clearing simply refers to the steps that are taken to determine who is paying what to whom and whether they have the funds to do so. It establishes the commitment for a payment to be made but stops before funds are actually transferred. Different payment types and payment schemes clear payments in very different ways and so it is hard to be any more specific. However, we cover several examples of clearing in this chapter.

Settlement is the process of transferring funds. There are various ways that this can be done. Settlement can occur at the same time a payment is cleared (or immediately afterward), in which case it is called real-time settlement, or it can take place later, in which case it is called deferred settlement. Usually settlement requires a central settlement party or agent where all of the participants and the scheme hold an account. In the UK, this is normally the Bank of England and in many other countries the central bank plays a similar role.

Furthermore, settlement is carried out either gross or net. Real-time settlement almost by definition is also gross settlement, in which the paying party transfers the full value of the funds to be paid to the receiving party. This means that the participants face little risk – either the payment is settled and is successful or it is not settled, and the payment is unsuccessful. For high-value payments, as we cover in Section 7.6.11, use of real-time gross settlement (RTGS) is common and since the 1980s has been a backbone of the payments ecosystem in several major economies.[33]

Deferred net settlement is common in payment schemes where there are large volumes of payments – and in fact real-time gross settlement in such schemes is not feasible. Periodically, the net position of each participant is calculated, based on the net flow of payments. This position can be calculated bilaterally, i.e. what each participant owes or is owed by every other participant, or multilaterally, in which the overall net position of each participant is calculated and those that have had net outflows pay into a central pot (or settlement account) and those that have had net inflows receive payment from that settlement account. Multilateral settlement is much more common, as bilateral settlement is only feasible with a small number of participants. For example, there are 190 possible combinations of two participants if there are 20 participants in total.

Participants in net settlement schemes carry the risk that another participant will default on a settlement payment. This is typically minimised by having each participant maintain a minimum balance in its settlement account at a level at or above the maximum likely net outflow of funds.

7.6   Interbank Payments

This section covers what were historically payments only between banks. However, many other types of institutions are now involved in making, transmitting and receiving payments and this section is just as applicable to them. As we saw in Chapter 2, technology has been used for making payments since at least the advent of money transfers using a telegraph network in 1871. The use of data networks and computer processing for payments between banks developed rapidly from the late 1960s, with schemes such as the UK's BACS (since renamed Bacs) automated clearing house launched in 1968, CHIPS in the US in 1970, the automation of credit card payments (specifically the messaging between acquiring and issuing banks via the scheme) in the 1970s and the launch of SWIFT's international interbank network in 1977. For retail customers, however, cash and cheque payments continued to dominate for several more decades.

Throughout the world there is huge variety among the various different national payment schemes. To cover all of these one would need to carry out a comprehensive review of such networks around the globe, a task that isn't possible in this book. Therefore, given our familiarity with it, we have used the British payment schemes as the basis of this chapter. The British schemes are not the most advanced in the world, but they are collectively one of the most varied in terms of the payment types they support and therefore provide a good example.

There are two ways in which payments can be sent: either individually or grouped together into a file. The latter approach is used by batch-oriented payment schemes, which include the oldest electronic payment schemes, and typically work on the basis of each participant sending a file of payments to the scheme at the end of each day, which then processes them (in effect recuts all the files into another group of files) and sends the relevant file to each participant. An example of this is the clearing process for card payments explained in Section 6.3; automated clearing house schemes often work in this way, including the UK's Bacs payment scheme (which we describe in Section 7.6.2).

Message-oriented schemes work on the basis of the participants sending in messages individually at any time during the period of operation of the scheme and routing them to the recipient immediately – we cover such schemes from Section 7.6.5 onwards.

7.6.1 Batch-oriented Payment Schemes

The basic process in a batch-oriented payment scheme is as follows:

1. A customer instructs their bank to make a payment for a specific amount to an account at another bank.
2. The paying bank validates and records the instruction. It collates all the instructions it receives and at the end of the day sends them to the payment scheme.
3. The payment scheme receives payment instruction files from all the participating banks and processes them into another set of files, one for each bank that is receiving payments. It also works out the net settlement positions of all the banks (i.e. the net amount to be paid to or paid by each bank).
4. The payment scheme sends the recipient payment files out, one to each recipient bank, along with details of their net settlement positions.
5. The banks that had a net outflow of money transfer funds from their accounts at the central bank to the settlement account of the scheme. The scheme transfers funds to the accounts of the banks that had a net inflow of money.
6. All banks credit the accounts of the recipients and debit the accounts of the payers.

This process includes multilateral net settlement.

7.6.2 Example – Bacs Direct Credits

Bacs was launched in the UK, initially as the Inter Bank Computer Bureau, in 1968 with a goal of automating the exchange of payment data between UK banks, supporting direct credits and direct debits. As one might expect for an activity begun in 1968,[34] the initial technical capabilities of Bacs were limited, based around the daily exchange of payment files on magnetic tapes with the clearing banks. The capabilities were extended in 1983 to enable corporate customers of the clearing banks to submit payment files directly to Bacs via a dial-up telephone connection – the Bacstel service – which was supplemented in 2003 (and subsequently replaced) by submission over the Internet in 2003 – unsurprisingly named Bacstel-IP. Banks and other payment service providers now send and receive files via the SWIFT network or via a secure direct connection with Bacs. The Bacs network and infrastructure is now operated by Vocalink, a subsidiary of Mastercard, with the Bacs scheme a subsidiary of Pay.UK, a company limited by guarantee (which means it is a not-for profit organisation) whose guarantors are members of the UK's payments ecosystem.

The original Bacs direct credit process is essentially the same as set out in Section 7.6.1, with some more specific timings. Files must be submitted between 7:00 a.m. and 10:30 p.m. on day 1 and Bacs sends out the files it creates by 6:00 a.m. on day 2. The recipient banks must process these on day 2. The payers' accounts are debited, and the recipients' accounts are credited on day 3. This is a push payment and is typically used by businesses when they want to make a batch of related payments, such as is often the case for the payment of salaries. As a push payment, a direct credit is relatively straightforward in terms of payment flow but using Bacs it takes three days to reach the recipient.

Typically, a business, such as an employer, will first need to sign up (at a cost) with a payment service provider (PSP) – either a clearing bank or a Bacs-approved bureau. Once this relationship has been established, the business can upload files of payment instructions to its PSP or directly to Bacs using Bacstel-IP, and the payments are pushed to the recipients. Transaction costs are relatively low, typically between 5p and 50p per payment.

However, despite their relative simplicity, as already mentioned, these push payments normally take three days to clear, which is not ideal but is well understood by participants and can therefore be accommodated – businesses just need to ensure that the transactions are submitted two working days prior to the date they want the recipients to receive the funds. Multilateral net settlement takes place on the morning of day 3 via the participant banks' settlement accounts at the Bank of England.

Bacs allows payment instructions to be submitted up to 30 days in advance of the payment date and will store such instructions until they are included in the relevant day's processing. Such payment instructions can also be cancelled up to a specific cut-off time.

As you would expect, Bacs has a process for dealing with direct credits that are rejected (e.g. because the recipient account does not exist). The timings stated before still apply, and the payer's account will still be debited on day 3. However, the recipient bank should include the rejected payment in its daily submission to Bacs on day 3, which Bacs sends in a so-called Automated Return of Unapplied Credits Service (ARUCS) report to the paying bank at the start of day 4. The payer's account is then credited with the returned payment on day 5.

Furthermore, recipient banks can also accept payments for which the account details were incorrect (e.g. because the recipient has transferred their account) and apply them to the correct accounts. When they do so they should inform the paying bank of the new account details by submitting a file with all changes to the Advice of Wrong Account for Automated Credits Service (AWACS) at Bacs. Bacs sends these details to the paying banks in AWACS reports, so that they can update the payers with the correct details.

There is another complication. A bank may decide that it has made some payments in error and can ask for them to be reversed by including the details in a file it submits to Bacs. If this is on or before day 1 of the process, either Bacs or the receiving bank can filter out the original payment and the reversal. For reversals that are submitted on day 2, the recipient bank has to act on them when it receives them in its daily files from Bacs on the morning of day 3, and not credit the accounts of its customers with the reversed payments.

Finally, with the addition of direct corporate access to Bacs in 1983, the Bacs file exchange processes and the files themselves were made more complex. Consider a business that submits a file directly to Bacs which contains instructions to pay salaries to its employees. Bacs has to forward the payment instructions onto the recipient banks as normal, and it also has to inform the business's bank that it has to debit the business's account to cover the salary payments. This was made possible by including what is called a contra payment instruction in the file submitted by the business, which provides details of its bank account. One contra payment instruction balances all the payments to be made by the business, and so the business will see just one transaction in its bank account for all the salary payments in this example. Having direct corporate access also complicates the distribution of ARUCS and AWACS reports.

7.6.3 Direct Debits

A direct debit payment is a payment from the bank account of a customer of a business, made automatically whenever requested by the business. They are often used to pay for regular bills such as monthly insurance premiums, utility bills and gym memberships. A customer must give a business that wishes to make such pull payments a direct debit mandate, which permits it to draw down variable payments on request from the account holder either for a set period or indefinitely.

In order to do this, the customer typically has to complete a direct debit instruction (DDI) form, which the business (or, in some schemes, the customer) has to submit to the customer's bank. Payment schemes that support direct debits collect DDIs from businesses and send them on to the customers' banks.

Then, when a business wishes to receive a payment, it must typically inform the customer in advance of the payment (e.g. by issuing a statement to the customer) and then submit the direct debit payment request either via its own bank or directly to the payment scheme, which forwards it to the customer's bank.

A bank that offers current or checking accounts must be able to process incoming direct debit mandates (e.g. checking their validity), deal with changes to mandates (e.g. customers cancelling them or closing or transferring their accounts), and process direct debit payment requests (including dealing with the situations where an account has insufficient funds to pay a direct debit payment request or a direct debit payment request has been made after the customer has cancelled the corresponding mandate). Similarly, businesses using direct debit payments must be able to handle changes to and cancellations of direct debit mandates and failed direct debit payments.

So, in summary, direct debits involve two sets of processes for the businesses that use them and the banks that handle them – those involving setting up, maintaining and ending direct debit mandates, and those involving requesting direct debit payments and making such payments.

7.6.4 Example – Bacs Direct Debits

Direct debit instruction forms for the Bacs scheme can be completed by the account holder either on paper (in which case the account holder must sign the form) or online (in which case no signature or other form of authentication is required). The layout of paper forms and the presentation of online forms must follow rules issued by Bacs. Once filled in, a business must retain a copy of the paper form or the information entered online and submit the information from the form via Bacs to the account holder's bank. To do this, a business submits a file of direct debit instruction data to the Automated Direct Debit Instruction Service (AUDDIS) at Bacs, using the same daily submission process it would use for submitting direct credit files. Bacs processes all the DDI data it has received by the cut-off time, first performing some basic checks to ensure all the required data has been supplied and is correctly formatted. Next, Bacs produces a new set of files from the valid DDI data so that there is a new file for each bank, containing DDIs that are to be applied to accounts at each bank, and sends these to the respective banks. A recipient bank may respond via Bacs if there is a problem applying the DDI, e.g. the account doesn't exist or the type of account doesn't accept direct debits, and the originator of the DDI will receive an AUDDIS rejection report containing all such rejections.

After a direct debit mandate has been established, at some point in the future the customer could cancel it by notifying their bank, or their account could be closed or transferred to another branch or bank. The customer's bank can notify the business that set up the direct debit by submitting a file containing such changes to the Automated Direct Debit Amendment and Cancellation Service (ADDACS) at Bacs. Each day a bank submits a file of such changes to Bacs, which collates all such files received up to the cut-off time and forwards the changes to the respective originating businesses.

Note that for banks and businesses operating direct debits it is possible to automate the processes involving AUDDIS and ADDACS, and we would expect most banks to do so. For a business, a decision to automate the processes may depend on the volume of direct debits it deals with.

We then move onto the second set of processes, direct debit payments. A payment starts on day 1, when the originating business creates a Bacs file containing all the direct debit payment requests due in two working days' time, and submits this file to Bacs before 10:30 p.m. Overnight, Bacs collates all the files and produces and sends a file for each paying bank, including a file containing a contra credit payment, to the bank of the originating business. The point of the latter is to tell the bank where the originating business has its account to get ready to credit the account with the value of the direct debit payments. On day 2, each paying bank processes the file it receives from Bacs, checking the existence of valid direct debit mandates and that each paying account has sufficient funds. On day 3, the paying banks debit the accounts of their customers who were listed in the files they received, and the bank of the originating business credits the business's account with the value of all the direct debits. On the same day, the banks settle between themselves via their settlement accounts at the Bank of England, as part of the overall Bacs multilateral net settlement process. Also, normally on day 3 but sometimes on day 4, the paying banks submit rejected direct debit requests to the Automated Return of Direct Debits (ARUDD) service at Bacs as part of their daily submission to Bacs. The originating bank and business will receive these rejections by the start of the next day, so on either day 4 or 5. Therefore a business that collects payments using direct debits via Bacs only has certainty on which payments were successful on day 5 of the cycle. As with all Bacs processing, the cycle only takes place on working days, i.e. Monday to Friday except English bank holidays. So, in the very worst case, day 5 could be 11 calendar days after submission of the original direct debit payment requests (with, for example, day 1 being Friday 24 December and day 5 landing on Tuesday 4 January).

A further complication of Bacs direct debits is that a customer can dispute a payment, and the direct debit guarantee that all participating banks operate means that they are refunded. The business that originated the payment is informed via yet another Bacs report, a Direct Debit Indemnity Claim Automation (DDICA) report, and the business's account will be automatically debited for the claim after 14 working days.

We should point out that Bacs is in the process of migrating to ISO 20022 messaging (see Section 7.6.7), although it will remain a batch-oriented scheme.

7.6.5 Message-oriented Payment Schemes

Message-oriented payment schemes accept individual payment messages from participants at any time during their hours of operation and process each message as it arrives. Clearing (the identification of the payer's and recipient's bank) happens when a payment instruction message is processed, but settlement can take place either at the same time (in which case the scheme provides real-time gross settlement – each payment is settled as it is processed) or at specific times (in which case the scheme provides net settlement – payments are collated and the net positions of participants calculated at each settlement time, similar to settlement in a batch-oriented payment scheme described in Section 7.6.1).

As we describe message-oriented payment schemes, we will use several specific terms: payment messages are exchanged between participants in a payment scheme (often abbreviated to scheme) and are transmitted over a payment network (or sometimes more than one network) that connects all the participants. A payment scheme may define many different types of message including payment instructions, which we cover next.

7.6.6 Payment Instructions

At its simplest, an electronic payment comprises a payment message containing a payment instruction carried over a payment network and the transfer of value between accounts maintained by an accounting platform, often at a central bank (historically, the Bank of England would move gold between different piles in its vaults to settle transactions between banks, but now records such transfers electronically[35]). In practice, an electronic payment is likely to involve more than one message, often because a confirmation message will be sent in return or because of the specific nature of the payment scheme (see, for example, how card payments work in Section 6.3).

7.6.7 Payment Message Formats

Each payment scheme has a set of standards that all participants must use to format, submit and receive messages, typically defining many different types of messages used for different purposes, including one or more types for payment instructions. The format of payment messages varies widely, although ISO 8583[36] is a standard that many schemes use, albeit with many differences in usage and meaning of the various data elements contained in each type of message. The ISO 8583 message format is compact (which was helpful when data networks were slow) but relatively inflexible and was originally defined for card payments. There is a general movement to the more modern, flexible format defined in ISO 20022 (see www.iso20022.org), which is based on XML (see Chapter 3 for more information on XML) and supports many different categories of financial messages.

It should be noted that just because a payment scheme uses a particular standard does not mean that it is possible to take the stated standard and start using it – in fact, we believe that this would be virtually impossible. In many cases, the scheme (or even the organisation that provides a connection to the scheme's network) may decide not to use all the fields defined in that standard and may apply different meanings to the fields compared to other schemes. If you are building a connection to a payment network, it is well worth investing some time to be sure of what the message formats and associated rules are before you start developing for them. We have also found that schemes don't necessarily have complete documentation on how they process messages or the meaning of certain combinations of values of fields in the payment messages, so developing and testing with real-world sample messages or files (if the scheme will supply them) is a good way of reducing the risk of errors. Some payment networks also provide facilities for testing, including certification of a new connection.

7.6.8   Payment Message Addressing

The payment network and recipient institution have to know how to route a payment message and, usually, the account to which it is to be applied. This can involve several pieces of information, some of which can overlap.

First, there is something that identifies a connection to the payment network. A participant in a payment scheme may have more than one connection to the payment network because it has different business units (or even legal entities) that need to receive or make payments and/or by virtue of mergers and acquisitions. One would expect these to have different business addresses. A participant may also have more than one physical connection to a payment network because it needs to ensure that its connection is highly available, so if one physical connection fails it has at least one other that can be used. One would expect such redundant connections to be represented by the same business address but technically, from a data network perspective, they may have different network addresses.

Second, once a recipient organisation has received a message, it may require information on where to route the message internally. For example, a large bank typically needs to know the branch an account is held at (or at least assigned to, if its accounts are all maintained centrally).

Third, the account of the intended recipient has to be identified, normally with an account number.

Historically, each scheme came up with its own system and format for this information, often drawing on what had been used on cheques to automate sorting them. So, the UK's Bacs scheme uses the same sort codes that appear on UK cheques for the first and second purposes above. Each sort code is uniquely allocated to a bank and also denotes the branch of a bank. Sort codes have the format of *aa bb cc*, with all characters being numeric. An example of this is 40 33 33 which is for a branch of HSBC in Milton Keynes. Similarly, banks in the US use nine-digit routing numbers that uniquely identify banks and their branches for cheques, Fedwire payments and ACH payments.

SWIFT assigns Business Identifier Codes (BICs), the format of which is defined in ISO 9362,[37] to financial institutions globally.[38] Until the 2009 version of ISO 9362 BIC stood for Bank Identifier Code[39] and this name is still often used. Each BIC is unique, and it is common for an institution to have more than one BIC. An institution does not have to be connected to the SWIFT network to have a BIC, but if it is connected it must have a BIC. A basic BIC has eight characters and three additional characters can be used to represent a branch or other internal structure. Therefore, a BIC comprises either three or four fields respectively; the first three fields represent a connection to the network and the last field internal routing information. An example of a BIC, for the same branch of HSBC in Milton Keynes as in the previous paragraph, is MIDLGB2176D. The first field represents a business or bank and has four characters which, according to ISO 9362, can be alphanumeric but which SWIFT limits to being alphabetical. In this case MIDL refers to HSBC (by virtue of the fact that HSBC acquired Midland Bank in the UK). The second field is a two-character country code and in our example GB refers to Great Britain. The third field comprises two alphanumeric characters with the first one originally indicating in what time zone the business was located, and the second one whether the business was connected to the SWIFT network (any value other than 0 or 1) or not (a value of 1) or whether the BIC was for testing purposes only (a value of 0). However, this field is now purely for additional segregation of BICs for the business indicated by the first field. In our example, this field has the value 21, with originally 2 indicating the UK's time zone and 1 indicating the bank was not connected to the SWIFT network. The fourth field has three alphanumeric characters and is used for internal routing or classification of messages. In our example, 76D is the identifier of the branch in Milton Keynes.

Banks have used many ways to number accounts (and historically often didn't number them at all). However, with the introduction of electronic cheque sorting equipment with machine-readable printing on the cheques, clearing banks in each country had to define a standard way of numbering accounts, as well as numbers identifying each branch. The UK clearing banks (i.e. those that operated the central cheque clearing process) settled on an eight-digit numeric account number (and a six-digit sort code as set out earlier), although there are some accounts with more or fewer digits, with rules on how to convert them to standard eight-digit account numbers. The account numbers are not totally random. To help identify mistakes in keying in sort codes and account numbers, there are various modulus checking algorithms that can be applied to a sort code and account number combination, which vary depending on the sort code. Vocalink, the company that operates the Bacs and Faster Payments networks in the UK, provides the lookup table that says what type of modulus check to run and what weighting to apply for any given sort code.[40] A successful check means that the account number is valid for the sort code (although it doesn't guarantee that the account is actually in use or open). While there are benefits of modulus checking (it reduces errors and the need for re-keying), the UK's implementation of it is complex and we suspect it was implemented that way because of differences in banks' processes and platforms. To complicate matters in the UK, historically a bank or building society that wasn't a clearing bank was allocated a single sort code and a single account number for the whole business and then had to use what was often called a roll number, in effect a reference number, to distinguish between its customers' accounts, and this uses the reference field in the Bacs file and Faster Payments message (see Section 7.6.9).

There is an international standard that combines a connection identifier, internal routing information and account numbering, the International Bank Account Number (IBAN), as defined in ISO 13616:2007.[41] This is in common usage in many European countries (including all countries in the Single European Payments Area) and has some support in the Middle East, Central America, the Caribbean and South America. Using an IBAN should remove the need to also use a BIC, although we note that some international payment providers insist on both pieces of information. The IBAN consists of up to 34 alphanumeric characters comprising a two-letter country code, two numeric check digits and up to 30 alphanumeric characters giving the Basic Bank Account Number (BBAN) whose format is country-specific. An example of an IBAN is GB98 MIDL 4033 3312 3456 78 (in which we have inserted spaces for readability). This code is, again, for an account at the Milton Keynes branch of HSBC in the UK. Each country has a different algorithm for constructing a BBAN from the equivalent of an account number and sort code or routing number. The UK's algorithm is a four-character code for the bank (MIDL in our example, as also used in the BIC for the same bank), followed by the six-digit sort code that historically represented a bank branch (40 33 33) and an eight-digit account number (12345678); these last two fields are the same as used in UK payment schemes, including on cheques and in submissions to Bacs.

7.6.9   Other Payment Message Fields

As well as routing information, the message normally has to indicate what it is about, using a message type indicator, and contain information on who sent the message (which may well be similar in format to the address information covered in Section 7.6.8). There may also be date and time fields.

If the payment message is a payment instruction, it will contain the value of the payment, plus for international payments a field indicating the currency of the payment. There will also be one or more freeform fields that can be used to provide further information on the payment, e.g. the account number that allows a utility company to allocate the payment to an account, a reference (often called a roll number in this context) for a building society to allocate a payment to one of its customers' accounts or an invoice number that allows a company to identify which invoice the payment is for. The UK's Bacs and Faster Payments schemes both have a single reference field with a maximum length of 18 alphanumeric characters, which is rather limiting, and do not check or enforce any specific formats for things like invoice numbers or roll numbers in this field.

Finally, you would expect there to be some way of uniquely identifying each payment message – in some schemes this was done through a combination of the value of other fields such as date, payment value, sending account and recipient account – but more modern schemes may provide rules for generating a unique identifier for each message.

7.6.10   Example – Faster Payments

The UK's Bacs payment scheme has one great drawback and that is the time it takes to send a payment. As we showed in Section 7.6.2, for a regular direct credit it takes three working days for the payment to get to the recipient, even if their bank is right next door to the originating bank – and this could mean, in some circumstances, it would take a whole week if there was a weekend with a bank holiday either side (such as at Easter and, from time to time, at Christmas). In the modern world three or more days for a domestic payment to complete is clearly not acceptable. The UK banking industry (with prompting from the UK government) recognised this and launched Faster Payments in 2008 with the goal of providing near-instantaneous payments.[42]

The Faster Payments scheme is simple to set up for customers of banks and other payment service providers, requiring only a sort code and account number to be correctly routed to their destination, and the recipient should receive the funds within two hours (and in most cases within seconds). The service is also free for retail customers. Consequently, it should come as no surprise that the Faster Payments service has proved to be hugely popular, to the extent that Bacs is no longer used for direct credits initiated by retail customers. The basic process of sending a payment and the periodic settlement that takes place is illustrated in Figure 7.1. Clearing takes place in steps 1 to 7 and settlement in steps 8 to 10. As is normal for a high-volume payment scheme, multilateral net settlement is used. Note, however, how the payer's account and recipient's account are debited and credited nearly immediately, before the banks at which the accounts are maintained settle with each other. The scheme operates 24 hours a day, 365 days a year.

Settlement takes place three times a day on every banking day (i.e. not weekends or bank holidays). Each participant settles with the funds in its so-called Reserves Account at the Bank of England. To minimise settlement risk, each participant in the scheme has what is called a Net Sender Cap (NSC), which is set above the predicted maximum net liability of that participant between settlements. An outbound payment will be refused by the scheme if it would cause a participant's NSC to be breached. In addition, each participant must have on deposit at least the same amount of funds as its NSC in what is called a 'Reserves Collateralisation Account (RCA), also at the Bank of England. Ordinarily, the funds in the RCA would not be touched but if a participant were to default on a settlement payment, the funds in the RCA could be used to settle.

The observant reader will note that the Faster Payments scheme operates very much like a single-message card payment scheme (covered in Chapter 6), but with more frequent, intraday settlement, and it even uses ISO 8583 as its message format (although it is in the process of migrating to ISO 20022). This is perhaps not a surprise given that Vocalink, the operators of the UK's LINK ATM network, built (and operate) the Faster Payments infrastructure. Like Bacs, the Faster Payments scheme is managed by a subsidiary of Pay.UK.

As well as the payment flow shown in Figure 7.1, businesses may connect directly to the Faster Payment network, using a platform that is similar to Bacstel-IP, and even submit payment files in the same format as Bacs payment files.

Faster Payments also supports the UK's standing order capability. Standing orders are a common payment facility (they also exist in Germany, Japan, New Zealand, South Korea and Spain, as well as many other countries) where a customer can set up future-dated payments, on a schedule, to pay a fixed amount to an account at any other UK bank or building society. The key difference between a standing order and a direct debit is that standing orders are set up and managed by the payer, rather than the recipient, and are typically used for making regular payments in which the value doesn't change. The big advantage of having standing orders run on the Faster Payments network is that they arrive just as quickly as any other Faster Payment – nobody has to wait three or more days for receipt of funds.

However, the Faster Payments scheme is not perfect. As we touch on in more detail later in this chapter, their near-instant nature makes them attractive to criminals. For example, authorised push payment fraud that became common in the UK relied upon convincing customers to send money to the fraudster's account and then moving the money on before the fraud was found out. Such fraud relied on the fact that the Faster Payments scheme did not check the name of the account holder of the destination account or provide a means for the initiator of a payment to check this either – it relied on the payment initiator entering the correct sort code and account number, so if they could be induced to use the wrong sort code or account number, payments could be diverted. The UK banking industry implemented Confirmation of Payee to reduce the prevalence of such fraud.[43] This relatively simple development allows the payee's name to be compared to the name of the account holder as registered at the receiving bank. If the two do not match, then the payer is warned that the recipient may not be who they claim to be.

278

FIGURE 7.1 Faster Payments payment flow.

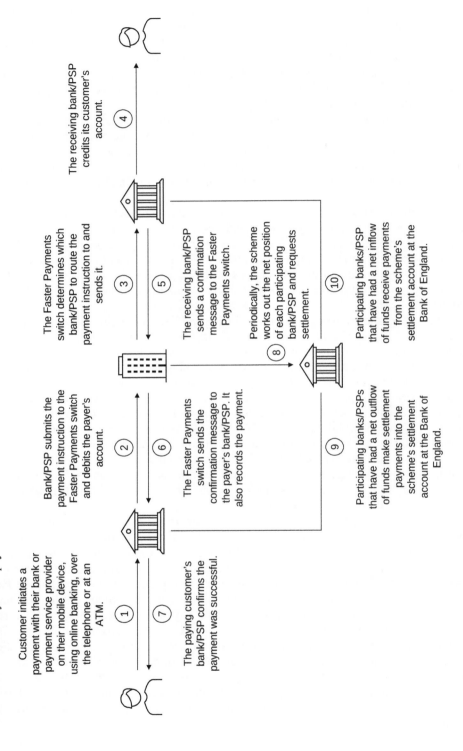

Customer initiates a payment with their bank or payment service provider on their mobile device, using online banking, over the telephone or at an ATM.

Bank/PSP submits the payment instruction to the Faster Payments switch and debits the payer's account.

The Faster Payments switch determines which bank/PSP to route the payment instruction to and sends it.

The receiving bank/PSP credits its customer's account.

The receiving bank/PSP sends a confirmation message to the Faster Payments switch.

The Faster Payments switch sends the confirmation message to the payer's bank/PSP. It also records the payment.

The paying customer's bank/PSP confirms the payment was successful.

Periodically, the scheme works out the net position of each participating bank/PSP and requests settlement.

Participating banks/PSPs that have had a net outflow of funds make settlement payments into the scheme's settlement account at the Bank of England.

Participating banks/PSP that have had a net inflow of funds receive payments from the scheme's settlement account at the Bank of England.

Another, very basic, way in which risk is managed in the Faster Payments scheme is through payment limits. The Faster Payments scheme itself has a limit of £250,000 per transaction (although in 2019, testing of payments up to £10m was carried out), but this limit is adjusted by individual banks for their customers and by which channel they are initiating a payment. For retail customers the limit is often set to £20,000, with small businesses and corporates having higher limits. Of course, £20,000 is still a lot of money for a retail customer to lose.

7.6.11 High-value Payment Schemes

High-value payment schemes such as Fedwire in the US and CHAPS in the UK typically process low volumes of payments but ones that can be of huge value. Having certainty that a payment has been successfully made is of paramount importance to the end users of such a scheme, and ensuring that settlement takes place is of paramount importance to the banks that exchange payments using it. For many retail customers of banks, the only time they are likely to make use of such a scheme is when they purchase or sell a property, and even then they may well rely upon a solicitor or notary or other professional to make or check such payments on their behalf.

Such schemes use real-time gross settlement and are message-based, because of the ad hoc nature of each payment and the need for it to be made in near real-time.

7.6.12 Example – CHAPS

The Clearing House Automated Payment System, or CHAPS, was established in 1984 and still runs today. CHAPS payments are relatively expensive, costing the end user as much as £35 to send, but are guaranteed to clear on the same day, assuming nothing goes wrong in the process and the payment is submitted before the cut-off time, which is at 5:40 p.m., with payments completed by 6:00 p.m.

The CHAPS network is actually a closed user group on the SWIFT network, which we cover in more detail later. The basic process of a CHAPS payment is that a customer requests that a payment be made and their participating bank submits a CHAPS payment request to SWIFT. SWIFT routes the message to the Bank of England, which transfers the funds between the paying and receiving participants' accounts using its RTGS system – which is in effect a banking platform that maintains a record of the accounts that each payment service provider has at the Bank of England. The Bank of England then sends payment confirmation messages to both participants via SWIFT. That is it – it is probably the least complex payment flow of all the payment systems we have considered so far.

7.6.13 International Payments

Within the UK and Europe there are two common ways to make international payments. Europe has its own payments network, the Single European Payments Area (SEPA). As of 2020, there were 36 members of SEPA,[44] which includes most European countries. The payments network allows any customer of a bank in any participating country to send Euro payments anywhere in the SEPA area. It supports batch credit transfers, instant credit transfers and direct debits. The first are cleared and settled overnight, the second means the payment is available to the recipient within 10 seconds, and direct debits work in a similar way to direct debits in the UK.

As we explained in Section 2.10.2, SEPA, like Bacs and Faster Payments, separates the scheme from the network and infrastructure used to operate the scheme but in an even more complex way, reflecting the federated nature of payment systems across its area of remit. SEPA allows payment service providers (PSPs, which are typically the banks whose customers initiate payments) to choose whatever clearing and settlement mechanism (CSM) they want to use as long as it adheres to the scheme rules, which include requiring CSMs to interact to ensure that all PSPs can exchange payments. A CSM typically comprises a central bank such as Banca d'Italia or Deutsche Bundesbank, the European Central Bank's TARGET2 Instant Payment Settlement (TIPS) and a domestic payments scheme such as Belgium's Centre for Exchange and Clearing or Spain's iberpay. In reality this means a bank can use its existing domestic payments scheme for both domestic and cross-border SEPA payments, with cross-border payments typically settled via its domestic central bank using TIPS.

For (almost) all payments involving a country outside SEPA there is the SWIFT network. SWIFT is not a payment scheme – all it does is transfer messages between financial institutions securely; it never handles money or performs settlement between financial institutions. It is used for various types of financial transactions, including payments. As a simple example, consider a customer who wishes to make a payment from their account at Barclays in the UK to an account at Commonwealth Bank of Australia (CBA). It is highly likely that these two banks have a correspondent banking relationship, in which they both agree to set up an account for the other bank for such payments. So, Barclays sends a SWIFT payment message to CBA informing it of the payment. It also transfers the funds from its customer's account to the account of the CBA at Barclays. CBA, having received the payment message via the SWIFT network and on seeing the transfer into its account at London (it can be notified by another SWIFT message or it may just check manually), makes a payment into the destination account in Australia. The messaging gets more complex when two banks don't have a correspondent banking relationship and have to use intermediate banks to transfer the funds. Figure 7.2 shows a more complex international payment, describing how the payment moves from bank to bank in order to reach its destination. In this diagram, a UK bank (A) makes a payment via a UK payment scheme to another UK bank (B), which then uses its correspondent relationship with a US bank (C) to send the payment internationally (like the previous Barclays and CBA example), which in turn uses a US domestic payment scheme to make the payment to the recipient's bank (D).

Routing an international message requires a different banking address format than national payments. An international payment is routed using a BIC and account number or an IBAN, as explained in Section 7.6.8.

As a network that has existed for over 40 years SWIFT is not without its problems, the two most often cited being that it can take several days for a SWIFT transaction to complete, depending upon the relationships between the sending and receiving banks, and there has historically been no easy way to understand where a payment has gotten to at a given point in time. SWIFT is looking to resolve this with the deployment of its Global Payments Innovation (gpi) initiative. This is targeted at decreasing transaction times, providing full transparency on costs (including foreign exchange costs) and allowing customers to track payments through a unique end-to-end tracking reference

FIGURE 7.2   International payment example.

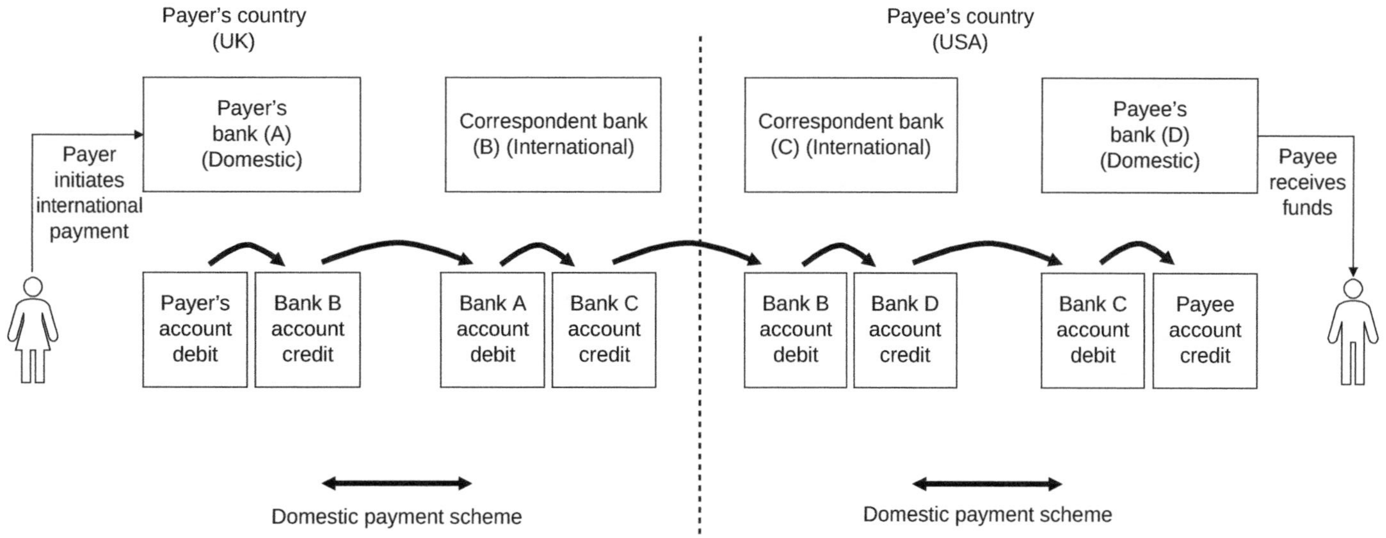

(UETR) that enables customers to understand exactly where their payment is at any given point in time.

There are also a number of organisations attempting to 'disrupt' the international payments space by providing alternative solutions. Probably the most noteworthy (as at mid-2020) of these is Ripple. Ripple's solution, RippleNet, is based upon Distributed Ledger Technology (DLT), a similar technology to that which underpins Bitcoin. In 2017 it was announced that Ripple, American Express and Santander had entered into an agreement to establish a payments route between the US and the UK that would enable almost-instantaneous settlement.[45] This solution is marketed to retail customers and has been proven to work but, to date, hasn't gained much traction in the wider payments community. We look again at the future of payments in Chapter 10 and provide our perspective on whether Ripple, one of its peers or another solution altogether will ever truly challenge the hegemony of SWIFT.

7.6.14   Options for Participating in Payment Schemes

For a new bank or financial institution, there are usually various different ways in which it can connect to local payment networks and participate in local payment schemes, remembering that the scheme and its network may be separate entities, as with Bacs and Faster Payments in the UK. There are typically four different approaches.

In the first approach, a bank or financial institution could become a full member of a scheme, with a direct connection to its network. In effect, it would become a clearing bank. The new bank is also required to open a settlement account at the settlement bank for the scheme (usually the central bank). This arrangement is typical of established banks (such as Barclays, Lloyds, HSBC and Santander in the UK). The UK's Faster Payments scheme calls this Direct Participation and calls such a participant a Directly Connected Settling Participant. Such a bank has to handle all the operational complexity of participating in the scheme and the technology complexity of connecting its systems to the scheme network with the potential advantages that it may mean it can offer its customers the best service levels and get the lowest prices for payments.

In the second approach, a scheme may allow a bank or financial institution to connect directly to its network but settle through a clearing bank (often called a sponsor bank) rather than with the settlement bank. The UK's Faster Payments scheme calls this Direct Agency and calls such a participant a Directly Connected Non-Settling Participant. It complicates the flow of a payment message, because the sponsor bank has to keep track of all payments to and from the so-called agency bank it is sponsoring so that it can monitor the agency bank's net settlement position at all times – in effect, it authorises each payment, typically allowing it if the agency bank is within its net settlement limit (see the discussion on the Faster Payments Net Sender Cap in Section 7.6.10). So an outbound payment message is sent from the agency bank to the payment network, which routes it to the sponsor bank, which checks it and sends it back to the payment network, which routes it to the recipient bank, and the confirmation message follows the same path in reverse. The potential advantage of this arrangement is that the sponsor bank can provide intraday liquidity to the agency bank, which can be useful if the agency bank doesn't have the capability to monitor its net settlement position internally. However, it requires the agency bank to connect its systems to the payment network.

The third approach is the traditional agency banking model. The agency bank or financial institution connects to the sponsoring bank's systems to submit and receive payments. The UK's Faster Payments scheme calls this Indirect Agency. So a payment instruction is sent from the agency bank (which may be in a simplified or different format from the standard messages used by the payment network), to the sponsor bank, which sends it on (after reformatting it if necessary) to the payment network, which routes it to the recipient. Similarly, messages such as confirmations and inbound payments destined for the agency bank are routed by the payment network to the sponsor bank, which forwards them onto the agency bank. The sponsor bank monitors the agency bank's net settlement position in the same way as in the previous paragraph. This model means that the agency bank's systems and processes may not need to adhere to the service levels dictated by the payment scheme – for example, the agency bank systems may not be available 24 hours a day. The sponsor bank can queue payments destined for the agency bank when its systems are unavailable (if permitted by the scheme's rules).

Note that in both of the previous agency banking models, the sponsoring bank does not have any knowledge of the customer accounts at the agency bank. The agency bank usually has to deposit funds into a settlement account at the sponsor bank and the sponsor bank draws down on these when it settles at the scheme's settlement bank (in which it includes the agency bank's net settlement position in its own net settlement position).

The fourth and final model is what we term an e-money model. In this model the agency bank or financial institution lodges all its customers' funds at a sponsor bank, in individual accounts. The agency bank relies on the sponsor bank to manage its customers' accounts, and in fact, the agency bank does not need a banking licence. This is a model used by several neobanks, as discussed in Section 2.8. The agency bank typically manages the relationship with its customers and provides them with servicing facilities (e.g. a mobile app). However, all transactions are undertaken by the sponsor bank. The agency bank must integrate its systems to those of the sponsor bank. However, it does not need to manage settlement at all.

There are (at least) two further ways of connecting to a scheme. A bank may choose to use a third-party payment gateway to connect to the scheme (or, indeed, to a sponsor bank). From the scheme's perspective, the same settlement arrangements as in the approaches above apply, but messaging to and from the participating bank goes via the payment gateway provider's connection to the network (or sponsor bank). This can simplify the connection and message formats for the participating bank. In the other model, a third party provides processing services for the participating bank, including managing all the customer accounts and connecting to the payment scheme. The participating bank still has to settle with the payment scheme, either directly or using a sponsor bank. This is a processor model, used often in the card payment industry (see Sections 6.3 and 6.4), and is common in some countries such as Germany and the US (see Section 2.10.3).

7.6.15 Hours of Operation

No discussion of payments would be complete without a mention of some of the timing constraints on interbank payments. While modern payment schemes tend to operate 24 hours a day 365 days a year, much of the banking world is still attached to the past, when banks shut at night, and this is particularly true of older payment schemes.

Depending upon the age of a payments scheme, many of the processes that support it may have been established at a time when either clearing and settlement were highly manual or relied upon what we would now regard as legacy banking platforms that worked on batch jobs and needed extended periods of downtime in order to complete operational procedures, updates and maintenance, the legacy of which is that many older payment schemes still use processing calendars based upon these constraints. Consequently, it is not unusual for payments schemes to be unavailable over weekends and on bank holidays as well as having cut-off times by when payments must be submitted.

This might sound trivial, but it has serious implications for the operations and technology teams in a bank. For example, if the submission cut-off for a payment is 4:30 p.m. and a customer submits one at 5:00 p.m. the bank must consider several things, including, for example, when the payment will show as having been sent on the customer's statement, the implications for any interest the customer's account should accrue, the reconciliation of the payment, and when it should clear the payments process.

Additionally, many bank holidays can move. Sometimes this is due to the date of the holiday being based upon natural phenomena (such as Easter and Eid al-Fitr), but there are also times when a bank holiday is either moved by government or even added in order to reflect a significant event such as the death of an important national leader or a notable commemoration. Systems and processes need to take this into account.

7.7   Payment Fraud and Sanctions

Some of the biggest risks faced by any payments operation are those posed by fraud, money laundering and terrorist financing activities. Failure to spot and intercept money gained from or intended for illegal purposes is a serious issue. Every business that manages money or payments is responsible for putting in place appropriate measures to ensure that it is doing everything reasonably possible to combat these activities. In many countries this extends well beyond just financial services. Every business is responsible for ensuring that, at a minimum, it completes appropriate due diligence on its counterparties. As well as being a legal and regulatory responsibility, financial services businesses have a moral obligation to ensure that illegal movement of money is curbed as much as possible.

In addition to detecting money laundering and fraud, banks and financial institutions must have controls in place to avoid sanctions breaches (see Section 5.6.2 for an explanation of sanctions lists). Arguably, controls on domestic payments are provided by the sanctions check performed when a new customer opens an account and usually repeated periodically. However, for international payments, the foreign party in the payment is unlikely to be known to the domestic bank or financial institution, and so all international payments should normally be screened for potential sanctions breaches.

Within the context of a payment operation, care should be taken to ensure that all payment activity is monitored for suspicious activity and action is taken swiftly when suspicions are raised. This is discussed further in Chapter 5.

7.8   Payment Reconciliation

As noted previously, a payment instruction is just a message on a network and, like any message, it can get lost or miscommunicated. For example, a participant in a payment scheme may be using manual processes and there can be a human error, or there could have been a system failure (depressingly common, as we discussed in Section 2.7), resulting in payment messages going missing or being sent more than once. Depending on where a payment message gets lost or miscommunicated, there is the potential for a customer or a bank to lose money. For example, in the Faster Payments message flow shown in Figure 7.1, if the first message sent from the paying bank to the Faster Payments switch is lost, this is potentially immaterial – the payer's account hasn't been debited, the paying bank won't have the payment included in its net settlement and the recipient bank is none the wiser. However, the customer who initiated the payment will be wondering what happened to it and whether it will eventually be paid, and the paying bank may have reduced the available balance of the paying customer's account. The paying bank may have a customer service issue on its hands. On the other hand, if the confirmation message is lost between the scheme switch and the paying bank, there will be an issue during settlement as the paying bank's view of its settlement position (assuming the paying bank maintains it) will differ from the scheme's view, as well as the customer service issue given that the paying customer still doesn't know what has happened to the payment.

There are various ways in which errors can be avoided, detected and mitigated. Some schemes require each payment message to have a unique identifier, so duplicate messages can be ignored by all participants who receive them. Payment messages may contain information (e.g. a checksum or hash value) that allows a recipient to determine if their content has been inadvertently changed. Account numbering standards such as the IBAN and the UK's sort code and account number combination have two checksum digits and must pass a modulus check respectively, thereby reducing the risk of a payment being sent to an incorrect account.

Another way to avoid errors is for each participant in a payment scheme to keep a list and sum of all incoming payments and another of all outgoing payments so that it can monitor its settlement position. At settlement time each participant reconciles its view with that provided by the scheme (or sponsor bank if routing payments through a sponsor). It may be sufficient to check that the sums match, but timing differences of payment messages around the settlement cut-off may mean not all payments match, although non-matching payments may still be honoured and reconciled in the next settlement. In other words, the goal of payment reconciliation is to ensure that all payments are accounted for and that the balances reported by the various different parties in a payment network tally. Note that the ability of an indirectly connected bank to perform payment reconciliation is dependent upon the capabilities of its sponsor bank, both in terms of quality of data and when it is made available by the sponsor bank.

From a timing perspective, intraday reconciliation is not standard in that not every organisation does it, unless the payment schemes in which they participate require it (e.g. because they use intraday settlement). However, particularly for a new bank, it can be useful to carry out intraday reconciliations in order to ensure that its platforms are performing as expected. If connected to a scheme through a sponsor bank the simplest way for an agency bank to perform intraday payment reconciliation is to receive a regular summary file that includes all payments since the last file and use that to compare with all payments that have occurred on the agency bank's platform. Where there are discrepancies the operations team need to determine what the next action should be – often a discrepancy may resolve itself when the next payment file arrives from the sponsor bank, but if it doesn't then the operations team will need a clear strategy for addressing unreconciled payments. It is important that payments are checked against recipient data, value, time and payments message data (as it is possible to receive two valid payments for the same value to the same recipient, for example).

7.9   Payment Technology

This section builds on the explanation of banking technology that we set out in Chapter 3, and uses the architecture shown in Section 3.15 and repeated in Figure 7.3. It isn't essential reading, particularly if you are not interested in how a payment platform works. Figure 7.3 shows the bank's Internet banking platform, which calls various other services, including a payment service, to provide banking functionality.

7.9.1   Creating a Payment Instruction

Let's assume the customer using the Internet banking service wishes to make a payment to an account at another bank. They select this option from the menu of the main Internet banking webpage, which sends an HTTPS message requesting the relevant page, which the web server sends to the Internet Banking object. The Internet Banking object requests a list of the customer's payees from the Payment service, then creates the page, populating it with the customer's accounts so the customer can select an account from which the payment will be made and with details of previous payees so they can reuse the details

FIGURE 7.3   Internet banking platform using services exposed by other platforms.

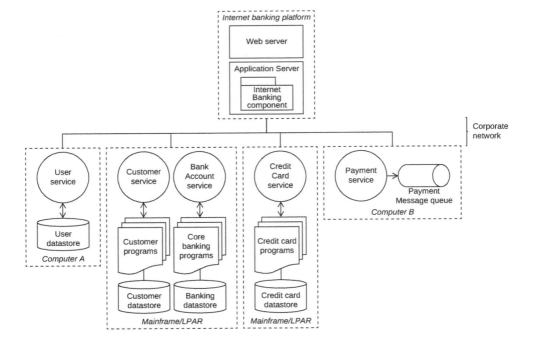

from one of these. It then sends it back via the application server to the web server, which sends it as an HTTPS message to the user's web browser. The customer can now select the account to use for the payment and a payee or enter the details of a new payee.

The customer does this and submits the payment. This results in the customer's web browser sending another HTTPS message to the web server, which forwards it to the Internet Banking object. The Internet Banking object then forwards the details to the Payment object. This process is shown in Figure 7.4.

Let's examine the concept of the Payment object putting a message into the Payment Message queue, the very last action in the process shown in Figure 7.4. A message queue is another type of datastore. Any program can put a message into a queue, and another program can remove the message from the queue at some point later in time and do something with the information contained in the message. When the Payment object puts a message onto the Payment Message queue, it receives an immediate response from the message queue software (normally called a *message broker*) confirming that the message has been put into the queue. Some other program, say a payment gateway, will remove the message at some point later, but nothing is sent back to the Payment object when it does so. Message brokers normally guarantee that every message will be kept safely until it is removed from the queue. This is why the Payment object can put a message into the Payment Message queue and then forget about it – the message will be processed at some point. So, the flow of the message is as illustrated in Figure 7.5. After the Payment object has put the payment message into the Payment Message queue, it sits there until the Outbound Payment processor program removes it from the queue. If the bank only processes payments overnight, e.g. as part of its end-of-day processing, the Outbound Payment processor may only be run at the end of every day. The payment messages created during the day are safely stored in the Payment Message queue until then.

The use of message queues to transfer information between platforms is very common, mainly because the sending platform can *fire and forget* the message without the receiving platform having to be available at the same time or working at the same rate, or the sending platform even knowing what receiving platform will process the message. So, for the user in our example, their payment appears to have been sent instantaneously. Of course, because it is only processed at the end of the day, the payee can only receive the payment on the next day at the earliest (or after whatever period the payment scheme dictates).

This is an example of what is called *loose coupling*. Conversely, remote procedure calls (see Section 3.12) represent a form of *tight coupling*, as both the sender and receiver have to be running and the sender has to wait for the receiver to respond.

Message brokers normally offer some other useful benefits:

- More than one program can be servicing each queue, i.e. removing messages from the queue and processing them. Normally, when a message is removed by one program, it is deleted from the queue and no other programs will receive it. This provides an opportunity to scale up the number of receivers to increase the throughput.
- It's possible for more than one receiving program to get each message, using what is termed publish and subscribe (colloquially pub/sub). The sending program publishes a message to the queue (i.e. puts the message into the queue as normal). Various other programs subscribe to the queue and can read a copy of message from it. The message broker ensures that every program that subscribes to the queue gets a

FIGURE 7.4 Creating a payment using Internet banking.

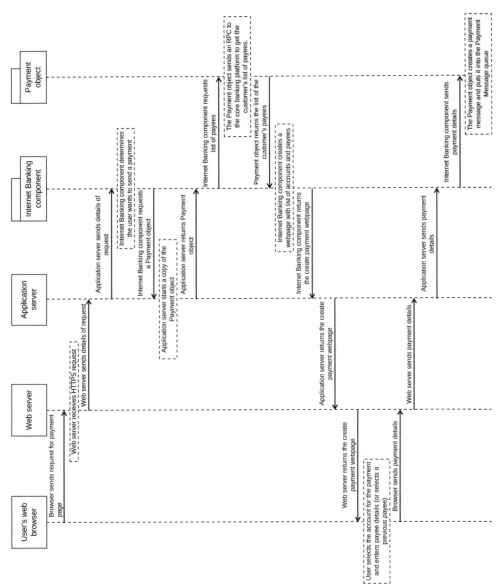

FIGURE 7.5   Outbound payment message flow.

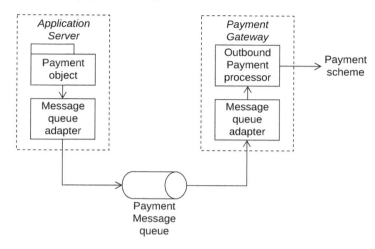

copy of the message. For example, we could get a logging program to read each payment message and save it to a file or datastore, as well as ensuring that each payment message is processed by the Outbound Payment processor. The converse to publish and subscribe – one program reading from several message queues – is of course also possible. Note also that more than one program can publish to the same queue, so publish and subscribe allows many-to-many communication.

- Message brokers often allow the action of putting a message into a queue to take part in a database transaction. So, a program can delete a record from a database managed by an RDBMS and put the information from that record into a message it places into a message queue in a single transaction. In other words, either the record is deleted from the database and the message is sent or, if an error occurs, the record is not deleted and the message isn't sent. Similarly, removing a message from a queue can be part of a database transaction – either the message is removed and information from it written to a database, or the message remains in the queue and nothing is written to the database. This helps ensure that programs do not lose information when sending or receiving using message queues.

Note that the guarantee that a message will be received can only really be implemented as a guarantee that the message will be delivered at least once. It could be delivered more than once, for example if there is a failure of the network or the message queueing software. This is an important consideration for the designers and programmers of platforms that use message queues. There are two ways of dealing with this typically. It may be that it doesn't matter if the same message is processed twice. For example, if the server program just overwrites an existing row in a database with the same data, this could be fine. This is an example of what is termed an *idempotent* operation (the same result happens from applying the operation more than once). Another way to guarantee a message is received is for the sender to include a unique identifier with each message so that the receiver can check if it has received the message before and ignore messages with identifiers that it has already processed. This consideration is, of course, very important for payment messages – we wouldn't want a payment to be sent twice due to a system or network error.

Traditional message brokers include IBM's WebSphereMQ (widely used in banks in our experience) and Teknekron's Information Bus (with a heritage in communicating information used in financial trading and now owned by Reuters) and there are a range of newer open-source message brokers such as Apache's ActiveMQ and Kafka, and Pivotal's RabbitMQ. Messaging is still very much in use in mainstream software and system development.

7.9.2   Processing Interbank Payments

In this section we cover technology relating to interbank payments. This does not include card payments, which typically use their own platforms, messages and networks, as covered in Chapter 6. As we discussed earlier in this chapter, a customer can make a payment to an account at a different bank in a variety of ways – via a low-value domestic payment scheme or via a high-value domestic payment scheme which differ in terms of their service levels such as time taken for a payment to clear and which may have different fees, and also via an international payment service via SWIFT (for example). Of course, the bank also has to process payments from other banks through the same schemes into its customers' accounts. Historically, the core banking platform would have managed all payments, and at a time when payments were processed during end-of-day processing in batches and customers could only initiate payments during banking hours, this was perfectly viable. However, in a world where customers can initiate payments 24 hours a day, payment schemes offer near-real-time payments and banks run multiple core banking platforms, many banks have separated the payment processing functionality onto dedicated platforms or even outsourced payment processing completely.

There are several benefits of doing so. Changes to payment processing (e.g. due to changes to scheme rules) can be made on just one platform rather than on all core banking platforms. The bank can also quickly get a total view of inbound and outbound payments in order to manage its liquidity more easily. The role of the core banking platform in processing a payment is limited to reducing the available balance of an account when an outbound payment is made or to increasing the balance when an inbound payment is received, thereby limiting the demands on the platform.

We illustrate the process of sending a payment to an external account in Figure 7.6, with a payment scheme that supports immediate credit transfers. It's worth noting how the account from which the payment is made is debited. In this example, the available balance is reduced before the credit transfer message is sent to the payment scheme, and if the payment is successful, the account is then debited. It would, of course, be possible to debit the account first of all and then, if the payment was unsuccessful, re-credit the account. The format of the credit transfer message sent from the payment platform to the payment scheme is dictated by the scheme, and, if the scheme is up to date, would be in a format that adheres with ISO 20022. Finally, there may be some time between the credit transfer message being received by the scheme and the scheme confirming the payment was accepted. This is because there may be a delay in the beneficiary bank processing inbound payments (e.g. because it is doing maintenance on its platforms).

This process is for a single immediate outbound payment. If a payment scheme operates for less than 24 hours a day or only on business days, outside these times the payment platform can store up outbound payments until the scheme is operating again. Many older payment schemes operate on a batch basis only, in which they expect to receive

FIGURE 7.6 Process of making a payment to an external bank account.

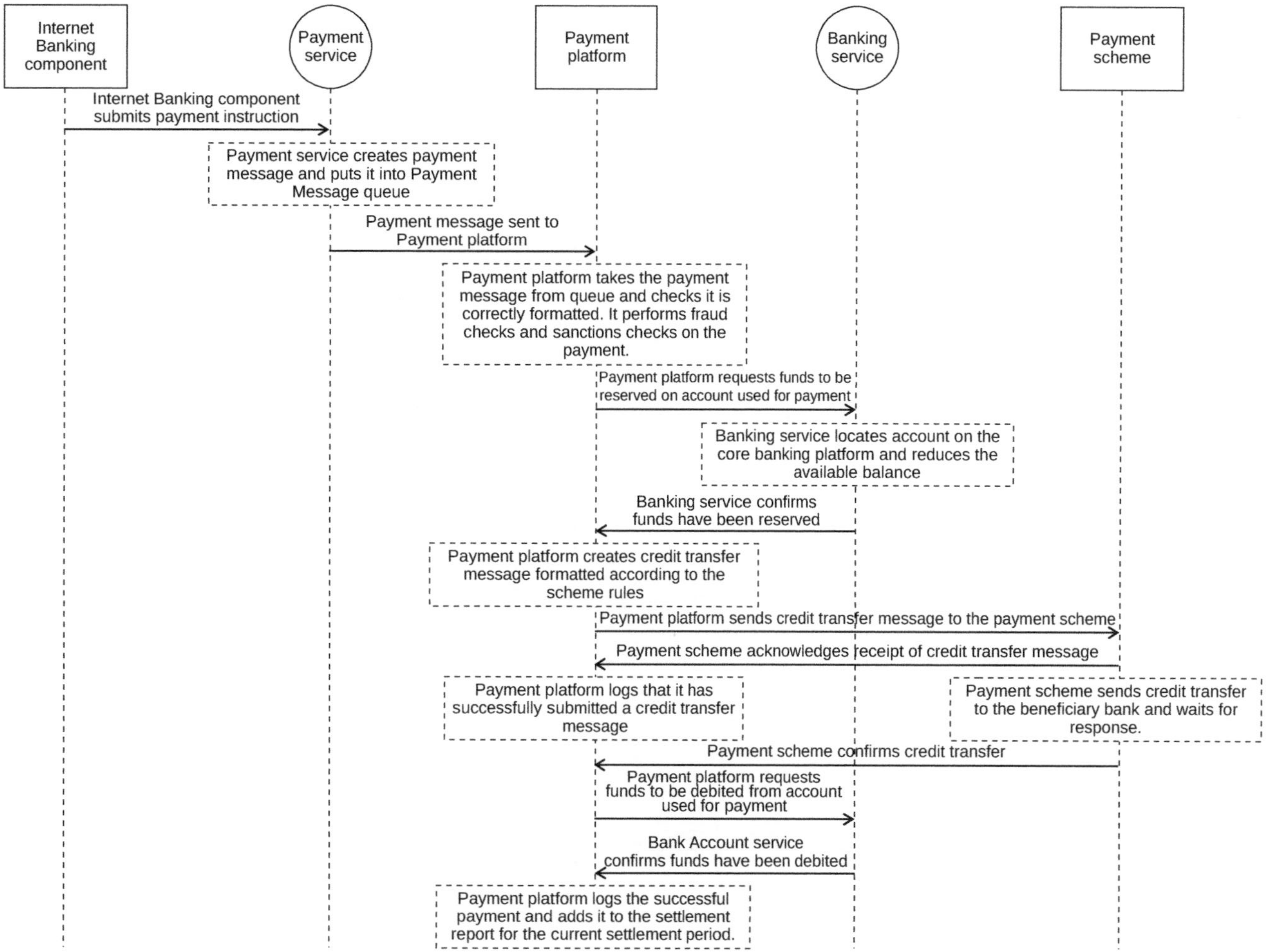

one file per day of outbound payments from a participating bank. For such a scheme, the payment platform can store up payment messages it receives during the day and send them as a single batch to the payment scheme at the appropriate time. In other words, the payment platform can provide a 24-hour service to internal platforms in the bank, even when the payment schemes to which it interfaces do not. If nothing else, this can make configuring and developing platforms that need to initiate payments much easier.

Payment platforms will typically accept batch payment files (i.e. files containing multiple payment instructions). For example, the bank's HR platform may generate a payroll file every two weeks or every month and a daily accounts payable file that contains payment instructions. The payment platform can separate such files into single payments and send them to the payment scheme as single immediate outbound payments, or, if the payment scheme accepts batch files, it can convert the files to the payment scheme file format and send them.

The payment platform can also be used to provide a payments service to business customers, enabling them to submit batch payment files (e.g. payroll and accounts payable).

In Figure 7.6 we set out the first steps that the payment platform carries out to process an outbound payment. The first step is to perform fraud and sanctions checks, which often use other platforms that the payment platform will call, although sophisticated payment platforms may have fraud and sanction checking functionality built in. Fraud checks could include alerting a customer to an outbound payment and seeking confirmation (e.g. by replying to an SMS text message). The ability to perform sanctions checks is particularly important with SWIFT messages given they are often used for international payments. See Sections 7.7 and 5.6 for more information.

The payment platform also handles inbound payment messages received from the payment schemes to which the bank belongs. The processing of an immediate inbound payment is shown in Figure 7.7. This is much simpler than an outbound payment.

Note that the payment platform could also receive credits to the credit card accounts held on the bank's credit card platform (representing the monthly payments from cardholders to their accounts), so it must have rules to decide which platform maintains the account it must credit.

Another function of the payment platform is reconciling settlement reports from the payment schemes with its own logs of payments.

It's a fairly standard service to offer customers the ability to make future-dated payments and periodic payments (called *standing orders* in the UK). Typically, this service would be offered by the core banking platform as each such instruction is associated with a specific account and the core banking platform can initiate such payments during its end-of-day (or start-of-day) processing. However, this need not be the case and they could be maintained on the customer platform, for example, in which case there would have to be a process to delete such instructions if the bank account from which they were to be made was closed.

7.9.3   The Technology Underlying Payment Platforms

A payment platform is fundamentally a platform that processes messages, including transforming messages between different formats. It also integrates with other platforms – for example, to receive payment instructions (from internal and external platforms), to check and reduce available balances on core banking platforms, to

FIGURE 7.7   Processing an inbound direct credit.

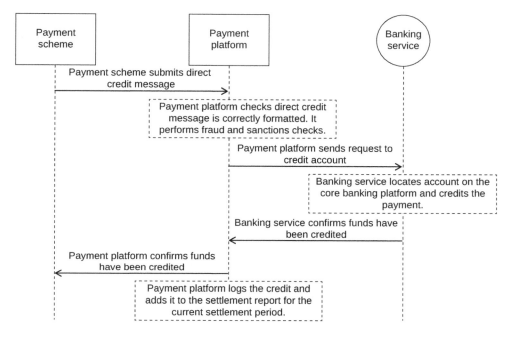

screen payment instructions for sanctioned entities and to assign a fraud risk score to a payment instruction. In effect, a payment platform has to have a lot of the functionality of an enterprise service bus (see Section 3.17), and, indeed, could be built using an enterprise service bus. In fact, IBM's Financial Transaction Manager is exactly that – a set of process flows running on IBM App Connect Enterprise (an enterprise service bus, formerly called IBM Integration Bus and, prior to that, WebSphere Message Broker, with a heritage from various other products) using IBM WebSphereMQ (a messaging technology) to exchange messages with other platforms, an IBM Db2 RDBMS to store information on payment instructions and process flows, and IBM WebSphere Application Server that houses applications to monitor and administer the platform. There are also other third-party payment platforms including ACI Worldwide's UP Real-Time Payments, Finastra's Fusion Global PAYplus, FIS Enterprise Payments, Fiserv's Dovetail Payments Platform and Temenos Payments.

For a greenfield bank, a fully-fledged payments platform would probably initially be overkill, and for one such bank we implemented a simple payment routing platform using IBM WebSphere MQ, routing payment messages between a core banking platform, a credit card platform and the finance platform and a clearing bank that provided the connectivity to the payment schemes. This approach was fast and low risk to implement, which were important factors in helping the bank launch quickly. We note that about five years after running with this simple solution and with several million customer accounts the bank decided to select and implement a more sophisticated third-party payments platform. With another start-up bank we decided to use a third-party outsourced payment gateway to connect to a clearing bank. At the other end of the spectrum, a large international bank we worked with had built its own international payments platform in COBOL, running on an IBM mainframe, at some point in the 1980s, and has maintained it ever since, updating it as payment scheme messages change and for new payment schemes. Another large international bank we worked with was rolling out its transaction banking offering to tens of countries around the world, using a centralised third-party payments platform and a third-party core banking platform.

7.10   References

1. Finance, U.K. (2019). UK Payment Markets Summary: 2019. https://www.ukfinance.org.uk/sites/default/files/uploads/pdf/UK-Finance-UK-Payment-Markets-Report-2019-SUMMARY.pdf (accessed 12 July 2020).
2. Peachey, K. (2015). RBS payment failure could last days. *BBC News* (17 June). https://www.bbc.co.uk/news/business-33162855 (accessed 12 July 2020).
3. AAP (2015). CBA tech fail leaves customers fuming. *The Australian* (11 September). https://www.theaustralian.com.au/business/latest/cba-tech-fail-leaves-customers-fuming/news-story/1f09a06d8fd1066bcf25afa737dc1dd5 (accessed 26 July 2020).
4. Robinson-Wall, N. (2019). We had problems with bank transfers on 30th May. Here's what happened and how we're fixing it for the future. Monzo (20 June). https://monzo.com/blog/2019/06/20/why-bank-transfers-failed-on-30th-may-2019 (accessed 12 July 2020).
5. Vilar, H. (2018). Starling faces payment and app issues, again. *Fintech Futures* (26 July). https://www.fintechfutures.com/2018/07/starling-faces-payment-and-app-issues-again/ (accessed 12 July 2020).
6. LearnVest (2015). Bartering in the modern day: How people are swapping skills and services ... for free. *Forbes* (20 July). https://www.forbes.com/sites/learnvest/2015/07/20/bartering-in-the-modern-day-how-people-are-swapping-skills-and-services-for-free/ (accessed 12 July 2020).
7. European Central Bank (2015). What is money? https://www.ecb.europa.eu/explainers/tell-me-more/html/what_is_money.en.html (accessed 26 July 2020).
8. European Central Bank. Issuance and circulation of euro banknotes. https://www.ecb.europa.eu/euro/intro/issuance/html/index.en.html (accessed 27 July 2020).
9. Bank of England. Scottish and Northern Ireland banknotes. https://www.bankofengland.co.uk/banknotes/scottish-and-northern-ireland-banknotes (accessed 27 July 2020).
10. U.S. Currency Education Program. The history of American currency. https://www.uscurrency.gov/history (accessed 27 July 2020).
11. Bank of England. What is legal tender? https://www.bankofengland.co.uk/knowledgebank/what-is-legal-tender (accessed 12 July 2020).
12. Committee of Scottish Bankers. Legal position. https://www.scotbanks.org.uk/banknotes/legal-position.html (accessed 26 July 2020).
13. Royal Mint. Legal tender guidelines. https://www.royalmint.com/aboutus/policies-and-guidelines/legal-tender-guidelines (accessed 26 July 2020).
14. Parliament of Canada (1999). Bill C-41. https://www.parl.ca/DocumentViewer/en/36-1/bill/C-41/royal-assent/page-16 (accessed 12 July 2020).
15. UK Finance. UK Payment Markets Summary 2019.
16. European Central Bank (2020). Banknotes and coins in circulation. https://www.ecb.europa.eu/stats/policy_and_exchange_rates/banknotes+coins/circulation/html/index.en.html (accessed 12 July 2020).

17. Bank of England (2020). Banknote statistics. https://www.bankofengland.co.uk/statistics/banknote (accessed 26 July 2020).

18. Board of Governors of the Federal Reserve System (2020). Currency and coin services. https://www.federalreserve.gov/paymentsystems/coin_data.htm (accessed 26 July 2020).

19. Capgemini. World payments report 2019. https://worldpaymentsreport.com/resources/world-payments-report-2019/ (accessed 29 July 2020).

20. Fiserv. Teller cash recycler. https://www.fiserv.com/en/about-fiserv/resource-center/brochures/teller-cash-recycler.html (accessed 12 July 2020).

21. Edmonds, T. (2014). The demise of the cheque. House of Commons Library Standard Note SN/BT/5318 (9 December). https://researchbriefings.files.parliament.uk/documents/SN05318/SN05318.pdf (accessed 13 July 2020)

22. Tellez, E. (2017). The ongoing decline of the cheque system. *Reserve Bank of Australia Bulletin* (June Quarter): 57–65. https://www.rba.gov.au/publications/bulletin/2017/jun/7.html (accessed 29 July 2020).

23. The Local (2016). Denmark officially kills the cheque (29 December). https://www.thelocal.dk/20161229/denmark-officially-kills-the-cheque (accessed 29 July 2020).

24. Reserve Bank of Australia (2020). Payments data C5.1: Cheques – Original series. https://www.rba.gov.au/payments-and-infrastructure/resources/payments-data.html (accessed 28 July 2020).

25. Reserve Bank of India (2012). *RBI Monthly Bulletin* (November). https://www.rbi.org.in/scripts/BS_ViewBulletin.aspx?Id=13764 (accessed 28 July 2020).

26. National Payments Corporation of India (2020). Retail payments statistics on NPCI platforms. https://www.npci.org.in/sites/default/files/RETAIL-PAYMENTS-STATISTICS-Jun-2020_0.xlsx (accessed 28 July 2020).

27. Cheque and Credit Clearing Company. Post 1985 – Cheques and C&CCC. https://www.chequeandcredit.co.uk/information-hub/history-cheque/post-1985-cheques-and-cccc (accessed 28 July 2020).

28. Pay.UK (2020). Annual summary of payment statistics 2019. https://www.chequeandcredit.co.uk/sites/default/files/annual_summary_of_payment_statistics_2019.pdf (accessed 13 July 2020).

29. Gerdes, G.R. and Walton, J.K. (2002). The use of checks and other noncash payment instruments in the United States. *Federal Reserve Bulletin* 2002: 360–374. https://www.federalreserve.gov/pubs/bulletin/2002/0802_2nd.pdf (accessed 28 July 2020).

30. Board of Governors of the Federal Reserve System (2019). The 2019 Federal Reserve payments study. https://www.federalreserve.gov/paymentsystems/2019-December-The-Federal-Reserve-Payments-Study.htm (accessed 28 July 2020).

31. Cheque and Credit Clearing Company. Types of cheque fraud. https://www.chequeandcredit.co.uk/information-hub/cheque-fraud-advice/types-cheque-fraud (accessed 13 July 2020).

32. Cheque and Credit Clearing Company. How to become an Accredited Cheque Printer. https://www.chequeandcredit.co.uk/suppliers/accredited-cheque-printers/how-become-accredited-cheque-printer (accessed 13 July 2020).

33. Dent, A. and Dison, W. (2012). The Bank of England's Real-Time Gross Settlement infrastructure. *Quarterly Bulletin* 2012 Q3: 234–243. London, UK: Bank of England. https://www.bankofengland.co.uk/-/media/boe/files/quarterly-bulletin/2012/the-boes-real-time-gross-settlement-infrastructure.pdf (accessed 30 July 2020).

34. Pay.UK. Access to payment systems – Bacs. https://www.accesstopaymentsystems.co.uk/what-payment-scheme/bacs-payment-schemes-ltd (accessed 12 July 2020).

35. Crowell, R. (2019). The Bank's golden evolution – A question & answer session with Victoria Cleland, Bank of England. *Alchemist* 95: 4–7. http://www.lbma.org.uk/assets/Alchemist/Alchemist_95/Alch95Complete.pdf (accessed 27 July 2020).

36. ISO 8583:2003 (2003). *Financial transaction card originated messages – Interchange message specifications*. Geneva, Switzerland: International Organization for Standardization.

37. ISO 9362:2014 (2014). *Banking — Banking telecommunication messages – Business identifier code (BIC)*. Geneva, Switzerland: International Organization for Standardization.

38. SWIFTRef (2017). BIC Plus & BIC directory 2018: SWIFTRef's solution to the revised ISO BIC Standard. https://www.swift.com/sites/default/files/documents/swift_swiftref_factsheet_bicplus.pdf (accessed 27 July 2020).

39. TransferWise (2019). What is SWIFT BIC? *The Telegraph* (12 February). https://www.telegraph.co.uk/money/transferwise/what-is-swift-bic/ (accessed 27 July 2020).

40. Vocalink. Modulus checking. https://www.vocalink.com/tools/modulus-checking/ (accessed 12 July 2020).

41. ISO 13616:2007 (2007). *Financial services – International bank account number (IBAN)*. Geneva, Switzerland: International Organization for Standardization.

42. Faster Payments. About us. https://www.fasterpayments.org.uk/about-us (accessed 12 July 2020).

43. Pay.UK. Confirmation of payee. https://www.wearepay.uk/confirmation-of-payee/ (accessed 12 July 2020).

44. European Payments Council (2020). EPC list of countries in the SEPA Schemes geographical scope. https://www.europeanpaymentscouncil.eu/sites/default/files/kb/file/2020-06/EPC409-09%20EPC%20List%20of%20SEPA%20Scheme%20Countries%20v2.6%20-%20January%202020.pdf (accessed 12 July 2020).

45. CNBC (2017). American Express, Santander team up with Ripple for cross-border payments via blockchain. https://www.cnbc.com/2017/11/16/american-express-santander-team-up-with-ripple-on-blockchain-platform.html (accessed 12 July 2020).

CHAPTER 8

Regulation, Finance and Compliance

8.1   Introduction

In Chapter 1 we introduced our banking model in which finance, regulatory reporting and compliance are all within the corporate functions tier. Within this chapter we do not provide a comprehensive review of all functions in the corporate functions tier but, instead, focus on covering those functions that we regard as most complex, interesting and requiring most analysis.

We start this chapter with a discussion of regulation, as this area has so much influence over the activities of any banking business and particularly within the two major functions that we cover in the rest of this chapter – finance, which typically takes much of the responsibility for risk modelling and regulatory reporting, and compliance, which must ensure that the bank is compliant with regulation (among other things such as law and industry standards). The chapter concludes with a brief summary of some of the other corporate functions.

8.2   Regulation

Regulation and regulatory change are a constant within any banking business. As we discussed in Chapter 2, there has not been a period in recent history where regulatory change has been absent from the industry. Even where deregulation has occurred, the reality is that regulation has been passed in order to make this happen.

The level of controls enforced by regulation in financial services is much debated and, depending upon the prevailing climate, varies considerably from country to country and time to time. Both the US and the UK went through periods of deregulation in the 1980s and 1990s, opening up opportunities for bigger banks to extend their businesses into new markets, products and services. This deregulation has since been blamed for many of the issues that led to the banking crisis of 2008.[1] Higher levels of regulation, while tending to provide more protections for the security of retail customers' finances and arguably also supporting the longer-term health of the economy, increase the cost of a banking business's operations and change budgets, and therefore also impact the banking industry's ability to deliver shareholder returns.

Since the 2008 banking crisis, regulation in the UK has tended towards enforcing more controls, with examples being the Client Assets Sourcebook (CASS),[2] the Mortgage

Market Review (MMR)[3] and retail bank ringfencing[4] (see Section 2.9) but, as we will see later in this section, there has also been regulatory focus on encouraging more competition.

Arguably neither scenario in its extreme, either heavy or light regulation, is helpful to the industry, but it would appear that we are destined to see the regulatory gauge swing from one side of centre to the other for some time to come, probably indefinitely.

The banking crisis also brought with it a focus on how banks behaved, not just what they did, or did not, do. In the UK the fixing of LIBOR (London Inter-Bank Offer Rate) and payment protection insurance scandals rocked the industry and the behaviours of bankers the world over came into question.[5] In 2019, the Royal Commission in Australia[6] returned the result of its review of the Australian banking system, describing an industry that would appear, to the interested observer, to be rotten to the core. One can only anticipate that this must result in a swing towards higher levels of regulation in that country, an industry that was previously often cited as a leading light in the world of retail banking, particularly in respect to its aggressive adoption of digital technology.

So, finding the right balance in regulation is an ongoing struggle for governments and regulators. While banking businesses should, rightly, be subject to regulatory oversight, too much of it risks stifling innovation while too little risks consumer welfare and, possibly, even their savings and the health of the economy at large.

Since the end of the first decade of the twenty-first century the pendulum has swung towards higher levels of regulation, but this does not mean that all new regulation has been to the detriment of the industry. Certainly, we were previously at a point where one could argue that the industry was out of control and, morally and ethically, established banks were found wanting. But the position of the regulators and the thrust of their new regulation appears to be producing some promising results.

In the UK, the response to the 2008 banking crisis saw a number of significant changes within the regulatory regime. The UK government and regulators determined that one way to reduce the long-term risk (beyond some of the more focused risk reduction strategies) was to diversify the industry by diluting the hegemony of the established banks and encouraging innovation. This resulted in a number of changes that spoke volumes about their intent.

One of the first major steps announced was the break-up of the Financial Services Authority (FSA) (see Section 2.4.1). The FSA was split into two entities: the Prudential Regulation Authority and the Financial Conduct Authority. The FCA has since gone on to engage with a host of financial services innovators, in particular through the regulatory sandbox it created in 2016.[7]

Following the split of the FSA came the creation of a new bank licencing process, driven by the UK government's focus on establishing more competition in banking. As odd as it may sound, the UK did not have a well-defined process for the licencing of new banks prior to this point. As a first-hand participant in the build of Metro Bank in 2009 and 2010, one of us can attest to the lack of clarity that the team at Metro Bank had to work through as it sought to achieve a banking licence in the immediate aftermath of the banking crisis.

The replacement of the LIBOR calculation process was also a key change as it marked a further move away from the established banks' control over the banking markets (see Section 2.4.1 for more information on the cartel activities of UK clearing banks). Although the banking crisis of 2008 is testament in itself to the terrible miscalculation of risk (arguably brought about by an institutional lack of understanding of products that the industry had itself created), one could argue that an even more damning outcome was the realisation that the setting of one of the most important financial interest rates in the world at the time, LIBOR, had been manipulated by a number of banks in order to favour their financial positions. The UK reacted to this by setting out to replace both the process and the provider through the Hogg committee, run by Baroness Hogg.[8] The goal of this process was to create a robust and reliable interest rate calculation mechanism that could not be manipulated by the banks.

The changes wrought in the UK system were some of the most fundamental changes to UK banking in over a century and have arguably brought about a renaissance in UK banking that has already impacted the established players through the creation of new competition and innovation in the sector. In their own right, these changes were substantial, but they have been made even more potent by changes brought about by the EU as well. EU legislators, often much maligned for their bureaucracy, have laid the seeds for change in banking and have, as a result, magnified the impact of the changes brought about in the UK. Two key pieces of legislation have the potential to bring about profound change in banking (and beyond).

8.2.1 PSD2

The Payment Services Directive (Part 2) (PSD2)[9] came into force on 12 January 2016 with the rules applying from 13 January 2018. Banks and other financial institutions had until September 2019 to implement the requirements, which we cover later in this section. In reality, the industry signalled that it would fail to meet the implementation deadline, and so the European Banking Authority and national banking regulators extended it twice, by a total of two years. It should be noted that PSD2 does not apply equally across all areas of banking but is focused on accounts that provide payments functionality, primarily current accounts and payment cards, although some other account types fall under PSD2 when they provide payment services. Most savings and lending products are therefore excluded from this definition if they do not support more general payments functionality. Like many forms of legislation there are broad-ranging implications of PSD2, but from our perspective there are three primary outcomes that any retail banking business should be aware of:

1. **Data sharing:** Under PSD2, banks must share customer data relating to payment accounts if the customer wishes to have this data shared. In the first instance the most obvious use of these new access rights is to provide customers with money management toolsets that draw data from multiple banks and provide the ability to categorise a customer's incomings and outgoings, but also to support budgeting and savings planning. This functionality is even referred to as account aggregation, clearly indicating the original intent, and a provider of such services is defined as an Account Information Service Provider (AISP). However, we believe that there is far more potential to this than there might appear on first consideration, a point that we return to later (see Chapter 10).
2. **Payment initiation services:** This functionality allows a Payment Initiation Service Provider (PISP) to create payments on behalf of a customer and that are carried out over the payment networks. While, on the face of it, this may appear to

be relatively basic functionality, it may have significant impacts for the banking industry, particularly payment cards businesses. One of the great benefits it provides for PISP businesses is that there is zero cost for these payments, as the banks themselves pick up the costs of payments using domestic payment networks. This can mean significantly lower costs than are associated with payment cards, which typically include a transaction fee that is payable by the merchant. Again, this feature of PSD2 offers a number of opportunities that we discuss in Chapter 10.

3. Strong Customer Authentication: One other key element of PSD2 is implementation of Strong Customer Authentication (SCA), which introduces additional security measures to counter payment fraud and covers both interbank and card payments. The significance of this change is yet to be fully understood, but in our opinion the additional friction that SCA introduces into the payments process may actually help the payments industry open up to alternative payments solutions, as it may mean that card payments are no more efficient than other forms of payment.

8.2.2   General Data Protection Regulation

The European Union's General Data Protection Regulation (GDPR)[10] came into force on 24 May 2016 and its requirements had to be implemented by 25 May 2018. Despite a great deal of publicity, it is a much-misunderstood piece of legislation. Most businesses still regard GDPR as a piece of data protection legislation (which it is, in name) but it has the potential to have much wider impacts. Much has been made of being GDPR compliant and the cost of not being so (for example, the UK's Information Commissioner's Office issued a notice that it intended to fine British Airways almost £200 million for a data breach that occurred shortly after GDPR came into force).[11] However, the core of GDPR is not just about data protection but is also focused on giving the consumer more control over who has access to their data, for what purposes and for how long.

While many businesses regard addressing GDPR as a test of compliance (essentially ensuring that customer data is well managed and secure, as well as providing consumers with a means of asking for their data to be erased), not much has been made of the consumers' right to share their data with other organisations, the so-called right to data portability. This ability to request that your data be shared with a third party is very similar to the provisions laid down for the banking community under PSD2 and could have the potential to significantly change the way that we, consumers, manage and share our data.

8.2.3   Open Banking and Open Data

So, why all the focus on a few pieces of European law? Well, the UK and European regulators are not alone in introducing legislation and regulation to open the banking industry up to more competition. In our view, this broader adoption of data-sharing principles should only be regarded as a good thing. As demonstrated in earlier chapters, history has been on the side of the big banks. Over the course of the past 200 or so years, we have seen a shift towards the hegemony of a small number of powerful brands in each major first-world market. This has led to where the established banks regard their position as invincible and have come to take their customers for granted. To support consumer interests, encourage innovation and develop better consumer outcomes, competition is vital to this industry. Regulation should never be a barrier to competition or innovation but should act as a safety net to discourage inappropriate behaviours and ensure a fair playing field. In our minds, the changes that have been brought about in the past decade certainly seem to be moving our industry in the right direction.

The innovation of open banking is no longer limited to Europe. It was clear from the outset that such changes have the potential to significantly change the financial world, and both regulators and industry participants across the globe have been quick to adopt similar principles. In Japan, Singapore, India[12] and South Korea[13] regulators have taken a softer approach on open banking, facilitating rather than forcing, yet businesses have started to adopt it anyway. For example, MAS, the state regulator of Singapore, has worked with the Association of Banks to create an API Playbook.[14]

Elsewhere, state regulators have actively started to push open banking. In Hong Kong, for example, the Hong Kong Monetary Authority (HKMA)[15] published an open banking framework in mid-2018 and in Australia the Consumer Data Right[16] was announced in 2017. Interestingly the Consumer Data Right has a greater scope than just financial services and, in our minds, has the potential to create similar opportunities to those of GDPR in Europe.

Of course, the activities of individual regulators can only really impact upon the area over which that regulator has jurisdiction, be that across the EU, in nation states such as the UK, Singapore or Australia or even at the individual state level such as in the US, but where regulators work together there is opportunity for change on a much more global level. Fortunately, we live in an era in which our regulators are enlightened and have recognised such an opportunity. Commencing in 2015, regulators began to experiment with the creation of regulatory bridges. The first such instance in the modern era was signed into existence by the UK and Singapore, arguably two of the most progressive regulatory regimes, in May 2016.[17] This bridge enabled UK and Singapore regulators to refer fintech organisations to each other and share data about them in order to speed up their regulation in each other's jurisdiction. Other regulators were quick to recognise the benefit of such bridges, and there are now dozens in existence.

However, simply opening up the industry to enable competition is not yet proving to be any kind of panacea. For example, while the introduction of new banks into the industry has certainly shaken up the established banks and forced them to start innovating (and start treating their customers like real people), it hasn't fundamentally changed the behaviours of those people that really matter, our customers. For example, UK customers are still not changing their current account provider in any great numbers.

The current account is most commonly regarded as the most valuable product that a bank can sell to its customers. This is not due to their profitability – though, contrary to popular opinion, even so-called free UK current accounts are profitable – but because they are regarded as a relationship account. If a customer holds their primary current account (that which their salary is paid into and the majority of their bills are paid from) with a given bank, then that bank would typically expect to be able to leverage the relationship in an effort to sell more products to that customer. Historically, there was some evidence to suggest that this was the case, and many consumers who have a current account with a bank have a greater propensity than non-current account holders to have at least one other product with that bank, often a credit card. However, in recent years the rise of the Internet has reduced this stickiness. After all, why would I take a loan from my current account provider if a cursory search of the Internet can serve up many other loan products at a lower rate? However, the current account still maintains its position as most valued product for many banks.

From an observer's perspective the UK is uniquely positioned to support the development of our understanding of customer behaviours when it comes to their current accounts. The launch of Metro Bank in 2010, followed by the launch of two new digital banks, Monzo and Starling, that have all placed the current account at the core of the customer engagement model, means that we have no shortage of alternative new banks for consumers to choose from. We also have a government-initiated bank switching service (the Current Account Switching Service, or CASS) that was established to support consumers in switching their current accounts. The Bacs scheme (that runs CASS) publishes data on a quarterly basis detailing, for most UK banks, the number of customers who have either switched to or from each bank.[18] Most mainstream UK banks participate in CASS and allow their data to be shared (the exceptions being Metro Bank and Handelsbanken). While CASS data is not comprehensive (switching probably represents only one in every four new primary UK current accounts each year), it does, at least, provide some directional guidance to the interested observer.

As we were going to print, the latest data for the UK had been published on 30 July 2020 and covered the second quarter of 2020. The data could be the subject of an essay in its own right, but the data tells us that most UK switchers, when they do move accounts, are moving from one long-established high street bank to another, with HSBC and Nationwide being the two biggest net gainers of current accounts. However, neobanks are taking some market share, Monzo and Starling both being featured in the top five net gainers of current accounts.

However, the key statistic is that, over the period from 1 July 2019 to 30 June 2020, there were 868,000 switches of primary current account in the UK. This represents less than 2% of UK adults.

Of course, the UK public is not necessarily indicative of populations elsewhere, but the data doesn't exactly present a rosy picture for prospective new entrants around the world. The UK is not alone in indicating that new entrant banks are going to have to work very hard to gain traction in the market. Moven, established by the renowned banking tech author Brett King, failed to gain much traction in the current account market in the US and eventually failed altogether as a bank.[19] It would appear that consumers were looking for more than just a new brand in the market.

While the focus in this section has been mostly on Europe and, more specifically, the UK, regulation is a global phenomenon and globalisation means that many of the concepts developed in one jurisdiction often get exported to others. After the 2008 banking crisis the UK led many of the reforms to encourage innovation (modifications to new banking processes, innovation initiatives by regulators, regulatory sandbox and regulatory bridges, to name a few), but it wasn't long before other regulators copied and then leapt ahead of the UK. Singapore, for example, has shown global leadership in its embracing of fintech over the past decade.

However, innovation has not been the only area of regulatory change. In the US, the Dodd–Frank Act[20] was established in the aftermath of the banking crisis by President Obama (and then partially repealed by President Trump). The act was broad and far reaching for US regulated entities and included comprehensive regulation of financial markets, consumer protection, increasing standards and cooperation, rationalisation of the country's regulatory agencies and more.

In 2010, the US also passed the Foreign Account Tax Compliance Act (or FATCA),[21] which required banks outside of the US to search their customer records and report on any customers with US connections. This is an extraordinary act in that it requires businesses with no connection to the US to provide these reports. Most interestingly, many national governments, particularly in Europe, have agreed to cooperate with it.

So, not only is local regulation a consideration for any banking business, but in some cases it must now comply with regulation enacted elsewhere!

8.2.4 Consequences of Non-compliance

Failure to comply with regulation can result in severe penalties for both businesses and responsible individuals (even down to custodial sentences in some jurisdictions). If regulation has been flouted one should expect the regulator to come down particularly heavily.

Of course, any penalty meted out by the regulator might only be the start of a bank's problems. The reputational damage of being censored by one's regulator can be even more substantial for a business than the regulatory punishment.

8.3 Global Standards

National regulation, even that as far reaching as FATCA, is not the only consideration when thinking about regulatory compliance. There are two other areas of consideration that should be borne in mind. Global standards tend to be either voluntary regulatory standards or enforced by industry participants. Examples include Basel III,[22] a global, voluntary (at a national level) regulatory framework that is focused on improving understanding of stresses on the banking industry, capital adequacy and liquidity risk for banking and investment firms. Developed by the Basel Committee on Banking Supervision, Basel III has been implemented in the US and Europe. The Payment Card Industry Data Security Standard (PCI DSS),[23] a worldwide standard on data security enforced by the payment card industry, is another good example.

There are also many national organisations that are available to support banking businesses seeking to improve their own standards. One such example is the Joint Money Laundering Steering Group in the UK. This is a trade organisation that provides guidance on the implementation of robust anti-money laundering rules and processes for UK businesses. Other examples include the Australian Finance Industry Association and the Canadian Bankers Association. These sorts of organisations normally do not enforce standards but can often provide a wealth of information.

8.4 Working with (and within) Regulation

From a technology perspective there are three significant implications of regulation. First is the area of business compliance. Many areas of a modern banking business have specific regulations that they must comply with. This could range from treating customers fairly (and thereby ensuring consistent treatment), through to know your customer and anti-money laundering requirements or meeting specific capital or liquidity targets as decreed by the regulator. The specifics of a bank's regulatory requirements will depend upon the jurisdiction(s) that it operates within and the regulated activities that it carries out. It should also be noted that some regulatory requirements must also be able to be met in a wind-down scenario – for example, being able to compile a report of all of the business's customers, the products they hold and the balances of those products.

Second, in many cases the technology function itself has certain regulatory requirements that it must meet. In the UK, for example, the technology function must ensure that any outsourcing arrangements are compliant with SYSC 8.1 of the FCA regulations.[24]

Finally, wherever a business is regulated there are likely to be reporting requirements associated with the kinds of business that are carried out. Typically, this might include financial data (annual reports, liquidity and capital), confirmation of the ownership structure, transactional data and information on instances of attempted or actual fraud and other criminal activities. Often these reports need to be submitted on a regular basis and must include data covering a specific period. Regulatory reporting is most often managed by the finance function within a bank, but the technology function must ensure that the data is readily available to support this.

One final note on reporting – in our experience, while smaller businesses can often meet their regulatory requirements by compiling data in spreadsheets, larger businesses often require the implementation of specialist toolsets in order to compile their reports. While there is currently a predefined schedule for regulatory reporting in many locales, some national regulators now have a longer-term vision of achieving real-time reporting. If you are currently in the process of building (or re-building) a bank you should consider how you will meet this obligation when it arrives.

8.5   Finance Functions – Introduction

Finance and treasury sit at the heart of a modern banking business. Should you ever have the good fortune to go through a regulatory approval process for a new bank you will see that a substantial amount of the work falls to these teams. The reason for this is obvious: for a bank to be able to make a strong argument that it will be viable requires a significant amount of financial analysis.

Not only must a prospective bank prove that it can be financially viable but it will typically also have to prove that it will be suitably capitalised and that it will always have sufficient liquidity to support its day-to-day business activities, even under extreme conditions. The capital and liquidity planning, and the nature of the conditions that a prospective bank must prove it should be able to accommodate, are set out by local regulators. In Europe, as part of a bank licence application (and, in fact, on an ongoing basis for existing banks) the business must submit both an internal capital adequacy assessment process (ICAAP) document and an internal liquidity adequacy assessment process (ILAAP) document, which both typically require the development and maintenance of large financial models in order to forecast the capital and liquidity requirements of the bank over a number of years into the future. The models may draw on extensive analysis of large amounts of data from within the bank and from third-party data feeds.

Before we look further into the finance and treasury functions of a banking business, it is worth looking briefly at these two words, *capital* and *liquidity*. Capital is a measure of the financial reserves that a bank has to support the business in the event of a loss. Such a loss could be brought about by a number of possible factors, such as a non-performing loan book, regulatory fines or even a mis-selling issue (such as the payment protection insurance scandal that hit UK banks).[25] A bank's capital is made up of its own funds – typically things such as share equity and retained profits. A failure in a bank's capital management could result in insolvency. A bank's liquidity is a measure of how much cash (or assets that can quickly be converted into cash) is available to meet financial obligations that fall due, regardless of whether those obligations are customer withdrawals or just the day-to-day activities of the bank. Liquid assets are typically made up of cash, central bank reserves and government bonds. An example of a significant liquidity event would be a run on the bank, where large numbers of customers are attempting to withdraw their money at the same time. This kind of event could happen through either physical cash withdrawals or bank transfers – both are equally applicable when it comes to liquidity as even with bank transfers the originating bank must have the cash to settle.

For those interested in understanding capital and liquidity in more depth, the Bank of England has produced a very good primer.[26]

8.6 Finance

A banking finance team bears many similarities to a finance team in any other business or market. The finance team (as distinct from the treasury team) takes responsibility for the business's accounting. This includes managing the general ledger (GL), which stores the financial transactions of the business, though sometimes at a summary level. For example, it does not keep a record of every transaction that occurs in the core banking platform. The general ledger consists of a number of sub-ledger accounts that are defined in the business's chart of accounts. Updates to the GL are carried out either through automated processes (for example, data from the core banking platform) or through manual processes known as journal entries. Much of the finance team's responsibilities revolve around ensuring that the GL is up to date and is an accurate reflection of the bank's current financial position.

8.6.1   Accounts Payable and Accounts Receivable

Accounts payable (AP), which includes payroll, although the latter is often done separately, and accounts receivable (AR) cover managing payments to suppliers (and to staff, in the case of payroll) and billing of third parties, respectively. In many cases the bank's income is mostly automated in a modern banking environment as it is carried out through the application of interest, fees and charges using the core banking or other platforms. However, the finance team will still track the bank's position in the GL to ensure that the business is making money and all fees and charges are being paid.

8.6.2   Book-keeping

While a modern GL is capable of receiving automated updates from a vast array of other systems, there are times where the finance team will have to apply manual adjustments to the GL. These are typically posted to the GL in what is called a *journal*.

8.6.3 Tax

Tax is rarely straightforward and is complicated further by the variable application of tax in banking, particularly where it comes to the various activities of a bank. In the UK, for example, many banking services are value-added tax (VAT) exempt, meaning that the bank can neither charge VAT nor recover VAT on many of the goods and services that it procures. However, there are other forms of taxation that apply to UK banks, such as corporation tax, so the finance team needs to maintain a strong understanding of the tax laws and how they apply to different products and services.

8.6.4 Financial Planning and Budgeting

The finance team is responsible for carrying out a significant amount of financial planning. This is not just scenario planning, but includes ongoing oversight of the business's financial position, movements in the assets and liabilities and forecasting. This activity is often carried out in close coordination with the treasury team (see Section 8.7).

8.6.5 Financial Reporting

The bank will need to periodically report its financial position, to the financial markets (if the business is listed) and to the regulators and tax authorities in the jurisdictions in which it operates. Financial reporting is required to meet defined standards. There are a number of financial reporting standards around the world, with Financial Reporting Standards (FRS) 102[27] being a standard for smaller businesses in the UK, and International Financial Reporting Standards (IFRS)[28] being used by listed companies and international businesses. It can be a major undertaking to update finance platforms and processes to new versions of reporting standards.

8.6.6 Regulatory Reporting

The finance function is responsible for the majority of the regulatory reporting requirements imposed upon a modern banking business. We cover regulatory requirements in more detail in Section 8.2.

8.6.7 Technology and Finance

The primary tool of the finance team is the general ledger (GL). The core of the financial accounting of any business, the GL holds all of the business's accounts. A GL is built on the basis of double-entry book-keeping and so has both a credits and a debits side. Every transaction in the bank will have a debit and a corresponding credit in the GL. From experience, we can tell you that if you are trying to build this capability from scratch it takes a little while to get your head around the impact that each transaction has on the debits and credits. A GL must be able to record transactions, run period-ends (to support reporting) and apply journals which represent daily activities and adjustments. There are many capable finance packages available in the market and few good reasons to spend time building your own.

Beyond the GL, a finance team will likely also require access to a payroll system. Payroll includes undertaking a complicated set of tax and benefit calculations, the payment of salaries and taxes collected directly from salaries and the issuing of payslips and other documentation. For a small company this can often be outsourced, but larger companies may want to run their own payroll.

As the business grows, the time might come where it requires additional tools, such as tax planning and budgeting tools, for the finance team to run effectively.

8.7 Treasury

The main role of the treasury function of a banking business is ensuring that the bank's financial position is stable over both the short and long term and that any risks associated with it are appropriately managed. It may sound odd to the uninitiated, but most of what the treasury function does is manage risk. To a technologist, the concept of risk is often about managing the people, technologies, timing and costs to ensure the success of a project or the long-term viability of a technical solution, but a treasurer looks on risk as a function of the various financial positions of the bank, how they, customer demand, local and global market forces and a number of other elements interact (or might interact) and what the implications for the bank might be.

As an example of the kind of work that the treasury team will do, consider the scenario of capital planning. Before a bank can launch it must be capitalised – it must hold in reserve an amount of money, agreed with the regulator, that can be used to underpin the operations of the bank should it hit a period of adverse trading conditions. This capital requirement is calculated using a complex model normally built by the bank's treasury team (using the ICAAP in Europe – see Section 8.5) which is based upon a projection of what the bank believes are likely forecasts for its business under a number of scenarios. This model is based on a number of factors, which likely include the range of products that the bank will offer and the (interest) rates at which it will offer them, the volumes of each kind of product that the bank expects to sell, the running costs of the business, underlying interest rates (typically set by a central bank), expectations on how financial markets might move and a whole series of other considerations and risks. The problem is that this is a forecast and, as we all know, forecasts rarely turn out to be correct.

For example, let us say that once this model was completed, the capital requirements were set (and met) and the bank then launched. From the very first day of trading it is likely that there will be some deviations from the model – customer uptake for some products will be higher or lower than anticipated, central bank interest rates might move in different directions than what was expected, and this might impact the rates that the bank offers its customers, or there might be worrying news about national employment trends that hits the value of one of the key currencies that the bank uses. Any of these changes could mean that the bank is exposed to financial risk. For example, if more people make deposits into savings accounts than borrow from the bank then the bank has spare capital that isn't working for it. If the bank leaves this money in an account with the central bank (or its sponsor bank) then it will not earn enough interest on it to cover its costs and pay out the interest owed to savers. The bank must therefore find a way to use these additional funds to earn interest. This could be through lowering the interest rate it offers to borrowers to make the lending products more attractive, or maybe through buying financial instruments (bonds, for example) to achieve a slightly better return on the extra capital, or a combination of actions. Any one of these changes is not only another change to the original model, but also impacts upon the current forecast and changes the risk profile and future forecasts of the bank. So, if the bank had bought extra bonds to help address the interest shortfall and then interest rates rise, what does this mean for the bank?

The forecast for the bank must therefore be regularly updated by the treasury team, but it is still only ever a forecast. The bank's assets and liabilities will change on a daily basis and markets and governments will do the unexpected. The bank treasury team must manage a long-term view of the business, but also adjust for the daily changes that occur at and to the bank.

To ensure that there is a coherent and consistent approach to how treasury manages risks, the function will have developed a strategy. The strategy will define what the business risk appetite is, how it approaches risk management and what products and strategies it will use to manage its risk. Modelling of risk is critical to that strategy. The treasury's middle office is typically responsible for defining the strategy, creating and running the models and for monitoring compliance with the strategy.

8.7.1   Risk Management and Modelling

As part of the ICAAP, the treasury team will produce a number of risk models. These models will typically include some or all of the following, though the local regulator will likely provide guidance on what it expects:

- Credit risk: This covers the risk that borrowers default on the loans made to them by the bank, therefore reducing the income of the bank (i.e. interest payments on loans made by its customers) and its assets (i.e. the recoverable balances of the loans). In reality, it is affected by a broad range of factors including those associated with the quality of lending, macro-level factors that might impact a particular part of the market (a sudden new punitive tax on the wealthy, for example) and geographic factors (an example of which might be a global bank with a concentration of lending in one specific geography). When determining the capital implications of a bank's credit risk position, historical lending performance is a vital input to a lender's credit risk model. If a business can prove that it has a historically low default or loss rate then it has a good argument for holding less capital in reserve.
- Operational risk: This covers a broad range of risks that typically include conduct risk, IT systems–related risks and compliance or regulatory risks – in effect, the risks that the business does not operate in the way that was intended because of failures, errors and incorrect actions. It identifies and manages the risks, including potential mitigants and resolution strategies and their financial impact. Examples might include a significant IT systems failure or perhaps a failure of the business to comply with local regulation and the ensuing sanctions that a regulator might impose.
- Interest rate risk (IRR): This is the risk associated with movements in interest rates. IRR can occur at any point, but one very simplistic example might be where longer-term fixed rate assets (loans, for example) are balanced against shorter-term fixed rate liabilities (short-term savings, for example).

- Market risk: This covers movements in financial markets that could damage the financial position of the bank. For example, political instability could mean funds are withdrawn from the bank by its customers and moved to other countries or into tangible assets (such as gold).
- Liquidity risk: These are risks associated with the business managing its liquidity position (i.e. its short-term access to cash). This might occur, for example, where a business holds a lot of short-term deposits (e.g. in instant access savings accounts) and long-term loans. In this situation if the depositors choose to withdraw their money then the business may not be able to fund the withdrawals of the depositors as it has lent the money out to long-term borrowers.
- Reputational risk: This is the risk associated with the bank's reputation that result in lost revenue and an inability to encourage new customers to engage with the business. For example, the bank's reputation may be damaged if a high-profile customer is associated with criminal activity or if its systems have a highly public outage which causes inconvenience to many customers.
- Strategic or business risk: This covers the business's inability to deliver on its planned business strategy. An example of this might be the failure of the business to raise enough deposits because a pricing assumption turns out to be flawed.

The various categories often overlap or impact each other – for example, market risks which reduce the flow of deposits into a bank impact its liquidity which in turn hamper its ability to achieve its business strategy.

The majority of the risk management activity sits within the treasury function, but as you will have noted, there are some elements that utilise inputs from other areas of the business. Of particular note is the operational risk category, which is likely to require input from right across the business.

In many of the smaller businesses that we have worked in, this function has typically relied on spreadsheets to support its activities. Of course, many of the risks are not binary. For example, a risk model associated with interest rate risk must enable the user to model changes to the interest rate across a variety of different rates – What if rates rise 50 bps (basis points, 1 bp, often pronounced 'bip', is one hundredth of 1%), or if they increase by 100 bps? In such a case the model needs to demonstrate the impact on all assets and liabilities that the business maintains across a period of time. As one might imagine, a spreadsheet that attempts to model this is complex, and this complexity only increases as additional variables are added.

It doesn't take long for these spreadsheets to become unwieldy, difficult to understand and to modify (particularly if the creator of the spreadsheet has moved on and somebody else has inherited it) and error prone. The problem is that there are few good alternatives available. In our experience, while risk management software does exist, it is often very specific in terms of its focus and often not oriented towards the needs of a bank. It is worth spending the time to seek out the right risk management tools for the business.

The risk team will tell you that the quality of the outputs from risk modelling is dependent upon the skills of the team members and their ability to understand and model risk (which is why they are paid so well). While to an extent this may be true, we are now moving into a period where data is becoming significantly more important. The reasons for this are twofold. First, we have access to much more data on our customers and markets than we ever used to. This is somewhat true within our banks (though we still haven't moved on much from understanding a name, address and identity details), but the real benefit is now just as likely to come from the data we can get from external data sources – credit agencies, demographic databases and industry researchers can now provide us with enough data to support our decision-making process down to the level of an individual member of the public (though possibly not by name). If you want to know how people who worked in retail outlet middle management coped the last time there was a credit crash, someone has the data and can sell it to you, or, if you are lucky, you might even be able to access it for free.

Second, we have the tools and the skills to utilise the data. The advent of big data, AI and modern data modelling and analytics (not risk-specific, but general data modelling – see Section 3.22) has improved our ability to gather, query and model data significantly. With the right data set it is now possible to ask all sorts of 'what if' questions and really start to understand the world of risk in ways that we could never do with a spreadsheet.

We pick up on the value of data in Chapter 10 and note here that risk modelling has the potential to benefit hugely from effective use of data in the future.

8.7.2   Asset and Liability Management

The treasury front office team is typically responsible for managing the various asset and liability positions, in line with the bank's strategy. The objective is to ensure that risks to the bank's overall position are minimised (or even negated) such that the bank remains profitable regardless of the circumstances it finds itself in. Of course, this may not always be possible, but within certain limits it should be.

The front office team will monitor and maintain the bank's status across a number of areas, which we look at now.

8.7.2.1   Cash and Liquidity Management

While the name *cash management* might imply that the treasury team is actually handling cash, this isn't the case. In treasury terminology, cash management is actually the process of managing what is done with the cash (and cash-like assets) that exist within the organisation.

A bank often holds a lot of cash, whether it be physical cash or balances within its bank accounts. Some of the bank's cash must be maintained in either a physical form (in ATMs and teller lines, for example) or a highly liquid form (such as the funds in its bank account, to allow the bank to make payments to suppliers and staff, for example). However, holding too much cash can be a bad thing. Financial returns on cash are typically terrible and therefore any business holding large quantities of cash is losing money. Within the context of cash management the treasury team will seek to find the right balance between the amount of cash held and investing any remaining cash in a variety of different places. The choice of investment will depend upon when the treasury team believes it might need to be able to access that cash, so how liquid that investment needs to be.

Liquidity measures how quickly the bank is able to access cash to support its business needs and is therefore closely related to cash management. So, for example, a government bond that could be exchanged for cash within 24 hours is regarded as significantly more liquid than funds that have been lent to investors for loans. When considering what to do with surplus cash the bank must ensure that it is prepared to respond should anything adverse occur in its cash position. For example, if lots of customers suddenly decide to withdraw their money from the bank, as they did with many banks during the crisis of 2008, then the bank will need access to a lot of cash very quickly in order meet the demand (or risk consequences similar to those experienced at Northern Rock).[29]

8.7.2.2   Balance Management

The bank will likely have a number of accounts with various third parties, including reserves held in accounts with central banks and at settlement banks (if different) and probably also with a sponsor bank if it has one. The bank might also have an account with another bank if, for example, it provides correspondent banking services for the organisation (see the discussion on international payments in Section 7.6.13 for more information). Some of these accounts, perhaps all of them, will have minimum balance requirements.

All of these accounts need monitoring and the balances will need topping up, or perhaps funds might need withdrawing when the balance is higher than the minimum required so that it can be used more efficiently. Where a minimum balance is required to be maintained, this process is critical, as failure to maintain a minimum balance can result in the scheme or partner taking action against the bank.

8.7.2.3   Products and Pricing

Of course, the core of banking is about the products that the bank offers to its customers, otherwise it isn't really a bank. These can be in the form of assets (loans to customers) and liabilities (savings accounts). The treasury team needs to know what volumes of products are held at which rates, when these products mature (when the customer can either withdraw their savings or finish repaying a loan) and under what terms a customer can close their account early. This allows the team to understand how the bank's products might be expected to perform.

Depending upon what kinds of products the bank deals in, the predictability of this element will vary dramatically. For example, a bank that offers long-term fixed rate deposit accounts and lends the deposits out in the form of mortgages has more predictability than a bank book that includes current accounts and instant-access savings accounts. Products that remain on the books of a bank for long periods and have a consistent (or predictable) balance are regarded as being *sticky*, whereas more volatile products, like instant access savings accounts, are not regarded as sticky. Current accounts are somewhat stickier, as we saw in Section 8.2.3, and although the balance of any current account may vary considerably over a month, the total balance across all current accounts may be remarkably consistent or follow a predictable monthly cycle.

However, if it were as simple as offering sticky, long-term products then few banks would offer anything else. The reality is that shorter-term products, while more volatile, often offer a greater opportunity for the bank to make money. For example, most instant-access savings accounts in the UK offer near zero interest currently, so being able to attract large numbers of savers to these products means that the bank is able to lend this *free* money out to borrowers and make money, but at a risk of more instability and risk on the books.

When considering the rates, maturity period and stickiness of the products of a bank, the treasury team will attempt to find a mix of products that provides the best balance between profitability and stability. To the outsider this might sound a little odd. One might expect that product pricing is set by the bank management and reflects upon what the bank believes it can charge (or offer) on a product based upon market forces (other bank offerings, customer loyalty, etc.). However, the treasury team plays a vital role in this process through its pricing and product mix models and its influence can be substantial.

8.7.2.4   Markets and Financial Instruments

It is not always possible for a bank to manage its entire business purely by finding the right blend of products to deliver the perfect mix of return versus stability. To account for this, many modern banks make use of financial instruments with which to raise funds or make use of surplus cash, for example.

Depending upon the nature of the bank, the types of financial instruments that are used may vary. For example, a bank that has significant exposure to a particular currency (perhaps because it has a branch network in the country) might invest in currency swaps to hedge against dramatic currency variations. Banks will also make use of financial instruments in order to make temporary use of excess cash (see Section 8.7.2.1).

The range of financial instruments available to a modern bank is extremely broad but it should be expected that, at a minimum, any bank will likely want to be able to trade in some forms of bonds and derivatives. It may also, from time to time, choose to raise capital through taking on debt in the market, i.e. taking a loan from a wholesale or investment bank at a low rate and lending it to customers at a higher rate.

8.7.2.5   Capital Management

Every bank is required to hold a capital reserve. The size of this reserve may vary depending on a variety of factors (for example, the product mix that the bank holds, the proven stickiness of products and local regulatory expectations), but it must be maintained at all times. The treasury team is responsible for tracking this reserve.

8.7.2.6   Fixed Assets

The fixed assets need to be represented among the rest of the assets of the bank to provide a full representation of the total assets and liabilities. Fixed assets include items such as buildings, land, equipment and plant. Some of these assets will depreciate over time, while some, such as buildings, may appreciate.

8.7.3   *Treasury Back Office*

The treasury back office is primarily an operational function. It will independently confirm the transactions that have been made by the front office, settle those transactions and carry out any reconciliations to confirm positions with counterparties.

8.7.4   Technology and Treasury

From a technology perspective, treasury is perhaps one of the more complex functions. Creating its own technology to support the various activities carried out by the treasury function is probably not something that most businesses will want to do as it takes time and money and delivers no capacity to differentiate in front of customers. To support treasury functions, a bank will likely need to have the following technology:

- **ALM platform.** Asset and liability management (ALM), as already mentioned, is a specialist practice in its own right that is dedicated to managing liquidity, funding and financial risks. There are plenty of off-the-shelf ALM platforms on the market and consequently there is no real need to develop your own bespoke solution. It may be possible to launch a new bank without an ALM platform at all, although it is likely to be necessary once the range of products grows.
- **Market data feed.** As most banks trade in financial instruments (and sometimes more) there is a need to track the market to understand the implications on the bank's liquidity position (among other things). To achieve this, it is normally necessary to have access to a market data feed, with Bloomberg and Reuters being by far the most popular. This requires little technical integration.
- **Payments and accounts data.** For a large bank there is often a degree of consistency in payment flows as a consequence of the large volumes that it manages, but for smaller banks there can be more relative variation in daily flows. To keep track of the net payment flows and reserve positions with schemes (be that interbank payment schemes or card payment schemes) the treasury team needs to be able to monitor both, ideally on a real-time basis. Incidentally it is normally necessary to monitor payment flows from risk and fraud perspectives anyway, so the technical capability to do this should already exist.
- **Risk modelling software.** This is rarely a necessity on day 1 of a new business and may never be a requirement for some forms of banking offerings. As mentioned previously, many small banks run much of their risk modelling on spreadsheets. However, as the bank grows it might require specialist software to support this function.

8.8   Compliance

The role of the compliance function within a banking business is to manage the business's compliance risk. Broadly, compliance risk can be defined as the risk of sanction, financial loss or reputational damage brought about as a result of a failure to comply with legal or regulatory requirements. The compliance role, under many regulatory regimes, is mandated.[30]

Both law and regulation, in whatever country the business is hosted or operates within, will be open to a degree of interpretation. The extent to which interpretation can be applied varies from jurisdiction to jurisdiction, but there is always an element of it.

The challenge for any compliance function is to find the right trade-off between compliance and giving the business latitude for innovation. Coming down too heavily on the side of compliance can result in heavy restrictions on a business's ability to make money and too much cost in monitoring existing business activities, whereas failure to enforce sufficient levels of compliance can result in a business operating outside of the law or regulation and a risk of significant damage to the business if (or when) things go badly – either the regulator identifies a failure to comply and implements sanctions against either the business or individuals or there is financial or reputational loss, or both.

8.8.1   History of Compliance

Historically, the role of the compliance function within banking businesses tended to be regarded as one of an advisory nature. The compliance team would be responsible for understanding the regulation and law that applied to the business and promoting this understanding across the business. In some cases, the compliance team would also carry out testing of the measures established to meet these regulatory and legal requirements but, more often than not, the obligation to design and implement appropriate controls was left to individual business managers. This created a system of patchwork implementation, with limited efficacy and inconsistent results.

The banking crisis of 2008 changed all that. Since then a lot of focus has been brought to bear on the area of compliance. Were banks too lax in their approach to compliance? Did compliance functions have sufficient understanding of what their businesses were doing? Did compliance functions have the authority to appropriately challenge business functions? In many cases the role of compliance within banking businesses was found to be insufficiently broad and lacked the authority to ensure regulatory and legal compliance.[31]

In a modern banking business, a compliance function covers a broad range of activities and should have the authority to ensure that both legal and regulatory requirements are met by the business.

8.8.2   Promulgation and Tracking of Compliance Objectives and Measures

This topic encompasses the identification of the regulatory and legal requirements that the business should meet and that may or will arise in the future. This includes not only identifying which rules are applicable, but also tracking them to ensure that it is understood where they apply in the business (which functions and processes need to meet them) and how they have been met. In a small business this can be carried out on a spreadsheet, but larger businesses may need a more sophisticated toolset.

8.8.3   Creation of Standards and Tools for Managing Compliance Risk

In a large business there may be many individuals responsible for either managing compliance or implementing solutions that need to meet various legal or regulatory requirements. It is important that the business has a consistent approach for meeting compliance obligations that ensures that applicable laws and regulations are considered wherever they apply. The compliance team is responsible for developing the standards and toolsets to ensure this.

8.8.4   Training

Ensuring that the workforce maintains robust and up-to-date knowledge and standards requires regular training on a broad range of subjects (everything from treating customers fairly to anti-bribery and corruption, and anti-money laundering). The compliance team is often responsible for ensuring that appropriate training exists to support the business's compliance obligations and, importantly, that staff training needs are met.

8.8.5 Assessment

The compliance team should carry out regular checks on business functions to ensure that the tools, standards and training have been implemented and are being regularly maintained. Assessment of these standards should be structured, with formal reporting.

8.8.6 Root-Cause Analysis and Enforcement

In the event that something does go wrong (and no complex system in which humans, technology and processes intersect is likely to be infallible), the compliance function may be engaged in a root-cause analysis exercise to understand what went wrong. This should include the definition of new measures, training or standards and could even result in disciplinary or legal action if someone is found to have acted in contravention of company standards, negligently or illegally.

8.8.7 Technology and Compliance

Compliance has a few specific demands on technology in terms of their own day-to-day use of systems. However, it can impact a broad range of the business's technology requirements. Compliance software, for example, helps track legal, regulatory and industry (and individual business) compliance requirements and allows the users to actively assess, track and monitor how the business meets those requirements. For a small business with relatively few regulatory permissions this might be as simple as tracking on a spreadsheet, but for larger businesses a custom toolset (there are many third-party solutions on the market) should be considered.

The compliance team will have some demands in terms of secure storage needs. While this is common across most areas of the business the compliance team's requirements may be somewhat more complex and there may be a need for access to such storage to be tightly controlled and proactively monitored. When dealing with cases of financial crime, for example, the compliance team must be assured that any storage it uses is secure and that any access (whether that is to view or to change content), even by members of the compliance team, is monitored.

The compliance team will also have strong views about what business processes should be monitored and how. This could include areas as diverse as contact centre recording to payments and finance or treasury processes and all the way through to segregation of duties and controls. In our experience there is a tendency for some compliance teams to over-engineer requirements, so it can be necessary to review such requirements and even require evidence, but all such requests from compliance should be taken seriously.

8.9 Human Resources

The human resources (HR) function is one of those areas that has seen a degree of re-invention in terms of role titles during the digital business era. For example, titles such as

Chief Happiness Officer or VP of Teammate Success now exist.[32] However, the activities of the HR function have not fundamentally changed during the modern era, even if some of the roles and the toolsets they use have. The key areas covered by HR are:

- Recruitment: Running recruitment activities, including advertising, recruiter engagement, process management (end-to-end), organising interviews and assessment centres, creating offers and onboarding.
- Employee lifecycle management: Beyond the recruitment process the employees will need support throughout their careers and even when they leave the business.
- Learning and development:Establishing and managing an appropriate training regime for all staff. In many locales there are specific regulations relating to the requirements for continuing professional development (CPD) for banking staff, particularly those that provide financial advice to retail customers.
- Performance management: Establishing performance management processes and ensuring that all such processes are run regularly and fairly.
- Compensation and benefits: Creating and managing compensation packages, pay rises, pay ladders, etc.
- Discipline: Creating an appropriate disciplinary process and the running of that process should the need arise.
- Well-being: Perhaps one of the newer functions of HR, well-being covers the emotional and physical health of staff and might include mental health support as well as physical health advice.
- Career planning: Establishing and managing the career paths within the organisation. This is often not something that is required until the organisation achieves a certain size.
- Maintaining safety: Establishing processes and controls to maintain a safe working environment. This includes workplace assessments and providing specialist equipment to support individuals with specific needs – for example, higher desks and chairs for those who are taller than average.
- Employer and employee relations: Managing the relationship between management and the general workforce is a critical activity. In a modern fintech environment much of this is taken on by the management team themselves – a lot of what makes a fintech a fintech is its working environment, and management take their responsibilities in this area very seriously. However, in some organisations the HR function must play a larger role.
- Labour law: Ensuring that the business is compliant with any law and regulations that apply in each jurisdiction within which the business operates.

In many cases these requirements can be supported through a suite of standard desktop office software, a common file share (for employee handbooks, staff processes and the like) and a secure file share (remember, this data relates to staff personal data). However, specific tools are also required in many cases. Typical tools that one should expect to provide to support HR will include:

- HR platform: Career management, holiday booking, rewards, self-service career management tools and more can be found in many off-the-shelf HR platforms. Pretty much every business we have worked with has bought, rather than built, its

HR platform. There are many good examples of cloud-based solutions that can be procured at a reasonable cost, often on a per-employee basis.

- Training platforms: Training comes in a variety of forms and there are a large number of cloud-based platforms that can be used to provide core or supplemental courses. In all cases you should ensure that HR can track staff training, but where CPD is mandated by regulation it is imperative that there is an auditable output that can be used to prove that staff are fulfilling their training obligations.
- Recruitment systems: Typically these come in the form of toolsets that support the HR team in running recruitment campaigns on popular recruitment sites, through to the point where the business is ready to make an offer.

8.10   Procurement

For some reason, procurement and supplier management are often confused with each other. They are, though, very different disciplines. Procurement manages the process of new supplier onboarding and ongoing contractual management, whereas supplier management is responsible for overseeing the delivery by third-party suppliers after contracts are signed. At certain times (e.g. during contractual negotiations with an existing supplier) these activities may overlap, but most of the time they run entirely separately. We would argue that supplier management should be done by the function or functions working with a supplier and not by the procurement team, although the procurement team may provide guidelines and set expectations about how it should be performed.

Beyond establishing processes and controls around procurement, the procurement team will often get involved to manage the contractual aspects of a procurement process, ensuring that good practice is followed and the organisation is getting good value and has appropriate contractual cover for the services or products to be supplied. Procurement will also get involved during any re-negotiation of services and at the point of contractual renewal (or, ideally, well before) to ensure that a competitive re-tender process can be run if required.

There are e-procurement tools available, but in a small to medium-sized business the procurement team usually only needs a secure file share in order to deliver. It can be of benefit to provide tools to track contracts, obligations etc. and remind staff to start a re-tender before the impending contractual renewal date forces you to renew with the incumbent (the option of a re-tender is useful in ensuring that your incumbent remains interested even if you have no intention to move to another provider).

8.11   Other Corporate Functions

As described in our bank model (Figure 1.1 in Chapter 1), there are a number of other functions that reside within what we describe as the 'Corporate Functions'. Some of these, such as marketing (see Chapter 4), we have covered elsewhere in this book. Each of the remaining functions could justify the writing of a book in and of themselves, but their role within a bank is very similar to the role they fulfil in any large business. From our perspective they require little bank-specific technology, although they do deserve a mention for the sake of completeness. These functions include:

- Communications: This includes press releases, media relations, publications and investor relations. In a smaller business this might be included within the marketing department, but larger businesses will typically have a specialist function.
- Corporate real estate: This area is responsible for managing any property associated with the business. This could include everything from managing large properties owned by the bank, right down to individual office leases. At its most sophisticated it might include managing estates of offices across the globe, reducing the corporate carbon footprint from its real estate, physical security of offices, cross-charging of office space to business functions and management of business continuity options should the normal premises become unavailable. At scale, this can require very sophisticated real estate management technology solutions, but these are outside the scope of this book.
- Internal audit: The role of internal audit is to provide ongoing evaluation of the bank's controls, accounting processes and governance. As such, internal audit requires a broad understanding of risk, accounting practices and local law. While there are audit-specific software tools, in the early days of a business, in much the same way as compliance, the audit function will primarily require a secure file storage area in which to store its data and findings.
- Legal: This department is responsible for ensuring that the business is compliant with any applicable laws within any countries the business operates within. This includes everything from contract reviews through to interpreting laws and agreeing on approaches to complying with those laws.
- Strategy and planning: In a smaller business most of the strategy and planning is carried out by the bank management team, with some support from other areas, such as product owners and treasury. However, in larger banks we have found specific business units whose only focus is working on business strategy and planning. Often these functions will carry out extensive market and product analysis, study developments in other markets and seek new ideas and third parties to work with. Strategy is one of those areas that, from the outside, seems glamorous, as the guidance they provide helps steer the business. However, despite the influence the function has, the amount and depth of work they carry out should not be underestimated. Strategic decisions are often underpinned by enormous amounts of data and analysis. It should come as no surprise, then, to know that strategy functions are huge consumers of business and external data, analytics tools and spreadsheets.

8.12   References

1. Robertson, J. (2016). How the Big Bang changed the City of London for ever. *BBC News* (27 October). https://www.bbc.co.uk/news/business-37751599 (accessed 30 July 2020).
2. Financial Conduct Authority (2015). Client money and assets. https://www.fca.org.uk/firms/client-money-assets (accessed 2 August 2020).
3. Financial Services Authority (2010). Mortgage market review: Responsible lending. https://www.fca.org.uk/publication/consultation/fsa-cp10-16.pdf (accessed 2 August 2020).

4. Financial Conduct Authority (2016). Ring-fencing. https://www.fca.org.uk/consumers/ring-fencing (accessed 2 August 2020).

5. Kampfner, J. (2014). Bad Banks: Greed, Incompetence and the Next Global Crisis review – a rogues' gallery of financial scandal. *The Guardian* (21 July). https://www.theguardian.com/books/2014/jul/21/bad-banks-greed-incompetence-next-global-crisis-review-alex-brummer-rogues-gallery-financial-scandal (accessed 2 August 2020).

6. The Royal Commission. Royal Commission into Misconduct in the Banking, Superannuation and Financial Services Industry. https://treasury.gov.au/publication/p2019-fsrc-final-report (accessed 27 July 2020).

7. Financial Conduct Authority (2015). Regulatory sandbox. https://www.fca.org.uk/firms/innovation/regulatory-sandbox (accessed 27 July 2020).

8. HM Treasury (2013). Hogg Tendering Committee for LIBOR. https://www.gov.uk/government/groups/hogg-tendering-committee-for-libor (accessed 29 September 2020).

9. European Commission (2015). Payment services (PSD 2) – Directive (EU) 2015/2366. https://ec.europa.eu/info/law/payment-services-psd-2-directive-eu-2015-2366_en (accessed 27 July 2020).

10. European Commission. Data protection. https://ec.europa.eu/info/law/law-topic/data-protection_en (accessed 27 July 2020).

11. Information Commissioner's Office (2019). Intention to fine British Airways £183.39m under GDPR for data breach (8 July). https://ico.org.uk/about-the-ico/news-and-events/news-and-blogs/2019/07/ico-announces-intention-to-fine-british-airways/ (accessed 29 September 2020).

12. Fintechnews Singapore (2020). Singapore leads Asia Pacific in open banking (28 February). https://fintechnews.sg/37980/openbanking/singapore-open-banking-apac/ (accessed 27 July 2020).

13. Hamilton, A. (2020). South Korea reports 20m subscriptions to open banking service. *Fintech Futures* (7 July). https://www.fintechfutures.com/2020/07/south-korea-reports-20m-subscriptions-to-open-banking-service/ (accessed 27 July 2020).

14. MAS. Application Programming Interfaces (APIs). https://www.mas.gov.sg/development/fintech/technologies---apis (accessed 27 July 2020).

15. Rothwell, G. (2018). Open banking Hong Kong – How open is open? *Fintech News* (17 October) https://fintechnews.hk/7225/open-banking/open-banking-hong-kong-accenture/ (accessed 27 July 2020).

16. Australian Competition and Consumer Commission. Consumer data right (CDR). https://www.accc.gov.au/focus-areas/consumer-data-right-cdr-0 (accessed 27 July 2020).

17. UK Government (2016). First ever FinTech bridge established between Britain and Singapore. https://www.gov.uk/government/news/first-ever-fintech-bridge-established-between-britain-and-singapore (accessed 27 July 2020).

18. Bacs. Account Switching Service. https://www.bacs.co.uk/Services/accountswitchingservice/Pages/AccountSwitchingService.aspx (accessed 27 July 2020).

19. Crosman, P. (2020). Why Moven, one of the first challenger banks, is calling it quits. *American Banker* (27 March). https://www.americanbanker.com/news/why-moven-one-of-the-first-challenger-banks-is-calling-it-quits (accessed 27 July 2020).

20. Smith, K. A. (2020). How the Dodd-Frank Act protects your money. *Forbes* (20 July). https://www.forbes.com/advisor/investing/dodd-frank-act/ (accessed 27 July 2020).

21. Kenton, W. (2020). Foreign Account Tax Compliance Act (FATCA). Investopedia (30 June). https://www.investopedia.com/terms/f/foreign-account-tax-compliance-act-fatca.asp (accessed 27 July 2020).

22. BIS. Basel III: international regulatory framework for banks. https://www.bis.org/bcbs/basel3 .htm?m=3%7C14%7C572 (accessed 27 July 2020).

23. PCI Security Standards Council. Securing the future of payments together. https://www .pcisecuritystandards.org/ (accessed 27 July 2020).

24. The Financial Conduct Authority. SYSC 8.1 General outsourcing requirements. https://www .handbook.fca.org.uk/handbook/SYSC/8/1.html (accessed 30 July 2020).

25. Wearden, G. (2011). How the PPI scandal unfolded. *The Guardian* (5 May). https://www .theguardian.com/business/2011/may/05/how-ppi-scandal-unfolded (accessed 27 July 2020).

26. Farag, M., Harland, D. and Nixon, D. (2013). Bank capital and liquidity. *Quarterly Bulletin* 2013 Q3: 201–215. https://www.bankofengland.co.uk/-/media/boe/files/quarterly-bulletin/2013/bank-capital-and-liquidity.pdf (accessed 5 July 2020).

27. Financial Reporting Council. FRS 102 The Financial Reporting Standard applicable in the UK and Republic of Ireland. https://www.frc.org.uk/accountants/accounting-and-reporting-policy/uk-accounting-standards/standards-in-issue/frs-102-the-financial-reporting-standard-applicabl (accessed 27 July 2020).

28. IFRS. https://www.ifrs.org/ (accessed 27 July 2020).

29. O'Connell, D. (2017). The collapse of Northern Rock: Ten years on. *BBC News* (12 September). https://www.bbc.co.uk/news/business-41229513 (accessed 26 July 2020).

30. European Central Bank (2020). Strengthening banks' compliance frameworks. https://www .bankingsupervision.europa.eu/press/publications/newsletter/2020/html/ssm.nl200212_1.en .html (accessed 30 July 2020).

31. Deloitte. (2015). The changing role of compliance. https://www2.deloitte.com/content/ dam/Deloitte/gr/Documents/financial-services/gr_fs_the_changing_role_of_compliance_en_ noexp.pdf (accessed 10 July 2020).

32. Campos, B. (2020). Chief Happiness Officer: What do they do and why are they important? Cyberclick (02 April). https://www.cyberclick.net/numericalblogen/chief-happiness-officer-what-do-they-do-and-why-are-they-important (accessed 27 July 2020).

CHAPTER 9

The Technology Function

This chapter covers the concepts associated with the implementation and management of technology. We highlight the key elements that should be considered in technology management and our thinking on what works and does not work. These thoughts are borne of several decades of working in technology within the banking industry, and we hope that you find them both pertinent and thought provoking.

9.1 Organisation and Governance

The technology function and associated governance structures within modern banking businesses are fundamentally no different than those of most other businesses, although with international banks they are often complicated (in the extreme) by geographic and business line divisions.

We have been exposed to a broad range of technology governance structures throughout our consulting careers working with national, regional and international banks but, despite their external differences, the way banking technology capabilities are organised follows a broadly consistent model, with most of the functions of a banking business's technology capability typically fitting under one of the following categories:

- *IT management and strategy*. This area includes senior management and will determine the technology strategy of the business. All key decisions relating to projects, programmes, investment, headcount and geography are made here. In international banks there will often be both a global management team and country management teams.
- *Architecture*. This ranges from strategic elements, such as the development and maintenance of technology roadmaps and standards, through to day-to-day assessments of new system designs and the governance of dispensations from the agreed standards (so, for example, if a project team believes it needs to vary from a standard in order to deliver, then it would need to seek a dispensation from the architecture team). This function usually consists of senior, experienced architects.
- *Development*. This includes the functions of the bank that focus on technology development, including the design and build of new networks, servers and platforms and the development of code. Traditionally this might include a broad range of architects and software specialists.

- *Change management*. This area includes project and programme management teams and can also include testing functions, although we have also seen testing included within the Development function.
- *Technology operations*. Responsible for the day-to-day management of the IT estate. Technology operations does everything from keeping the lights on (backups, restores, issue resolution, maintenance and patching) to accepting new systems into service and also often provides the support functions (service desk, desktop support and applications support). Networks and telecoms might also reside within this function in a large bank, although sometimes it is a separate function.
- *Information security*. Historically, the security function was often included as a sub-set of the technology operations function (or possibly design), but these days security has become such an important element of IT that most financial businesses will have a designated security, or cybersecurity, function with a chief information security officer (CISO) reporting to the CTO or CIO. It should be noted that there is a trend for security teams to also report in to risk functions.
- *Supplier management*. Not to be confused with procurement, the supplier manage-ment function is responsible for ensuring that technology service suppliers deliver what they are contracted to. This is not just about ensuring that the technology or services they provide do as they are expected to; it is much more complex and includes delivery against service-level agreements (SLAs), security requirements, resilience and recovery, correct staffing and more.
- *Service management*. Service management is the interface to business users. Service managers are responsible for reporting on SLAs agreed upon between technology and the business, agreeing to changes and ensuring that the business receives a level of service appropriate to its needs.

An organisational model of a simple bank's technology function could therefore be drawn as shown in Figure 9.1.

The technology function is there to support the needs of the business, and it is com-mon in international banks to find that the business lines demand some direct control over the technology function, particularly in the domains of change and development, resulting in the structure shown in Figure 9.2.

Of course, many banks are also geographically dispersed, and it is often the case that each geography requires its own requirements to be met and therefore insists on control of elements of the IT environment specific to the services that it consumes. This results in the example shown in Figure 9.3 of geographic alignment added to the business-aligned organisational model.

It's not hard to see where this is going and yet many of the international banks still work on the basis that this structure is in some way manageable and efficient (it's not, for the record) and even go to lengths to split each of the other functions into business and country-aligned units. This is hopelessly inefficient and creates a culture of conflict for resources and funding as well as a complex web of matrix management. International businesses are difficult to manage at the best of times and breaking the technology func-tion into a thousand different pieces so that everyone can have the control they believe that they need turns the function into a hopeless mess.

FIGURE 9.1   An organisational model for a simple bank's technology function.

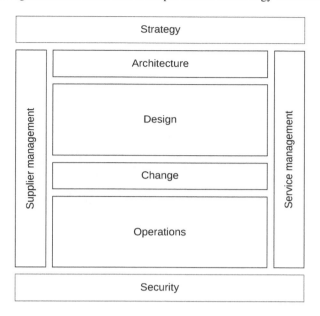

FIGURE 9.2   A business-aligned organisational model for the technology function.

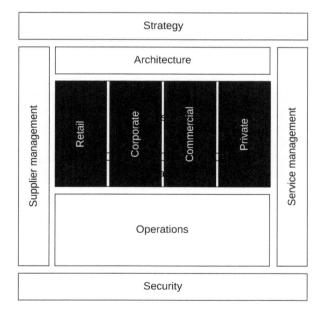

FIGURE 9.3   Business and geography-aligned organisational model for the technology function.

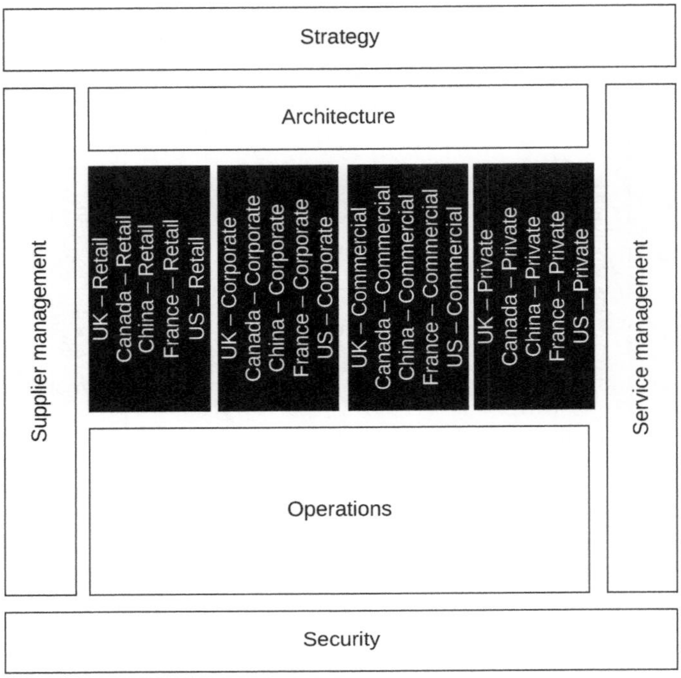

As ex-consultants, we ought to point out that such chaos is a boon for consulting. On a regular basis, and particularly when new management comes in, consultants are rolled in to optimise the technology function. In the process they make large sums in fees and invariably the result is no better a structure than the original one. We have seen some of the world's largest banks paralyse themselves for years and spend huge sums of money restructuring their technology function rather than focusing on making real progress. Ultimately, this is one of the fundamental reasons why big banks struggle with their technology: poor management.

For the record, there is no ideal structure for the technology function of a large bank. The one thing that has stood out to us during our many years in the business is that the effectiveness of the technology structure is actually a composite of three key elements: the strength of the management team as a team (not as individuals, but working together), the culture of the technology function, and its alignment to the business.

When building a technology function, beyond consideration of these three key elements, the best recommendation we can give is to keep it as simple as possible. Reducing the number of lines of management facilitates the flow of information, reduces the risk of political infighting, and improves alignment to the strategy.

9.2   Conway's Law

When considering the organisational design of technology functions, it would be remiss of us not to mention Conway's Law, which was a hypothesis made by Melvin Conway in 1968 in his article "How Do Committees Invent?"His thesis states:

> *Organizations which design systems […] are constrained to produce designs which are copies of the communication structures of these organizations.*[1]

Although he wasn't talking about computer systems specifically, his hypothesis has long been discussed in that context.* After much academic discussion on the truth of the thesis it was actually tested, as it applied to the software industry, in 2007 by Alan MacCormack at MIT and John Rusnak and Carliss Baldwin at Harvard Business School.[2] Their analysis showed that a commercial software organisation with a high degree of structure and shared goals and behaviours typically produced tightly-coupled code, whereas an open-source software community, with geographically dispersed members and little organisational structure, typically developed loosely coupled code, strongly indicating that Conway's Law is based on more than a grain of truth. Here, tightly coupled means that the various components that comprise a software product or application have a high number of dependencies on each other, whereas loosely coupled means they don't. We can envisage why this is the case – commercial software teams that communicate all the time can reuse each other's components (and programming code), and they are also developing a common software product. On the other hand, members of open-source communities work more independently of each other and typically develop components or code that interest them, and they may dip in and out of working on an open-source product. There isn't the same compulsion to reuse other people's code, and integration of components is typically via a few interfaces.

Conway's Law has significant implications for the organisation of a technology function in any business, including small and large banking businesses. Consider a large, international banking business with a big, monolithic core banking platform. It has hundreds or even thousands of people in the technology function maintaining and operating the platform, keeping it running, and adding new functionality. However, it takes forever (well, a year or two) from specifying a requirement for a new piece of functionality to it being delivered, because of the layers of governance any change goes through and because the platform code is tightly coupled, and making a change requires extensive design and testing efforts to make sure it doesn't break anything. All changes have to be bundled into one or two big updates a year, because doing it any faster is impossible. Changes could be made much more quickly if fewer people were involved and if the platform wasn't a big monolith. That's where neobanks have an advantage – they can build small multiskilled teams, each of which owns, maintains, tests, deploys, monitors and operates a service (or microservice – see Section 3.20) that is loosely coupled with the other (micro) services.

---

*There are other, similar hypotheses made by other authors, and the general concept is sometimes called the *mirroring hypothesis*.

As long as they respect the interfaces of the microservices that their microservice calls, and maintain the interface that other microservices use to call their microservices, they can deliver changes as often as they like.

There is a big movement among the software development community away from large, monolithic platforms towards building platforms or applications from small, relatively independent microservices to deliver the pace of technology change that many businesses want. The challenge for incumbents is the investment they have already made in big shared platforms, and the challenge we see for the proponents of microservices is the management of large, complex networks of microservices – after all, a complex system is a complex system whether it is a huge mainframe application or a cloud-based set of microservices.

9.3   Cost of Technology

The one element of technology that preoccupies the mind of business and technology management even more than governance structure is cost. Since the introduction of technology into businesses over half a century ago the cost of buying, maintaining and managing technology has risen inexorably. Not because technology is becoming more expensive (quite the opposite on a cost per processing unit basis, as articulated by Moore's Law[3]), but because we use so much more of it. Periodically, every business makes efforts to rein in its technology costs, but with the world at large moving more and more towards the use of technology in our everyday lives the best a business can hope for is to maintain efficiency.

Technology cost is not a bad thing when technology is well managed. Many of the advances in technology result in cost savings elsewhere. Whether it is through automation of manual processes or the closure of bank branches and offices that are no longer required, technology can be a force for enterprise cost reduction. Of course, there is the human side to this point – when technology replaces humans there is an inevitable cost to those individuals.

Most bank technology functions that we have encountered tend to measure cost, at its simplest, in two major categories (often called buckets) at the highest level, run cost and change cost. In some large banks there is also a regulatory change bucket that is managed separately as a third category. This additional category is an odd one because there are a thousand reasons why change might be forced onto an organisation in many areas, including legal, competition and industry standards, to name a few. That is not to say that there isn't benefit in knowing what the change budget is being spent on, just that breaking out regulatory change into a third top-level category doesn't make much sense in its own right. We have seen other banks use a two-tier model, with the top tier being 'run' and 'change', and the second tier breaking run down into 'keeping the lights on' and 'growth' and change breaking down into 'mandatory' and 'discretionary'. This, we feel, better represents the categorisation of technology cost at the highest level of the bank.

The basic, and very sound, working assumption is that any business should work to reduce the run cost to as low as possible, so that a greater proportion of the technology cost is spent on change. This makes complete sense: run cost is about keeping the lights on, whereas change can be an opportunity to innovate, grow and take market share.

To put this in perspective, the World Economic Forum published a report in 2017 that highlighted the fact that US banks typically spend about 78% of their technology budget on run-the-bank activities and only 22% of it on change-the-bank ones.[4] Big banks are literally burning billions of pounds a year just to keep the lights on in the technology functions. Imagine what could be achieved if these banks could even up this balance.

In a small banking business tracking technology costs is relatively straightforward, but as the business gets larger and more complex (e.g. a multinational, multi-business-line bank) things get much more complicated. Our experience of large banks is that this often becomes an industry in itself – with large numbers of staff building complex cost models and attributing costs to different business units. Trying to build an exact, or even approximate, cost for running a single system (including the costs of electricity, data centre space, enterprise software licences, maintenance, operational support and applications) and then splitting that cost among multiple business lines on the basis of the number of users, some form of pre-agreement, payload or some other arbitrary split inevitably ends in disagreement and more confusion than clarity. This is particularly the case when this exercise is run on spreadsheets, as it is in some of our biggest banks.

Tracking the costs of running the technology estate is a 'must do' exercise. Not doing so will result in runaway costs and poor efficiency. As a start-up it may be possible to get away without tracking cost for a short period, but it will quickly cause problems. However, tracking it successfully shouldn't require a cottage industry. To our mind there are only two ways to track costs.

The simple way: For small organisations that don't need to re-charge business units, managing cost is as simple as working with the finance team and project managers to identify all the technology costs and then track them. However, if the business is likely to scale, or is already operating at scale, and recharging is required, then a more sophisticated approach may be required.

The sophisticated way: Implementing a specialist toolset (there are good technology financial management tools on the market) that is designed to support technology financial management is the only way to manage technology cost management efficiently at scale. This will save a fortune over the long run. Spreadsheets only work up to a certain size before they become unwieldy, inefficient and error strewn.

On a final note, the one thing that we have learnt, more than anything, working with start-ups is that a good employee never regards any spend as someone else's money. They manage every penny and every contract with care. Unfortunately, there are many bigger businesses that have cultures that don't follow this approach.

9.4   Working with the Business – It's about the Service, Not the Technology

In a modern business, the consumption of technology by the business should never be about specific technologies, computing hardware (be that CPUs, RAM, storage or any other element) or even software. Instead, business users expect a service that delivers to their needs. A good technology function understands, at some depth, what their business and users need.

Fundamentally it is that last point that marks out new entrant banks from their established competition. When you build a fintech from scratch as a technologist you cannot hide from the need to develop a fundamental understanding of how every area of a banking business works. You must engage risk, compliance, retail banking, business banking, operations, marketing, finance and treasury (and everyone else) to understand not just what they do, but how they come together to ensure that the bank operates effectively at every level. It can be frustrating having to learn everything about how a bank works but when you do this you then understand how every decision, every change and every technology solution impacts the bank. This is incredibly powerful and it's a far cry from large banks where each technology team focuses on one discrete area of the bank for years at a time. Yes, they become experts in that area, but they often have little understanding of how it integrates with the rest of the business or what the upstream and downstream implications of decisions are. Big banks do contain some very capable technologists, it's just that those technologists very rarely really understand how the bank actually works.

Understanding how the business works is key to delivering technology because the business should consume services appropriate to its needs from the technology function. That doesn't mean that it hands off responsibility to the technology function for all elements of technology; it is still very much about a partnership, but it is a partnership of peers with a mutual respect and understanding for each other. The service is an agreement between the two business units that defines what the business needs and the service levels that underpin it.

A small organisation may not even define the services initially, but as the business grows they will be needed and the sooner a structure is put in place the easier it will be. In fact, our experience with building a bank in the UK actually required us to define business services at a basic level in order to define service levels and structure an effective business continuity plan.

A service can be as simple or complex as the two parties need. At its simplest a service description should include a summary of the business activity carried out by the service, some basic availability data and the names of key contacts associated with it. The elements of an example simple service might be as shown in Table 9.1.

TABLE 9.1   A simple business service.

Name	eKYC
Description	Electronic Know Your Customer service, used for identification of customers and checking of identity documents as part of the customer onboarding process. Used both in-branch and through the mobile app.
Service Owner	Jane Smith (Contact Details)
Business Unit(s)	Retail Banking, Business Banking
Business Owner	Frank Jones (Contact Details)
Service Hours	24 hours
Availability Service Level	99.99%
Recovery Time Objective	4 hours
Recovery Point Objective	0 (data can be recovered from partners in the event of local data loss)

Of course, a service can be more complicated than that shown in Table 9.1 and even the service description can become quite complex if allowed – adding business data, prioritisation, issue escalation data, key contact details and more. However, for a basic service model, something along the lines shown should suffice.

A service could also be broader than this. For example, it could cover the whole onboarding process. This has benefits in that fewer services need to be defined to cover the whole bank, but it also has drawbacks in that it allows less specificity and runs the risk that technology components that serve a number of elements of the business end up with more than one service level covering them.

There may be hundreds of services delivered by the technology function across the bank, from supporting the ATM network through to regulatory reporting. Each one should be defined as simply as possible (we don't want to make an industry out of this), with a clear set of performance metrics around it.

9.5   Service Management

Underpinning the business services is the technology service management regime. There are many examples of service management regimes and standards, including COBIT (Control Objectives for Information and Related Technologies),[5] ISO 20000 (the international standard for managing and delivering technology services)[6] and Microsoft Operations Framework (MOF),[7] to name a few, but ITIL[8] (Information Technology Infrastructure Library) is probably the best known of all.

This book is not targeted at teaching the reader about service management, but it is important that we look at this discipline before moving on. Not only is good service management the bedrock of technology management, but it also provides a framework which can be used to standardise and measure the quality of services.

ITIL was first developed in the late 1980s and has gone through a number of iterations since then. The foundation edition of the current version, 4, was released in February 2019, with additional elements released over the course of 2019. However, as ITIL v3 is still better known to many we have elected to use this version as our model for service management. It should be noted that while ITIL v4 is presented quite differently than ITIL v3, many of the principles are the same and, in fact, the ITL v4 practices are very similar to the processes identified in ITIL v3.

ITIL v3 has many similarities to a technology delivery programme – there is a strategy element, a design element, a change element and a run element and then a feedback loop (continual service improvement or CSI) to allow us to gather and act upon feedback relating to the efficacy of the service. However, rather than being a programme with a start and finish, every activity in a service management process model is focused on how technology delivers to the day-to-day needs of the business on an ongoing basis. Understanding whether the service model is delivering what the business needs every day requires a means of measuring the performance of that service.

The following example covers a customer onboarding process for which we will then define the performance metrics. You will note that we have illustrated a composite service here, broader than the eKYC service defined previously. Neither approach is more correct (they both have their merits), but using a composite allows us to provide a little more detail in our example. A customer onboarding process typically includes a number of key steps:

1. [START] Customer clicks on 'Create Account' for a specific account type.
2. Key service information – The business may need to share some key information (depending on local law and regulation) with the customer before onboarding them, such as how it will manage their data.
3. Gathering customer data – depending on the process this might include taking details of name, age, address, profession, contact details and a photo and/or video.
4. Gathering supporting documents – This used to be a question of taking hard copy to the local bank branch but can now normally be completed electronically (see Chapter 4 for more information).
5. Identity checking – This includes confirming that the identity document is valid and has not been tampered with and also verifying that the person's photo matches that on the identity document.
6. PEP and sanctions checking (see Section 5.6.2 for more information).
7. Decision – Can the business take this individual on as a customer? There may be some time between step 6 and this final step, because the identity-checking systems sometimes throw exceptions that need manual reviews. Many banking businesses actually pause the process at this point and then notify the customer of their decision once the identity and PEP/sanctions checks are completed.
8. [STOP] Process complete. The account will now be set up. Actions relevant to specific account opening processes now follow.

Looking at this from a business perspective, there are a number of key performance indicators (KPIs) that could be applied:

- Page loading time – each page must load within X milliseconds of the customer hitting 'next' or equivalent.
- Identity check – X% must complete within Y seconds. Remember that some identity checks need manual intervention, either by the eKYC provider or from the banking operations team.
- PEP and sanctions check – must respond within X seconds.
- Entire end-to-end process – must be available 24/7/365 with an uptime target of 99.99%. You can target higher than this (and many do!), but bear in mind that 99.99% equates to less than an hour of downtime a year.
- Onboarding process – must be able to handle X simultaneous users at any given time.

In order to produce these results the technology function will need guidance from the business. It will need to understand what capabilities the business requires and what responsiveness, volumetrics and uptime it needs as a minimum. The key is in keeping the business honest and this is where the relationship with business owners is very important. Naturally, business owners will want the best for their staff and customers, but 100% uptime on an internal HR platform for 200 people is almost certainly not a real requirement. A business can typically manage without the HR platform for a day or two and it is important that a level of honest and objective evaluation is maintained. Trying to get a technology function to spin all of the plates, all of the time, can result in some odd decisions – imagine losing your contact centre and HR platforms on the same day and then realising that the KPIs meant that the HR platform recovery was prioritised!

9.6 Mapping Services to Applications

Once the services have been defined, the next step is to map those services to applications. At the end of the day, a technology function's ability to deliver a service and meet the KPIs and SLAs agreed upon with the business is dependent upon understanding how the applications in the estate support that service (and, of course, the infrastructure that underpins those applications).

In some instances, this mapping is simple. For example, the ability to check the status of a relationship with a customer might be wholly reliant upon a single platform, the customer relationship management (CRM) platform. However, there are many instances where a service may rely upon a large range of platforms. As an example, let's look at customer onboarding again. In this case we are looking at customer onboarding as the creation of an initial customer profile and are not including any specific account creation.

The process will require a number of different platforms, which might include:

- Web and app presentation server – to interface to the customer device and feed and gather content.
- Content management platform – holding the content that the presentation server shares with the client device.
- Customer database – to store data about the customer.
- Identity validation platform – to check the image of the identity documents and also confirm that the likeness in the image is the same as the customer photo.
- PEP and sanctions checking platform – to check the name of the customer against known PEPs and sanctions targets.

However, this isn't all. There may well be other platforms involved, including the core banking platform, various microservices and datastores, file stores (for storage of the uploaded customer image files, for example) as well as network components and security devices (such as firewalls). It is clear that delivering the service requires a number of systems all working in union.

Now that we understand what systems are involved, understanding the KPIs and SLAs will aid in deciding how those systems need to be architected. This, in turn, flows through into the non-functional testing that will need to be carried out prior to deployment, but also periodically in respect to disaster recovery testing.

The process of mapping business outcomes to services and then services to applications is tedious (as we know all too well) but is imperative in order to ensure that technology will deliver what it needs to in order to support the business. This is particularly true when systems fail. Knowing what business capabilities will be impacted, and how much of a priority each is, is key to defining how you address such a failure.

It is also worth remembering that the team that is working for the bank now is not the team that will be working there in five years' time. People move on, systems change and new systems are implemented. If the team are carrying around this data in their heads then gaps will develop in due course and mistakes will be made.

Building this mapping as soon as possible, and maintaining it as the environment changes, will save the business (and the technology function) a lot of heartache and pain in the long run.

9.7   Governing the Application Estate

Now that we understand how the applications deliver to the needs of the business, we need to determine how we will manage each of those applications. By *manage* we actually mean everything from sourcing through to administration, development, rate of change and many other considerations.

It is possible to manage every application separately, with a custom approach in every case, but this is inefficient. Again, at a small scale this might work, but over time, and with scale, it becomes cumbersome and costly. To address this there are a number of different approaches, but we have used *pace-layered models* to good effect in the past and we will therefore use these as the basis for this discussion. Stewart Brand documented the idea of pace levels (which had come from the architect Frank Duffy) as they relate to buildings in his book *How Buildings Learn*[9] – different levels change at different rates or paces and are managed differently. For example, the site on which a building is constructed doesn't change, whereas the services in a building (e.g. the elevators and air conditioning) may be changed every 7 to 15 years, and the stuff inside the building (chairs, desks, appliances) change all the time. One of the points behind this is that the slowly changing levels are in charge of the rapidly changing levels – the site of the building controls its structure which controls its boundaries (or skin) which control its services which control the internal layout (the space plan) which control where the stuff that's in the building can go. Gartner adapted Brand's approach to a classification of applications found in the technology estates of businesses, terming the groups that change at different rates as layers (rather than levels described by Brand), and making the point that different layers require different management approaches.[10]

In the pace-layered model as applied to applications there are three layers:

1. *Systems of innovation* – applications that are built to address transient or new opportunities. Systems that typically fall into this category are customer apps, social media components and other portals. In the case of banking the rich mobile apps touted by the neobanks sit in this category. These systems change very regularly.
2. *Systems of differentiation* – these are applications that are either unique to the company or exist to support medium-term industry-specific opportunities. In a banking environment you might find a custom credit scoring engine or open banking API. These systems are regularly reconfigured, but new code deployments occur less regularly than with systems of innovation.
3. *Systems of record* – these are typically long-term, established systems that support core processing or hold important data. For a banking business this might include core banking platforms, payment platforms, finance platforms and treasury platforms. Change in these systems is infrequent by comparison to the systems of innovation.

In the case of a bank or e-money business, the pace-layered model might look like the one in Figure 9.4. It should be noted that where a system sits in the hierarchy is not

FIGURE 9.4 A simple banking pace-layered model.

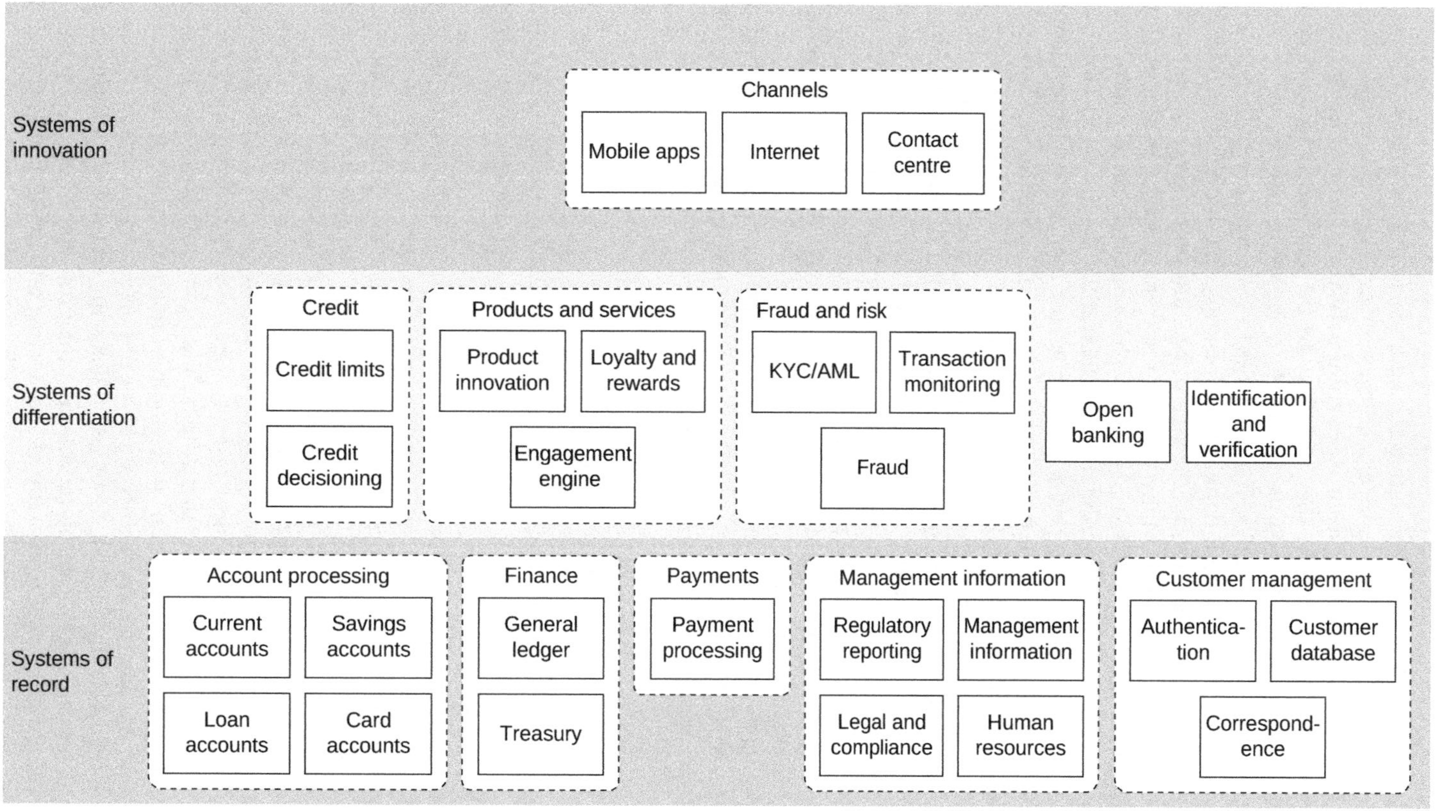

Systems of innovation

Channels
- Mobile apps
- Internet
- Contact centre

Systems of differentiation

Credit
- Credit limits
- Credit decisioning

Products and services
- Product innovation
- Loyalty and rewards
- Engagement engine

Fraud and risk
- KYC/AML
- Transaction monitoring
- Fraud

Open banking
- Identification and verification

Systems of record

Account processing
- Current accounts
- Savings accounts
- Loan accounts
- Card accounts

Finance
- General ledger
- Treasury

Payments
- Payment processing

Management information
- Regulatory reporting
- Management information
- Legal and compliance
- Human resources

Customer management
- Authentication
- Customer database
- Correspondence

consistent across an industry. Instead, individual businesses will have different priorities, and this might push applications into different levels in the hierarchy.

The different layers of the model lend themselves to different approaches to governance. For example, the systems of innovation will typically undergo frequent updates that are deployed quickly. So, they are likely to be well suited to agile development methodologies and a less formalised approach to change management.

In consideration of the different approaches to governance we will use two examples of bank applications: the core banking platform and the mobile app. The core banking platform (which covers at least the area of account processing, but sometimes much more) is a system of record. Many (though far from all) core banking platforms are commercial-off-the-shelf (COTS) platforms. The work that these platforms carry out must be 100% reliable and they aim to be available all of the time. Therefore, any change is very carefully scoped, developed in a controlled manner and implemented under strict change control. Even where the core banking platform is primarily made up of microservices they will still be tightly managed, and changes will be tested and deployed in a controlled fashion. Change programmes for systems of record will likely be scoped in advance of work starting and may well be implemented through a conventional waterfall methodology. By contrast, the bank's mobile app development must be adaptive to enable rapid changes of direction as early testing delivers customer feedback. The budget for such change can't easily be predicted in advance so a pooled budget, with individual projects drawing down on it, often works better. An agile development methodology is ideal for managing this kind of system.

Fundamentally it does not matter whether you choose to adopt this approach or one from elsewhere. What does matter is that there is an underlying structure to the applications governance to ensure consistency and efficiency across the estate.

9.8   Insourcing and Outsourcing

The approach to sourcing should be informed by the governance model to a large extent. However, as we will see in this section there are additional considerations when sourcing technology hosting, solutions, software and people.

To understand outsourcing in technology, it helps to have a little bit of the background. In the early days of technology adoption there were no technology departments. Often technology would be implemented by a department or business unit, and it would be managed locally by the unit that commissioned it. However, by the 1960s, technology was becoming centralised and banks were building data centres to house it.[11]

Centralising the management of technology made a lot of sense for a whole host of reasons (skills pooling, efficiency, buying power and more). One of the other upsides was that it had started to become clear just how much was now being spent on technology and the cost benefits that could therefore be had from centralisation.

By the 1980s, centralisation of technology functions was in full swing and businesses were starting to look further afield for opportunities to improve their technology bang for the buck. In the 1990s and early 2000s the technology industry realised that there was money to be saved by outsourcing the provision of a whole host of technology services – everything from networks to hosting and desktop support to coding was considered for potential outsourcing. Typically, this required engagement with a large technology services provider such as Accenture, EDS or IBM, where the expectation was that it would have an even larger skills base and could deliver economies of scale on top of its margin for running the service.[12,13]

However, in those early years the results were often sub-optimal. Nobody (and we're including the outsource providers here) really knew what they were doing, and the resultant poorly delivered services would often end up with the relationship between supplier and customer descending into acrimony and animus. A great example of an early failed outsource is JPMorgan Chase and IBM, who signed a $5 billion, seven-year outsourcing deal in late 2002, only to cancel that deal in 2004.[14] This was not a one-off, with large numbers of other outsourcing deals suffering similar outcomes.

With time and experience the second and third generation of outsource contracts moved to a more mature level and started to deliver more in line with expectations. Once outsourcing contracts proved that they could work, the next step was to look for further cost savings, and this is where the IT outsourcers starting offshoring. This, of course, was not a new idea. The process of offshoring was already in full swing in the contact centre arena. Initially in India, offshoring has spread to pretty much every location that has a combination of both a good education system and (comparatively) low salaries.[15]

It was not long, though, before the bigger banks realised that they could achieve the same benefits in-house by developing their own offshore development centres, which they duly did.[16] The technology estates for larger banks are often so large and complex that bank technology functions (when in-house) were as large as some of the outsourcing providers. Banks could therefore gain the benefits of offshoring without having to pay a supplier's margin!

However, that's not the end of the story. With the surge in cloud and as-a-service models, the sourcing landscape for many banking businesses has become a complex and often nuanced affair. These newer models provide businesses with the ability to minimise capital expenditure and move to a pay-as-you-go operational cost base and it is this that has powered many of the neobank models – whether that is through consuming e-money as a service (cards and e-wallets provided by the likes of PaySafe, PrePay Technologies and Wirecard) or through the ability to build highly scalable solutions within the cloud.

Decisions around sourcing will be very specific to the business, but as a general rule:

- Never outsource the unique selling proposition (USP). If an application is critical to the success of the business and actively contributes towards the competitive advantage, the business should be developing (and probably also managing) it in-house. However, hosting it in the cloud, thereby outsourcing the infrastructure element, is perfectly reasonable. In our pace-layered model, the USP would typically be delivered by systems of differentiation or innovation. A new or small business may need to be prepared to be a little flexible on this guidance until it has the scale to deliver this in-house.
- Look to buy 'pay-as-you-go' wherever possible. Sourcing hardware and software that is billed on the basis of what is used, when well-managed, minimises capital costs and creates a cost base that is both predictable and scales with the business. This is as true of cloud hosting as it is of individual applications. Many third-party providers now deliver solutions that can be bought on a per-user or some other usage basis. However, some of these solutions have a minimum volume requirement which should be understood before going too far down the procurement path.

- Only consider custom coding of applications that are either the interface to the customer or offer a means of differentiating in the market. If possible, source as much of the rest from specialist third parties and integrate with it. This significantly reduces the amount of work needed to be put into management, maintenance and operations and also means that the business doesn't need to maintain as much knowledge within in-house technology teams.

Applying pace layering to outsourcing might result in the following approaches.

Systems of record rarely offer any individual banking business a means of differentiating from other businesses (unless you believe you can genuinely create a whole new class of banking product). All of these systems require a large amount of specialist knowledge to design and build, are already well represented in the market by a number of very capable third-party providers and can now be sourced in the cloud (even core banking platforms are now commonly cloud sourced – good examples are those from ClearBank, FIS, Fiserv, Mambu and Temenos). In most cases, there is no reason to build, manage or even host the systems of record.

The decisions are less consistent when considering systems of differentiation. Some systems of record, such as eKYC platforms, are highly specialist, require significant investment and are already provided by capable third parties. However, if the bank provides specialist lending or believes that it has a unique approach, for example, then it may well be worth building a custom credit decisioning engine. Decisions need to be taken on a case-by-case basis in this category.

Systems of innovation are typically customer-facing systems and are therefore the primary point of contact with them. Every aspect of these applications should be carefully managed by the business to ensure that customers get the very best service. Typically, unless a business is just too small to maintain an in-house development team, or the business differentiator sits elsewhere, we would suggest that these applications be in-sourced. That is not to say that they should be coded from the ground up in-house; there are plenty of capable web servers, for example, on the market. However, the overall solution should be put together and managed in-house.

Before we finish on sourcing, there are a few elements to keep an eye out for when agreeing on third-party contracts. Once something is outsourced it can be hard to move off that provider to an alternative, so careful consideration should be given before entering into a relationship with them. A few key thoughts are:

- Documentation and intellectual property (IP): If outsourcing coding to a third party, it is important to ensure that code and documentation are contractual commitments from the third party and that IP for any customisation is owned by the business or, at worst, shared.
- Bait and switch: A common enough tactic when outsourcing for particular skills is for a supplier to put their A-team in front of the client during the pitch and then replace it with the C-team for delivery. Check that the team at the pitch is the team that will deliver the solution being bought.
- Lock-in: Once in a contract with a third party, how locked in does the bank become? If the answer is anything more than very little, then be very careful when considering the following points:

o Renewals: Look out for auto-renewing contracts. Where there is an auto-renewal clause ensure that a reminder is set to review the contract long in advance of any cut-off date for notice.

o Pricing reviews: Remember that pricing will change over time. Understand how it will change and place restrictions on by how much if possible. We like to try to peg the price changes to something reasonably reliable and fair, like inflation.

One final perspective on outsourcing. It sounds obvious, but always read the contract carefully. It is tempting to skip some of the more obscure paragraphs. However, having seen suppliers invoke force majeure during the coronavirus pandemic, we can attest to the fact that every clause in a contract could become relevant at any time and it is therefore critical that each one is reviewed in that light. Contract exit clauses are another key area that we would suggest require attention. This may not seem all that important at the time of contract negotiation but at some point the bank will need to exit the contract and these clauses will become very important. Time spent negotiating these points during the procurement phase will pay off later.

9.9   Managing the Estate

9.9.1   The Importance of Standardisation and Order

The bedrock of a strong technology capability is reliability. To achieve this, a technology function must ensure that appropriate standards are in place, from architecture and design to coding and through to the day-to-day operations. We have already touched on service management, but there is another element that is also important, namely, standardisation.

Through standardisation it is possible to improve consistency, reliability and the ability for staff to understand how the environment functions. Standardisation can be applied across architecture (using a roadmap and patterns), coding (choice of languages, structure of coding, commenting, documentation, deployment methods), operations (naming standards, documentation, operational processes) and throughout the broader technology function. Implemented correctly, standards should not constrain innovation or hinder efficiency but should complement them.

9.9.2   The 'Agile' Excuse

The development of agile methodologies was a huge step forward in software development, but it has since been used as an excuse for a multitude of sins. It should be noted that the methodology itself is not at fault. Instead, it is often misunderstanding or laziness that brings the issues. This is never truer than when it comes to standardisation and good order within the technology estate. We have found many examples where poor practice has been justified through agile. None of these examples stand up to interrogation. Agile is heavily reliant upon discipline and teams working to consistent standards and processes. It is not anti-standard or even anti-documentation. In many cases agile actually has little to say about broader technology documentation, but in development it is clear about the need for it and even proposes very strong standards to ensure that code is well constructed. Agile is about efficiency in documentation, creating the minimum required in order to serve the purpose it exists for.

9.9.3   Elements of Standardisation

A banking technology estate is rarely a small or simple affair. Supporting a robust and ever-growing technology estate requires a degree of standardisation. While every organisation needs to look to embrace new approaches and technology, it should do so with a view to how it will manage the estate on an ongoing basis. If every system is architected to different standards, using different coding languages, different operating systems and databases, this will create complexity and is often a recipe for disaster. Under such a scenario, over time, it becomes impossible to manage all of these systems or even retain the right skills to do so. Instead, an organisation should maintain a roadmap that clearly articulates which technologies are acceptable, which will be adopted in the near future and which are to be tombstoned (no further development) and removed from the estate. The smaller the number of development languages, operating systems and applications run in the estate the lower the cost of maintenance and operations and the more the business can spend on adding real value through change projects. This is not to say that one should ignore opportunities to use new technology (they should be embraced), but always take a measured approach to assessment and adoption of new technologies rather than establishing a free-for-all. Architects and coders should be encouraged to investigate and experiment with new technologies, but these should never be adopted before a rigorous appraisal and agreement with senior technologists, who should assist them in finding and agreeing on the right tools for the job.

The need for naming in a technology estate is a fundamental aspect of good technology management. Servers and services must all have a 'name' and a lack of standardisation can make understanding the technology estate extremely difficult. We have seen instances where entire environments have no discernible naming standards. This covers everything from server names to services (and microservices) and code functions. The defences for this activity vary, but one we heard is that this process provides additional security. Security is best delivered through other means. What this lack of standardisation does do is render the environment almost unmanageable to all but the people who built it and it takes forever to get new staff up to speed. Failure to implement a nomenclature across the technology estate will cause problems: it will be inefficient, costly and likely to result in human-generated failures as a result of misunderstandings.

The challenge is in finding the right level of standardisation for each organisation. If in doubt we would recommend that you err on the side of caution initially. It is easier to relax standards later than it is to tighten them once the technology estate is out of control.

The Agile Manifesto states *working software over comprehensive documentation*.[17] This is a sound principle but is often used as an excuse for poor documentation or even no documentation at all. That was never the intention of the community that came up with agile. Their focus was, rightly, on producing code, but serious practitioners of agile know that any development requires some documentation to support it. In our view, the principles that should be applied when considering documentation are:

- Keep it to a minimum. Documentation should be enough to understand the requirement/design/application, but no more. It should be concise and clear.
- Document code in code. In other words, code should only ever have very limited external documentation. The majority of code should be simple and clear enough for another coder to understand and supported by tests that provide additional clarity.

- Document after the fact. In many cases much of the documentation should be completed as elements of the solution mature (document what was done, rather than what the team thought they were going to do). Throughout development of any technology solution things will change. Continually rewriting documentation to reflect changes is time consuming and inefficient. Of course, there are some elements, such as requirements, that need to be written during the project.
- Documentation is not inefficient in its own right. The architecture of the IT estate, requirements, operational manuals and so on are all required in order to run an efficient and reliable technology service. Document the elements of the estate that require documentation but do so as efficiently as possible. For example, environmental data should be held in a configuration management database (CMDB) which can be updated easily and used as the basis of automated build processes.

It should be noted that none of the deficiencies identified above are solely the product of poor agile implementations. It just seems that in recent years poorly managed environments usually hide behind agile as a reason for explaining their deficiencies. In fact, we, having spent several decades working with international banks, have seen that many established, long-running firms suffer from similar issues, though in those cases they are compounded by the complexity of the environment and years of accumulation. These environments have been in existence since long before agile was dreamt up!

9.9.4 Non-functional Capabilities

Non-functional capabilities are an element of the technology estate that is rarely mentioned outside of the technology function and often only get noticed when something horrible happens, such as during security breaches or IT failures. Within the technology function they should be regarded as being just as critical as the functional capabilities of the estate.

There is a large range of non-functional capabilities that any business must address; everything from usability (including compliance with local disability rights laws) to security. Each of these elements needs to be taken just as seriously as the functional capabilities of the technology estate. Within the bounds of this book we cannot present a comprehensive overview of all of the non-functional capabilities, but it would be remiss of us not to provide some coverage.

9.9.4.1 Usability

Usability includes a range of elements from general usability (screen layout, readability of text), to performance (particularly responsiveness) and accommodation of disabilities (large fonts, etc.). While some of these are open to individual interpretation (screen layout for example), in many jurisdictions there are specific laws that will require businesses to accommodate certain disabilities.

9.9.4.2 Security

Frequently, when a business technical failure hits the headlines, it is security related. Nothing makes better news than a juicy data breach, particularly one where customer data has been taken. Not so long ago, security was often something of an afterthought.

After all, before the Internet came to the fore in the mid-1990s there was very little for anyone to attack. However, as Internet-facing applications, intranets, extranets and now cloud computing have pushed more and more elements of the estate into the public domain, the security perimeter of the business has become much broader. Security, of course, is not just about border management, or even demilitarised zones (areas of the network that hold the systems that need to be exposed to the outside world) anymore. The attack surface and variety of channels open to attackers means that we must assume that at some point either an external attacker will gain access to our network or, more likely, one of our own employees will wittingly or unwittingly be the cause of a security incident. Every business must work on the basis that at some point a security breach will occur and plan for that event. However, that doesn't mean that you shouldn't make it is difficult as possible for such an event to occur.

9.9.4.3   Systems Monitoring

Systems monitoring is another area that has changed considerably over the years. At one time you were ahead of the game if you could centrally monitor system event logs and possibly, if you were lucky, a few application logs. Today, done well, systems monitoring is a sophisticated and highly valuable part of a modern technology function. While the original premise behind systems monitoring was to monitor and alert on the health of a server or application, this has expanded to track virtual servers, microservices, containers, network components and much, much more. It is also often combined with automated response mechanisms that will manage load, auto-scale and implement fault-remedying solutions without human intervention.

However, in line with many of our previous comments, monitoring is not just about managing the technology. It is just as important to consider how it can support the business. This idea links back to the service concept that we discussed earlier in this chapter. Monitoring of a discrete system, IT service or microservice does not provide much benefit if its contribution to each business service is not understood. This extends across both internal systems and interfaces with third parties.

Monitoring those interfaces should not just be about the basics of 'is the endpoint up, responsive and performant?' but should consider much more sophisticated monitoring that supports our understanding of how the interface is performing and what it tells us about the business.

So, for a given service we might seek to monitor the following:

- Is the link up, in other words, are the two ends of the connection up and connected?
- Is the connection functional, in other words, are the two ends sending the normal kinds of traffic to each other?
- Is the connection performant, in other words, is the communication functioning at the normal levels of performance (response times, traffic levels, etc.)?

So far, this is consistent with normal technology monitoring, but we can go further. We could ask whether the data in the messages is consistent with prior messages. Is the content in the messages the same as it always has been or does it differ in any way? Are any of the fields or content of the fields changing? Are we receiving data in fields that used to be empty or vice versa? This is as much a security question as it is a business one, but it helps us to understand whether the interface is working the way it usually does or whether we should take a closer look to ensure that it doesn't or isn't starting to impact business processes.

We could also ask if the balance of response types is changing, either over the course of a given period or over the longer term. Again, this can really help the business to understand how the service is being used and whether there is anything that needs to be responded to. For example, in our eKYC service there are a number of possible responses from the service provider. Simplistically these could be (a) Okay – the customer's details appear valid and supporting documents cross-verify; (b) Not okay – something is wrong with the data provided or the customer's identity is that of a known fraudster; or (c) Not sure – something can't be confirmed by the service provider so someone in the business needs to check the data and make a decision manually. There are variations, but broadly speaking, these are the three normal outcomes. Once a business has been using a service like this for some time it should have an understanding of what proportions these responses typically come back. So, for example, normally 95% come back with an okay response, 3% Not okay and 2% Not sure, but what if these proportions start to change? From a pure technology perspective, we don't care. After all, the interface is up and functioning. However, from a business perspective this could be critical information. It could indicate that the service provider's systems are not functioning correctly or it could be that there is an attack underway on the business (for example, if the number of Not okay responses climbs, then that could indicate a concerted attack in an effort to open bank accounts for fraud or money-laundering purposes). In either case the business needs to know so that it can act either to increase support centre staffing while issues with the service provider are being addressed or to establish countermeasures against the fraudsters and a check on recently opened accounts to see whether they managed to successfully set up any accounts.

Monitoring the technology is just plain good sense. Monitoring to support the business is where the technology function can provide additional value to the business.

9.9.4.4 Performance

History has abundant examples of people who never saw the popularity of a given technology or channel, from Thomas Watson in 1943, who stated *I think there is a world market for maybe five computers*, to the development of the Internet, and all of those CEOs that thought their business was safe before seeing them eaten alive by a new entrant competitor.[18] This lack of ability to see the future (and nobody has a crystal ball) has a habit of encouraging people to build for what they can see and not worry about the future, and nowhere is this more prevalent than in technology.

Designing for scale and, most importantly, testing to ensure that systems perform at scale is important, but is often left until late in a project and then not carried out due to lack of time. Non-functional testing is even less of a priority for many businesses than functional testing. We are not saying that every service should be designed to scale to support the whole of the planet, just that it needs to have been designed to scale beyond where the business reasonably expects the upper limit to be and then tested to ensure that it can actually support those levels.

Performance testing is also not just about ramping up a test suite to maximum load. There are a large range of tests that can be carried out, including soak testing (testing over a long period), stress testing (testing at an overload level), spike testing (testing over a sudden burst of very high throughput) and scalability testing (ramping up over time to see how the system performs as it scales). In each case the goal is to understand the limits of system performance, how the system performs as it nears those limits and how gracefully the services provided by the system fail once those limits are exceeded.

This does not mean that all systems must be treated and tested equally. A decision should be taken in consideration of criticality for the business, likely loading, potential for reputational damage, criticality, and so on.

No critical system should ever go live without having undergone some level of performance testing.

9.9.4.5   Resilience and Recovery

However well architected a solution is, it is almost inevitable that it will fail at some point. This could be due to a software failure, a system upgrade, hardware fault or even a performance failure (see the previous section). The basis of good resilience and recovery planning is in knowing and accepting that failures are inevitable and designing resilience into the architecture. Before we continue, the reader should be aware of what we mean by the terms resilience and recovery (for an explanation, see Chapter 3).

Both resilience and recovery should be designed into the environment but, as with performance, this always needs to be balanced against cost. The more stringent the requirements the more it will typically cost to achieve and maintain them.

Testing of both resilience and recovery is a necessity. Systems should be tested both before going live and also after any significant change. They should also be tested on a regular basis even if no changes have occurred.

Testing of resilience can be as simple, for example, as switching one of the nodes in a cluster off to ensure that the remaining node(s) continue to deliver the service. However, there are now much more sophisticated ways of testing resilience. One of the most noteworthy of these is chaos engineering, where software in production is experimented upon to ensure it is resilient – yes, people actually trigger failures in their own environment to ensure that the systems are resilient. The extreme end of this scale are toolsets, such as Chaos Monkey,[19] that actually run in live environments and randomly impact live systems. We cover Chaos Monkey in more detail in Section 4.16.2.

Testing of recovery used to be as simple as failing the service over from a primary data centre to the business's secondary data centre, or that data could be recovered from a backup. However, with the advent of cloud services the former approach is no longer as clear-cut. If using cloud services, then the cloud services provider should automatically fail services to an alternative site in the event of a data centre failure, so a failover now feels more akin to a resilience problem than a true recovery scenario.

9.9.5   *Conclusion*

Operating within the banking domain typically requires running highly reliable, secure and performant systems and services. To that end it is imperative that the technology function puts sufficient focus on the non-functional elements of the solution to ensure this. When working to tight timescales it is easy to push the non-functional design and testing to the periphery of thought. After all, the business is looking for a functional system. However, failing to design and test non-functional criteria will result in disaster for the business at some point. The problem for the technology function is that the business would have forgotten the pressure that everyone was under to launch the solution and would now be asking why the technology function has failed so badly!

9.10   Following the Rules – Regulation, Law and Technology

The financial press is awash with stories of new tech companies that have successfully developed and deployed innovative solutions into the banking market. These financial technology or fintech companies include the likes of Monzo, PayPal, PayTM, Revolut and Venmo – businesses that seem to grow in value almost daily.

While these businesses are rightly proud of their ability to innovate and outmanoeuvre the incumbent businesses, there is often another area in which they have innovated en route, that of regulatory and legal compliance.

We are not suggesting that these businesses have flouted or are not compliant with applicable law and regulation, but rather that as a new business they have been able to take a fresh look at the industry and apply different, more efficient, approaches to the same problems that the incumbent banks have often struggled with. In some cases this has been through the new entrant's ability to select which regulatory authorisations to work within (for example, e-money regulations are less onerous than a full banking licence) but also that by taking a fresh look at regulation, often without the corporate baggage of having operated to the rules for generations, and through appropriate use of new technologies, these businesses can often solve what are almost insurmountable issues for established businesses.

We have covered regulation and the bank in Chapter 8, and here we look at some elements that are specific to technology.

9.10.1   Regulation and Technology

One of the things that we have found in our experiences of working with and in fintech businesses is that a significant proportion of people who have worked within banking for a long time have established in their minds a view of what the regulations require of them. This mindset is often formed by working in established banking businesses where much of the wisdom is received rather than established upon the basis of first principles. Often staff in legacy businesses don't re-read the regulation or challenge the established mindset; they just accept it and then work to ensure that any proposed change is compliant with their understanding of the regulation.

This is a problem. Regulation in many jurisdictions is often open to interpretation. It does not provide a single prescriptive solution that must be implemented. Instead it determines the outcomes that must be achieved and then leaves it open to the individual business to determine how best to meet that outcome. This means that while many large banks are mired in solutions that are far too complex and long winded to be effective, smaller, more agile businesses that are prepared to check the regulation and then challenge both it and themselves can often find innovative solutions that are quicker, simpler and much more cost effective.

In a conversation with the UK regulator we asked why it was that UK regulation was so open to interpretation. The answer we received, which we must make clear was not a formal position of the regulator, was that by leaving the solution to a requirement open, there were two beneficial outcomes possible. First, to come up with a workable solution the regulated entity must first understand that requirement. This ensures that regulated entities understand not just the desired outcome but what the intention is behind the requirement. Second, it gives the entity the opportunity to innovate in order to achieve the outcome.

While technology is often instrumental in enabling a banking business to meet its regulatory obligations, there are often aspects of technology that are regulated in their own right. When considering regulation from the perspective of technology, one should always bear in mind the following perspectives:

- Regulation as it relates to the requirements for a specific project or deliverable – so, for example, if the business is about to launch its first current account there will be a number of regulations that would be applicable to this product, including not just the product itself but the take-on process, how the bank calculates any overdraft interest, how it manages the customer and so on.
- Regulatory reporting requirements – every regulated business must produce regulatory reports periodically. Whenever a change is implemented the impact on regulatory reporting must be considered.
- Tracking – it is good practice to track all of the regulatory requirements that the business must adhere to and how they are being met. Clearly this needs to be reviewed regularly (for changes to regulation) and updated when changes are applied to the environment.
- Technology compliance – there are very few specific technology-related regulatory requirements because most regulation applies specifically to banking activities and products. However, there are some and these should always be considered. One of the most obvious of these is regulation in respect to outsourcing of technology and services (covered under the SYSC 8.1 regulation in the UK[20]). In Europe, the European Banking Authority (EBA) and local regulators have written a great deal on the responsibility associated with managing key services that are outsourced and ensuring that the regulated entity has the skills, experience and contractual rights required to provide appropriate oversight of these services.[21] As with the business requirements, any regulation that applies to technology should be noted and tracked. One might also argue that the Open Banking rules are also a technology regulatory requirement.[22]

The head of a technology function can be a regulated role. In the UK, for example, the chief information officer (CIO) of a bank is often a regulated role, falling under the Senior Manager's Regime (a formal regime that defines and regulates senior roles in financial services) as an SMF24 (which is actually a chief operations role, but covers technology and can be shared between individuals). As a senior manager an SMF can be held personally responsible if is determined that the technology function was responsible for a bank's failure to meet regulatory standards.

For more information on regulation see Chapter 8.

9.10.2 Law and Technology

Regulation is only part of the story in any jurisdiction, because financial services are also bound by the same laws as every other business and must therefore comply with them as well. The guidance provided earlier is equally applicable to law and the consequences of failure to comply can be just as profound.

Beyond the laws that apply to various elements of business practice, technology is often responsible for addressing many of the data-related laws. There are a number of areas that must be considered.

9.10.2.1 Data Protection

Data protection is not as simple as just ensuring that all data is kept securely, because there are many instances where the business needs its customers to have access to data. The key elements of a good data protection policy are:

- Categorising data: Defining the different types of data that could be held by the business – for example, public data (e.g. marketing campaigns), customer data, proprietary business data (trade secrets), internally sensitive data (e.g. payroll) and so on.
- Defining security for each category of data: Once the categories are agreed the level of data associated with the different categories needs to be defined.
- Implementation of roles: Different roles within the organisation need access to different data and sometimes even need different permissions on that data (for example, someone might have read access whereas someone else might have the ability to change the data).
- Tracking and auditing: All access to systems should be logged, with access to sensitive data tracked, monitored and reported upon.

Data breaches now occur with alarming regularity and the consequences go well beyond the fines that can be applied (which can be significant, particularly if the business operates in a jurisdiction where GDPR applies[23]). The real damage is the loss of public confidence in the organisation as the result of a data breach. These events could be terminal for even large businesses.

9.10.2.2 Data Retention

Different types of data need to be retained for different periods. With storage being so cheap, one of the easiest ways to address data retention requirements might be to keep all data (albeit archiving older data to the cheapest storage devices). However, data privacy laws around the world mean that there is often the need to justify retention of data – if it can't be justified then you shouldn't be keeping it. This even extends to scenarios where data has been shared or processing has been outsourced to a third party. In such instances the bank must know who has its customer data and have an agreement with it that it will delete the data if required.

We have worked in a number of organisations where nobody was able to define for how long data needed to retained, when it should be deleted or even if this was possible (for example, data held in a relational data model can be very hard to delete). Not only is this in contravention of retention laws, but it can make a response to a customer's request for their data (under GDPR) to be deleted very difficult.

9.10.2.3 Data Access Requests

Changes to laws, but also a growth in public awareness, has meant that subject matter requests are becoming more common. Customers in many parts of the world now have a right to know what data a business is keeping on them. In response to a customer request, the business must be able to state what data is held on that individual within a defined timeframe.

9.10.3 Industry Rules and Technology

Above and beyond regulatory and legal compliance, there is often also the need to comply with industry rules. While the law and regulation vary from location to location, the industry rules can often be consistent. The need for connectivity to enable money to be used effectively throughout the world requires a degree of standardisation and the enforcement of minimum levels of capability and compliance and it is often industry consortia that enforce this. So, the existence of industry rules has real value.

Some good examples of industry rules are the Payment Card Industry Data Security Standard,[24] a common set of security standards enforced by (not surprisingly) the payment card industry. Card-related fraud is a serious issue for the financial services industry, so, frustrating as the certification process can be, we can all agree that PCI DSS is a good thing.

Another good example is SWIFT,[25] which is responsible for ensuring that payment messages can traverse the globe (reasonably) quickly and reliably. As such, it is obvious that a common messaging standard must be enforced to ensure interoperability between all members.

9.10.4 Regulation and Law – Conclusion

From a technology perspective, not only must all applicable rules, regulation and law be complied with as a business (thereby requiring the technology function to provide suitable solutions to support this), but the technology function itself must be compliant.

It is worth considering the implementation of a tracker to identify and track compliance with all of the applicable rules that impact technology in each of the jurisdictions where the business operates. Clearly, the compliance function should already be doing this for the rest of the business, so there may be an opportunity to use its platform!

9.11   References

1. Conway, M. (1968). How do committees invent? *Datamation* 14 (5): 28–31. http://www.melconway.com/Home/pdf/committees.pdf (accessed 3 August 2020).
2. MacCormack, A., Rusnak, J., and Baldwin, C. (2007). Exploring the duality between product and organizational architectures: A test of the "mirroring" hypothesis. Harvard Business School. https://www.hbs.edu/faculty/Publication%20Files/08-039_1861e507-1dc1-4602-85b8-90d71559d85b.pdf (accessed 16 July 2020).
3. Intel. Fueling innovation we love and depend on. https://www.intel.co.uk/content/www/uk/en/silicon-innovations/moores-law-technology.html (accessed 16 July 2020).

4. World Economic Forum (2017). Beyond Fintech: A pragmatic assessment of disruptive potential in financial services. http://www3.weforum.org/docs/Beyond_Fintech_-_A_Pragmatic_Assessment_of_Disruptive_Potential_in_Financial_Services.pdf (accessed 16 July 2020).

5. ISACA. Effective IT governance at your fingertips. https://www.isaca.org/resources/cobit (accessed 16 July 2020).

6. ISO/IEC 20000-1:2018 (2018). *Information technology – Service management – Part 1: Service management system requirements*. Geneva, Switzerland: International Organization for Standardization.

7. Microsoft. Microsoft Operations Framework 4.0. https://docs.microsoft.com/en-us/previous-versions/tn-archive/cc506049(v=technet.10) (accessed 16 July 2020)

8. Axelos. ITIL – IT service management. https://www.axelos.com/best-practice-solutions/itil (accessed 16 July 2020).

9. Brand, S. (1994). *How Buildings Learn: What Happens After They're Built*. New York, NY: Viking Penguin.

10. Gartner. Pace-Layered Application Strategy. https://www.gartner.com/en/information-technology/glossary/pace-layered-application-strategy (accessed 16 July 2020).

11. Barclays. Technology. https://www.archive.barclays.com/items/show/5412 (accessed 16 July 2020).

12. Patterson, J. (2017). How IT outsourcing has changed over time. Transcosmos (27 March). https://transcosmos.co.uk/blog/evolution-of-it-outsourcing-infographic/ (accessed 16 July 2020).

13. Gonzales, A., Dorwin, D., Gupta, D. et al. Outsourcing: Past, present and future. https://courses.cs.washington.edu/courses/csep590/04au/clearedprojects/Dorwin.pdf (accessed 16 July 2020).

14. Finextra (2005). JPMorgan Chase's excessive tech spending killed IBM outsourcing deal. *Finextra* (8 February). https://www.finextra.com/newsarticle/13203/jpmorgan-chases-excessive-tech-spending-killed-ibm-outsourcing-deal (accessed 16 July 2020).

15. Gonzales et al. Outsourcing.

16. Mccue, A. (2006). HSBC outsourcing designs in India. Bloomberg (27 November). https://www.bloomberg.com/news/articles/2006-11-27/hsbc-outsourcing-designs-in-indiabusinessweek-business-news-stock-market-and-financial-advice (accessed 16 July 2020).

17. Agilemanifesto.org (2001). Manifesto for agile software development. https://agilemanifesto.org (accessed 16 July 2020).

18. CB Insights (2019). Foot in mouth: 59 quotes from big corporate execs who laughed off disruption when it hit. https://www.cbinsights.com/research/big-company-ceos-execs-disruption-quotes/ (accessed 16 July 2020).

19. Netflix. Chaos Monkey. https://netflix.github.io/chaosmonkey/ (accessed 16 July 2020).

20. The Financial Conduct Authority. SYSC 8.1 General outsourcing requirements. https://www.handbook.fca.org.uk/handbook/SYSC/8/1.html (accessed 30 July 2020).

21. European Banking Authority (2019). EBA publishes revised guidelines on outsourcing arrangements (25 February). https://eba.europa.eu/eba-publishes-revised-guidelines-on-outsourcing-arrangements (accessed 16 July 2020).

22. European Banking Authority. Payment services and electronic money. https://eba.europa.eu/regulation-and-policy/payment-services-and-electronic-money (accessed 16 July 2020).

23. Wolford, B. What are the GDPR Fines? GDPR EU. https://gdpr.eu/fines/ (accessed 16 July 2020).

24. PCI Security Standards Council. Securing the future of payments together. https://www.pcisecuritystandards.org/ (accessed 16 July 2020).

25. SWIFT. https://www.swift.com/ (accessed 16 July 2020).

CHAPTER **10**

The Future of Banking

We don't claim to have a crystal ball and can't claim to have a completely clear understanding of what future development the banking industry might see. However, as industry participants and commentators we do have some views on where the banking industry is heading and what the likely changes and innovations of the next decade might be.

To put the following section into context, we are now in 2020. What we would regard as neobanks (businesses such as Ant Financial, Monzo, N26, Revolut and Starling) are all significantly less than 10 years old, with the challenger payments businesses (the likes of Klarna, PayPal and TransferWise) being a little older. In early 2020, Pay.UK released account switching data for the last quarter of 2019 which revealed that Monzo was the single biggest net recipient of current account switching in the UK.[1] For those not familiar with the UK current account switching service, we cover this in more detail in Section 8.2.3.

Mobile-only neobanks are currently in the ascendency, funky debit cards (coral pink[2] and portrait[3] versions, for example) are all the rage, expense management and forecasting are becoming sophisticated (for example, identifying individual merchant spending, spending by sector and balance forecasting) and it's possible to travel the world without paying a fortune in foreign currency charges.[4] An entire industry of neobanks that supports small businesses is offering expense management, invoicing (including automated follow-ups to customers who are late in paying) and integration with common accounting platforms, but currently mostly for sole traders and owner managers.[5] As we explored in Section 2.9, neobanks may have an opportunity given that some of them can operate current accounts at a cost comparable to that of much larger legacy banks, but only if they can grow scale.

However, the future of neobanks is far from certain. The Covid-19 pandemic wrought significant damage and banks such as Monzo had to make considerable cuts to their workforces.[6,7]

Open banking also seems to be catching on, at least with the regulators, across the globe. The big question now is *where next?* Some things are easier to predict than others.

10.1 Broad Trends

As detailed in Chapter 2, the history of the banking industry around the world is one of significant consolidation to the point where it is dominated by a relatively small number

348

of international banks and between three and five large domestic banks in each major economy and an even smaller number of payment card schemes. There always have been smaller financial institutions (building societies, credit unions and local banks), but they have never threatened the dominance of the large banks. From a pure volume of accounts perspective the big banks still dominate, but arguably the status quo across the industry is changing and we see a number of possible outcomes.[8]

10.1.1   The Payment Card Industry

As discussed in Chapter 2, payment cards are used and accepted around the world.[9] However, cards are not the only way of making payments. In China, card usage is vastly overshadowed by the Quick Response (QR) code[10] and elsewhere around the globe there is a rise in other forms of mobile to mobile payments and open banking-related services.

The reason for the dominance of card payments in the West really comes down to two primary factors. First, their cultural and merchant acceptance: payment cards have been around for so long that recognition of them among the general public and acceptance by merchants is almost ubiquitous. It took payment cards several decades to achieve this level of acceptance on the UK high street (see Section 2.5.7). Second, their practicality: they are very easy to use and only require a piece of plastic, a card reader and an Internet connection.

However, mobile payments are on the rise.[11] Although there are concerns among the general public about running out of battery power on their smartphones, it still seems inevitable to us that the age of plastic cards is coming to an end and there will be, over the coming years, a wholesale move to payment by phone, wearable or perhaps even something else, like facial recognition.[12] The question, then, is what this means for businesses that currently operate in the payment card sector.

It is a certainty that new businesses will continue to start up and attempt to innovate in the payments space. Some of these will use the established payment networks and infrastructure, some will use structural changes (such as those created by open banking and immediate payment schemes) and some will seek to establish entirely new means of making payments – P2P and QR-based methods already exist, but others will also come into being. A frequent challenge that such businesses face is the so-called network challenge. Merchants will only accept a payment mechanism (and spend the money to integrate it into their online stores, or pay for the infrastructure to accept it in their physical stores) if their customers are keen to use it, and customers are often only keen to invest their time and personal data in a new method if it is widely accepted. Furthermore, there appears to be a large array of payment methods already available, with acquirers offering tens of different methods to merchants. It's hard to know what payment methods to accept if you are a merchant or what to use if you are a consumer. If you are a payment start-up, raising your profile to stand out among a large group of incumbents, both large and small, is difficult.

Therefore, moving from niche offering to challenging the established card schemes is always going to be hard. As mentioned earlier, cards are accepted almost everywhere, in the Western Hemisphere at least. The payment card schemes also have significant investment capital and capable research and development functions.[13] While the plastic card may disappear, the payment card schemes are actively working on new solutions that use their established infrastructure but take advantage of the same consumer shifts that their start-up competition seeks to leverage. However, they face a dilemma – they don't want to cannibalise their existing business and they have to be careful not to compete with their own customers, the card issuers and payment acquirers. We are not sure they are as hungry as many start-ups, although they have deep pockets given their per transaction revenue model and could probably afford to acquire any rising threats. Is it possible that a start-up service will step into the space and truly challenge the hegemony of the established players? Yes, it's possible, but in our view it is not likely, unless that new player brings something truly special to the game.

As we see it, something truly special could come in a number of forms. Businesses such as Ant Group have enormous capital behind them.[14] Although pushing QR code payments (or any other new payment technology) from East to West represents a significant challenge, not just from the established payment card schemes but also from suspicious Western governments, it may be possible. Of course, Ant Group is not the only well-financed business out there that is eyeing this market. The challenge could equally come from Google, Amazon, Facebook and Apple (GAFA) or any other well-funded global consumer business. Although both Apple[15] and Google[16] have consumer cards programmes there is a long way to go from having a card product to producing a genuine alternative to cards or even just the card schemes – but it may be possible.

The cards businesses do have an Achilles heel. They have to charge for their services. Being essentially monoline businesses they must generate an income from this business to remain viable. This isn't the case for a business like Amazon,[17] which has proven previously that it is happy to take a loss on a product or market offering in order to gain market share. Setting merchant fees to zero on the Amazon marketplace, as an example, would be a tempting proposition for merchants and would allow Amazon to build a payment business that isn't based on a payment card from one of the payment card schemes.

Another possible entry route is the populist one. Neobanks have already demonstrated that catching the zeitgeist can be a route to considerable success. A start-up that could catch the mood of the times, as Monzo has in banking in the UK, might be able to compete successfully with the incumbents but it would still require a considerable amount of capital and the ability to successfully deploy the model over a broad geography.

A specific route that we think several will attempt to take in Europe is the use of open banking and immediate payment schemes – such as Faster Payments in the UK – as an alternative to card payments at online merchants initially and then at physical merchants. The basic approach is for the merchant to accept an immediate payment that is initiated and authenticated using the open banking application programming interface (API). For the merchant, the advantage is that the merchant fee could on average be a quarter or less of the fee the merchant pays for a card payment and for the user, it is the seamless user experience available when using a smartphone. At a physical point of sale, the near-field communication (NFC) device in a smartphone or a QR code generated by the smartphone could be used to communicate with the point of sale card reader.

The most likely outcome is that the established payment card schemes will change with the times and deploy new solutions and strategies to defend against any new arrivals – or acquire them. For example, Mastercard acquired Vocalink, the operator of the UK's Faster Payments scheme, in 2016. However, we would not bet against the GAFA four, Ant Group or another Internet behemoth entering the market and giving the incumbents a run for their money.

10.1.2 Banks

The situation in banking is somewhat different from that of the global payment card industry. While there are a number of banks that operate internationally, even then the actual banking services are typically delivered to a country, state or regional market. Banking is also a composite of a large number of different products and services, each of which is open to specific challenges and opportunities. It is this nature which makes banking more susceptible to challenge, either on a local level or on a product, feature or functional level. The rise of open banking compounds this risk for large banks, by forcing them to open up access to customers' accounts and payments.

But what does this mean? After a slow start, the large banks are certainly fighting hard to retain control and market share. By and large they are keen to fund innovation within their businesses,[18,19] so isn't the obvious outcome that they will fight off the smaller start-ups? In our opinion, no. That doesn't mean that all large banks are doomed, more that they will inevitably cede services to the newcomers in certain areas. In fact, over the shorter term we expect many of the large banks to remain competitive, but they will see reversals in certain areas.

We envisage a new market structure emerging where a variety of business models are likely to exist. We classify these in four categories:

1. The niche specialists are businesses that identify and focus on specific elements of banking that are inefficient or open to competition. A good example of this is Revolut, which has focused on the consumer foreign exchange market (and expanded from there), but there will be others. Many of these might use open banking to provide their services, be that in account aggregation value-added services or perhaps payment services (using established banks' payments capabilities) and could end up owning the customer relationship, even where the core banking services are provided by an established bank.
2. The platform bank will provide the basics of the banking model including commodity products (current accounts for example), payments, and regulatory compliance and will act as processing banks for the niche specialists (as above). This is a volume play and could result in a low-margin business, but at volume this could still be very successful. Those large banks that fail to stay abreast of market changes may well find themselves forced into this position.
3. The market specialist – the establishment of the market specialist is already occurring. New entrant banks that cover some elements of the core banking services, enhanced through relationships with complementary third parties (either as add-on services or providing retail banking products that the new entrant does not want, or is not ready, to offer themselves) are already much in evidence. Monzo and N26[20] are examples of this and are demonstrating an active interest and some success in growing beyond the borders of their country of origin.[21]
4. The full-spectrum large bank – for those large banks that prove nimble enough to stay competitive with the new entrants, there is still an opportunity to continue to operate with a significant share of the banking sector in their domestic markets. Some of the models identified above may erode market share and profit margins, but the massive scale of some of these businesses, combined with capable management, should allow them to continue as they have for some time, albeit perhaps less profitably.

Many of these roles already exist today, of course. However, our belief is that the proliferation of niche and market specialist roles that we expect to see over the next decade or two will eventually force the creation of the platform model. So, we will see more niche and specialist banks, the same large international and domestic banks and the creation of the platform bank.

10.2   Changing Products, Features and Functions

Of course, change at the market level can only really be realised by changes within the products, features and functions offered in the banking market (though a good backstory and great marketing goes a long way[22]). Here we see great potential for change, but less so in products and more in the areas of features and functions. Why is this?

The banking industry has been remarkably stable in the products offered for a long time. It is arguable that the last great innovation in retail banking products was the invention of the payment card over half a century ago. Considering the advances made in technology over the last couple of decades this might sound odd to an outsider, but it is worth considering a number of aspects of banking. First, as we discussed in Chapter 2, banking has been around for a long time, giving plenty of opportunity for the products to arise and develop. Second, banking products are actually pretty simple, with there being really only a handful of products: current accounts, savings accounts and lending accounts. Third, within most industries technology tends to enable greater efficiencies, improved features and better customer engagement but it doesn't necessarily revolutionise the products themselves – for example, Uber is still delivering taxi rides to customers despite all of the technology and press coverage.[23]

We have struggled to think of any genuinely new retail banking products over the past three decades other than offset or current account mortgages in the UK.[24] One could argue that open banking might enable monetisation of money management solutions instead of charging for the financial products themselves (and this would be new), but it is unlikely that the core product set of a bank will be fundamentally re-imagined.

However, where technology has had a massive role to play is in the development of new features for established products and services as well as having had a huge impact on the way that modern banks are run.

10.3   The Future of Payments

10.3.1   Instant Free Payments Anywhere

Digitisation of our payments networks is already generating significant improvements in terms of speed of completion within a limited geography and also in terms of cost. Everything but international and high-value payments is trending towards being free these days. If this speed of service and efficiency can be achieved nationally then it can also be achieved internationally, albeit with banks likely to continue to take a commission on foreign currency conversions.

It can be argued that considerations such as money laundering and terrorism monitoring will mean that international payments will always suffer delays. However, most anti-money laundering, fraud and payment monitoring is today carried out by systems. Yes, those systems still have a way to go in terms of sophistication and they will still throw exceptions that will require human intervention that will sometimes slow the process down but that doesn't mean that near-instant payments can't be made available, just that some exceptions may mean that some payments take a little longer than others.

Delays in international payments today do not add extra security, they just reflect an inefficient process. Between improved levels of automation and some of the anti-fraud initiatives outlined in the following pages there is no reason why international payments can't give the impression of being instant, or at least near instant.

10.3.2   Payment Anti-fraud Measures

Fraud is a constant concern for the banking industry and, as we covered in Chapter 7, instant payments can be a facilitator of such fraud. Not only is fraud bad for custom, but in many cases the banking businesses themselves carry much of the loss. It is therefore an area that participants are constantly looking to improve. One area of fraud that has seen significant growth in recent years, particularly as a result of the digitisation of payments, is authorised push payment crimes in which criminals convince their targets to send them money.

The exact mechanism for this varies, but a typical attack might include hijacking a solicitor's email address and sending payment requests to customers with modified bank account details. Unfortunately for the victim there is often no means of validating that a given bank account is correct for the intended recipient (short of speaking to them) and this form of attack can prove to be devastatingly effective. Combined with the ability to move payments quickly a fraudster can escape with the money before the victim even realises that they have been targeted.

The UK is one of the few countries that tracks this kind of fraud in detail and, according to UK Finance (a trade association),[25] there was almost £500 million of push payment fraud in 2019 and this figure had risen by about £100 million from the previous year. While not as prevalent as card fraud, this is a significant, and worrying trend.[26]

The UK is not alone in experiencing this kind of fraud and as the banking industry pushes the use of digital payments over cash and cheques in the years ahead this kind of fraud will only get worse on a global level.

Although push payment is only one kind of fraud it does demonstrate that the convenience of new, instant, payment methods and online banking bring significant new opportunities to fraudsters. In the fraud versus fraud prevention arms race this can only mean that banks will have to step up their anti-fraud game. We foresee a number of significant changes occurring in the next decade.

An obvious solution, and one the UK implemented, is to confirm the name of the recipient when the payer submits the banking details for a payment.[27] So, if the payer submits what they believe are payment details for F. Bloggs & Co, their solicitor, and the system returns with a statement such as *This does not match the recipient's name, please check the recipient's details before sending any money* (or words to that effect), then this should reduce instances of fraud. There is nothing to stop this service being implemented globally, but it does require cooperation on a global scale.

While national fraud databases have existed in some countries for many years, true collaboration on anti-fraud measures has been slow to emerge. However, there are examples of it. In September 2019, five Dutch banks (ABN AMRO, ING, Rabobank, Triodos Bank and de Volksbank) announced a collaborative agreement to set up an organisation to monitor their combined transactions with the goal of more effectively identifying and stopping suspicious transactions.[28] Such collaborative efforts have been under discussion for some years but had never previously come to much. Implementing such a solution is quite straightforward (as the technology for payment monitoring already exists) and the added data from having significantly more payments to monitor should provide better insight and an ability to spot suspicious activity at a broader level much earlier. With the creation of a specialist organisation one should also expect the benefits typically associated with centres of excellence such as the development of specialist skills pools. In theory there is nothing to stop the members of SWIFT implementing such solutions to counteract global fraud or money laundering, except that global politics and state-sponsored fraud, money laundering and sanctions breaches are likely to cause issues in both the implementation and execution.

Artificial intelligence and machine learning (AI/ML) technologies excel at parsing large quantities of data, building a model of how the data works and then spotting anomalies. We expect to see much greater use of AI/ML technologies in the area of transaction monitoring in the coming years. This should significantly assist in reducing the delays currently associated with international payments.

Of course, there is a more cynical view of the delays in international payments that we have heard made more than once. By slowing those payments down, and thereby holding large amounts of funds in their own accounts overnight, the correspondent banks earn a tidy sum in interest. It is not necessarily in their interest to invest time and money into improving efficiency in a process where they actually benefit from the existing inefficiencies.

10.4   Technology in Operations

A huge amount of the manpower in operations functions is dedicated to relatively mundane and repetitive tasks. For those who work in banks this won't come as much of a surprise and it is something that banks have been working hard to automate for many years. The idea of applying AI and automation in operations is not new and is something we expect to see significantly increase in years to come.[29]

We don't expect people to be entirely replaced by computers in operations, but we can see a position where they start to become something of a rarity. While it is often claimed that the implementation of automation, AI (and machine learning for that matter) into banks will allow humans to be re-tasked with activities more closely aligned with our skills (people skills, innovation and so on), the reality is that there will inevitably be a reduction in headcount in many banks as a consequence of the deployment of these sorts of technologies.

With reductions in headcount in operations (and other areas of the bank) and the shift to computer-driven processes we should also expect to see the numbers of exceptions thrown by those computer systems decrease – it stands to reason that if computers are governing the inputs and are managing the operational elements of the bank then there is less room for human error and therefore a lower likelihood of an exception.

Of course, there will still be some computer-driven exceptions, but these can be isolated, fixed and then should not recur. The question then becomes one of the reliability of the software.

10.5   Regulation

Regulatory reporting is always carried out in retrospect, covering the past month/year (or other period) of data. The issue that this creates for the regulators is that they only ever discover issues when they either find it in a business's data after the fact or somebody tells them. This causes a problem, because it means that action can only really be taken after the event and not as a corrective while an event is occurring.

However, it doesn't have to be this way. The holy grail of regulation is to be able to identify when an event is occurring and act immediately, but the only way to do this is to receive and analyse data from banking businesses in real time.

Achieving this requires two steps forward. First, the ability to create a regulatory return in real time. Much of the data required to support this might make up transactional and event data that could be communicated to the regulator in real time fairly easily, but some things need to be calculated. For example, the exposure that a bank has to movements in an underlying exchange or central bank base rate may require multiple calculations to be applied before it can be submitted. To achieve even near-time submission requires a level of technical capability that does not currently exist (show us a single bank today that never checks or amends the outcome of its regulatory reporting platforms before submitting).

The regulator must also be able to make sense of the data being submitted. Again, this is not simple. Most regulators around the world are responsible for many hundreds of financial institutions. Taking all of the real-time submissions from all of these businesses and turning those into usable data for a regulator is going to require a lot of work. This will require a high degree of automated analysis of reporting data and the ability for those analytics systems to alert when issues are identified.

Real-time regulatory reporting is going to become a reality in due course. However, we believe that the complexities associated with managing, reporting and understanding the data mean that a phased approach is the most likely. Regulators will likely start by consuming the simpler transactional data, before moving on to ask for calculated 'dynamic' position submissions.

10.6   Finance

As covered in Chapter 8, the finance function is governed by a clear set of rules in respect to accounting, general finance and regulatory reporting. Anything that can be codified in this way lends itself well to being programmed. As with operations we expect significant headcount reductions in finance departments, as many of the more junior and day-to-day activities are replaced by computers.

We do, though, still see roles for specialist and experienced finance operatives. While much of the modelling can be codified, for example, the definition of risks and some of the complex *what if* modelling will still need to be led by an experienced practitioner.

10.7   The Technology Function

The increasing use of technology in banking, as with many industries, shows no sign of abating. There are clearly many opportunities to make further use of technology through artificial intelligence, machine learning, and automation or robotics as well as the possibility of further proliferation of digital channels. It seems fairly certain, then, that the technology function is one of the few areas of banking that is likely to see increases in headcount and overall cost.

It also seems likely that much of this additional headcount will be employed by the bank rather than outsourced. As the influence, and therefore importance, of technology to the institution continues to grow the development capabilities required to build and maintain these services will be regarded as core to the business and maintained internally. To be clear, we are not predicting the end of outsourcing, more that the balance of sourcing, particularly in the development functions, will shift more to in-house development.

Having said that, we do expect to see continued movement of hosting towards the cloud and greater use of third-party and open-source toolsets, code and platforms. So, while headcount shifts towards being internally sourced, the hosting and large elements of the codebase are likely to come from outside. Coders will, instead, focus on writing and maintaining the elements of code that either represent business-specific capabilities, particularly where they offer opportunities to differentiate, or provide the glue that binds the third-party code together. This implies a greater swing towards the use of smaller, more discrete, code sets (microservices) and away from the monolithic platforms of the past. That is not to say that third-party applications won't be used. Our personal belief is that third-party applications ought to be used for all non-differentiating business capability such as HR, finance and treasury.

The other area that will undoubtedly continue to grow is data science and analytics. While much has been made in the press about the value of data and the shift towards analytics, the reality is that we have only just started to scratch the surface. Not only do we see continued development in banks seeking to make better use of their own data, but there will be a significant increase in the combination of in-house data with data sourced from elsewhere – be that explicitly through (approved) use of customer data held by other businesses or from open-source data. Such examples might include personal data from other sources (through open banking[30] or GDPR[31]) or data released by companies or government organisations, such as the UK House Price Index supplied by the Land Registry in the UK[32].

While we expect there to be a reduction in headcount across many functions in banks due to automation, technology will be the clear winner. To produce, manage and maintain all of the technology that will replace the people in other functions of the bank will inevitably mean that the technology function must grow.

10.8   A Short Digression on Data

The data story is one that has seen significant development over the past 10 to 15 years and, to a large extent, has been driven by sovereignty and ownership.

It is generally acknowledged today that some of the larger Internet businesses had limited respect for an individual's rights in respect to their data until very recently.[33] Data that they held was used as they saw fit and could be sold to anyone who wanted to buy it, with no consent from the individual required. However, the balance of power has shifted significantly in the past decade. This shift is best demonstrated in Europe, although many other states are clearly treading similar paths.

As covered in Chapter 8, within Europe there have been two significant pieces of legislation that have the potential to play a significant role in how we use data, namely PSD2[34] and GDPR[35], that enable open banking and open data.

Open data has a large range of potential applications within the banking industry. Just a few possible examples include personal lending, with a decision to offer a loan drawing on the applicant's financial data obtained using open banking APIs from accounts they hold at other financial institutions. Also, in business lending with the potential for using not just financial data from other institutions, but also open data. For example, a bank might also choose to assess footfall data (including volumes, timings and even wealth assumptions from mobile phone data) in deciding whether to grant a loan to a restaurant to pay for an extension to the dining area. Finally, in financial well-being where data can be aggregated from a range of the customer's bank accounts (and potentially other sources) to support planning for future goals. For example, analysing spending to propose ways to cut costs in order to save for a child's future university education. This could even include suggestions to change suppliers of certain services in order to reduce outgoings.

Of course, these examples are just a tiny fraction of the potential that open data offers to the banking industry. If a large tech or retail company (Amazon, for example) were to enter the banking industry more comprehensively than it already has, it could leverage the data it holds on customers, with their consent, to provide a broad range of financial products and services tailored very specifically to their needs.

10.9   Banking Products and Services

Although we see limited prospect of a fundamental overhaul of the products in banking, there is still room for innovation within existing product features.

10.9.1   Current Accounts

In recent years the current account has arguably been the most heavily innovated product in banking. Led by neobanks we have seen the addition of instant notification of payments, budgeting, account aggregation and much more. However, there is still room for further innovation.

Possibilities include cardless accounts. As touched on in Chapter 5, the days of plastic payment cards appear to be numbered. In the next few years, we expect to see the emergence of current accounts that have no physical payment card. This is not to say that there is no payment card functionality on the account, merely that the card account will be entirely virtual.

Second, programmable payment accounts are not a new concept, with products like root[36] having offered the capability for some years. However, we see this concept becoming more mainstream through the creation of much simpler If This Then That (ITTT) accounts where customers can set up rules to help them manage their money.

For example, if there is more than £500 in my account on day 25 of the month then move £300 to my savings account.[37]

With our world seemingly becoming ever smaller, the need for access to money in a variety of currencies and locales is becoming more and more commonplace. At the moment this is typically addressed through bureaux de change, traveller's cheques, travel cards and no-fee payment cards. However, there is nothing to stop the banking industry (particularly international banks) establishing multiple accounts for customers, in different currencies, under a single umbrella account and enabling the customer to seamlessly move money from one account to another (at spot rate) as they wish and accessing the cash locally (without additional charges) wherever their currency is supported. A European business, Ipagoo, attempted to achieve something along these lines and, although it went into administration in 2019, we see the concept having the potential to become a popular option in the future.[38]

Finally, the family mortgage already exists in some countries around the world.[39] We see the potential for current accounts where family money is either pooled or exists in a series of nested accounts, with different members having varying rights to access and control the funds – essentially a mandate at the family level. This would enable parents to manage their children's access to money as well as enabling adults to have some control over the funds of vulnerable relatives without having to stop them having the freedom they need to get on with their everyday lives.

10.9.2   Loans

Probably the single greatest opportunity to innovate in lending will come through the loan origination stages, specifically in the area of credit decisioning. The existing credit scoring and decisioning solutions are limited by the fact that they can only really assess customers on the basis of a limited set of historical performance data and some current facts (such as salary).

In recent years there has been much talk about using radical new approaches to credit score customers, such as assessing data sourced from social media profiles.[40] While some of these new approaches may provide additional insight, they also come with a large number of constraints and concerns which may make them impractical to implement.[41]

However, open data and open banking, as noted before, do offer significant potential for use in credit decisioning as they can provide a current, and comprehensive, understanding of the customer's position. They have also been enshrined in law in many countries, meaning that there are significantly fewer obstacles, once a customer's consent has been given, for an organisation to navigate in order to provide these kinds of features.

It would seem likely that sharing banking-related data will be the obvious first step down this path, but tapping into open data or social media feeds could enable banking businesses to make better informed decisions across a whole range of credit scenarios.

10.9.3   Mortgages

Mortgages also have potential for some degree of change. For example, in many countries mortgage terms are typically based upon the likely income-generating lifespan of a single generation. However, this isn't the case everywhere and in Japan, for example, a 100-year intergenerational mortgage was introduced in the 1990s.[42] With property prices in many parts of the world getting to the point where younger people are finding them extremely difficult to afford, we see intergenerational mortgages as a possible next step for the mortgage industry. With property becoming a major source of intergenerational wealth it would seem reasonable that an element of the debt associated with the purchase of a property could also be passed down from one generation to the next.

As discussed in Chapter 3, robots have already taken a hold in the banking industry with contact centres being one of the areas in which robots were adopted. However, they are also creeping into other areas of banks, such as supporting customers with basic money management activities. At the moment these robots are relatively simplistic, but they are already making inroads into more advanced functions such as mortgage advice services.[43] As robotics and AI become even more sophisticated, we see significant opportunity for them to expand across the areas of advice. One such area is likely to be in the provision of support for the mortgage process. Currently many geographies recognise advised sales (supported by a person who provides advice) and non-advised, or execution only, mortgages. However, regulators are open to the idea of robo-advice[44] and we expect robo-advised sales to start to become more common. Of course, over time one should expect these robots to become much more sophisticated, enabling mortgage advisers to extend their range of services to offer fully robo-advised journeys as well as using robots to automate aspects of human-advised journeys.

10.10   Distributed Ledger Technologies and Cryptocurrencies

Blockchain, as with many emerging technologies, was over-hyped at its outset. In the eyes of its fans, it quickly became a potential answer to almost any problem in almost any industry. However, over time both distributed ledger technologies (DLTs), of which the blockchain is just one example, and crypto currencies, of which Bitcoin is an example, have started to find their place, both more broadly in other markets and but also directly within the banking industry.

While many of the implementations in banking currently reside within commercial banking functions, there are a few notable exceptions, as discussed next.

10.10.1   Payments

One of the original goals of the blockchain was to create a means of exchanging value without there being any need for either party to trust either each other or even a third-party intermediary. This clearly has the potential for use in mainstream banking as well as crypto currencies. Indeed, several businesses have attempted to build commercial implementations of DLTs to compete with or replace national and international payment systems. Probably the best-known example of this is Ripple, a US-based technology company founded in 2012. Ripple has seen moderate success, with banks such as Santander[45] and Bank of America[46] trialling services based upon the technology. In fact, Ripple now claims to have more than 300 financial institutions using its RippleNet technology.[47] Ripple is not the only business pushing blockchain-based payments networks. For example, JPMorgan Chase is leading a separate push that also claims over 300 members.[48] There is clearly potential in these initiatives, but the jury is still out on whether they can supplant the established networks such as SWIFT. The advantage that SWIFT has is its huge user

base, numbering over 11,000 institutions across the globe,[49] and it will require a huge
effort or a demonstrably far superior solution in order to seriously challenge a network
of this size.

10.10.2 Currencies

There is no shortage of different cryptocurrencies, with new ones being invented seemingly every week. Although most fail to gain any real adoption, there are some that have
achieved a degree of success. Among the current hopefuls are Bitcoin, Ethereum and
Ripple, to name just a few. However, all of the most successful cryptocurrencies share a
common trait – volatility – and this means that they currently have more in common with
a speculative asset than a true currency. Attempts have been made to create stablecoins,
cryptocurrencies that are tied to the value of other assets (be that a particular currency,
a basket of currencies or some other relatively stable item).[50] However, none of these has
yet seen much success.

Despite the current lack of success as a true currency, we still see a potential future
for cryptocurrencies. The two most likely avenues to success are either through being
launched as a currency by big tech (Facebook-backed Libra, for example[51]) or through
being launched by a national government. While the idea of big tech launching an
all-conquering global digital currency is tempting, the practical reality is that national
governments are highly likely to reject, and actively fight, any such offering.[52] It is much
more likely that national governments will launch their own digital currencies. These
will likely be relatively mundane affairs but, being government backed, they will likely
be stable and therefore have the potential to see widespread adoption.

10.11   The Future of the Branch

Having worked at Metro Bank we have seen the power of a branch network in engaging
the general public. Where a bank can optimise its branch footprint, as Metro Bank has,
then there is an opportunity to make it a profitable endeavour. There may always be
a proportion of the public that will want, or even need, the ability to meet the bank
face to face.

However, we also see an opportunity to bring computers further into branches.
ATMs, for example, can be significantly enhanced to provide a much broader range
of services. As discussed in Chapter 4, facial recognition (or other biometric logon
capabilities) can be embedded to enable an ATM to not only recognise the customer,
but also greet them by name. Add robo-advice to the solution and you have a platform
that can now greet a customer, engage them in conversation and solve any question they
might have. Such solutions could be used to reduce some staffing levels in large branches
or as a complete replacement for smaller branches. Initially, while the technology
proves itself, there may be the need for embedded video conferencing capabilities, but as
computers become better at reading facial expressions and intonations, we can see even
the need for that waning.

We believe that the branch is here to stay, for a while at least, but the manned branch
footprint will decrease to cover only towns of above a certain size and the format of those
branches will change to accommodate greater digitisation.

10.12   Headcount, Skills and Career Progression in the Bank of the Future

As should now be abundantly clear, our expectation is that headcount, as a rule, in modern banks will inevitably be lower than it is today. Automation, AI and machine-learning technologies will replace many of the operational and back office roles that we see today. There will still be opportunities for smaller numbers of staff to augment the machines where specialist knowledge supports questioning, querying, innovation or troubleshooting, but the day-to-day activities will be provided by technology. In and of itself this is a considerable cost saving for banks. Despite the human cost, the reduction in human error, employment-related costs and improvements in efficiency are just too great a prize to give up.

In the channels, too, we expect reductions in headcount. Reductions in the branch network might initially result in a shift towards greater use of contact centres (which will require some reskilling to accommodate video calling), but over time we expect a significant amount of contact centre engagement to be completed by computers as well, either through automated resolution of simple issues and questions or through robo-advice and AI.

The only function in banks that we expect to continue to grow is the technology function. However, even here the change is not all one way. Programming will be the significant growth area, but elements such as desktop support and operations should wane as either demand drops (fewer staff at the bank results in fewer support calls) or computer support activities are digitised – many technology operations functions lend themselves well to being run by computers.

While the reduction in headcount across the bank will bring financial efficiencies, there are some new problems that could arise as a result. With significant digitisation of many activities there is a risk that the skills and knowledge associated with those activities are lost. This generates two significant problems for the organisation. First, without the in-depth skills and experience of operating a function, it is hard for any business to innovate in that space and, second, without appropriate experience, if the computer systems fail, then understanding the issue is harder if the knowledge of how that function works no longer exists in-house. Of course, some of this knowledge will have transitioned into the technology function but technologists are a fickle lot and once a piece of code is cut the engineer often moves onto another project and much of the knowledge they held about the specifics of that activity is quickly lost.

Industries such as banking draw upon their large workforces to find the right people to retain, promote and drive their business in the future. With significant reductions in more junior roles there is a question mark over the ability of those businesses to find the right skills and capabilities to develop into the specialists and managers of the future. Does this brain drain mean that our future banks will lack the depth of capability to find the right people to build into future leaders? If so, what does this mean for their future?

Technology can deliver massive benefits and the digitisation of the banking industry is inevitable. However, one can't help but wonder whether we might lose something among all the gains and that something could have a significant impact upon the industry in the years ahead.

10.13   References

1. Pay.UK (2020). Current account switch service statistics. https://www.bacs.co.uk/Resources/FactsAndFigures/Pages/CurrentAccountSwitchServiceStatistics.aspx (accessed 17 July 2020).
2. Kobie, N. (2018). The inside story of Monzo's fluky bright coral bank cards. *Wired* (19 November). https://www.wired.co.uk/article/monzo-card-design (accessed 17 July 2020).
3. Starling (2018). Introducing our new card. https://www.starlingbank.com/blog/new-bank-card-design/ (accessed 17 July 2020).
4. Burrows, L. (2020). Revolut Review – Is it the best way to take money abroad in 2020? *Money to the Masses* (1 July). https://moneytothemasses.com/quick-savings/travel-quick-savings/revolut-review-is-it-the-best-way-to-take-money-abroad (accessed 17 July 2020).
5. Monck, M. Compare business bank accounts. *Moneyfacts*. https://moneyfacts.co.uk/business/business-bank-accounts/ (accessed 17 July 2020).
6. Hinchliffe, R. (2020). Monzo cuts 120 jobs in its UK head office. *Fintech Futures* (4 June) https://www.fintechfutures.com/2020/06/monzo-cuts-another-120-jobs-in-the-uk/ (accessed 17 July 2020).
7. O'Hear, S. (2020). Monzo to shutter Las Vegas customer support office, 165 employees being let go. *TechCrunch* (9 April). https://techcrunch.com/2020/04/09/monzo-to-shutter-las-vegas/ (accessed 17 July 2020).
8. Statista (2018). Number of customers at selected banks in the United Kingdom (UK) from 2007 to 2017. https://www.statista.com/statistics/940560/number-of-customers-at-select-banks-in-the-united-kingdom/ (accessed 17 July 2020).
9. UK Finance (2019). UK payment markets summary: 2019. https://www.ukfinance.org.uk/sites/default/files/uploads/pdf/UK-Finance-UK-Payment-Markets-Report-2019-SUMMARY.pdf (accessed 17 July 2020).
10. Yuzhe, Z. (2019). In depth: The fight for dominance in China's mobile payment market. *Caixin* (23 September). https://www.caixinglobal.com/2019-09-23/in-depth-the-fight-for-dominance-in-chinas-mobile-payment-market-101464880.html (accessed 17 July 2020).
11. UK Finance (2019). Rise in mobile banking and contactless as consumers take pick 'n' mix approach to payments. https://www.ukfinance.org.uk/press/press-releases/rise-mobile-banking-and-contactless-consumers-take-pick-n-mix-approach-payments ().
12. Lee, Y. N. (2019). Forget the QR code. Facial recognition could be the next big thing for payments in China. *CNBC* (19 November). https://www.cnbc.com/2019/11/19/tencents-wechat-china-may-soon-use-facial-recognition-for-payments.html (accessed 17 July 2020).
13. Halpin, P. (2020). Mastercard to add 1,500 technology jobs in Ireland. *Reuters* (24 February). https://www.reuters.com/article/us-ireland-jobs-mastercard/mastercard-to-add-1500-technology-jobs-in-ireland-idUSKCN20I0XA (accessed 17 July 2020).
14. Crunchbase. ANT Financial. https://www.crunchbase.com/organization/ant-financial#section-overview (accessed 17 July 2020).
15. Apple (2019). Apple Card launches today for all US customers. https://www.apple.com/newsroom/2019/08/apple-card-launches-today-for-all-us-customers/ (accessed 17 July 2020).
16. Constine, J. (2020). Leaked pics reveal Google smart debit card to rival Apple's. *TechCrunch* (17 April). https://techcrunch.com/2020/04/17/google-card/ (accessed 17 July 2020).
17. Stone, B. (2013). *The Everything Store: Jeff Bezos and the Age of Amazon*. Transworld Publishers Ltd.
18. Finextra (2016). HSBC establishes Hong Kong R&D lab. https://www.finextra.com/newsarticle/29696/hsbc-establishes-hong-kong-rd-lab (accessed 17 July 2020).

19. Barclays. The Home of FinTech – celebrating five years of innovation. https://rise.barclays/ (accessed 17 July 2020).

20. N26. The bank you'll love. https://n26.com/en-eu (accessed 17 July 2020).

21. Browne, R. (2020). Peter Thiel-backed mobile bank N26 says it's luring deposits from US titans like Chase and Citibank. *CNBC* (27 January). https://www.cnbc.com/2020/01/27/n26-the-mobile-bank-backed-by-peter-thiel-has-gained-250000-us-users.html ().

22. Bloomfield, K. (2018). Monzo: The rise and rise of the coolest challenger in the class. *The Fintech Times* (21 December). https://thefintechtimes.com/monzo-challenger/ (accessed 17 July 2020).

23. Uber. https://www.uber.com/gb/en/ (accessed 17 July 2020).

24. Kagan, J. (2020). Offset mortgage. *Investopedia* (21 February). https://www.investopedia.com/terms/o/offset_mortgage.asp (accessed 17 July 2020).

25. UK Finance. UK Finance: Cross-sector cooperation needed to tackle rise in authorised push payment fraud. https://www.ukfinance.org.uk/uk-finance-cross-sector-cooperation-needed-tackle-rise-authorised-push-payment-fraud (accessed 17 July 2020).

26. UK Finance (2020). Fraud – The facts 2020. https://www.ukfinance.org.uk/system/files/Fraud-The-Facts-2020-FINAL-ONLINE-11-June.pdf (accessed 18 July 2020).

27. Pay.UK. Confirmation of payee. https://www.wearepay.uk/confirmation-of-payee/ (accessed 18 July 2020).

28. Hamilton, A. (2020). Major Dutch banks launch AML joint venture. *Fintech Futures* (13 July). https://www.fintechfutures.com/2020/07/major-dutch-banks-launch-aml-joint-venture/ (accessed 18 July 2020).

29. Ntansa (2019). 7 practical application of robotic process automation in banking today. https://www.ntansa.com/7-practical-application-of-robotic-process-automation-in-banking/ (accessed 18 July 2020).

30. Open Banking. https://www.openbanking.org.uk/ (accessed 18 July 2020).

31. EUR-Lex (2016). Document 32016R0679. https://eur-lex.europa.eu/legal-content/EN/TXT/?qid=1595072588841&uri=CELEX:32016R0679 (accessed 18 July 2020).

32. Land Registry. UK House Price Index. https://landregistry.data.gov.uk/app/ukhpi (accessed 18 July 2020).

33. BBC (2018). Facebook's data-sharing deals exposed. https://www.bbc.co.uk/news/technology-46618582 (accessed 18 July 2020).

34. European Commission. Payment services (PSD 2) – Directive (EU) 2015/2366. https://ec.europa.eu/info/law/payment-services-psd-2-directive-eu-2015-2366_en (accessed 18 July 2020).

35. EUR-Lex. Document 32016R0679.

36. root. Programmable banking for software developers. https://root.co.za/card (accessed 18 July 2020).

37. Monzo. Monzo and IFTTT. https://monzo.com/features/ifttt/ (accessed 18 July 2020).

38. Binham, C. (2019). Ipagoo falls into administration. *Financial Times* (2 August). https://www.ft.com/content/c1a6a924-b529-11e9-8cb2-799a3a8cf37b (accessed 18 July 2020).

39. Warden, P. (2018). Best mortgages for multi-generational families. *The Mortgage Reports* (24 February). https://themortgagereports.com/36095/best-mortgages-for-multi-generational-families (accessed 2 October 2020).

40. Packin, N. G. (2019). Social credit: Much more than your traditional financial credit score data. *Forbes* (13 December). https://www.forbes.com/sites/nizangpackin/2019/12/13/social-credit-much-more-than-your-traditional-financial-credit-score-data (accessed 18 July 2020).

41. Euronews (2020). Social scoring: Could that Facebook post stop you getting a loan or a mortgage? https://www.euronews.com/2020/06/24/social-scoring-could-that-facebook-post-stop-you-getting-a-loan-or-a-mortgage (accessed 18 July 2020).

42. Moffat, S. (1990) Japan's 100-year bank loans. *Fortune* (21 May). https://money.cnn.com/magazines/fortune/fortune_archive/1990/05/21/73567/ (accessed 2 October 2020)

43. Cheung, C. (2020). Robo-advice 'gaining traction' in lifetime mortgage sector. *FT Adviser* (14 May). https://www.ftadviser.com/mortgages/2020/05/14/robo-advice-gaining-traction-in-lifetime-mortgage-sector/ (accessed 18 July 2020).

44. FCA (2017). Robo Advice: an FCA perspective. https://www.fca.org.uk/news/speeches/robo-advice-fca-perspective (accessed 18 July 2020).

45. Ripple. Santander becomes first U.K. bank to use Ripple for real-time cross-border payments. https://ripple.com/files/case_study_santander.pdf (accessed 18 July 2020).

46. XRP Arcade (2020). Bank of America confirms Ripple partnership. https://www.xrparcade.com/news/bank-of-america-confirms-ripple-partnership/ (accessed 18 July 2020).

47. Ripple. RippleNet. The world's most accessible global payments network. https://ripple.com/ripplenet (accessed 18 July 2020).

48. Ledger Insights (2019). Deutsche Bank joins JPMorgan's blockchain payment network. https://www.ledgerinsights.com/deutsche-bank-joins-jpmorgans-blockchain-payment-network/ (accessed 18 July 2020).

49. SWIFT. About us. https://www.swift.com/about-us (accessed 18 July 2020).

50. Hayes, A. (2020) Stablecoin. *Investopedia* (30 June). https://www.investopedia.com/terms/s/stablecoin.asp (accessed 18 July 2020).

51. Libra. Welcome to the Libra project. https://libra.org/en-US/ (accessed 18 July 2020).

52. Paul, K. (2019). Facebook supports delay of embattled Libra project, Zuckerberg to tell Congress. *The Guardian* (22 October). https://www.theguardian.com/technology/2019/oct/22/libra-facebook-zuckerberg-delay-congress (accessed 18 July 2020).

About the Authors

Tim Walker and Lucian Morris have been working together for over a decade, using their complementary expertise and experience on the application of technology in the banking industry.

Tim is an expert on the use and implementation of technology in banking and payments organisations. After setting up one of the UK's first websites as a student in the early 1990s, he started his professional career at Logica, ultimately leading the development of a customer relationship management platform that was implemented in various financial services call centres. He then moved to Deloitte where he consulted to a wide range of banks and payments organisations, including a role as the lead solution architect for a new pan-European mass affluent online bank and leading the system integration of a new card payment authorisation platform for a global payment scheme. After becoming a partner at Deloitte, Tim set up and became the global leader of its core banking practice, providing advice to a wide range of banking institutions from small, single-branch banks to the largest international banking groups, as well as writing articles, presenting at conferences and undertaking pre-acquisition due diligence reviews of the technology and operations of various banking and payments organisations. During his time at Deloitte he worked across Europe, in the United States, and in the Middle East. Since leaving Deloitte, Tim has undertaken various roles including leading a large programme to implement a new finance platform for an international bank and as a non-executive director for a start-up bank in the UK. He lives in the Wye Valley with his wife and two children.

Lucian has been consulting, presenting, and writing on technology and retail banking related topics for more than 15 years and is a specialist in the building and management of technology solutions and services in financial services organisations. As a director at Deloitte, Lucian worked with many UK and European top-tier retail banks but is best known for his role as chief information officer during the build and launch of Metro Bank, for which Deloitte won a prestigious Management Consulting Association award. After spending more than a decade as a consultant at Deloitte, Lucian then worked on another start-up bank and led the build and launch of a UK-based fintech, LQID. He enjoys presenting on banking-related topics and writes a regular blog on LinkedIn where he comments on developments in UK retail banking, particularly the current account market. Lucian is currently the chief information officer at Mortgage Advice Bureau in the UK. He lives in Bedfordshire with his wife and two children.

Index